LOVE REVEALED

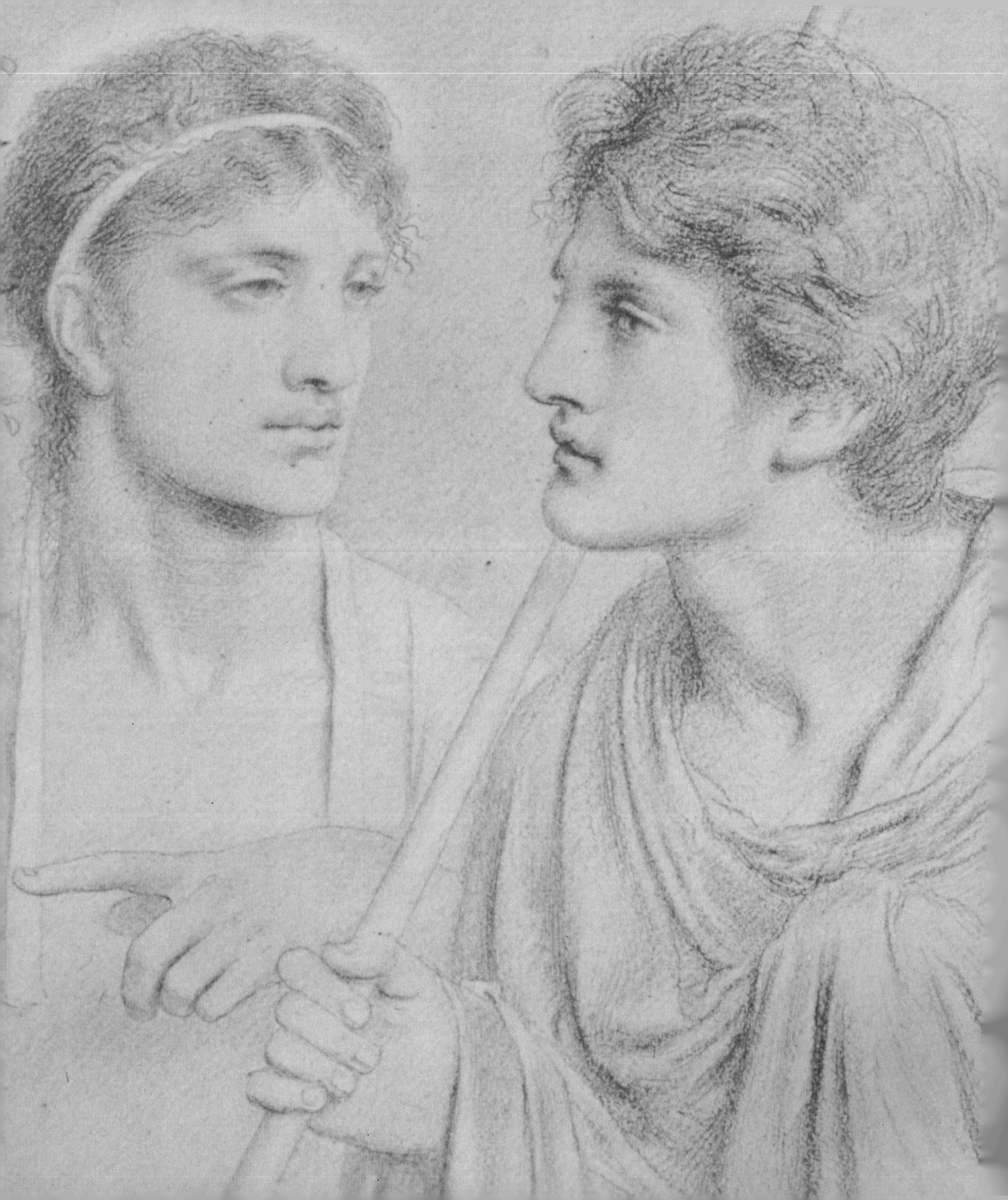

LOVE REVEALED
Simeon Solomon and the Pre-Raphaelites

Colin Cruise

with

Roberto C. Ferrari
Debra N. Mancoff
Elizabeth Prettejohn
Gayle M. Seymour
Frank C. Sharp

and Victoria Osborne

MERRELL
LONDON • NEW YORK

First published 2005 by Merrell Publishers Limited

Head office:
81 Southwark Street
London SE1 0HX

New York office:
49 West 24th Street, 8th Floor
New York, NY 10010

www.merrellpublishers.com

in association with

Birmingham Museums & Art Gallery
Chamberlain Square
Birmingham B3 3DH

Published on the occasion of the exhibition
Love Revealed: Simeon Solomon and the Pre-Raphaelites
organized by Birmingham Museums & Art Gallery
and shown at

Birmingham Museum & Art Gallery
1 October 2005 – 15 January 2006

Museum Villa Stuck, Munich
9 March – 18 June 2006

Ben Uri Gallery, The London Jewish Museum of Art
11 September – 26 November 2006

Exhibition curated by Colin Cruise
and Victoria Osborne

British Library Cataloguing-in-Publication Data:
Love revealed : Simeon Solomon and the Pre-Raphaelites
1.Solomon, Simeon, 1840-1905 - Exhibitions
I.Cruise, Colin II.Osborne, Victoria III.Birmingham Museums and Art Gallery
759.2

ISBN 1 85894 311 6 (hardback)
ISBN 1 85894 312 4 (paperback)

Produced by Merrell Publishers
Designed by Tim Harvey
Edited by Elisabeth Ingles and Barbara Roby
Indexed by Diana LeCore
Printed and bound in Spain

Front jacket/cover:
The Sleepers and the One who Watcheth (detail)
1870
see p. 150

Back jacket/cover:
Self-portrait
1859
see p. 84

Page 2:
Frontispiece from *A Vision of Love Revealed in Sleep*
1871
see p. 158

Publication supported with help from The Isaacson-Draper Foundation

Contents

Acknowledgements

The exhibition curators would like to acknowledge their debt to Lionel Lambourne, whose long-standing research into Solomon was fundamental to the important exhibition *Solomon: A Family of Painters*, organized by the Geffrye Museum in 1985; to Simon Reynolds, whose book *The Vision of Simeon Solomon* has been a key reference work and who has generously and untiringly supported this exhibition project in many ways; and to Gayle Seymour, whose PhD thesis was a pioneering work in the study of Solomon.

Thanks go also to: Graham Allen, Nicola Bailey, Dr Michael Richard Barclay, Martin Barnes, Tim Barringer, Martin Beisly, Mike Berry, Kate Best, Mark Bills, Charles Bingham-Newland, Peter Boughton, Nicola Bown, Albert Bowyer, Susan Brady, Xanthe Brookes, Peter Brown, Ruth Brown, Stephen Calloway, Simon Cane, Terry Cartlidge, Gill Casson, Claire Chandler, Irene Cockcroft, Kath Cockshaw, Mr and Mrs Andrew Coltart, Holly Congdon, Phyllis Connors, Peter Cormack, Claire Daly, Michelle Draycott, Harriet Drummond, Helen Dunstan, Robert Ebbutt, Colin Edmonds, Jason Edwards, Martin Ellis, Donato Esposito, Jane Farrington, Laurin Federlein, Jill Fenwick, Ciara Fitzgerald, Jane Fletcher, Charlotte Gere, Carmel Girling, the late Peter Gross, Audrey Hall, Lee Handley, Haydn Hansell, Julian Hartnoll, Mark Haworth-Booth, The Hearn Family Trust, Eric Holder, Carmen Holdsworth Delgado, Neil Holland, Julian Honer, Christine Hopper, Anthea Ingham, Alisa Jaffa, Pete James, Reyahn King, Julia Kirby, Mr and Mrs Lionel Lambourne, Dr Dennis T. Lanigan, Val Lecky, Ruth Linton, Henrietta Lockhart, Jane Luke, Rupert Maas, Jennifer Marin, Jan Marsh, Louisa Martin, Sharn Matthews, Hugh Merrell, Robert Meyrick, Andrew Milner, David Morris, Gregory Morris, Rachel Moss, Peter Nahum, Christopher Newall, Barbara O'Connor, Ayala Oppenheimer, Grant Palmer, Varshali Patel, Sandra Penketh, Alison Plumridge, Rodney Richardson, Haydn Roberts, David Rowan, Rebecca Seabrook, Paul Shinn, Tessa Sidey, Anthea Snow, Seymour Stein, Richard Swift, Annabel Thomas, R.K.R. Thornton, Simon Toll, Peter Trippi, Sharon Trulock, Carl Turner, Robert Upstone, Glennys Wild, Stephen Wildman, Pam C. Williams, Patsy Williams, Christopher Wood, Ben Woodhams, Vikki Woolrich, Sam Wythe, Amelia Yeates, and lenders to the exhibition who have asked to remain anonymous.

Foreword

Birmingham Museum & Art Gallery has a long-standing association with Simeon Solomon. It acquired its first work by him, *A Saint of the Eastern Church* (a gift from the Birmingham artists Myra and Kate Bunce) in 1900 when the artist was still living, although in poverty and obscurity. The museum's holdings of Solomon's work have since grown, thanks to the generosity of subsequent donors and benefactors, to become the largest public collection in the world. Birmingham is, then, an appropriate venue for this exhibition, the first full-scale retrospective of Solomon's work in almost a century.

We are delighted that the exhibition will also travel to two most appropriate partner venues. At Museum Villa Stuck, Munich, it will be shown in the artist villa of Franz von Stuck, allowing Solomon's work to be assessed in the context of the development of Symbolism in Germany. At Ben Uri Gallery, The London Jewish Museum of Art, it will explore Solomon's place as a Jewish artist, both within the Victorian art world and in wider non-Jewish society.

The exhibition would not have been possible without the help and support of many organizations and individuals. We extend warm and grateful thanks to the Trustees of The Isaacson-Draper Foundation, which provided a substantial grant to enable the production of this beautiful accompanying book. Malcolm Gibb has encouraged the museum's interest in Solomon over a number of years, and we are indebted to him for his generous support. Our thanks go, too, to Andrew Milner for his assistance in funding an introductory guide to the exhibition in Birmingham.

Many public and private lenders have kindly agreed to make their works available for the exhibition. To all those named, and to those who wish to remain anonymous, we extend our grateful thanks.

Our guest curator, Colin Cruise, has selected the works for the exhibition and written the illuminating accompanying catalogue. He has traced paintings and drawings that have not been exhibited since Solomon's lifetime, and his research into the reception of the artist's work and ideas has allowed us to make accessible much previously unavailable material. We are grateful to him for the knowledge, energy and imagination he has brought to the project. We acknowledge, too, the contributions of Gayle Seymour, Roberto Ferrari, Debra Mancoff, Elizabeth Prettejohn and Frank Sharp, who have provided new insights into Solomon's life and work in their respective essays.

Thanks go to Victoria Osborne, Curator of Prints and Drawings at Birmingham Museum & Art Gallery, who has co-curated and organized the exhibition, and to the many colleagues at the museum who have contributed to its realization.

Finally, our thanks go to Hugh Merrell and the staff at Merrell Publishers who have designed and produced this elegant accompanying book.

Rita McLean, *Acting Head of Birmingham Museums*

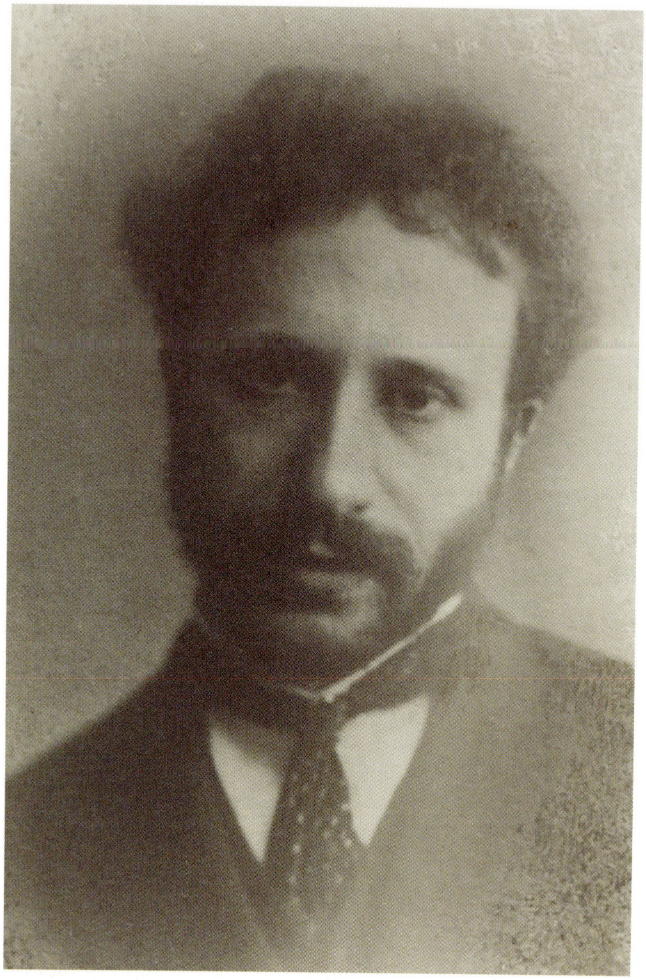

Introduction

It is tempting to start an account of the life of Simeon Solomon at its notorious end: with the disgrace, infamy and poverty that replaced respectability, fame and financial security. Such is the sensational detail that makes a life remembered, even – as is the case with Solomon – when there is so much more to remember and celebrate. William De Morgan, writing to Henry Holiday on the occasion of the publication of Holiday's memoirs in 1914, noted "an element of Aeschylean tragedy" in the events of his own life, adding: "However, nothing comes near poor Simeon in tragedy" (quoted in Stirling, 1922, p. 351). The tragedy was Solomon's arrest in February 1873, aged thirty-two, in a public lavatory in London. He was charged with indecent exposure and "attempting to commit sodomy". The incident ruined his professional career and led him to the workhouse and ignominy.

This exhibition refocuses attention on Solomon's achievement as an artist, his career and his contribution to the history of Pre-Raphaelitism and related late nineteenth-century movements such as Aestheticism. In recent essays surveying his life and work Solomon has been judged central to two thematic strands in nineteenth-century British painting: the emergence of Jewish art and the tentative development of an openly 'gay' imagery. Both of these manifested themselves at a time when training, career opportunities, professional art journalism and criticism, as well as the rise of the published art monograph, were new and distinctive characteristics for the production of a modern view of art. Artists increasingly became identified with new, sometimes startling, styles and subject-matter; critics, patrons and, eventually, private art dealers responded by identifying with particular factions. This is as true for Pre-Raphaelitism in mid-Victorian England as it was to be for Cubism in early twentieth-century France. So, while Solomon was not an 'easy' artist – as a study of contemporary art criticism reveals – he had his supporters and patrons who, at least up to the 'tragedy', could identify with the experimental nature of his works.

Although the aim of the exhibition is to re-examine Solomon as a professional artist, it does not, of course, overlook his intentions as a painter of Jewish subjects, or as a painter of subjects that promote a kind of sensibility of which, arguably, he was the first to attempt a pictorial representation – same-sex desire. The intention of the six introductory essays that preface this catalogue is to focus afresh on Solomon's career and the circumstances in which his works were produced. Thus, no single essay simply deals with Solomon as a 'Jewish' or 'gay' artist; rather, each attempts to see stylistic innovations and pictorial inventions and interventions in the genres and categories of contemporary painting as part of a wider exploration of the artist's contribution. They use a wide range of evidence, contextual material and illustrative matter – letters, hitherto overlooked reviews, comparative

Frederick Hollyer
Portrait of Simeon Solomon
c. 1866
(see p. 179)

material from Solomon's contemporaries, for example – to provide a new overview of the artist's place in the history of the art of the period.

The vital Old Testament subjects that formed an important part of Solomon's earliest inspiration are the starting-point for the opening essay by Gayle Seymour. She identifies the impact of Jewish emancipation on Solomon, finding a particular Jewish sensibility evident in his works that allows her to reflect on the manner in which various kinds of identity – religious, cultural and sexual – can be uncovered from a close reading of them.

Frank Sharp's essay deals with Solomon's early friendships with artists outside his family circle while he was still a student at the Royal Academy Schools. He concentrates on the special friendship with Henry Holiday but makes links as well between the student circle and the Pre-Raphaelite Brotherhood, and positions the young Solomon as central to the development of a new subject painting in England in the late 1850s and early 60s.

Debra Mancoff notes the artist's early contact with the Pre-Raphaelite Brotherhood and accounts for its impact on him. She traces the use of the term 'Pre-Raphaelite' in connection with Solomon's exhibited work and detects some ambiguity in his relations with the members of that group, particularly in their recollections of the period.

Elizabeth Prettejohn's essay places Solomon's exploration of Classical literature and culture and their various meanings in the context of British art practice and criticism of the time. She sees Classicism as finding some reconciliation with the 'Hebraic' element in his work, examining depictions of Sappho, Bacchus and Heliogabalus, among other subjects, in order to assess their significance for him.

Roberto Ferrari concentrates on the relationship between the painter and his patrons, examining, in the latter part of his essay, some of the most important and revealing exchanges between an artist and a patron of the period. Ferrari shows us an artist torn between pleasing the patron and creating transgressive and innovative works.

The role of religion and ritual in Solomon's works of the 1860s and 70s is the focus of my own contribution. Such subjects were also to have a presence in many of the paintings and drawings produced in his last years. These religious and spiritual allegories have often been seen as 'mystical', yet relate, too, to Solomon's consciousness of his own sexuality.

The sections of the exhibition are organized to reveal important developments in the artist's career – his active role in the life of the Dudley Gallery and his exploration of Classical imagery, for example. In all these sections it is clear that the works have their own peculiar fascination; they are never the slave of convention or stereotype, and present new, sometimes odd, interpretations of their subjects. Employing innovative drawing and painting skills and a vivid imagination, the artist realizes ideas in particularly striking images. Where works have not been traced, were unavailable for loan or are known to have been destroyed, we are fortunate to have photographs, for the most part taken during the artist's lifetime. In other cases wood engravings preserve alternative compositions.

The exhibition presents extraordinarily diverse works, and we find Solomon working in a variety of different modes and media at any one time. The great revelation to those who do not know Solomon's work well will be its wide and confident span of subjects, and its compositional and iconographic inventiveness. Although these qualities are present particularly in the juvenilia and the works of his early professional career, the final section of the exhibition is not to be read simply as the record of loss of power, a token glance at the 'shipwreck' of a career. True, the works in this section are often of strange and esoteric subjects, but they are by no means negligible. In the 1880s and 90s, and indeed up to the very end of his life, Solomon produced images that relate to his innovative works of earlier decades; yet they also have a visionary quality that allies him to the pre-Modernist avant garde in Europe and America, the Symbolist painters Franz von Stuck, Gustav Klimt, Fernand Khnopff, Jean Delville and Lucien Lévy-Dhurmer, and the photographer Fred Holland Day. Solomon's first serious biographer, Julia Ellsworth Ford, observed: "We might call [him] the psychic portrait-painter of Death, Night and Sleep, which are so frequently the subjects of his conceptions" (Ford, 1908, p. 17).

One of the most remarkable features of Solomon's career was how often the word 'genius' was used to describe him. For his admirers – and even for his many critics – his works were evidence of prodigious talent elevated, to a greater or lesser degree, by this rare quality. Thus, each of the six sections of this exhibition catalogue is prefaced by a text that describes the artist or his works in this way. By the end of the exhibition visitors will see why William Blake Richmond would remember Solomon as "the greatest genius of our set" or why Edward Burne-Jones might consider him "the rising genius". Despite these accolades, the rehabilitation of the artist's reputation was slow and perhaps compromising for those who heralded it, and the critical reception of the two memorial exhibitions – at the Royal Academy and at the Baillie Gallery – was certainly mixed. The *Studio* – by the time of Solomon's death the leading supporter of Arts and Crafts and late Pre-Raphaelite subject painting – reviewed the exhibition at the Baillie Gallery in terms that hint at the vagaries of Solomon's life with some sensitivity:

> In places nothing more than languidly sentimental, his art at other times rises to heights of a proud and remote mysticism which only meets its equal in Blake. The artist's ideal is one of Hellenic beauty always, and though comparison has been made between his early work and the drawings of Rossetti, his adherence to this ideal and his love of the abstract is in antagonism to the spirit of Rossetti's art. Rapid transitions from weakness to greatness and then again to weakness gave an extraordinary character to the artist's work as a whole, as it was to be seen in this exhibition. It is an inequality to some extent explained by the unhappiness for which the artist's temperament seemed fated in its curious incompatibility with life's daily traffic.
>
> (*Studio*, XXXVII, 1906, p. 67)

This is the first major exhibition dedicated to Solomon alone since those memorial shows. Some of the works have not been seen in public widely, if at all, since their first exhibition at the Royal Academy or the Dudley Gallery in the 1860s and 70s. Such is the case with *The Child Jeremiah* (RA 1862, cat. 38) and *Offering the First-Fruits of the Harvest* (1864, cat. 42). Other works have gained a popularity through exhibition or frequent reproduction – *Carrying the Scrolls of the Law* (1867, cat. 94), *The Sleepers and the One who Watcheth* (1870, cat. 106) and *Love in Autumn* (1866, cat. 100) are examples – yet this overview will help to recontextualize and refresh them. This process of recontextualization has led the curators to include in this exhibition works by Solomon's contemporaries – Dante Gabriel Rossetti, Frederick Sandys, Burne-Jones and Khnopff, among others – whose art influenced, or was influenced by, Solomon's visual imagination. For clarity, these works appear after the main Solomon entries in each section.

The curators hope that Solomon's genius, in all its difficult complexity, and for all its flaws and foibles, has found an opportunity, through this exhibition, to impress itself on a different age.

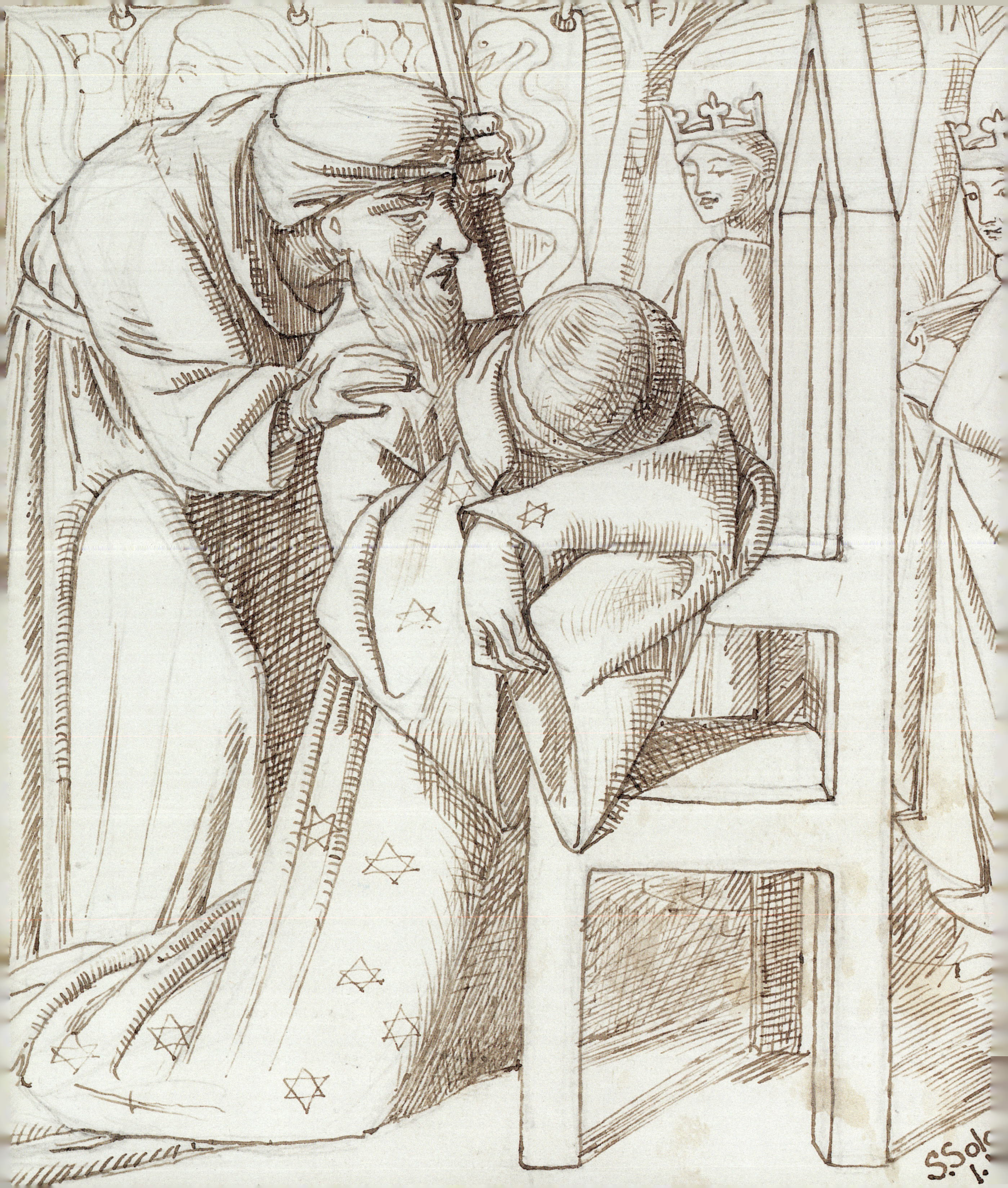

Gayle M. Seymour

The Old Testament Paintings and Drawings: The Search for Identity in the Post-Emancipation Era

In May 1858, at the age of seventeen, Simeon Solomon made his debut at the Royal Academy, the most prestigious art exhibition space in England, with a painting entitled *Isaac Offered* (see cat. 19 and fig. 23), the first in a series of Old Testament subjects that made his reputation as a rising star. This milestone in the life of the young artist was certainly significant on its own merits; however, when considered from a wider historical and cultural context, the event must be considered momentous since 1858 marked the point at which Lionel de Rothschild took his seat in Parliament – the first Jew to do so[1] – and thus the culminating moment in the emancipation of the Jews in England. With this painting Solomon not only announced his arrival as an artist, but also dared to claim his public position as a Jewish artist. For the next five years, and occasionally throughout the rest of his life, Solomon continued to explore Old Testament themes, often choosing subjects that addressed the paradox of Jewish emancipation – the fact that Jewish–Gentile interaction both fostered Jewish survival and undermined it. In the ancient stories of Jeremiah, Moses and David, among others, Solomon discovered themes that resonated with the issues and attitudes facing contemporary Jews and their problematical status. He also used these themes as an outlet to explore and acknowledge his own emerging homosexual identity. In so doing, Solomon's Old Testament paintings and drawings (1856–63) comprise a unique body of work that sheds light on those trying to construct new identities in the post-emancipation era.

In the nineteenth century the Jewish community in England underwent a profound transformation of its status and identity.[2] Jews were expelled from England by Edward I in 1290, but readmitted in 1656 during Cromwell's Protectorate.[3] From the mid-seventeenth century, Jews who lived in England were comparatively fortunate, saved, for the most part, from the overt persecution that plagued their Central and Eastern European co-religionists.[4] At the beginning of the nineteenth century, however, all municipal offices and election to Parliament, as well as professions such as teaching, medicine and the bar, were still closed to professing British Jews, since these vocations required a Christian form of oath.[5]

Emancipation came piecemeal between 1828 and 1858.[6] In December 1830, for example, Jews gained the right to become freemen of the City of London, which entitled them to engage in retail trade within the metropolis. Significantly, Michael Solomon (1779–1854), a London hatmaker and Simeon's father, was the first Jew legally admitted under this Act.[7] Men like Michael Solomon were thus able to ascend from humble circumstances at the start of the nineteenth century to largely middle-class respectability by mid-century, advancing from street traders and migrant salesmen to become proprietors of fixed retail outlets, able to mingle with the middle and upper classes of

Simeon Solomon
Nathan Reproving David (detail)
1859
(see p. 80)

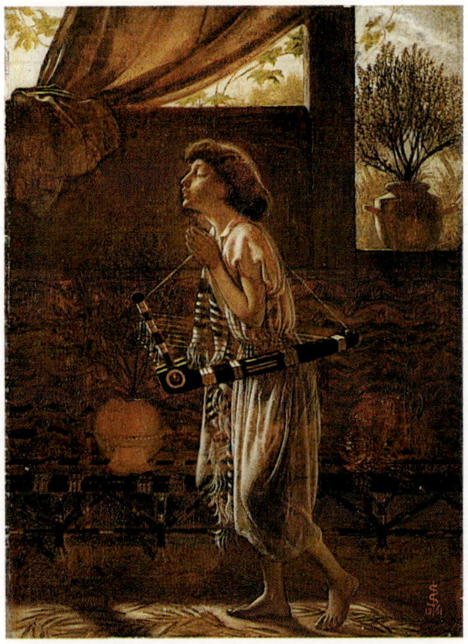

Fig. 1
The Child Jeremiah
1862
(see p. 89)

Gentile society. While previously Jews had thought of themselves primarily as Jews, members of a distinct and separate people whose affairs were regulated by their own laws, now they sought to create new identities for themselves as both Jews and Englishmen.[8]

Only as the legal restrictions on Jews were lifted in the first half of the nineteenth century did it become possible for a few of them to enter the profession of art.[9] Although not the first Jewish artist in England,[10] Solomon was the first Anglo-Jewish artist who self-confidently drew attention to his Jewishness by promoting himself as a painter of Hebraic subjects and scenes of contemporary Jewish life.[11]

As a pioneer Jewish artist – as art historian Larry Silver has pointed out about Maurycy Gottlieb (1856–1879), "the first Jewish artist" in Poland – Solomon essentially had "to invent the concept of what it meant to be a Jewish artist" since "there was no established model for being [one] ... available in his time and place".[12] Solomon's surprising strategy was to exploit his Jewishness. Unlike the ethnically and racially marginalized American artist Edmonia Lewis (*c.* 1843–after 1909), for example, who typically Europeanized the features of her African- and Native-American figures in order not to draw attention to her own ethnicity (she was a mix of Native- and African-American descent),[13] Solomon did precisely the opposite. Because he specialized in themes taken from the Hebrew Bible and insisted on using Jewish models with Semitic features, the visual signifier of his own Jewish ancestry, his Old Testament paintings and drawings were often read as autobiographical, as a kind of 'self-portrait'.[14] Solomon's open affirmation of his Jewish origins, as expressed in his Old Testament paintings and drawings, may well be one of the most significant aspects of his early work.

One of the difficulties of being a Jewish artist in nineteenth-century Britain was the dearth of Jewish collectors of art. This indifference to the visual arts was due in part to a restrictive understanding of the Second Commandment, prohibiting graven images and their worship, which also influenced observant Jewish patrons, since the spectator's experience of pleasure and desire in response to the art object was considered tantamount to idol worship.[15] This ethical constraint meant that Solomon had to create works appealing, for the most part, to Christian collectors.[16] Solomon's only patron from the well-to-do Jewish community was Ernest Abraham Hart (1835–1898), the eminent surgeon and brother-in-law of Abraham Solomon.[17] It is unknown if Hart actively commissioned works by other Jewish artists, or if his interest in Solomon's art was actually little more than familial obligation to his sister's brother-in-law; however, Hart owned one of Solomon's most poetic pictures, the 1862 Royal Academy oil *The Child Jeremiah* (fig. 1). Instead of depicting Jeremiah as a mature bearded man, as other artists invariably did, Solomon shows the prophet as a sensitive and shrinking adolescent who receives a message from God that he is a child of destiny: "Now the word of the LORD came to me saying, 'Before I formed you in the womb I knew you, and before you were born I consecrated you; I appointed you a prophet to the nations.' Then I said, 'Ah Lord GOD! Behold, I do not know how to speak, for I am only a youth'" (Jer. 1:4). In this cabinet picture, Solomon presents the viewer with a single figure in a darkened interior so pared down that it seems stripped of a narrative. The meditative figure thus invites the viewer's contemplation through its evocative colouring and the glowing light that caresses just the edges of the figure and is especially visible along the forehead, nose and lips of the young prophet. Solomon skilfully uses this Caravaggesque lighting technique to indicate that Jeremiah is having a conversation with God: "Then the LORD put forth his hand and touched my mouth; and the LORD said to me, 'Behold, I have put my words in your mouth'" (Jer. 1:9). God is thus signified in this painting as the phenomenon of light, rather than portrayed in material form. In this way, Solomon

Fig. 2
The Mother of Moses
1860
Oil on canvas
56.6 × 48.2 cm (23 × 19 in.)
Signed with monogram lower right
Delaware Art Museum, Wilmington, USA,
Bequest of Robert Louis Isaacson;/ Bridgeman
Art Library

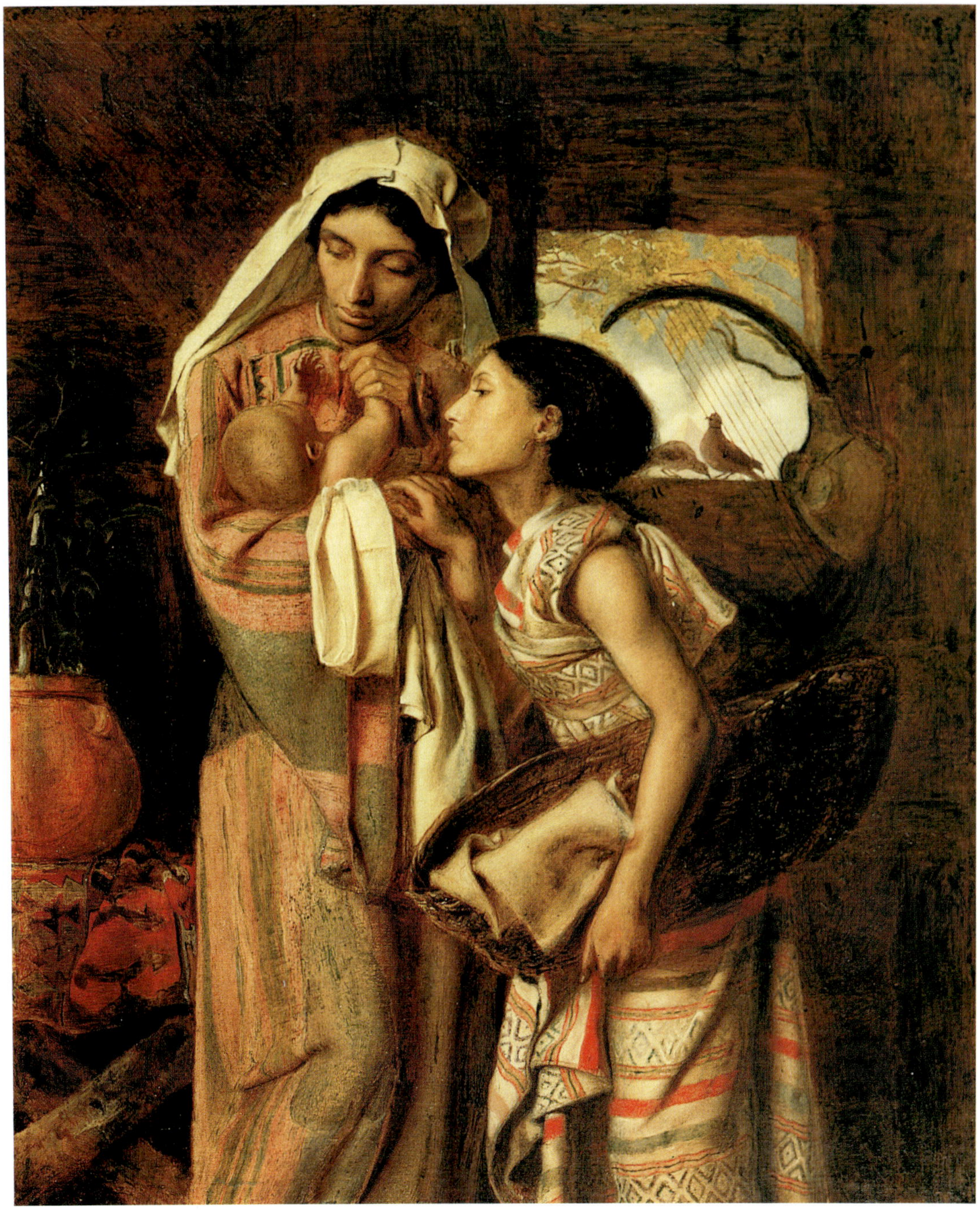

created for his distinguished Jewish patron a work that cleverly avoided the Second Commandment's most serious injunction against idolatry, the prohibition against representing God.

The Old Testament paintings and drawings attest to Solomon's ambition to seek acceptance in the highest form of artistic practice, the ambitious field of history painting.[18] Such a goal would not have been unusual, since Solomon received advanced training from his co-religionist Solomon Alexander Hart (1806–1881), professor of painting at the Royal Academy Schools, a leading exponent in the field of history painting.[19] While Hart specialized in canvases depicting English history and literature, the young Solomon essentially tried to create a new hybrid, Jewish history painting, in which the stories of the Old Testament could be mined, not only for their historicity and narrativity, but for their didactic intent.[20] Inspired by Hart's example, as well as those of his Pre-Raphaelite colleagues, Solomon sought to create biblical themes of great significance, using highly expressive figures and archaeologically accurate artefacts.

Solomon's principal preoccupation in his exploration of Jewish history was finding appropriate moments or actions in the Old Testament stories that might provide some kind of moral instruction, especially for those who were trying to cope with the challenges of life in the aftermath of emancipation. *The Mother of Moses* (fig. 2), for one, exhibited at the Royal Academy in 1860 when the artist was only nineteen, addresses the dilemma of acculturation that faced mid-century Anglo-Jewry – the desire to be both Jewish and British. On the one hand, Moses's birth and adoption are stories that acknowledge that the patriarch – who was raised by and lived among Gentiles in Egypt after he was given up by his mother in order to save him from Pharaoh's decree of infanticide – benefited from his contacts with a tradition other than his own; Moses was able to become Israel's deliverer precisely because of his knowledge of the religious traditions and political systems of an alien society.[21] Indeed, by the mid-nineteenth century, the favourable circumstances of emancipated middle-class Jews – including the Solomon family – allowed them to integrate into wider society, which attracted them and expanded their opportunities and experiences. On the other hand, the depiction of a loving mother caring for her infant stresses the bonds that linked Moses to his family and therefore to his racial and religious roots.[22] During his formative years, Moses lived with his mother and his sister who, according to the Jewish Commentary, instilled in him the essential tenets of Judaism, "ensuring that he remained a Hebrew".[23] Thus, Solomon's *Moses* makes visible the ambivalence felt by many middle-class Jews as they struggled to retain elements of their traditional heritage while enjoying a measure of freedom and equality in the secular and Christian culture of Victorian London.

Moreover, on a personal level, Solomon's image of a protective mother and a watchful sister may have autobiographical significance. Although he was not from a strictly orthodox family,[24] Solomon's knowledge of the stories of the Hebrew Bible, as well as his fondness for the Jewish customs and rituals (which he evoked with great conviction for the Victorian periodicals *Once a Week* in 1862, and *The Leisure Hour* in 1866; see cat. 83 and figs. 19 and 38),[25] can be attributed to the influence of his mother, Kate, and his sister, Rebecca.

As the artist typically did in his Old Testament oil paintings, in *Moses* the figures are posed in a classical manner (either frontally or in profile), and arranged against a flat architectural background, parallel to the picture plane. Solomon suppresses the action of the narrative in favour of creating the impression of a 'fruitful moment'.[26] In this way he adheres to one of the essential principles of history painting, whereby the artist selects a moment of the story that would suggest both the antecedents and consequences of the action shown.[27] In choosing to depict Jochabed, the mother of Moses, as she silently holds her infant son for one last time before launching him in a basket on the Nile, Solomon causes the viewer to contemplate also the emotionally intense moments that must have led up to this scene of last goodbyes. Thus the viewer meditates on what is not actually depicted in the painting: the intense psychological dilemma of a troubled individual who has been forced to make an agonizing decision of far-reaching implications.

A deep sense of melancholy and longing underscores most of Solomon's early Old Testament paintings and drawings. Richard I. Cohen, in his study of Jewish artists, has theorized that the melancholy present in much nineteenth-century Jewish art reflected the dying Judaic culture of post-emancipation Europe.[28] It is conceivable that Solomon, in paintings such as *A Young Musician*

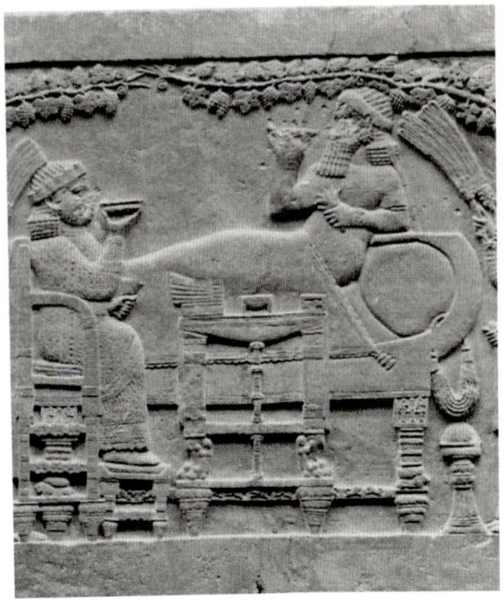

Fig. 3
Ashurbanipal Celebrates his Victory over the Babylonians (The Garden Scene)
c. 645 BC
Relief from the North Palace of Ashurbanipal, Nineveh
Stone
58.4 × 139.7 × 15.2 cm (23 × 55 × 6 in.)
The British Museum, London

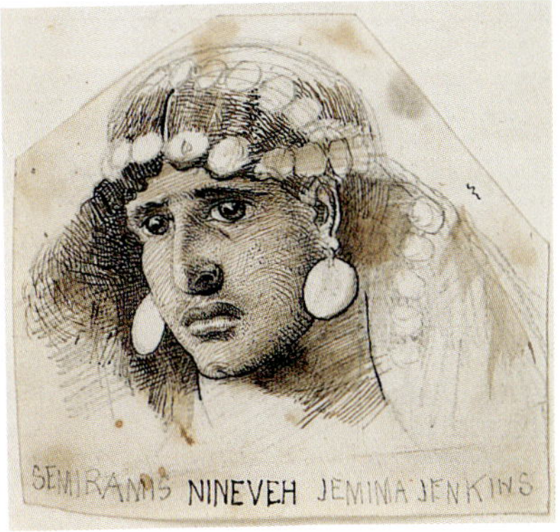

Fig. 4
Semiramis
c. 1858
Pen and ink on paper
From a sketchbook
Mishkan Le'Omanut Museum, Ein Harod, Israel

Employed in the Temple Service During the Feast of Tabernacles (cat. 36), exhibited at the Royal Academy in 1861, intended the solemn mood of the picture – a combination of pious reverence and introspection experienced by the faithful during the Feast of Tabernacles – to be an analogue for the feelings of sorrow and loss experienced by certain Jews as they sought to hold on to the vanishing past by visualizing it in painting.[29] In *A Young Musician* Solomon evokes the seventh day of the Feast of Tabernacles, during which time the faithful recite a prayer with the refrain "Hosannah!" ("Please save us!") to the accompaniment of flutes, harps and cymbals.[30] By stressing the archaeologically accurate accessories (such as the ivory-inlay harp, pictured in Assyrian relief sculpture found in the British Museum)[31] and the costume (called a *tallit*, a prayer shawl), as well as the gentleness and fervour of the expression of the model, Solomon intended to retrieve for his viewers an evocation of an 'authentic' Jewish experience that might connect acculturated London Jews to a pristine past, "more pious and more sincere than the vacuous present".[32]

Solomon's *Babylon Hath Been a Golden Cup* (1859, cat. 17) also addressed the experience of Jews as they struggled with the serious issues of assimilation and secularization, the twin centrifugal forces that were threatening the very survival of contemporary London Jewry. Although set in the archaic past, as recounted in Jeremiah 51:7, the subject allowed Solomon to present a cautionary tale for contemporary middle-class Jews, warning that Jewish–Gentile interaction might have deleterious consequences – temptation, laxity and religious corruption – potentially corrosive of Jewish identity. The historian Todd Endelman has documented with precision the "continual decline in synagogue attendance, home observance, Hebrew literacy, and other fundamental hallmarks of Jewish knowledge and practice" that accompanied emancipation over the course of the nineteenth century.[33] Many Jews, according to Endelman, could not resist the temptations British society presented. By integrating into the mainstream of society and associating with Gentiles at "professional gatherings, in lecture halls, and in countless other predominately Gentile surroundings, emancipated Jews encountered values and outlooks that undermined their faith and forged personal relationships that eroded their communal allegiances".[34]

Babylon was exhibited in November 1859 at Gambart's French Gallery. The catalogue quoted the entire verse with the picture: "Babylon hath been a golden cup in the hand of God, which hath made all the earth drunken: the nations have drunken of her wine, therefore the nations are mad" (Jer. 51:7).[35] The drawing, as I have explained elsewhere,[36] evokes the outcome of one of Jeremiah's earlier prophecies of disaster lamenting that while the Jews were held captive in Babylon for seventy years they would succumb to the luxurious and sinful life of their captors:

> Will you steal, murder, commit adultery, swear falsely, burn incense to Baal, and go after other gods that you have not known, and then come and stand before me in this house, which is called by my name, and say, "We are delivered!" – only to go on doing all these abominations?
>
> (Jer. 7:9–10)

As Solomon typically did with his early sepia drawings, in contrast to the more realistic rendering of the figures in the oil paintings, in *Babylon* he outlines the main figures, causing them to appear almost in silhouette against the densely crowded background plane. In the centre of the composition, a bearded man in strict profile, reminiscent of the treatment of the figures in Assyrian relief sculpture (fig. 3),[37] has succumbed to the sensual music of a harp being played by the legendary queen and builder of Babylon, Semiramis (fig. 4), whose symbol, the dove, is perched on the man's knee.[38] As if to account for the ecstasy of his posture and to underscore his apparent

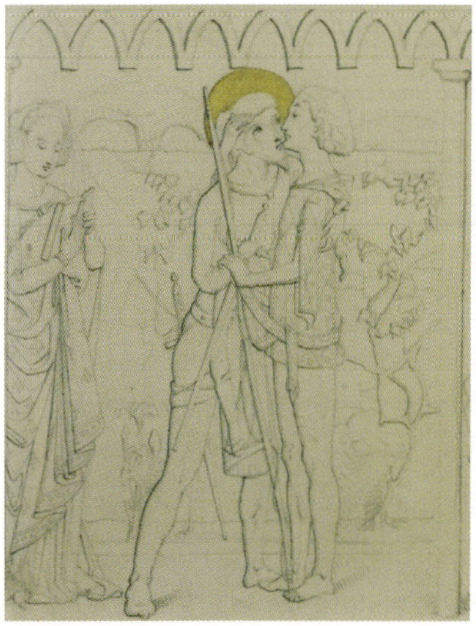

Fig. 5
Eight Scenes from the Story of David and Jonathan (detail)
1856
(see p. 73)

moral weakness, Solomon surrounds him with hedonistic pleasures: wine, spilt from an amphora in the left foreground, a metaphor for the corrupting influence of Babylon; dancing girls in the background, reminiscent of the Bacchantes, the followers of Dionysus,[39] representing the corrupted 'nations' who have drunk of Babylon's wine; and perfumed smoke from an incense-burner at the right, which creates a billowy design interweaving with the tendrils of the grapevines (also inspired by Assyrian relief), alluding to the fiery sacrifice to Babylon's gods. Solomon leaves no question that the bearded man is a Jew by depicting him wearing the phylactery, or *tefillin*, the cubelike capsules worn on the arm and the forehead by observant Jewish men during their morning prayer; however, the strap, which is ritually wrapped seven times around the arm and three times each around the hand and middle finger, is shown loosened,[40] as if to imply that when the restraints of Jewish moral law are allowed to slacken, religious adaptation and national disintegration follow close behind.

As usual, Solomon's Old Testament story carries an autobiographical significance; the cautionary message of *Babylon*, however, was lost on the artist. Indeed, Solomon gradually cut his ties with the Jewish community over the course of the 1860s as his Jewishness became a burden, especially after he moved away from his family home in 1862 and as he associated more with his Gentile colleagues. The very fact that Solomon employs a nude figure (although it appears sexually ambiguous),[41] still considered unacceptable for Jews living in traditional societies, must be considered in itself emblematic of the relaxing of religious barriers for Jews.[42]

While the Old Testament themes reflect the concerns and tensions of the wider Jewish community in preserving their identity in the post-emancipation era, on a more personal level they also illuminate Solomon's internal struggle to define and, ultimately, legitimize his own homoerotic yearnings. In certain examples, as I have elsewhere explained in detail,[43] Solomon used biblical themes to express his emotional states – anxiety, isolation, shame – as a way, perhaps, to overcome his feelings of despair and confusion engendered by his peripheral standing in the wider, essentially heterosexual, society. Solomon's early fascination with the heroic figure of David is perhaps understandable since in David's story Solomon found a legitimizing model for the love between men. According to the First Book of Samuel, David and Jonathan (the son of King Saul) openly displayed their love by swearing a lifetime pact together: "Then Jonathan made a covenant with David, because he loved him as his own soul" (I Sam. 18:3). In his 1856 drawing *Eight Scenes from the Story of David and Jonathan* (fig. 5), Solomon illustrated this episode by showing the men locked in a tender embrace.

Solomon's struggle to construct his homosexual identity is evident through further examination of the Old Testament drawings. In *Nathan Reproving David* (1859, cat. 21), for example, Solomon employed complex narrative structures in which the dialogue between a speaker and a listener contributes to our understanding of the artist's personal journey of self-definition.[44] The drawing depicts two men, King David and his trusted adviser, Nathan, having a conversation. In order to reveal the evil of his master's actions (David had allowed Uriah the Hittite, the husband of Bathsheba, to be killed in battle so that he might conceal his responsibility for her pregnancy), Nathan told the king the parable of the "rich man, the poor man, and the ewe lamb", shown in the roundels at the left, in which a rich man slaughters a poor man's cherished lamb in hospitality for a traveller (II Sam. 12:1–4). In the drawing, Solomon visualizes the emotional intensity of the highly charged moment as David, after hearing the parable and proclaiming with anger that the rich man should die for his selfish behaviour, sinks to his knees as he registers the shocking truth of Nathan's four-word reply, "You are the man" (II Sam. 12:7). Solomon thus gives Nathan's spoken word a leading role. As he lightly touches David's right shoulder, while with force he pushes down on David's back with his staff, Nathan makes his words unmistakably clear; the full weight of their meaning causes the listener to shield his ears, as if from frightening thunder.

The significance of this story for Solomon, a sexually unsure adolescent of eighteen, must be understood as more than that of the unjust landlord or of royal arrogance. In depicting the climax of the dialogue, Solomon highlights David's transformative moment of recognition; the impact of Nathan's spoken words causes David to acknowledge the secret he was keeping, even from himself.[45] The theme of David's moment of heightened self-awareness – of who he was – may have had for Solomon an autobiographical significance; the agonizing image of David may reflect the artist's own crisis and, perhaps, acceptance of sexual self-definition.

Simeon Solomon's Old Testament paintings and drawings reflect the special problems of an individual operating at an intersection of identities as a gay Jewish artist. Despite the obstacles that these marginal identities created for him, especially living in the Christian, heterosexual culture of Victorian England, Solomon succeeded in making a name for himself in a profession uncommon for Jews in previous centuries. Through his pictures, Solomon expressed the often contradictory experience of post-emancipation Anglo-Jews who, like Moses, both benefited from their association with the broader society and yet identified firmly with the history and traditions of the Jewish culture. Solomon's willingness to promote his Jewishness through his Old Testament pictures demonstrates powerfully that acculturated British Jews did not abandon all aspects of their identity. Rather than relinquish the Jewish world, Solomon used it as a source of inspiration and forged a new Jewish emphasis in the field of history painting, using art to reclaim a vanishing past. In many of these Old Testament works Solomon experimented with complex narrative devices to heighten the psychological intensity of his themes, reflecting the young artist's considerable skill as a draughtsman and story-teller and giving evidence of his intellectual depth. Solomon's images of melancholy mothers, yearning prophets and agonizing kings become all the more poignant when we consider that they open up a path to the thoughts and emotions of their maker.

NOTES

1 Lionel de Rothschild (1808–1879) was elected to the House of Commons in 1847 but was unable to take his seat until the requirement to swear a Christian oath was repealed in 1858. See M.C.N. Salbstein, *The Emancipation of the Jews in Britain: The Question of the Admission of the Jews to Parliament, 1828–1860*, East Brunswick NJ (Associated University Presses) 1982.

2 Out of a vast literature, the essential texts on the history of the Jews in England are Todd M. Endelman, *The Jews of Britain, 1656 to 2000*, Berkeley and Los Angeles (University of California Press) 2002; and Todd M. Endelman, *Radical Assimilation in English Jewish History, 1665–1945*, Bloomington (Indiana University Press) 1990. Recent studies that have examined the economic, social and political background of the Jewish community include: Israel Finestein, *Anglo-Jewry in Changing Times: Studies in Diversity, 1840–1914*, London (Valentine Mitchell) 1999; Jonathan Frankel and Steven J. Zipperstein, *Assimilation and Continuity in Nineteenth-Century Europe*, Cambridge (Cambridge University Press) 1992; Tony Kushner (ed.), *The Jewish Heritage in British History: Englishness and Jewishness*, London (Frank Cass) 1992; and Vivian D. Lipman, *A History of the Jews in Britain Since 1858*, New York (Holmes & Meier) 1990.

3 Jewish resettlement was negotiated by Menasseh ben Israel (1604–1657), known as the founder of the modern Jewish community in England. Interestingly, Solomon created a drawing entitled *Christ and the Rabbi, Ben Israel* (untraced), which was exhibited in 1906 at the Whitechapel Art Gallery, London. *Jewish Art and Antiquities*, exhib. cat., London, Whitechapel Art Gallery, 7 November – 16 December 1906, p. 51, cat. 852.

4 David Feldman has argued that British Jews were not disadvantaged simply because they were Jews but because they were not members of the Church of England. As such, Jews suffered from the same disadvantages that burdened Catholics and Protestant Dissenters who refused to swear an oath. David Feldman, *Englishmen and Jews: Social Relations and Political Culture, 1840–1914*, New Haven CT (Yale University Press) 1994, p. 2.

5 Numerous Relief Acts replaced the requirement to take the sacrament and give oaths "on the true faith of a Christian", using the New Testament Bible. David Cesarani, *The 'Jewish Chronicle' and Anglo-Jewry, 1841–1991*, Cambridge (Cambridge University Press) 1994, p. 5.

6 According to Geoffrey Alderman, emancipation can be defined as "the setting free from legal, social and political, or intellectual disabilities". In 1828 Jews were granted entry into the major professions such as law; in 1835 Jews achieved the right to vote in parliamentary elections (for males aged twenty-one and over); in 1845 Jews were given the right to hold any and every municipal office; in 1846 Jews were granted indisputable entitlement to own land; and in 1854 and 1856 Jews were allowed to take degrees at Oxford and Cambridge respectively. Geoffrey Alderman, 'English Jews or Jews of the English Persuasion? Reflections on the Emancipation of Anglo-Jewry', in *Paths of Emancipation: Jews, States, and Citizenship*, ed. Pierre Birnbaum and Ira Katznelson, Princeton NJ (Princeton University Press) 1995, pp. 128–30.

7 An Act of Common Council was passed on 10 December 1830, "enabling all persons born within the Kingdom ... not professing the Christian Religion ... to be admitted to the Freedom of the City of London ...". Michael Solomon obtained his freedom in the Gold and Silver Wyre Drawers Company on 7 January 1831 and was finally admitted to the Freedom of the City of London, 16 June 1831. Common Council (UK), 'Petition of Michael Solomon for Admission to the Freedom of the City of London', Corporation of London Records Office, 16 June 1831. A large silver salver with dedicatory inscription from Michael to his solicitor, Charles Pearson, thanking him for his legal services, exists in the Jewish Museum, London. For illustration, see R.D. Barnett (ed.), *Catalogue of the Permanent and Loan Collections of the Jewish Museum, London*, London (Harvey Miller) 1974, cat. 671.

8 Endelman, *The Jews of Britain*, p. 95.

9 The most comprehensive studies of nineteenth-century Jewish artists are Susan Tumarkin Goodman (ed.), *The Emergence of Jewish Artists in Nineteenth-Century Europe*, London (Merrell) 2001; and Richard I. Cohen, *Jewish Icons: Art and Society in Modern Europe*, Berkeley and Los Angeles (University of California Press) 1998.

10 Simeon Solomon was not the first Jewish artist in England: he was preceded by Solomon Alexander Hart (1806–1881) and Simeon's older siblings, Abraham Solomon (1823–1862) and Rebecca Solomon (1832–1886). Hart has the distinction of being the first Anglo-Jewish artist to exhibit at the Royal Academy in 1826 and the first to be elected to full membership in 1840. At the Royal Academy Schools, Hart was the professor of painting, 1854–63, and later became the librarian, 1864–81. According to Julia Weiner, as early as 1830 Hart created a painting depicting Jewish ritual entitled *The Elevation of the Law in the Polish Synagogue in London* (Tate, London); however, not wishing to be identified solely as a painter of Jewish themes, he switched to British history and literary themes. It was only after he was safely elected to the Royal Academy in 1840 that he produced a small number of paintings of Jewish ritual, such as *The Feast of the Rejoicing of the Law at the Synagogue in Leghorn, Italy*, 1850 (The Jewish Museum, New York). As for Abraham and Rebecca, neither was known for depicting Jewish themes. There are no known examples by Rebecca and only two works with Jewish – although not Old Testament – themes by Abraham. Julia Weiner, '"An artist of strong Jewish feeling": Simeon Solomon's Depictions of Jewish Ceremonies', in *From Prodigy to Outcast: Simeon Solomon – Pre-Raphaelite Artist*, London (Jewish Museum) 2001, p. 15.

11 Solomon's annual submissions to the Royal Academy between 1858 and 1863 always included one Old Testament theme – if not two. During this time he exhibited only one painting not on an Old Testament theme, his 1863 *Juliette* (no. 506); however, it was exhibited alongside the artist's 1863 *Isaac and Rebekah* (no. 567). Solomon exhibited at Gambart's French Gallery: 1858, *The Shadow of Death* (no. 115), based on Longfellow's *Golden Legend*, and *By the Waters of Babylon* (no. 116); 1859, *'And it came to pass when the evil spirit from God was upon Saul'* (no. 143), *Dante and Beatrice* (no. 144) and *Babylon* (no. 145). He did not exhibit at Gambart's again until 1865.

12 Larry Silver, 'Jewish Identity in Art History: Maurycy Gottlieb as Early Jewish Artist', in *Jewish Identity in Modern Art History*, ed. Catherine M. Soussloff, Berkeley and Los Angeles (University of California Press) 1999, p. 87.

13 Kirsten P. Buick, 'The Ideal Works of Edmonia Lewis: Invoking and Inverting Autobiography', *American Art*, IX, 2, Summer 1995, p. 14.

14 Many of Solomon's friends and contemporaries mentioned the artist's Jewish appearance, often using off-hand comments. See Debra N. Mancoff, 'As Others Saw Him: A Self-Portrait by Simeon Solomon', *The Art Institute of Chicago Museum Studies*, XVIII, 2, 1992, pp. 147–55.

15 Scholars have discussed the ambivalence of Jewish artists towards mimesis, arguing that while the Second Commandment prohibits the creation and worship of images, Mosaic Law both permits and forbids images. For a detailed explanation of the biblical polemic against idolatry, see Lisa Saltzman, 'To Figure, or Not to Figure: The Iconoclastic Proscription and Its Theoretical Legacy', in Soussloff, *op. cit.*, p. 69. Kalman P. Bland has also argued that the lack of Jewish visual art has less to do with religious prohibitions and more "to do with the experience of diasporan minorities and subordinate peoples" who have been excluded from the art establishment. See Kalman P. Bland, *The Artless Jew: Medieval and Modern Affirmations and Denials of the Visual Arts*, Princeton NJ (Princeton University Press) 2000, p. 11.

16 Solomon's well-known Christian collectors from this early period were Thomas E. Plint of Leeds and James Leathart of Newcastle. Plint owned six of Solomon's best Old Testament pictures: *The Mother of Moses* (1860, oil, Delaware Art Museum, see fig. 2), *David Dancing Before the Ark* (1860, sepia, private collection), *A Hebrew Musician* (1860, sepia, Huntington Library, San Marino), *Queen Esther Hearing the News of the Intended Massacre of the Jews* (1860, sepia, cat. 47), *Ruth, Naomi and the Child Obed* (1861, oil, untraced but see cat. 34) and *A Young Musician Employed in the Temple Service During the Feast of Tabernacles* (1861, cat. 36). Leathart owned four drawings: *By the Waters of Babylon* (1858, sepia, untraced), *Queen Esther Hearing the News of the Intended Massacre of the Jews* (formerly owned by Plint), *Isaiah Reproving the Women of Jerusalem* (1861–63, sepia, untraced) and *'Who is he that cometh from Edom with dyed garments from Bozrah?'* (1862, watercolour, untraced). Dianne Sachko Macleod has shown that both men were "eager to buy whatever was offered them", arguing that their enthusiasm for collecting was a way for rich businessmen to exonerate themselves from the guilt associated with the grim reality of the factories they oversaw. Dianne Sachko Macleod, *Art and the Victorian Middle Class: Money and the Making of Cultural Identity*, Cambridge (Cambridge University Press) 1996, pp. 179, 275.

17 Ernest Hart was brought into the Solomon family on 10 May 1861 when Abraham Solomon married Hart's sister, Ellen. Hart was already a respected surgeon at the North London Ophthalmic Infirmary as reported in the *Jewish Chronicle and Hebrew Observer*, 30 April 1858, p. 157. Hart practised as a surgeon until 1863, when he became dean of the medicinal school at St Mary's Hospital, London. He later became the editor of the *British Medical Journal* from 1866 to 1898. *Oxford Dictionary of National Biography*, s.v. 'Ernest Abraham Hart'.

18 My reading of Solomon as a 'Jewish history painter' is indebted to Larry Silver's discussion of Maurycy Gottlieb's history paintings; see Silver, *op. cit.*, p. 87.

19 The *Jewish Chronicle*, which followed the careers of Jewish artists in London, reported on a lecture given by Solomon Hart, professor of painting, at the Royal Academy in Trafalgar Square on 25 February 1858. The lecture was on the subject of history painting and how elevated subjects of spiritual history had the ability to improve the minds of men. 'Professor Hart's Lectures', *Jewish Chronicle and Hebrew Observer*, 5 March 1858, p. 93.

20 Burnham and Giese have defined 'historicity' as the use of archaeologically accurate details in order to claim 'historical truth'. 'Narrativity' is the "temporal sequence of several events cohesively organized, involving a specific time and place". "Didactic intention assumes there is a moral center, a hortatory aim, an exemplar or principles to teach." For an excellent introduction to the tenets of history painting, see Patricia M. Burnham and Lucretia Hoover Giese (eds.), *Redefining American History Painting*, Cambridge (Cambridge University Press) 1995, pp. 6–14.

21 The eminent Victorian religious scholar Patrick Fairbairn, whose *The Typology of Scripture* went through five nineteenth-century editions, made a particular point of emphasizing that Moses benefited by this early association with Gentiles whose "lessons in organization and government helped him set the future course of his people". Patrick Fairbairn, *The Typology of Scripture* [1845–47], Grand Rapids MI (Zondervan) 1967, p. 178.

22 The emphasis on the gentleness of Jochabed's caress may have been inspired by Solomon's understanding of the original Hebrew text: "She put the child in it [the wicker basket] and placed it among the reeds by the bank of the Nile" (Exod. 2:3). In using the Hebrew *s-y-m*, 'she put', the text implies gentle loving actions, as opposed to the harsh verb *hishlikh*, 'to abandon'. See Nahum M. Sarna, *The JPS Torah Commentary: Exodus*, Philadelphia (Jewish Publication Society) 1991, p. 9.

23 J.H. Hertz (ed.), *Pentateuch and Haftorahs*, London (Soncino Press) 1981, p. 210.

24 Assessing the orthodoxy of the Solomon family is complex. Based on evidence contained in correspondence and other primary documents, the orthodoxy of the Solomon family was fairly typical for middle-class, native-born, mid-century Jews in London. Endelman describes the situation: "Most were not Orthodox Jews by the standards of Central and East European Orthodoxy at the time or the standards of British and American Orthodoxy today, but were respectful of religious tradition and far more observant than wealthy Jews elsewhere in the West. They were not in any sense Jews in name only, nor was their Jewish identity merely a lingering ethnic allegiance. They observed the major Jewish holidays, kept the Sabbath, and adhered to the dietary laws, although their manner of doing so did not always agree with Jewish tradition and was considerably influenced by contemporary Christian practice." Endelman, *Radical Assimilation*, p. 81.

25 Solomon created two wood engravings illustrating scenes of contemporary Jewish life for an article entitled 'Jews in England' by G.L. (identity unknown), published in *Once a Week: An Illustrated Miscellany for Literature, Art, Science, and Popular Information*, VII, 9 August 1862, pp. 190–96. This was followed by ten illustrations of Jewish religious ceremonies, as conducted under the altered conditions of modern life, for a series of articles entitled 'Illustrations of Jewish Customs', published in *The Leisure Hour: A Family Journal of Instruction and Recreation*, XV, 1866: 3 February, pp. 72–74; 17 March, pp. 167–69; 7 April, pp. 216–18; 26 May, pp. 328–30; 16 June, pp. 376–77; 28 July, pp. 475–77; 25 August, pp. 539–41; 23 September, pp. 603–05; 13 October, pp. 652–54; 29 December, pp. 823–25; the authoritative series was written by Dr Hermann Adler (1839–1911), son of Nathan Marcus Adler (1803–1890), Chief Rabbi of the Great Synagogue in London. Hermann Adler later became Chief Rabbi from 1891 to 1911. For more information on these engravings, see Weiner, *op. cit.*, pp. 15–22; Gregory R. Suriano, *The Pre-Raphaelite Illustrators*, New Castle DE (Oak Knoll Press) and London (The British Library) 2000, pp. 237–46; and Paul Goldman, *Victorian Illustration: The Pre-Raphaelites, the Idyllic School and the High Victorians*, Aldershot (Scolar Press) 1996, pp. 56–57, 89–92, 311.

26 For a discussion of the 'fruitful moment', also known as the 'pregnant moment', see Diana Strazdes, 'Washington Allston: Great Painting as Mute Poetry', in Burnham and Giese, *op. cit.*, p. 150.

27 A distant pyramid, seen through the window on the background wall, alludes to Moses's future role as the deliverer of the Children of Israel from bondage in Egypt.

28 Cohen, *op. cit.*, p. 156.

29 The painting, exhibited at the Royal Academy in 1861 as *A Young Musician Employed in the Temple Service During the Feast of Tabernacles*, is now often known as *Hosannah!*

30 Hertz, *op. cit.*, p. 817.

31 The reviewer for the *Athenaeum* described the harp as Assyrian, inspired by the "Ninevite Bas-reliefs" in the British Museum. *Athenaeum*, 25 May 1861, p. 698. Solomon was not alone in his fascination with Mesopotamia. The public fad for all things Assyrian was fuelled by the archaeological discoveries of Austen Henry Layard (1817–1894) and their subsequent display in the 1850s at the British Museum. For a thorough discussion of the nineteenth-century discovery and reception of Assyrian art, see Frederick N. Bohrer, *Orientalism and Visual Culture: Imagining Mesopotamia in Nineteenth-Century Europe*, Cambridge (Cambridge University Press) 2003.

32 Cohen, *op. cit.*, pp. 156–58; also expanded in Susan Tumarkin Goodman, 'Reshaping Jewish Identity in Art', in Goodman, *op. cit.*, p. 16.

33 Endelman, *Radical Assimilation*, p. 94.

34 *Ibid.*, p. 109.

35 Curiously, the verse as quoted in Gambart's catalogue is not found in any of the well-known versions of the Bible. The catalogue also misprinted the citation, as 'Jeremiah 15:7'. Ernest Gambart, *Seventh Annual Winter Exhibition of Cabinet Pictures, Sketches and Watercolour Drawings, the Contributions of British Artists*, London (French Gallery) 1859, p. 14, cat. 145.

36 This interpretation is generated from a chapter in my dissertation; see Gayle M. Seymour, 'The Life and Work of Simeon Solomon, 1840–1905', PhD diss., University of California at Santa Barbara, 1986, pp. 48–50.

37 The correspondent for *The Times*, 24 November 1859, p. 9, in his review of Solomon's drawing at Gambart's French Gallery, noted Solomon's "pursuit of the Ninevitish".

38 The identification of the harpist as Semiramis is based on a drawing of the same head, contained in Solomon's famous sketchbook (now in the collection of the Mishkan Le'Omanut Museum attached to the Kibbutz Ein Harod in Israel, see fig. 4), labelled 'Semiramis Nineveh Jemima Jenkins'. This identification seems logical since the Babylonian queen was remembered, among other things, for creating a false religion by imposing the Babylonian cult of Nebo on the Assyrian religion. Some legends say she was raised by doves in the desert, hence the adoption of the dove as her symbol. *Encyclopaedia Britannica*, 11th edn, s.v. 'Semiramis'.

39 The possibility of a metaphorical linkage with the Dionysiac orgies of ancient Greece was not lost on Solomon: the drunken leopard, a frequent guest at Orphic rites, is shown in a state of amiable stupor. Seymour, 'The Life and Work of Simeon Solomon', p. 49.

40 The wearing of the phylactery commemorates God's commandment: "And it shall be to you as a sign on your hand and as a memorial between your eyes, that the law of the LORD may be in your mouth; for with a strong hand the LORD has brought you out of Egypt" (Exod. 13:9). See Sarna, *op. cit.*, pp. 270–72.

41 Lionel Lambourne was the first scholar to point out the sexual ambiguity of the harp player. See Lionel Lambourne, 'Abraham Solomon, Painter of Fashion, and Simeon Solomon, Decadent Artist', *Jewish Historical Society, Transactions*, XXI, 1968, p. 280. Colin Cruise has expanded on the sexual ambiguity of Solomon's figures; see Colin Cruise, 'Simeon Solomon: A Drama of Desire', *Jewish Quarterly*, Autumn/Winter 1998, p. 66.

42 Susan Tumarkin Goodman, in her discussion of Max Lieberman's *Bathing Boys* (1900), makes this point about the near absence of nudity in nineteenth-century Jewish art. Goodman, *op. cit.*, p. 26.

43 See Gayle M. Seymour, 'Simeon Solomon and the Biblical Construction of Marginal Identity in Victorian England', co-published simultaneously in *Journal of Homosexuality*, XXXIII, 3/4, 1997, pp. 97–119; and *Reclaiming the Sacred: The Bible in Gay and Lesbian Culture*, ed. Raymond-Jean Frontain, New York (Haworth Press) 1997, pp. 97–119.

44 For a discussion of the phenomenon of speakers and listeners in the art of Rembrandt, see Julius Held, 'The Spoken Word in Rembrandt', in *Rembrandt Studies*, Princeton NJ (Princeton University Press) 1991, pp. 164–83. I am indebted to Larry Silver, who noted a similar use of this narrative structure in his analysis of Gottlieb's work; see Silver, *op. cit.*, p. 94.

45 Eve Kosofsky Sedgwick has shown that in the late eighteenth century "'knowledge' and 'sex' [became] conceptually inseparable from one another – so that knowledge means in the first place sexual knowledge and secrets sexual secrets". See Eve Kosofsky Sedgwick, *Epistemology of the Closet*, Berkeley and Los Angeles (University of California Press) 1990, p. 73. Solomon makes the connection between knowledge, sexuality and transgression by illustrating the Expulsion of Adam and Eve on the background tapestry. See Seymour, 'Simeon Solomon and the Biblical Construction of Marginal Identity in Victorian England', p. 113.

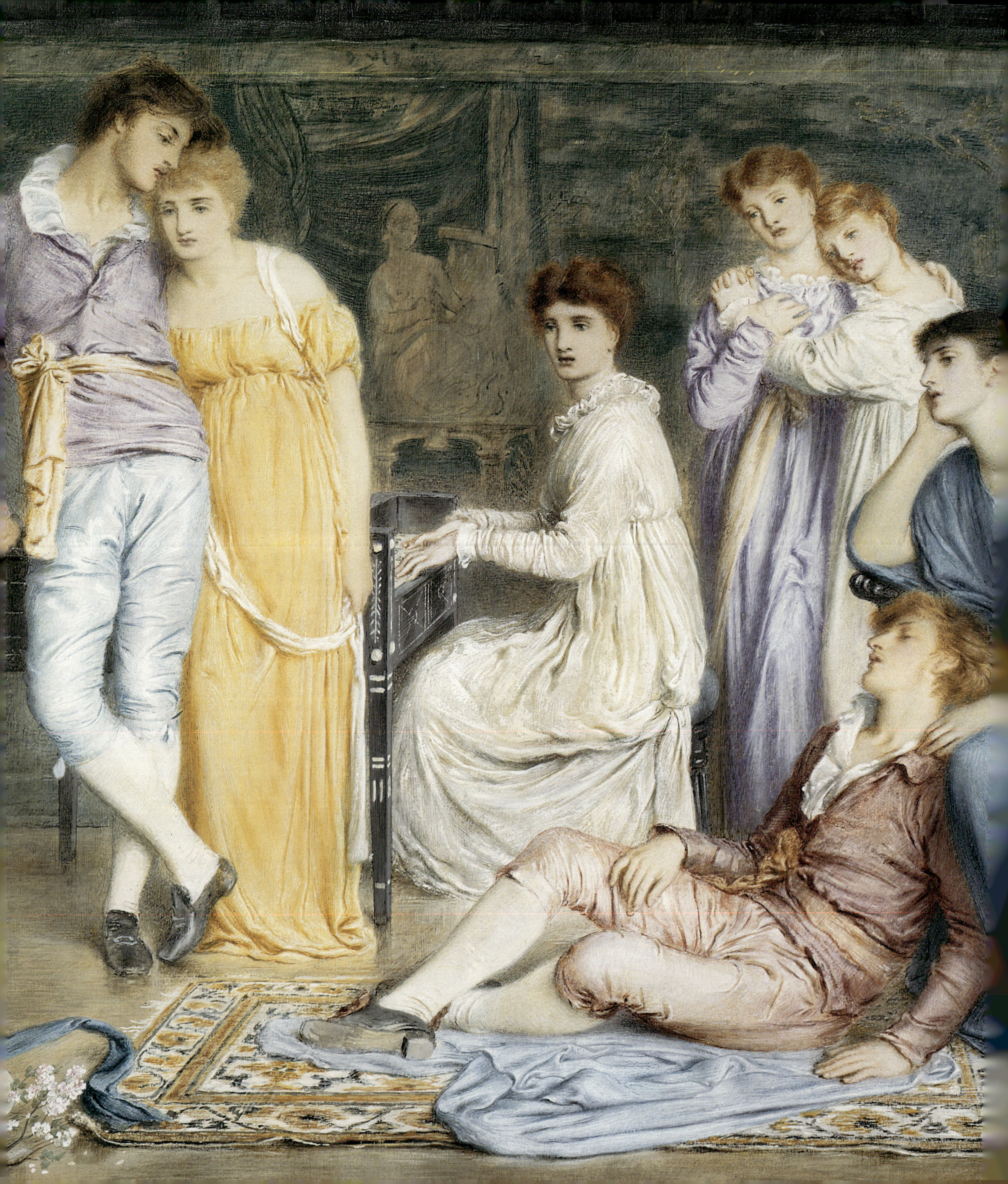

Frank C. Sharp

"A friendship I held dear": Simeon Solomon and the Royal Academy Circle

Simeon Solomon's earliest significant artistic connections outside his own family were made at the Royal Academy Schools. He was regarded as the most gifted of the group of Royal Academy students who became part of the Pre-Raphaelite circle in the late 1850s and early 1860s. Henry Holiday (1839–1927), his contemporary at the RA Schools, recalled:

> S.S. entered the R.A. schools as a probationer in the spring of 1855. I had done the same Dec. 1854, and, perhaps because we were the two youngest students in the schools, our ages being 15? & 14?, we sat next each other & began a friendship which lasted over 20 years. He missed the probationer tests & had to try again the Dec. following when he was successful and became a full student early in 1856 at the age of 15.[1]

A deep and lasting bond grew out of this early meeting. The two young men had similar tastes in art and shared a passion for music, frequently attending concerts together. Holiday recalled that he first heard Beethoven's Ninth Symphony with Solomon (see fig. 6).[2] Holiday would remain Solomon's closest friend for many years. Solomon also "became a favourite in [Holiday's] family, both on account of his abilities and his excellent qualities".[3] Holiday included Solomon in a family trip to Wales in 1862, and also enjoyed a warm relationship with his friend's family. He was welcomed in the homes of both Solomon's mother and his brother Abraham. Holiday found Abraham to be "one of the kindest of men, an excellent brother to Solomon and very friendly to me".[4]

Holiday discovered the gentleness, charm and mischievous sense of humour that would draw other artists to Solomon. He found that "[t]hose qualities which endeared him to all his friends, and with which I was intimately familiar, his straightforward nature, his faithful friendship, his devotion to his art and his fund of original humour – these qualities were the true character of the man".[5] Over fifty years after their first meeting, Holiday would remember his relationship with Solomon as "a friendship I held dear".[6]

Solomon first met William De Morgan (1839–1917) in 1859, when Solomon came back to the Royal Academy Schools to "compete for the draped model prize". De Morgan became part of Solomon's circle and accompanied Holiday and Solomon on a second journey to Wales in 1863. De Morgan and Solomon also formed a deep friendship that lasted until De Morgan "lost sight of him somewhere in the late sixties".[7]

It was also at this time that Solomon came to know William Blake Richmond (1842–1921). Holiday stated that his and Solomon's "most intimate friends in the schools were Albert Moore & William Richmond" and that they "were on friendly terms with many others such as G.D. Leslie,

Simeon Solomon
A Prelude by Bach (detail)
1868
(see p. 115)

Fig. 6
Solomon and Holiday Paying Homage to Their Heroes
Undated
Pen and ink on paper
Private collection

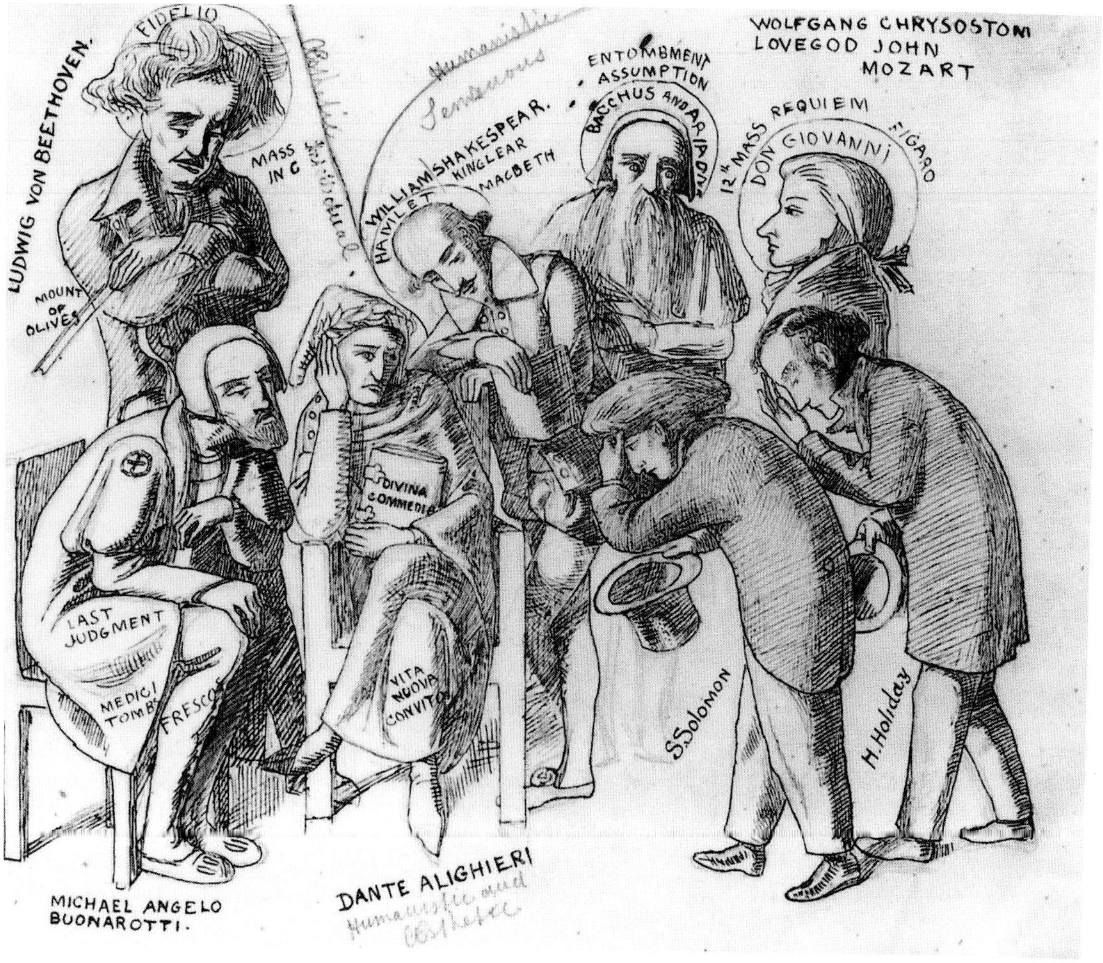

G.A. Storey etc".[8] Richmond would remember Solomon as:

> [a] fair little Hebrew, a Jew of the Jews, who seemed to have inherited a great spirit, an Eastern of the Eastern, facile and spasmodically intense, sensitive to extreme touchiness, conscious of his great abilities, proud of his race, but with something of the mystic about him which was Pagan, not Christian. Quaint with his humour. He touched all subjects lightly and with so much brilliancy that the follies he uttered and wrote seemed to be spontaneously wise and witty sayings. He twisted ideas, had a genius for paradox, and when in a humorous vein, speaking with assumed seriousness, he convulsed his friends with laughter by his strange weird imagination.[9]

The instruction at the Royal Academy Schools disappointed Solomon and his friends: "Masters we had none there. Charles Landseer sauntered through the rooms once a day and made some perfunctory remarks and an occasional pun but was not inspiring."[10] To a certain extent, for Richmond and De Morgan this void was filled by Solomon who, although with only a few years of experience, became a mentor to the two artists. Because of limited space, "students were not allowed promotion to the life schools for years merely because there was no room". Holiday and Solomon "soon found work in our studios more attractive than in the gloomy R.A. Schools".[11]

All of these young artists were heavily influenced by the Pre-Raphaelites. Holiday recalled, "I was beginning to feel the influence of the Pre-Raphaelite School at this time."[12] Richmond would "remember the keen admiration with which I and my friends regarded everything that came from

Millais's brush, and the almost worship with which we regarded his pictures. Fred Walker, Albert Moore, Simeon Solomon, Henry Holiday and I fed our young minds upon such pictures as the *Return of the Dove to the Ark*."[13] The young artists joined together to form a group, critiquing and inspiring each other. As Holiday remembered, "it must have been about this time that Marcus Stone, Simeon Solomon and I started a sketching club, meeting once a week at our respective houses in rotation. The host gave a theme on which we each had to make a sketch in two hours and he became the possessor of the sketches. We were afterwards joined by Albert Moore."[14]

Solomon was the first of his Royal Academy contemporaries to know Rossetti, Burne-Jones and William Morris, and it was through Solomon that the young artists moved into their orbit in the early 1860s. As Holiday remembered, "The original work of [Solomon] soon attracted the attention of such Pre-Raphaelites as Rossetti and Burne-Jones by whom he was much interested."[15] Georgiana Burne-Jones in her biography of her husband credited Solomon with bringing these artists to him: "Younger men now began to frequent the studio, some of them students of the Royal Academy, whose interest and curiosity had been aroused by Edward's work at the Exhibition of the Hogarth Club: they were brought in the first instance I believe by Simeon Solomon."[16] Holiday was one of the artists who came to know Burne-Jones through Solomon: "Simeon had met him first and he took me to meet him in Russell Place."[17]

For reasons that are unclear, William Michael Rossetti made a concerted effort to mislead early writers on Solomon as to when Solomon first met his brother and Burne-Jones. He told Julia Ellsworth Ford that "Solomon was in my Brother's Studio every now and then, like any other visitor, between such dates as 1863 and 1871".[18] In response to the question by Everard Meynell, author of the original entry on Solomon in the *Dictionary of National Biography*, as to what was "[t]he period of his friendship with the Rossettis, the Burne-Jones and Swinburne", William responded: "I fancy So[lomon] may have known Swinburne before (& after) he knew Gabriel & me. Our acquaintance with him began I think early in 1863 & continued until (say) 1869."[19] While William Rossetti's attempts to indicate that the connection ended before Solomon's arrest in 1873 are perhaps understandable, why he would wish to hide contacts made while Solomon was a young artist fresh out of the Royal Academy Schools in the late 1850s is a mystery. Possibly it is nothing more than an attempt to show that the relationship was of a shorter duration than it was. In any event, his statements citing 1863 as the beginning of the relationship are clearly false (see Mancoff's essay, p. 32).

It can be argued that Solomon was the last of the artists who can be definitively identified as Pre-Raphaelite to become part of the circle. Although his contemporaries certainly interacted with the circle's members, Solomon directly embraced their work in ways the others did not: Richmond and Holiday would both have careers that took them far from Pre-Raphaelite ideals, while De Morgan gave up painting for his work in the decorative arts. Solomon, however, produced a number of works that are instantly identifiable as 'Pre-Raphaelite', the poses, treatment and positioning of figures having direct similarities with the art of Burne-Jones and Rossetti.

The documentary record relating to Solomon is more fragmentary than that of any of the other artists associated with the Pre-Raphaelite group. What survives, however, gives ample evidence that Solomon was an integral part of this community of artists. Clearly they socialized together: Solomon hosted parties both when he lived alone in the early 1860s and later jointly with his sister Rebecca, and was a perpetual visitor in Burne-Jones's and Rossetti's studios. Ford Madox Brown's diary mentions more than one occasion when he spent five hours in Solomon's company.[20] Solomon also had a warm relationship with William Holman Hunt: a surviving letter from Solomon to Holman

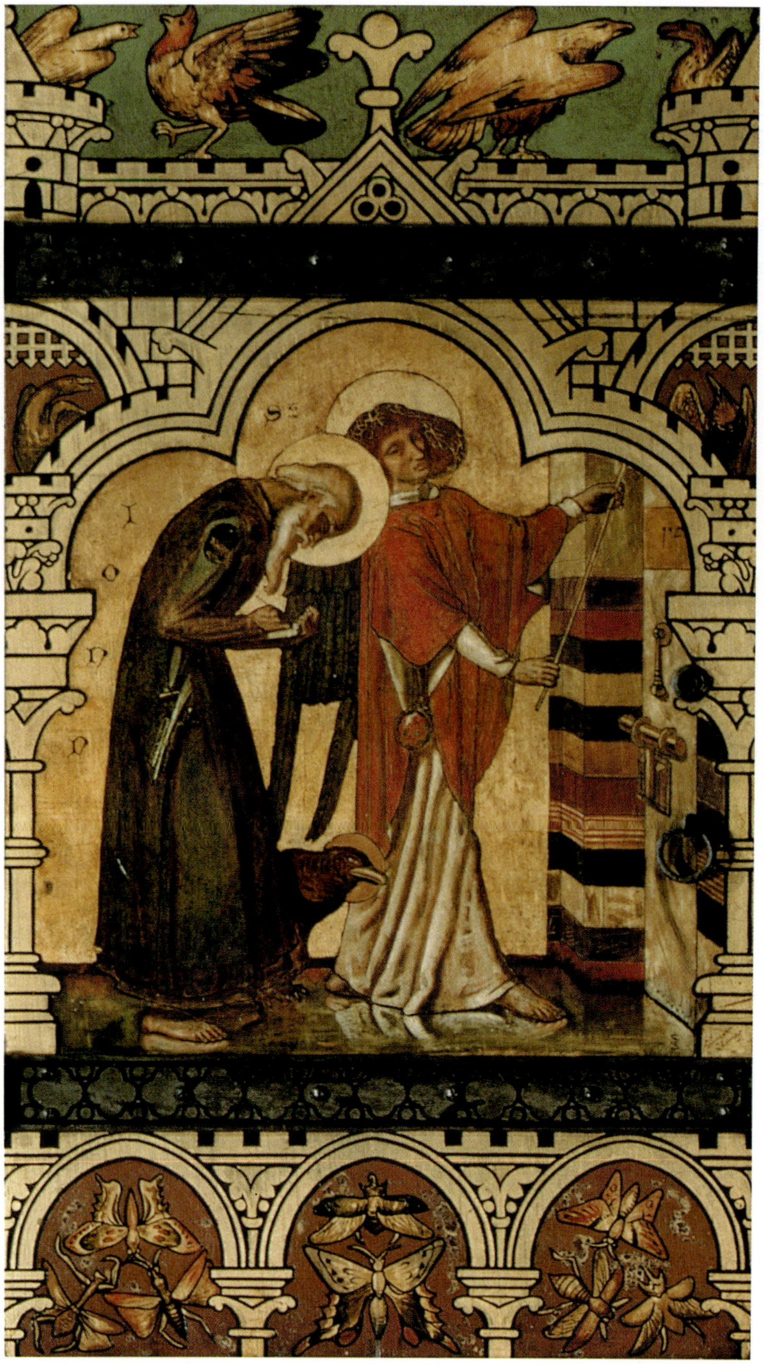

Fig. 7
Architecture: St John and the Angel Measuring the Heavenly Jerusalem
Detail of panel painted by Solomon for William Burges's 'Great Bookcase'
1859–62
Carved, painted and gilded wood
The Ashmolean Museum, Oxford

Hunt discussing plans to visit the elder artist's studio to view his work gives the impression that this was a regular occurrence.[21]

In common with the other artists in his circle, Solomon created designs for the decorative arts. His first work in this vein was probably the designs he created for William Burges's 'Great Bookcase' (see cat. 51 and fig. 34). Solomon was one of fourteen artists working on the project – the others included Burne-Jones, Rossetti, Albert Moore, Edward Poynter and Holiday – producing panels on the theme of Pagan and Christian art. Solomon's panels depict subjects such as Pygmalion and Galatea, St John and the Heavenly Jerusalem (fig. 7), and St Augustine.[22] Solomon went on to create glass and tiles for Morris, Marshall, Faulkner & Co. (few of these have been identified);[23] but he seems not to have been involved in designing ceramics for his friend De Morgan. De Morgan had only started his own firm in a small way by 1873, the year of Solomon's arrest, and would subsequently state that "Solomon never had anything to do with my pottery work".[24]

The most significant works for the Morris firm that can be definitively attributed to Solomon are his designs in stained glass for All Saints Church, Middleton Cheney, Northamptonshire. The windows were installed in 1865, so it is likely that the designs were created some time in 1864. The panels of the main part of the window are decorated with pairs of figures. Solomon designed those for two panels, one depicting Abraham and Moses and another with figures of David and Isaiah (cat. 51). He also designed a group of four panels depicting a procession of the twelve tribes of Israel across the top tier of the window.[25] William Morris's appreciation of Solomon's designs is proven by his decision to reuse Solomon's designs for windows for the North Church, Greenock, Renfrewshire, later in 1865.

The artists in Solomon's circle traded resources and skills. Solomon borrowed costumes for his paintings from Rossetti,[26] and also sought advice, especially from Burne-Jones. In the sole surviving letter from Solomon to Burne-Jones, Solomon seeks his guidance: "I also much want you to see a little picture I have been painting since my return, I want your advice about some colour."[27] It is clear that such assistance was a routine feature of the two artists' interaction. Solomon, too, was sometimes able to advise other artists: on at least one occasion, William Holman Hunt sought his help with getting details correct in a painting involving Jewish themes.[28]

Solomon often shared models with other artists in his circle: Nelly Smith, for example, was also employed by Burne-Jones, Poynter, Spencer Stanhope and several others.[29] Several of Solomon's works show a woman with features similar to Jane Morris's, and it is possible that she, too, modelled for him. Solomon was responsible for introducing to his circle the model (and later artist) Gaetano Meo, whom he discovered in 1865. Besides sitting for numerous works by Solomon including *A Prelude by Bach* (cat. 69), Meo appears in Burne-Jones's *Love Among the Ruins*, Rossetti's *Dante's Dream* and Richmond's *Prometheus Bound* and *The Watchers*, and in works by Ford Madox Brown, Frederic Leighton and possibly Holman Hunt. Henry Holiday made nude studies of Meo in preparation for stained-glass cartoons and for his illustrations to Lewis Carroll's *Hunting of the Snark*, and in the preparation of his *Dante and Beatrice* Holiday took the "colouring for Dante from Meo".[30]

Like some of the female models in Solomon's circle, Meo came from a humble background. Born in southern Italy to a Greek-speaking family, he was discovered by Solomon working as a street musician in London, playing a small harp. Struck by his handsome features, Solomon persuaded Meo to sit for him and introduced him to other artists. This discovery has something of the romance of Walter Deverell finding Elizabeth Siddal in a milliner's shop or Burne-Jones and Rossetti stumbling on Jane Burden in the theatre. Like these female 'stunners', Meo had the striking looks to attract the attention of an artist. Given Solomon's sexual orientation, it is difficult not to consider that there was a sexual element in the attraction; however, heterosexual artists in the group also appreciated Meo's qualities. William Blake Richmond, for example, referred to him as "the beautiful boy".[31]

Holiday told one of Solomon's early biographers that Solomon "continued to be my intimate and valued friend after my marriage in 1864 & until his tragic lapse".[32] While Solomon was in Italy in 1867, Holiday travelled to Rome, and on arrival "called first on Simeon Solomon".[33] The two men travelled together, immersing themselves in classical and medieval art. They travelled to Perugia and Assisi and made an extended stay in southern Italy visiting Naples and Pompeii.[34] From his published memoirs, Holiday remembered this as an idyllic episode. There were, however, stresses on the relationship. A surviving letter from Solomon to Holiday, probably from the period 1869–72, records

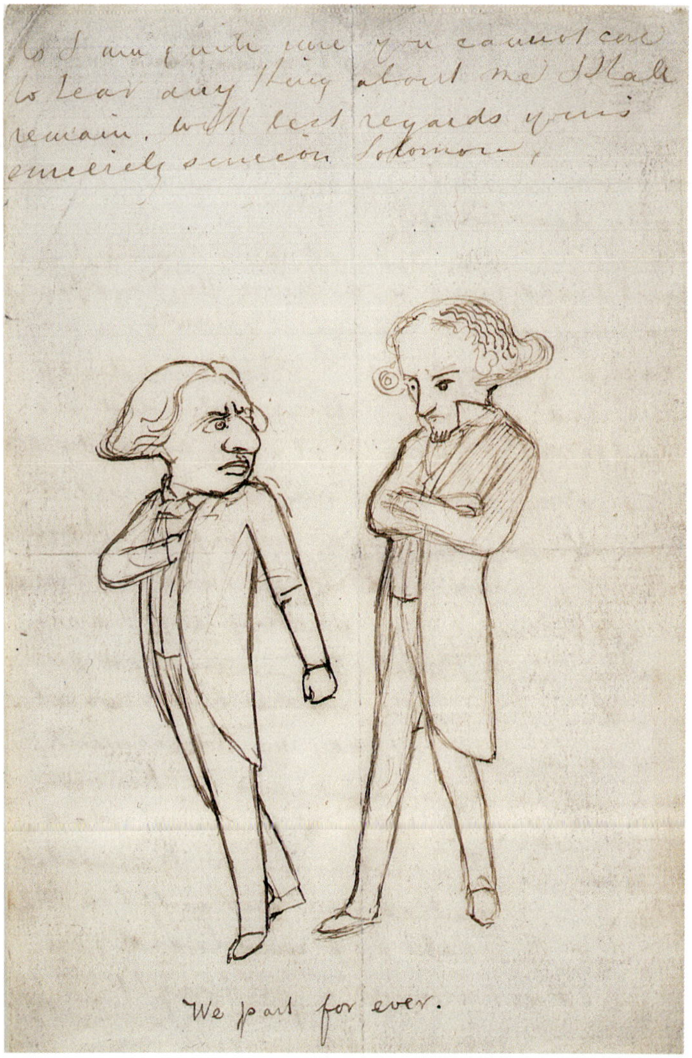

Fig. 8
We part for ever
c. 1869–72
Pen and ink on paper
Caricature drawing in an undated letter from Solomon to Henry Holiday
Private collection

a serious break in their friendship. The cause can be only a matter of speculation but it corresponds with his increasingly erratic behaviour under the influence of Swinburne, so Solomon may have said or done something that offended Holiday. Solomon's letter is clearly a plea for reconciliation:

> What is the reason I have not heard from you since the last time so long ago? Have I given you any cause for offence? Are you disappointed in me? Have I turned out differently from what you expected? Do you dislike me very much? Am I not worth writing to? I cannot believe that you have no time or opportunity for writing. If I were away and thought you wished for a letter I would make both or else make a sacrifice, you certainly cannot be very anxious to know how I did what I am doing, whether I am in Madagascar or Kamchatka.[35]

Solomon ends the letter with a humorous caricature showing him leaving Holiday, entitled "We part for ever" (fig. 8). Although the two men apparently resolved their differences, the caricature in this letter gives an interesting insight. Solomon's features are an obvious exaggeration of those found in his self-portrait and Holiday's are also a whimsical parody. The setting of the figures in an obviously dramatic way has echoes of such Pre-Raphaelite compositions as Hunt's *Claudio and Isabella* (1850, Tate) or Arthur Hughes's *Aurora Leigh's Dismissal of Romney* (1860, Tate).

Holiday was, later, one of the few artistic acquaintances of Solomon's to maintain contact with him after his "tragic lapse". Holiday recalled that he "made an earnest attempt to reclaim him about 1880 when I found him after a long disappearance, persuaded him to come see us an invitation cordially confirmed by my wife & backed by some of my friends, but the success was only temporary. He disappeared again without a sign."[36] Holiday was also instrumental in re-establishing Solomon's friendship with the Burne-Joneses. As Rossetti reported to Jane Morris:

> Ned Jones looked in for a minute and a half the other day and told me that poor SS wrote to him from a hospital. He did not answer but wrote inquiries to his doctor and learned that S. had arrived at the hospital not only ragged but actually without shoes! I must say Ned's conduct as a correspondent is hardly consistent with the penultimate piece of news he gave me on the subject: viz: that he and his wife had judicially gone to view this Hebraic phenomenon at a friendly meeting planned for this purpose by Holiday and his wife![37]

Simeon Solomon was a central figure in the group of young artists who met at the Royal Academy Schools and worked together in the late 1850s and early 1860s, and the relationships he had with these other artists were some of the most important of his life. Solomon's work was deeply admired and respected by his contemporaries: in 1867, Holman Hunt visited Spencer Stanhope in Italy and reported to Millais that Stanhope "quite believes in the inferiority of all men in England to [Burne-] Jones, Solomon and Val Prinsep",[38] while Richmond believed that "the greatest genius of our set was S. Solomon".[39] The regard in which these artists held Solomon and his work highlights his importance in his own artistic circle, and the impact that his innovative talent had on those around him.

I would like to thank Colin Cruise, Roberto Ferrari, Scott Thomas Buckle and Peter Cormack, Deputy Keeper, William Morris Gallery, for their assistance with this essay.

NOTES

1 Handwritten 'Memoir of Simeon Solomon' by Henry Holiday ('Holiday Memoir') prepared for Everard Meynell in connection with his compilation of the entry in the *Dictionary of National Biography* on Solomon. This is part of the collection of papers used by Meynell for the entry and currently held in a private collection (Meynell papers).
2 Henry Holiday, *Reminiscences of My Life*, London (William Heinemann) 1914, p. 42.
3 'Holiday Memoir', Meynell papers.
4 Holiday, *op. cit.*, p. 37.
5 *Ibid.*
6 Henry Holiday to Meynell, 20 July 1911, Meynell papers.
7 William De Morgan to Meynell, 19 July 1911, Meynell papers.
8 'Holiday Memoir', Meynell papers.
9 A.M.W. Stirling, *The Richmond Papers*, London (Heinemann) 1926, pp. 160–61.
10 'Holiday Memoir', Meynell papers.
11 *Ibid.*
12 Holiday, *op. cit.*, p. 41.
13 John Guille Millais, *The Life and Letters of Sir John Everett Millais*, London and New York (Methuen) 1899, II, p. 140.
14 Holiday, *op. cit.*, p. 40.
15 'Holiday Memoir', Meynell papers.
16 Georgiana Burne-Jones, *Memorials of Edward Burne-Jones*, London (Macmillan) 1906, I, p. 260.
17 Holiday, *op. cit.*, p. 65.
18 W.M. Rossetti to Julia Ellsworth Ford, 7 February 1903, in *Selected Letters of William Michael Rossetti*, ed. Roger Peattie, University Park (Pennsylvania State University Press) 1990, p. 635.
19 This claim is also untrue: as late as 23 May 1872, William Rossetti could meet Solomon in the street and speak to him on apparently cordial terms. *The Diary of W.M. Rossetti, 1870–1873*, ed. Odette Bornand, Oxford (Clarendon Press) 1977, p. 203.
20 *The Diary of Ford Madox Brown*, ed. Virginia Surtees, New Haven CT and London (Yale University Press) 1981, pp. 211, 213.
21 Solomon to Holman Hunt, n.d. Princeton NJ, Princeton University Library.
22 See J. Mordaunt Crook, *William Burges and the High Victorian Dream*, London (John Murray) 1981, p. 321.
23 A.M.W. Stirling, *William De Morgan and his Wife*, London (Thornton Butterworth) 1922, p. 77.
24 De Morgan to Meynell, 18 July 1911, Meynell papers.
25 See A. Charles Sewter, *The Stained Glass of William Morris and his Circle*, New Haven CT and London (Yale University Press) 1975, p. 133.
26 Solomon to D.G. Rossetti, 1860s, Harry Ransom Humanities Research Center at the University of Texas at Austin.
27 Solomon to Burne-Jones, 1860s, University of Manchester, John Rylands Library, Fairfax Murray Papers.
28 Holman Hunt to Solomon, 1860s, London, National Art Library, Victoria and Albert Museum.
29 *The Diaries of George Price Boyce*, ed. Virginia Surtees, Norwich (Real World) 1980, entry for 21 November 1864, p. 48.
30 Holiday, *op. cit.*, p. 292.
31 Stirling, *Richmond*, p. 272.
32 'Holiday Memoir', Meynell papers.
33 Holiday, *op. cit.*, p. 123.
34 *Ibid.*, pp. 130–31.
35 Solomon to Holiday, Collection of Scott Thomas Buckle.
36 'Holiday Memoir', Meynell papers.
37 Rossetti to Jane Morris, 29 February 1880, in *Dante Gabriel Rossetti and Jane Morris: Their Correspondence*, ed. John Bryson, Oxford (Clarendon Press) 1976.
38 Holman Hunt to Millais, 26 April 1867, University of Manchester, John Rylands Library.
39 Introduction by Richmond to Stirling, *De Morgan*, p. 9.

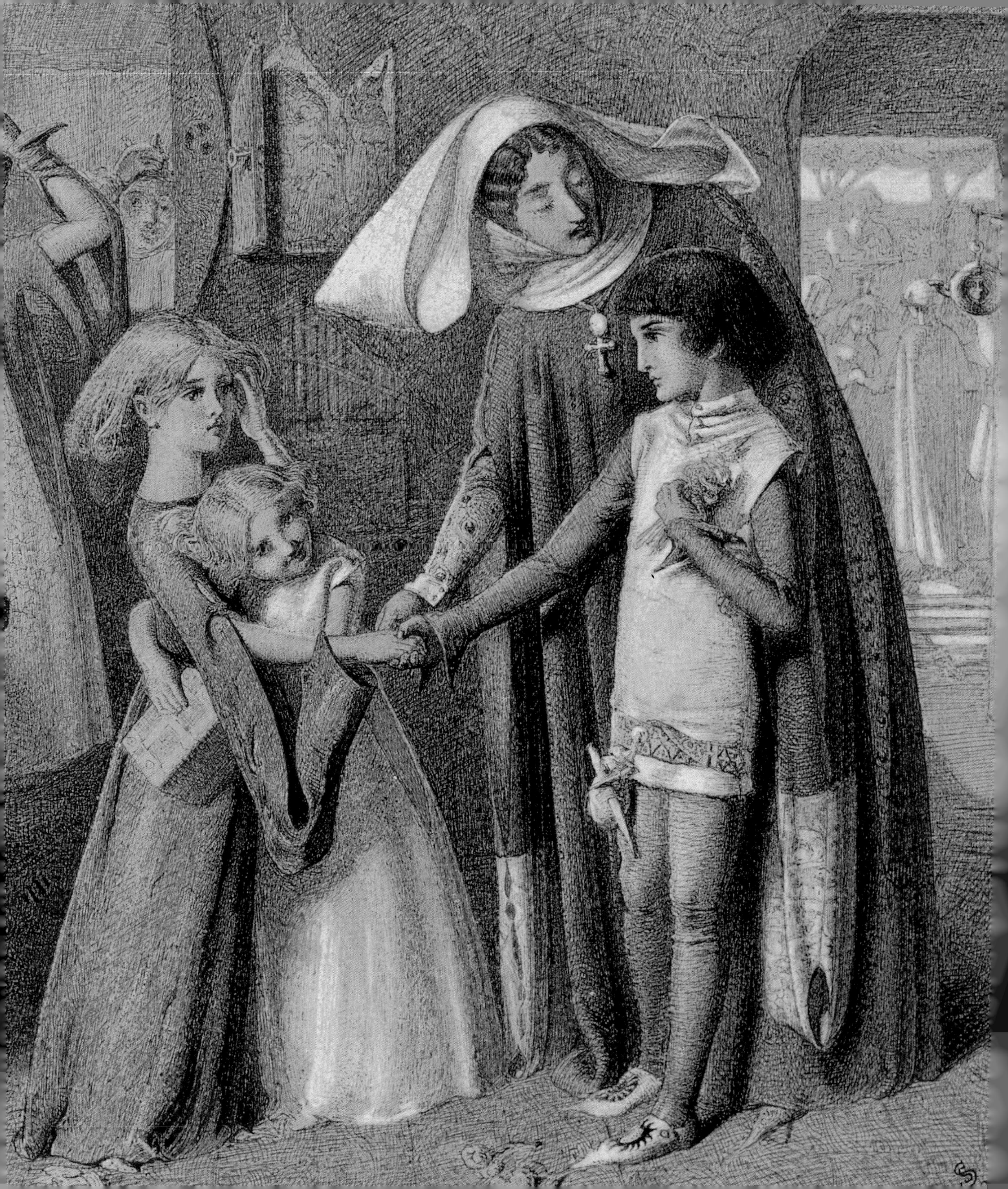

Debra N. Mancoff

Truth to Nature with a Difference: Solomon's Pre-Raphaelite Identity

Simeon Solomon came late to the Pre-Raphaelite circle. He was a mere boy in 1848 when the original seven brothers united to revive authentic principles and elevate sincere expression in English art, and barely an adolescent in 1851 when John Ruskin wrote his letter to *The Times* in their defence. By the time Solomon became an art student – enrolled at F.S. Cary's Academy aged twelve, he was accepted by the Royal Academy Schools aged fifteen in 1856 – the Pre-Raphaelite Brotherhood, as originally conceived, had ceased to exist. Well aware of his own youth and inexperience, he shied away from an initial invitation from the sculptor Alexander Munro to meet Dante Gabriel Rossetti in the autumn of 1857, writing with self-deprecating humour and charm, "Mr. Boyce has given you to understand that I am a man, but I am only just turned 17 and am very small and not advanced enough in manners to become the guest of grown up gentlemen at such a late hour."[1] Yet within a year, when Solomon made his Royal Academy debut, the few critics who noticed his work associated him with the Pre-Raphaelite Brotherhood.

Throughout Solomon's career, as well as over the course of the century since his death, critics and scholars have struggled with the appropriate way to frame his Pre-Raphaelite identity. Lionel Lambourne noted that in the twentieth century he had come to occupy "the invidious position of an *enfant terrible* in most chronicles of the Pre-Raphaelite Movement".[2] This is true, since in much of the literature on the Pre-Raphaelites and their circle Solomon's art has been studied through the lens of his personal biography. Solomon's relationships with Rossetti, Algernon Swinburne and Edward Burne-Jones have been well documented as the foundation for the interpretative discussion of Solomon's selection of subjects and the development of his distinctive expression, as well as the integral role these relationships seemed to have played in the choices he made in his life. The stylistic affinities between his work and that of Rossetti and Burne-Jones have been well mapped, and his contribution to the Pre-Raphaelite aesthetic in the creation of a sexualized male counterpart to the Rossettian ideal of female beauty has been persuasively established.[3] But the perception of him as a Pre-Raphaelite, specifically in the years that he rose to critical attention and in the decades that bracket his death, was by no means monolithic. That Solomon was regarded as a Pre-Raphaelite is a given factor in the analysis of his position in the movement's history, but over the course of his career the term was used equally to praise and condemn him. More than an *enfant terrible*, Solomon's late critics came to regard him as the irredeemable Brother who squandered his artistic potential. This perception of a tarnished Pre-Raphaelite identity, based as much on his personal behaviour as on his artistic achievement, was seen as a metaphor for lost innocence, for both his life and the artistic circle that gave his youthful endeavours context and meaning.

Simeon Solomon
Dante's First Meeting with Beatrice
(detail)
1859–63
(see p. 76)

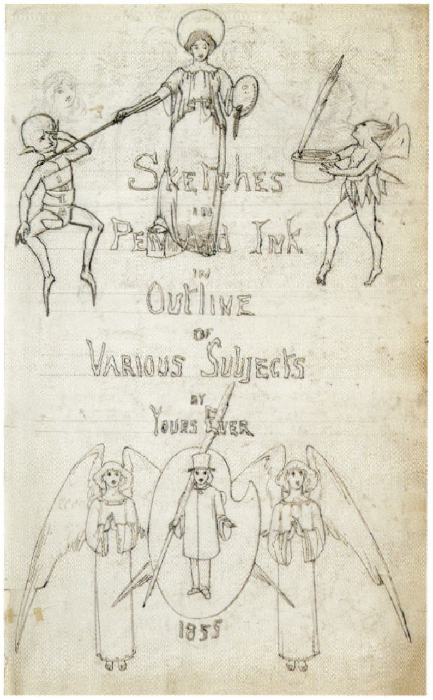

Fig. 9
Sketches in Pen and Ink in Outline of Various Subjects
1855
Pen and ink on paper
Frontispiece to a sketchbook
Mishkan Le'Omanut Museum, Ein Harod, Israel

In an anecdotal account of Solomon's life, Bernard Falk observed that the artist, "for convenience' sake", was "usually bracketed with the Pre-Raphaelite Brethren, though in reality having little in common with their ideals or aspiration".[4] Yet, as an adolescent, Solomon seemed to have formulated his artistic direction – in style, subject, sentiment and even ambition – on the Pre-Raphaelite model. Although it is impossible to pinpoint exactly when he discovered Pre-Raphaelite art, his early experiences provided many opportunities to see the work of the initial circle and to cross paths with some of the original brothers. Solomon's older brother Abraham, an established painter by 1846, had a studio at 18 Gower Street, the same street where John Everett Millais had lived with his parents and kept a studio when the Brotherhood was founded in 1848. Artistic life was sociable in the 1850s, and studio visits linked artists of divergent affiliations. It is reasonable to assume that Solomon's initial acquaintance with artists of any sector of the art world took place in his brother's studio.

According to his diary entry of 7 April 1857, George Price Boyce met Solomon on a visit to Abraham's studio to see his new painting *Waiting for the Verdict*. "Went to Solomon's," he noted, "saw some remarkable designs by his younger brother showing much Rossetti-like feeling."[5] The designs to which Boyce referred are likely to be the drawings contained in the sketchbook Solomon compiled between the years 1854 and 1857, now in the collection of the Mishkan Le'Omanut Museum, Ein Harod, Israel. The sketchbook's contents bear evidence of Solomon's range of interests, including scenes from works by Shakespeare and Dickens, as well as imaginative and witty vignettes (fig. 9). The subjects reflect some of the preferences of the Pre-Raphaelite circle, but literary imagery was popular throughout the Victorian art world at this time. Boyce's recognition of "Rossetti-like feeling" may have referred to Solomon's aesthetic choices. His figures – slender, lively, but oddly stiff – and his crowded compositions – filled with historically suggestive detail – recalled Rossetti's first endeavours in oil, such as *Ecce Ancilla Domini! (The Annunciation)* (1849–50, Tate), as well as his current work in watercolour, such as *Arthur's Tomb: The Last Meeting of Lancelot and Guenevere* (1855, The British Museum, London). But the same stylistic affinities may be cited with Millais's initial Pre-Raphaelite paintings, such as *Isabella* (1848–49, Walker Art Gallery, Liverpool) and *Christ in the Carpenter's Shop* (1849–50, Tate). Like any young artist of his generation, Solomon would have been well aware of the Pre-Raphaelite Brotherhood's romantic rebellion and admired them as a cutting-edge model of advanced style and artistic identity. And, even without his brother's professional connections, Solomon could have seen their works at any number of London art venues or in reproduction, in copies of *The Germ* or the newly published Moxon edition of Tennyson's *Poems* (1857).

Late in his life, William Michael Rossetti noted that he first became acquainted with Solomon's precocious talent around 1856 or 1857, when "an album stuffed full of a number of his designs, was handed about at a big gathering of men, including myself".[6] But there is no documented evidence to substantiate this early date, the names of those present at this "big gathering of men" were never recorded, and, with the exception of Boyce, Rossetti and the other members of his brother's circle, only noted their first encounters with Solomon and his work in retrospect. In any event, it is clear that Solomon's sketches served as his passport into the art world. In May 1858, when he made his debut at the Royal Academy with the Old Testament subject *Isaac Offered* (see cat. 19 and fig. 23), the critic for *Bentley's Miscellany* identified him as "well-known among artists as a first rate draftsman, but a neophyte painter", suggesting that his sketches had established his initial reputation. Among the young artist's "merits", the critic cited colour, expression and the authentic presentation of "oriental" costume and details of Jewish ritual. But the work, he lamented, was "in the Pre-Raphaelite guise", and although he voiced his objections to "the young painter's tendencies", he described Solomon as "the last rose of summer, for the brotherhood are no where this year".[7] It was true that neither Millais nor William Holman Hunt was represented in the exhibition that year, and Rossetti, as always, refrained from submitting his work for consideration. Solomon was received as a representative of the once daring but now declining rebellion just as he was becoming acquainted with the members of Rossetti's circle.

By 1858, although the original Brotherhood had completely disbanded, a younger group of artists had gathered around Rossetti, giving new vitality to the Pre-Raphaelite movement and new meaning to Pre-Raphaelite identity. Among Rossetti's new associates were Edward Burne-Jones and William Morris, who had recently worked with Rossetti in Oxford, painting murals with Arthurian subjects on the wall of the new Debating Hall, as well as Swinburne, Boyce and William Burges.[8] The desire to reform English art that had shaped the founding Brothers' mission had now been eclipsed by romantic medievalism. In contrast to Ruskin's charge that artists "go to Nature with all singleness of heart ... rejecting nothing, selecting nothing, scorning nothing", the source of the dictum 'Truth to Nature' that had inspired the meticulous rendering of the Brotherhood's initial endeavours, the new Pre-Raphaelites saw nature through the distinctive filter of individual imagination.[9] To be a Pre-Raphaelite in 1858 meant to embrace medieval subjects, to express a heightened aesthetic sensibility and to pursue artistic freedom. In his attempt to define the roles of the founding Pre-Raphaelite Brothers, Percy Bate observed that Holman Hunt had been the "reformer", Millais the "executant", and Rossetti the "dreamer".[10] When Solomon entered the circle at some point in 1858, the "dreamer" was the undisputed leader of the Pre-Raphaelites, and for Rossetti artistic truth was found in the exploration of the artist's own nature – his inner life and emotional state – rather than the appearance of the natural world. Solomon readily adopted the idea of truth to one's own nature, giving Ruskin's dictum a different nuance.

Over the next few years, Solomon forged his career on the Pre-Raphaelite template. He had already established his awareness of Pre-Raphaelite subjects and sensibility as seen in the sketch *Chiaro and his Soul* (c. 1857, Mishkan Le'Omanut Museum, Ein Harod, Israel), based on Rossetti's story 'Hand and Soul', published in the first issue of *The Germ*, and the modern-life subject featured in the highly finished drawing *I Am Starving* (c. 1857, private collection). The composition of an undated drawing, *The Death of Sir Galahad* (fig. 10), suggests a more deliberate association; the kneeling figure of Galahad evokes Rossetti's image of the young knight worshipping at a wayside altar in his illustration of Tennyson's 'Sir Galahad' in the 1857 edition of *Poems* (see cat. 119). Solomon's rendering of *Dante's First Meeting with Beatrice* (1859–63, cat. 16) reveals a denser, more claustrophobic composition, and his handling of pen and ink, balancing finely wrought details with the strong contrast of shadow and light, may mark Rossetti's direct influence. This was the style that Burne-Jones adopted when he first entered Rossetti's studio, watching and emulating him. Although it is not possible to cite the exact date, it is clear that, by this time, Solomon was doing the same. Entries in Boyce's diary also reveal that, as early as January 1859, Solomon felt sufficiently confident to express his opinions on Rossetti's work at the Hogarth Club, and on 30 April he met Boyce in Burges's studio, where he showed him a caricature he had made of Morris and his wife.[11]

Even as a young acolyte, an element of irreverence tempered Solomon's high seriousness about the Pre-Raphaelite mission. He produced sly satires of the original Brotherhood's idealism, such as his drawing *A Pre-Raphaelite Studio Fantasy* (fig. 11), representing himself as a young artist, armed with

Fig. 10
The Death of Sir Galahad While Taking a Portion of the Holy Grail Administered by Joseph of Arimathea
Undated; *c.* 1857–59
(see p. 76)

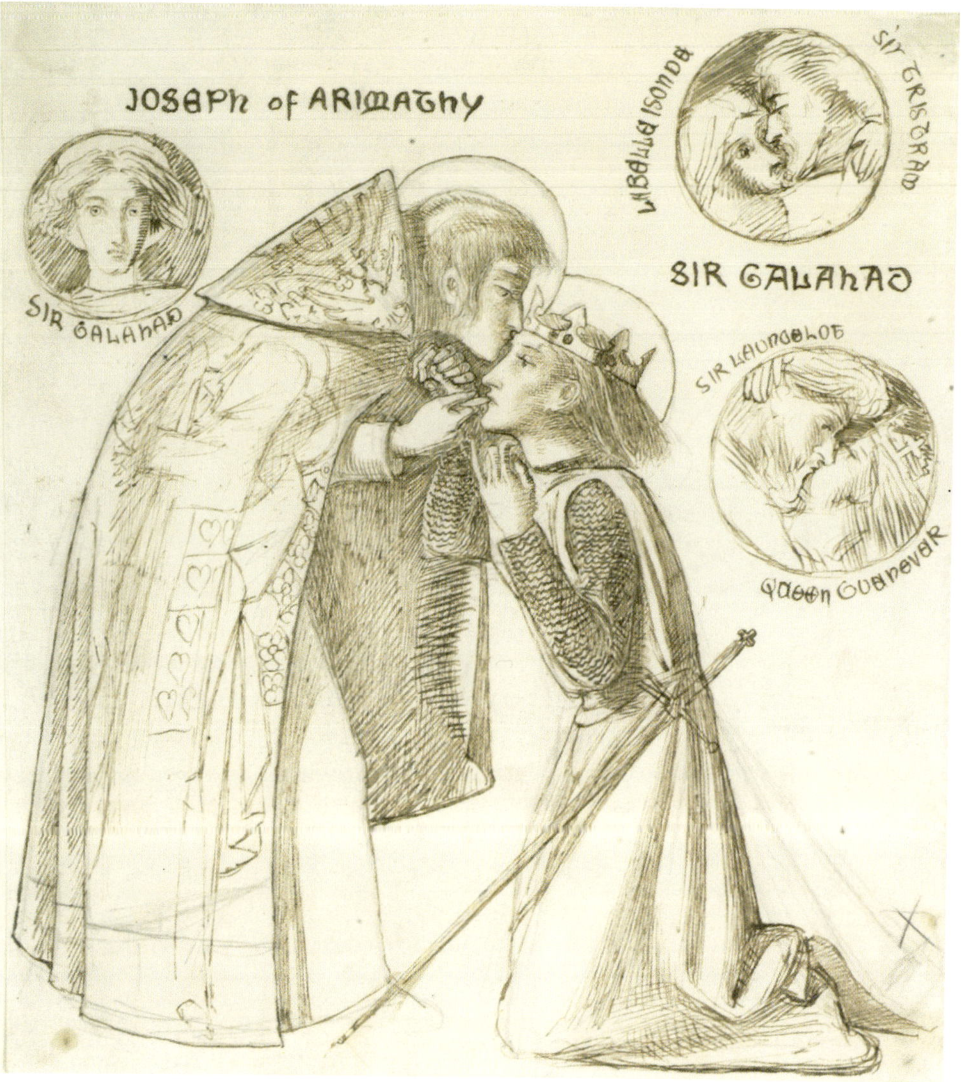

paintbrushes, a palette and a volume of Ruskin's *Modern Painters*, being subjected to a father's lament about a wasted education. He composed 'The PRB Catechism for the Use of Disciples of that School' (undated [1859], private collection), which revealed his complete understanding of the founding principles of the movement, but undercut his full endorsement of them with mockery, recommending that tests be administered by a monitor with red hair as well as raining blows on those who do not admire "red hair and green eyes".[12] He made a puckish jab at the favourite knight of the circle in the caricature *Sir Galipot bearing the holy Gruel* (fig. 12). Humour, particularly self-deprecation, had always enlivened the Pre-Raphaelite attitude; Rossetti and Burne-Jones both wielded wicked pens, and it is plausible that Solomon's satires stand as evidence of his acceptance in the circle. But there was one significant way in which he differed from his new and more established associates. Although he mocked the exhibition of Pre-Raphaelite work at the Royal Academy in his 'PRB Catechism', writing, "We exhibit there in order that the love for true art may not perish. We should hold it a duty to pat ourselves on the back for such consideration and self-sacrifice", after his debut in 1858 – unlike Rossetti and Burne-Jones – he participated in every annual exhibition from 1860 to 1872 except that of 1868.[13]

Fig. 11
A Pre-Raphaelite Studio Fantasy
Undated
Pen and ink on paper
18 × 22 cm (7 1/16 × 8 5/8 in.)
Private collection

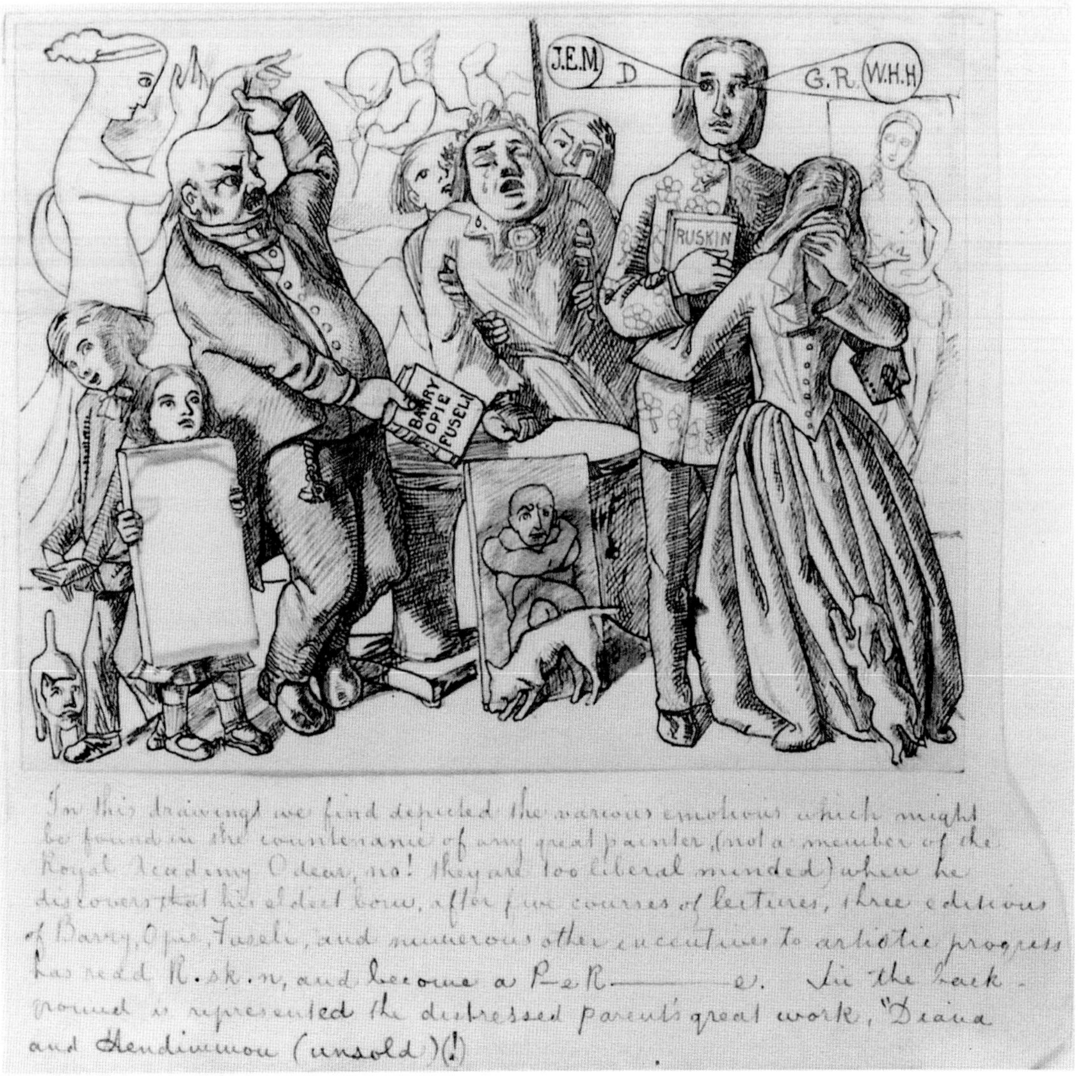

By the middle of the 1860s, the Pre-Raphaelite circle that Solomon had entered had drastically changed. Rossetti, now a widower, had largely abandoned his decorative, brittle watercolours for lush, rich-toned oils and traded his medieval narratives for the celebration of female beauty. Morris had turned to writing, as well as the business of design, and Burne-Jones embraced a new classical lyricism without relinquishing his fondness for the Middle Ages. As Elizabeth Prettejohn has observed, by this time the term Pre-Raphaelite was used by the Victorian press as a term of convenience, more as "an attribute of an artist's identity" rather than to distinguish an identifiable style.[14] In 1866 a critic for the *Gazette des Beaux-Arts* dubbed Dante Gabriel Rossetti the "high priest of Pre-Raphaelitism". But Rossetti saw it otherwise, writing to Ford Madox Brown: "The epoch of preraphaelitism [*sic*] was a short one which is quite over yet and will never be renewed."[15]

Solomon had changed, too. Although he maintained his friendship with Rossetti and his circle, he was widening his artistic acquaintance; further, in his art he began to pursue an aesthetic of difference in his exploration of androgynous and homoerotic beauty. To Robert Buchanan, writing under the pseudonym 'Thomas Maitland', Solomon's transformation was evidence of Pre-Raphaelite corruption. The target of his screed, 'The Fleshly School of Poetry: Mr. D.G. Rossetti', published in

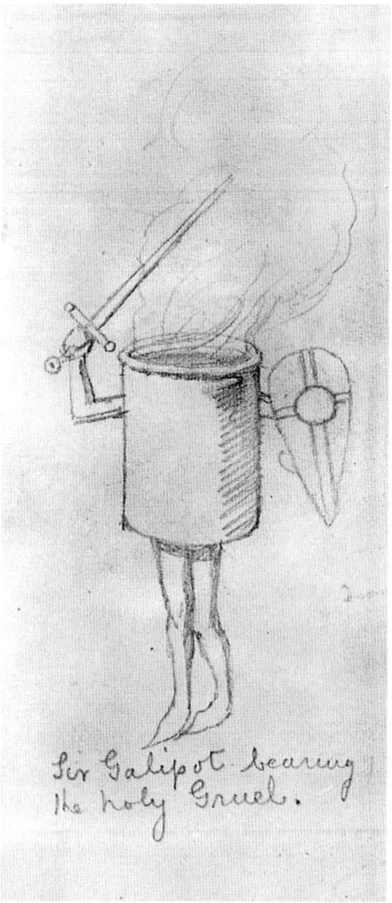

Fig. 12
Sir Galipot bearing the holy Gruel
Undated
Pencil on paper
13.5 × 5.8 cm (5⅚16 × 2⅚16 in.)
Birmingham Museums & Art Gallery

Contemporary Review (1871), was obvious, but those who had come under Rossetti's influence were equally guilty of the aesthetic crime of sensualism. Buchanan linked Rossetti with "the so-called Pre-Raphaelite school", and while admitting that he had seen little of his painting other than in photographic reproductions, he declared Rossetti was "an artist who conceives unpleasantly, and draws ill". According to Buchanan, these were weaknesses shared by "Mr. Simeon Solomon". Buchanan then turns to poetry, and after he judges Swinburne's poetry as "neither poetic nor manly", but "simply nasty", he identifies the same quality in Solomon's work: "pretty pieces of morality, such as 'Love dying by the breath of Lust'", in which Solomon's genius is put to such twisted use that the result produces "veritable monsters – like the lovely devils that danced around Saint Anthony".[16]

Although Solomon's suggestive subjects confounded and offended Buchanan, the critic passed his judgement on the basis of guilt by association with Rossetti and what he discerned as Pre-Raphaelite perversity. Just two months later, at Solomon's request, Swinburne penned a sympathetic review for *The Dark Blue* of his friend's recent work and his privately published prose poem, *A Vision of Love Revealed in Sleep*. Swinburne did not hesitate to characterize the strange and provocative quality he noted in Solomon's figures, a "supersexual beauty in which the lineaments of woman and of man seem blended as the lines of sky and landscape melt in the burning mist of heat and light".[17] But the name 'Pre-Raphaelite' was notably absent from Swinburne's descriptive and critical vocabulary. After Solomon's public humiliation, decades would pass before his name was linked with the Pre-Raphaelite movement in any considered critical sense.

In a letter to Félix Fénéon in 1891, the poet John Gray suggested that if the French critic came to London they could seek out drawings by Solomon, whom he described as "a Pre-Raphaelite, but also something else".[18] The issue of "something else" proved an obstacle for those who wanted to understand the position Solomon occupied in the Pre-Raphaelite circle. Percy Bate included him in *The English Pre-Raphaelite Painters: Their Associates and Successors* (1899) in his attempt to make his critical assessment of the movement fully comprehensive. But he admitted that Solomon was never "Pre-Raphaelite in the true sense of the word", explaining that "work less realistic never came from the easel of a painter".[19] By Bate's definition, there were two types of Pre-Raphaelite artists. When used in reference to the founding Brethren, the term evoked "the qualities of sincerity and directness", "honesty and definite inspiration", modelled on the example of the early Italian painters. But with the demise of the original Pre-Raphaelite Brotherhood, the public chose to ignore the "earlier meaning" and associate the term with the "eclectic and poetic school" of Rossetti, Burne-Jones and the lesser artists who followed in their wake.[20] This was the sense in which Bate positioned Solomon as a Pre-Raphaelite; the innocence and sincerity that were the core of the original Brotherhood were lost as the term changed meaning. Solomon's late entry into the circle placed him outside the authenticity of the original movement. And in the eyes of Bate and others, his personal history cast him in the role of Pre-Raphaelite after the fall.

At the time of his death, the discussion of Solomon's abandonment of Pre-Raphaelite idealism served as a code through which critics could refer to his social transgressions and explain his artistic decline. In his notice of the memorial exhibition at the Baillie Gallery, Robert Ross acknowledged that Solomon's best works were made "when he was associated with the Pre-Raphaelites and great things were expected of an inheritor of unfulfilled renown".[21] The romantic theme of the young, promising artist who squandered his potential also shaped the recollections of those who knew him. The comment credited to Burne-Jones, made when Solomon entered the circle – "You know, Simeon, we are mere schoolboys compared to you" – is balanced by that of his wife Georgiana; in 1904 she recalled that her husband had felt a pang of envy in his recognition of Solomon as "the rising genius". She confessed that "the tragedy of his broken career is one before which I am struck dumb; but all the more I do cling to recollections of hope and promise surely not false, though unfulfilled in this world".[22] The lament for what could have been replaced the need to speak of what happened.

G.C. Williamson, in his gossipy account of *Murray Marks and his Friends* (1919), declared that a true account of Solomon's artistic achievements "would be a revelation to the world of the skill of poor Solomon and the genius which he allowed to run to waste", placing the blame squarely on the artist.[23] In 1925 Arthur Symons, who does not mention the term Pre-Raphaelite, also struck a chord of regret, stating that Solomon "has his place, not far from Burne-Jones, in any record of the painting of the nineteenth century. Had circumstances been kinder to him, or had he been other than himself, he would have been a formidable rival."[24] The retrospective assessments had a common theme: in failing to fulfil his promise, Solomon failed the Pre-Raphaelite movement. Measured against an intangible standard of Pre-Raphaelite idealism, Solomon could not help but fall short of their expectations, allowing them to express distaste for his actions in the guise of talking about his art.

I would like to acknowledge the suggestions of my colleague Professor Thomas L. Sloan at the School of the Art Institute of Chicago and the research assistance of Farris Wahbeh and Elizabeth Shingleton.

NOTES

1 Solomon to Alexander Munro, *c.* October/November 1857, as quoted in Lionel Lambourne, 'A Simeon Solomon Sketchbook', *Apollo*, LXXXV, January 1967, p. 60. "Mr. Boyce" refers to the painter George Price Boyce (1826–1897), a friend of Rossetti's with whom Solomon became acquainted some time in 1857.

2 Lambourne, *op. cit.*, p. 59.

3 See Colin Cruise, '"Lovely Devils": Simeon Solomon and Pre-Raphaelite Masculinity', in *Reframing the Pre-Raphaelites: Historical and Theoretical Essays*, ed. Ellen Harding, Aldershot (Scolar Press) 1995, pp. 195–210.

4 Bernard Falk, 'The Tragedy of Simeon Solomon', in *Five Years Dead: A Postscript to 'He Laughed in Fleet Street'*, London (Hutchinson) 1937, p. 311.

5 *The Diaries of George Price Boyce*, ed. Virginia Surtees, Norwich (Real World) 1980, p. 17.

6 As quoted in Julia Ellsworth Ford, *Simeon Solomon: An Appreciation*, New York (Frederic Fairchild Sherman) 1908, p. 20. The date was more likely 1857 than 1856. Rossetti, who had not mentioned Solomon in his other writings, gave Ford permission to quote from one of his letters. He claimed not actually to have met Solomon until 1863 or 1864.

7 *Bentley's Miscellany*, May 1858, as quoted in *Solomon: A Family of Painters*, exhib. cat., ed. Jeffery Daniels *et al.*, London, Geffrye Museum (Inner London Education Authority) 1985, p. 6.

8 In 1857, Rossetti organized a group project to design and execute a programme of ten murals based on the Arthurian legend for the interior of the new Oxford Union Debating Hall. He assembled a group of six other artists to participate. Their inexperience with mural painting led to a technical fiasco. After a few months Rossetti abandoned the project, leaving his murals unfinished. The other artists soon followed, and the Debating Society hired William Riviere to finish the work.

9 John Ruskin, *Modern Painters*, 5 vols., Orpington (George Allen) 1888, I, pt. 1, p. 417.

10 Percy Bate, *The English Pre-Raphaelite Painters: Their Associates and Successors*, London (George Bell & Sons) 1899, p. 5.

11 Boyce, *op. cit.*, pp. 26, 27. The caricature has disappeared.

12 For a fuller discussion of these, see Gayle M. Seymour, 'The Life and Work of Simeon Solomon, 1840–1905', PhD diss., University of California at Santa Barbara, 1986, pp. 38–42. "Red hair and green eyes", as quoted on p. 42.

13 As quoted in Seymour, *op. cit.*, p. 41.

14 Elizabeth Prettejohn, *The Art of the Pre-Raphaelites*, Princeton NJ (Princeton University Press) 2000, p. 110.

15 As quoted in Jan Marsh, *Dante Gabriel Rossetti: Painter and Poet*, London (Weidenfeld & Nicolson) 1999, p. 277.

16 Robert Buchanan, 'The Fleshly School of Poetry: Mr. D.G. Rossetti', *Contemporary Review*, XVIII, October 1871, pp. 334–50, quoted in Carolyn Hares-Stryker (ed.), *An Anthology of Pre-Raphaelite Writings*, New York (New York University Press) 1997, pp. 238–39, 240.

17 Algernon Charles Swinburne, 'Simeon Solomon: Notes on his "Vision of Love" and Other Studies', *The Dark Blue*, I, July 1871, p. 574.

18 As quoted in J.H. McCormack, *John Gray: Poet, Dandy, and Priest*, Hanover NH (Brandeis University Press) 1991, p. 28.

19 Bate, *op. cit.*, p. 59.

20 *Ibid.*, p. 8.

21 Robert Ross, 'Fine Art: Simeon Solomon', *The Academy*, 23 December 1905, p. 1336.

22 The comment attributed to Burne-Jones is generally repeated without documentation. I have taken the quotation from Falk, *op. cit.*, p. 320. Georgiana Burne-Jones, *Memorials of Edward Burne-Jones*, London (Macmillan) 1906, I, p. 260.

23 G.C. Williamson, *Murray Marks and his Friends: A Tribute of Regard*, London (John Lane) 1919, p. 163. Williamson devotes a full chapter to Solomon at a time when most other writers are nearly silent about his life and career, but he states that he died in 1895, a full ten years in advance of his actual death.

24 Arthur Symons, *Studies on Modern Painters*, New York (William Edwin Rudge) 1925, p. 6.

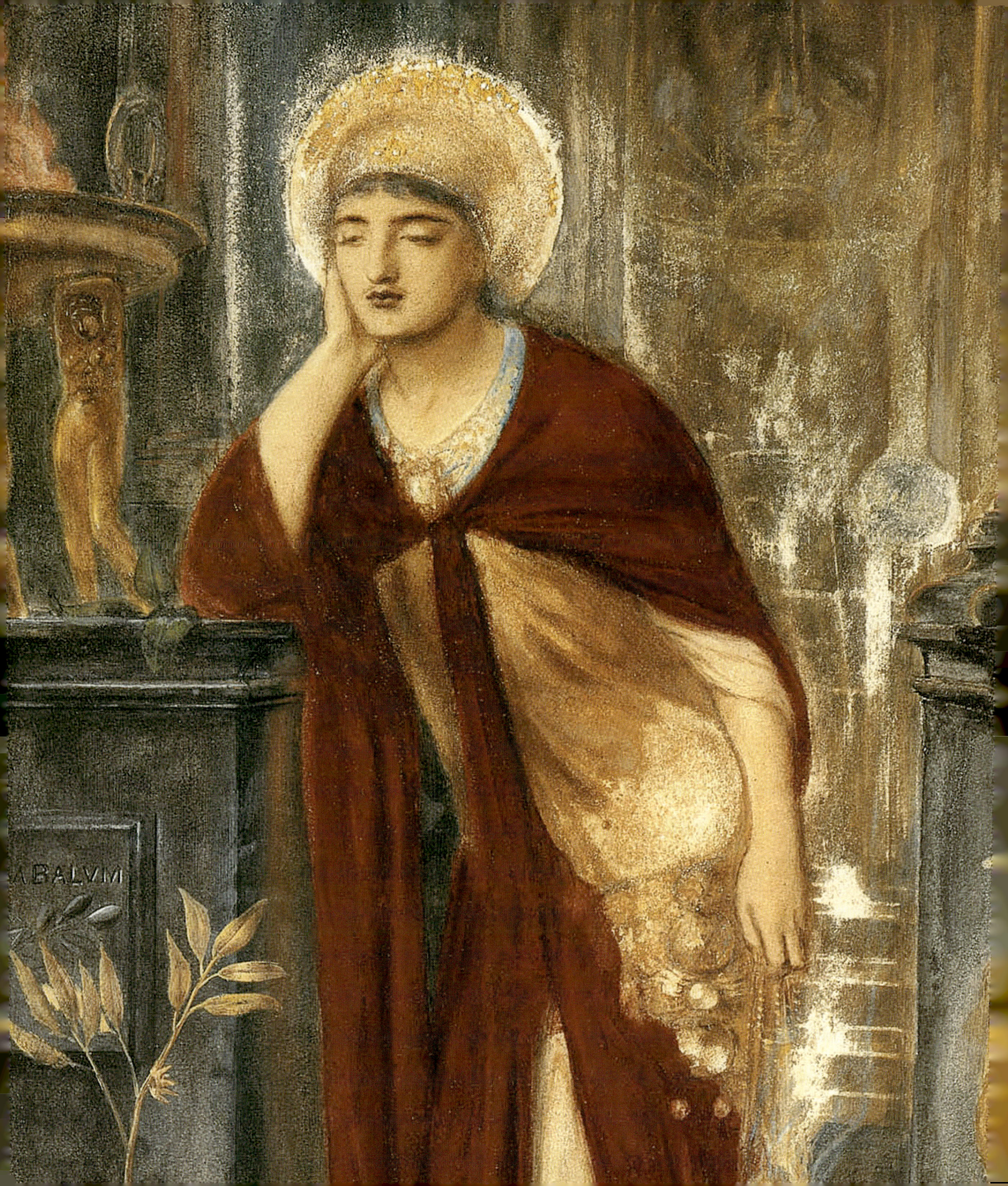
ABALVM

Elizabeth Prettejohn

Solomon's Classicism

"Hebraism and Hellenism, – between these two points of influence moves our world."[1] Thus the Victorian poet and critic Matthew Arnold names two fundamental principles of Western society and culture, equally great, but antithetical in their influence. Hebraism for Arnold involves action, conscience, law, and obedience to duty; Hellenism is the principle of thought, of beauty, of 'sweetness and light'. They are associated respectively with the Judaeo-Christian and the Greco-Roman traditions in Western culture, but for Arnold they are also living presences in the contemporary world he anatomizes in a series of essays, collected in his volume of 1869, *Culture and Anarchy*.

Simeon Solomon was unique among Victorian artists and writers for the balance, in his work, of Hebraism and Hellenism. Such a picture as *Carrying the Scrolls of the Law* of 1867 (cat. 94) gives powerful visual expression to the Hebraic principle: the young man, apparelled in the prayer shawl and hat of Jewish custom, is wholly absorbed in his religious duty, reverently embracing the scrolls of the Torah in which are inscribed the laws and observances of his community. In a painting of exactly the same date, Solomon presents the Hellenic god *Bacchus* (cat. 91) with the accessories of his pagan cult: the thyrsus or staff, balanced on his shoulder, entwined with vine-leaves and luscious purple grapes, which also wreathe his head. The two works, then, seem to divide along Arnold's lines, the one Hebraic and the other Hellenic. There is a moral difference, too: the scrolls of the law denote, above all, obedience to duty, while the grapes and vine-leaves allude subtly to the licence and intemperance associated with the ancient cult of Bacchus or Dionysus, god of wine. Yet both works are in some sense religious images; to that extent they are both Hebraic, and the expressions of both figures hint at inward spirituality or contemplativeness. On the other hand, despite the slight differences in skin-tone and physiognomy that perhaps differentiate them as Semitic and Aryan, both figures display a youthful male beauty that can be associated with Hellenism. Together the two works seem to propose a reconciliation between the tendencies that Arnold thought so dangerously divided in Victorian England.

But this was not an easy reconciliation. Solomon's Old Testament subjects and his scenes of Jewish religious ritual were widely approved as appropriate to his religious and racial background. Yet even some of Solomon's friends were much less sympathetic to the Classicism that began to appear in his work early in the 1860s, in pictures such as the various versions of *In the Temple of Venus* (cat. 72 and 73). Solomon's turn to the Classical coincides with the earliest signs of a more general Classical revival in British painting, seen in the work of such artists as Frederic Leighton, George Frederic Watts, Edward John Poynter and Albert Moore by the middle of the 1860s. Critics generally

Simeon Solomon
Heliogabalus, High Priest of the Sun and Emperor of Rome, 118–122 AD (detail)
1866
(see p. 137)

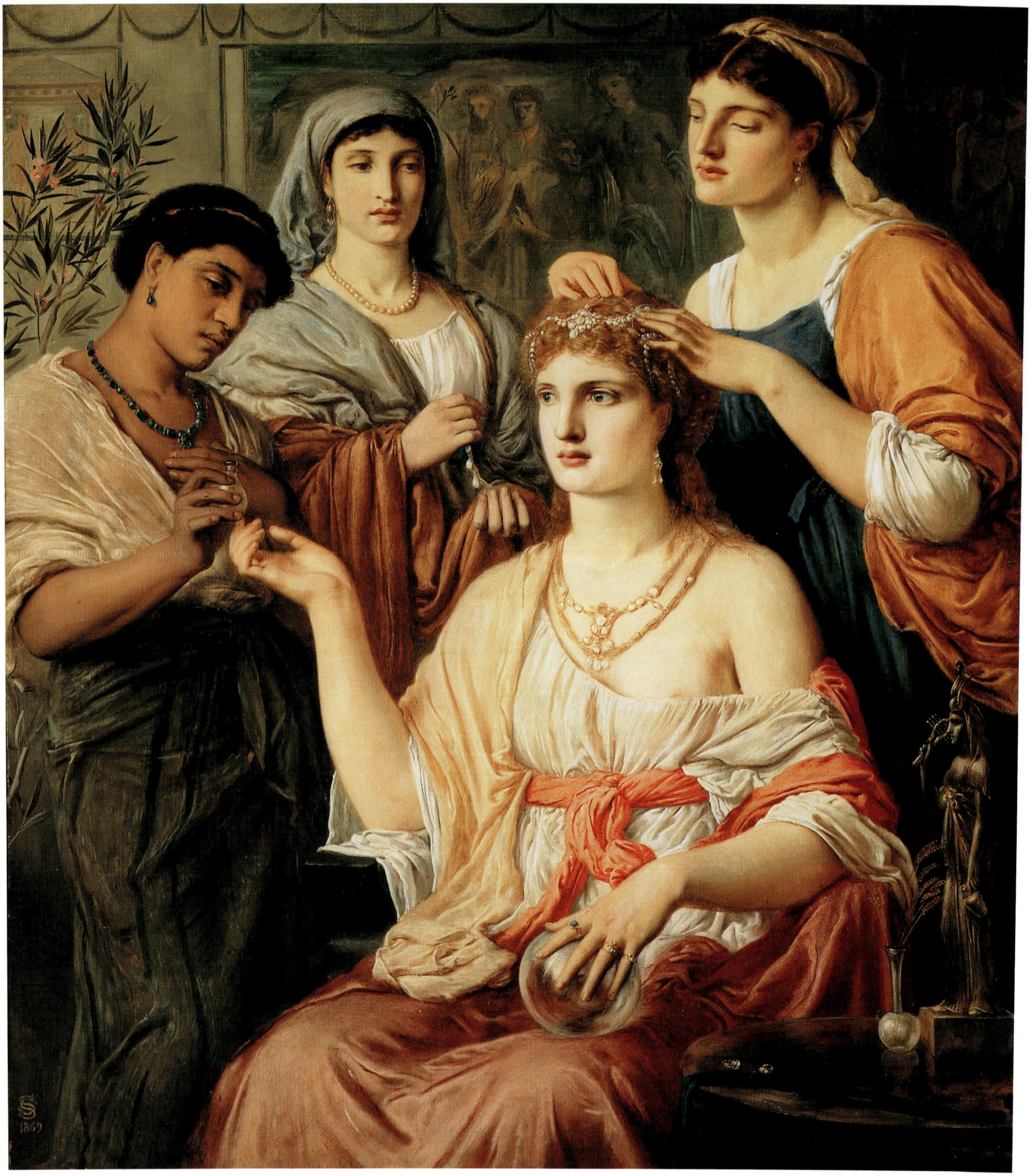

regarded the Classical revival as a salutary development, a worthy emulation of the ideal qualities attributed to the Greco-Roman artistic tradition. This was not so in Solomon's case. Sidney Colvin, in 1870 the first critic to publish an article on Solomon's work, uneasily described his shift to Classicism: "The decadence of Rome, the history of Rome under the Empire, with its frenzy of luxury, its life alternating between ferocious passion and feverish lassitude, offered an ample range of such subjects."[2] Much later, the painter William Blake Richmond, a close friend of Solomon's in their student days, praised Solomon's early pictures, "wholly inspired by the Hebrew Bible", but continued: "Unfortunately Solomon departed from his simple genius to accept an artificial and neurotic vein of late and debased Roman Art."[3]

Perhaps we may detect a hint of anti-Semitism in such remarks; Solomon the Jewish painter was thought to be at his best when he restricted himself to Jewish themes. Yet it is true enough that the first of Solomon's exhibited Classical subjects dealt, not with the Greek ideal, but rather with the decadence of the Roman Empire. Solomon's first important painting at the Royal Academy was *Habet!* (cat. 75), a scene of Roman patrician women watching a gladiatorial combat from their seats in the amphitheatre, exhibited in 1865.[4] The title would have been readily intelligible to its first audience, since it occurs frequently in Victorian historical novels about Rome: *habet!* ("he has it!", "he is hit") is the cry of the spectators when a gladiator falls, the sign of his defeat. Moreover the basic subject-matter would also have been familiar from historical novels set in ancient Rome; beginning with the founding novel of the genre, Edward Bulwer-Lytton's *The Last Days of Pompeii* of 1834, such novels commonly included a scene of Roman ladies in the amphitheatre. Solomon's painting does not depict the bloodshed in the arena; instead it concentrates on the reactions of the women, ranging from sadistic pleasure in the face of the blonde woman to the right of the central figure to the dismay of the fainting figure on the other side. This has the effect of placing us, the viewers of the picture, in the position of the fallen gladiator, appealing for mercy to the women who face us at such close range. But two of the women are turning their thumbs down, and the extravagantly bejewelled central figure, whom most Royal Academy critics described as the empress, appears too languid to intervene. The women's faces have the full-lipped, heavy-lidded sensuality of the female figures of Dante Gabriel Rossetti, a close friend of Solomon's at this date, and their gazes may combine desire with cruelty; love affairs between decadent Roman women and gladiators were another frequent motif in Victorian historical novels. The conjunction of violence and eroticism is disturbing, yet also compelling. Represented at life size, the figures face the viewer with uncompromising immediacy; there is no escaping the beauty of their cruelty.

Habet! was followed, at the Royal Academy exhibition of 1869, by another subject from the Roman decadence, *The Toilette of a Roman Lady* (fig. 13). This, too, gives visible form to a scene familiar in historical novels, in which a Roman woman demonstrates her vanity and luxury by dressing herself extravagantly with the help of slaves. The principal figure has brilliant red hair, perhaps with the hint that it is dyed; hair-dyeing was censured by the ancient Roman moralists as a sign of irredeemable vanity. On the table next to her is a statuette of Isis, suggesting that she is a devotee of a mystery cult, and perhaps sexually lax as well; Isis was a popular divinity among *demi-mondaines*.

In the Victorian Classical revival as it developed in the 1860s, there emerged a division no less sharp than Arnold's Hebraism and Hellenism, between the Greek ideal (as in the paintings of Leighton and Watts) and the Roman decadence. *Habet!* and *The Toilette of a Roman Lady* were pioneering examples of the latter category, and led the way for painters such as Lawrence

Fig. 13
The Toilette of a Roman Lady
1869
Oil on canvas
111.7 × 96.5 cm (44 × 38 in.)
Delaware Art Museum, Wilmington, USA, F.V. DuPont Acquisition Fund;/Bridgeman Art Library

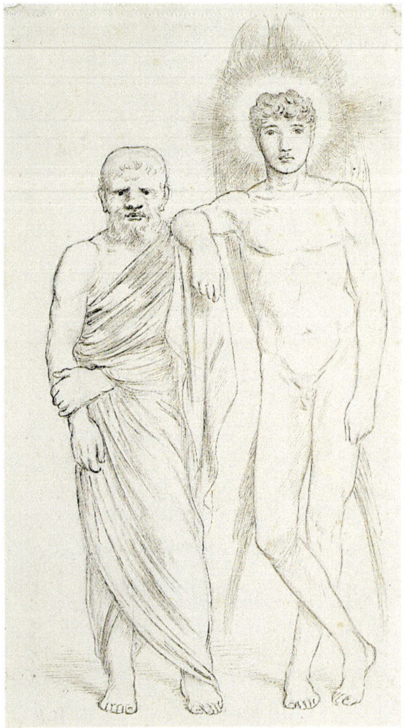

Fig. 14
Socrates and his Agathodaemon
Undated; c. 1865
(see p. 148)

Alma-Tadema, later the most prominent painter of such subjects. Moreover, the two Roman paintings were the largest and most important paintings of Solomon's career, his major statements at the Royal Academy exhibitions. Thus Solomon would seem, at least in public, to have chosen the decadent Roman side of Classicism, not its ideal Greek side. But that is not the whole story, for Solomon was powerfully attracted, too, to Greek antiquity.

An obvious reason for this was the tolerance of male same-sex desire in ancient Greek literature, something that attracted increasing attention in Victorian England, particularly in the universities, where such questions were discussed in élite intellectual circles well versed in the Classics.[5] In the 1860s Solomon cultivated a number of friendships among Classicists, including Walter Pater at Oxford, Oscar Browning at Eton, and the poet Algernon Charles Swinburne, who, despite failing to take his Oxford degree, was exceptionally learned in Greek and Latin literature. In the middle of the decade Solomon made a number of drawings of Classical subjects with sexually daring implications; the original drawings, as well as photographic reproductions by the skilled photographer Frederick Hollyer, circulated among the erudite and sexually sophisticated. For example, *Socrates and his Agathodaemon* (fig. 14) presents the most august of ancient Greek philosophers as a wizened old man, together with his 'good spirit', represented as a handsome young nude; this refers to Socrates' dalliances with beautiful young men, familiar from ancient texts such as Plato's dialogue *The Symposium*. The drawing treats this light-heartedly, contrasting Socrates' ugliness with the beautiful body of the Agathodaemon, who towers above him; its select audience presumably found it both humorous and mildly titillating.

But there was a more serious side to Solomon's interest in same-sex desire in ancient Greece, seen for example in his sensitive drawing of the head of the poet *Sappho* (cat. 65), and the watercolour *Sappho and Erinna in a Garden at Mytilene* (cat. 64). The watercolour is remarkable for its celebration of two female poets of antiquity, as well as for its frank depiction of their love; in both respects, too, it is closely related to Swinburne's poems of the same period, 'Anactoria' and 'Sapphics', which presented Sappho as fervently or even aggressively passionate towards women, while at the same time paying tribute to her poetic genius in verse of dazzling metrical complexity. Scholars now believe that Sappho (whose poetry is usually dated to about 600 BC) was not a contemporary of the poet Erinna, who may have lived two or three centuries later, and Solomon has sometimes been taken to task for the apparent anachronism. But Solomon is drawing on another tradition that links Sappho with Erinna; while its origins are obscure, traces of this tradition are found in an encyclopedia of the tenth century AD,[6] and Erinna often appears among Sappho's lovers in more modern poetry and literature. Both Swinburne and Solomon were no doubt aware of the surge of interest in Sappho, both as a poet and as a lesbian, in French literary circles from the mid-1840s onwards.[7] The most famous example is Charles Baudelaire's poem 'Lesbos', suppressed for indecency when it appeared in his collection *Les Fleurs du mal* in 1857. Baudelaire does not mention the names of Sappho's female lovers, but others, including Swinburne in 'Anactoria', refer to Erinna; a poem of 1861 by Théodore de Banville represents Erinna as transmitting Sappho's poetic legacy to a new generation of female poets.

Solomon takes up this literary tradition, but turns it in a new direction: his watercolour brings poetic genius and same-sex desire into closer, and more lucid, conjunction than ever before. Thus Erinna, usually identified as just one of Sappho's lovers, comes to the fore due to her fame, attested in ancient sources, as a poet. The statue of Aphrodite, to the right of the figures, refers both to female sexuality and to Sappho's most famous poem, an 'Ode to Aphrodite'; the lyre leaning on the

Fig. 15
Bacchus
1867
(see p. 134)

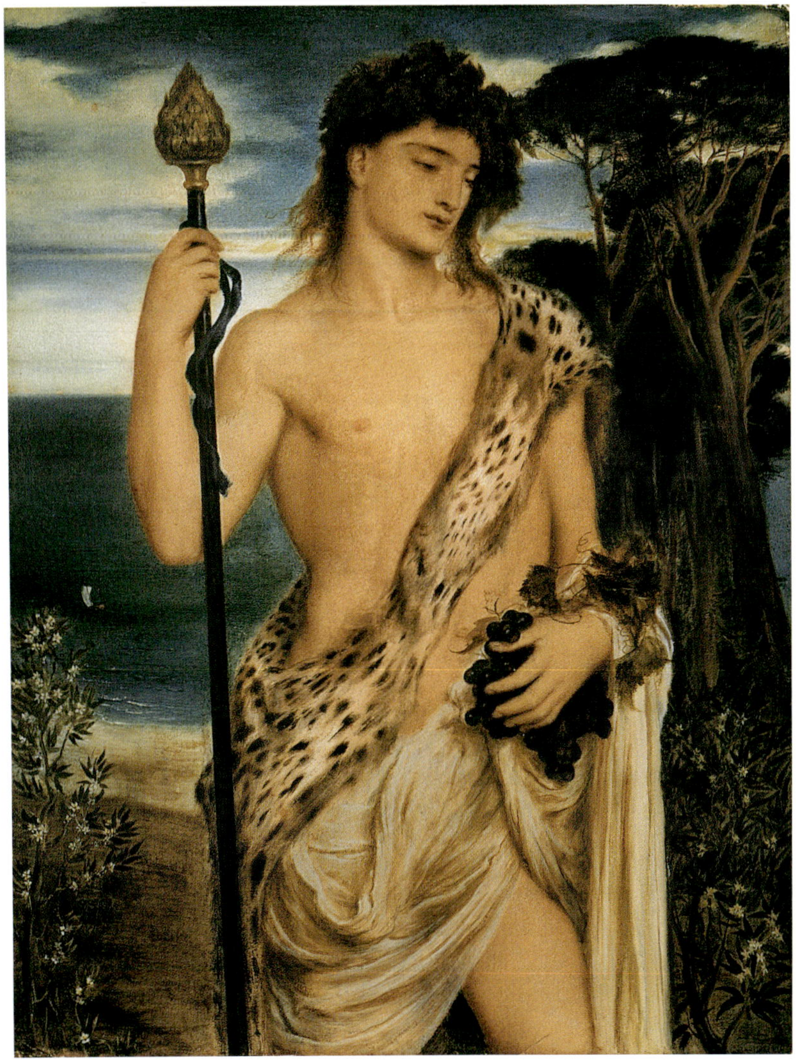

pedestal and the laurel wreath around Sappho's head are also symbols of poetry. Thus we can read the intimacy between the two figures as involving their art as well as their love, and the fact that they are of the same sex reinforces the sense of a special affinity between them. In a slightly later drawing, *Erinna Taken from Sappho* (cat. 66), the setting with statuette and lyre is repeated, but Erinna appears in a man's embrace, to Sappho's jealousy; the scenario recalls the only substantial fragment of Sappho's poetry, apart from the 'Ode to Aphrodite', that was then extant.[8] The two drawings demonstrate the depth of Solomon's Classical erudition. No doubt he consulted his Classicist friends, but in these and other examples he drew confidently on ancient literary texts ranging from the Greek philosopher Plato to the Roman lyric poet Catullus.

Solomon did not attempt to display his drawings of Sappho in public, but he did exhibit two representations of the wine-god Bacchus, a figure who seems to have had special importance for him; the oil painting, which we have already mentioned, appeared at the Royal Academy in 1867, and the watercolour (fig. 15) at the Dudley Gallery the following year. The wine-god was inevitably associated with the pleasures of the senses, in both ancient and modern representations, and his revels were seen to involve sexual as well as bibulous licence. But Solomon adds a distinctive touch of melancholy to the erotic appeal of his beautiful Bacchus. In the watercolour, the leopard-skin and drapery seem to slip from the fleshy forms of the torso, the hair is dishevelled, and the god looks pensively downwards. He is not carousing, but rather seems lost in reverie; or we might fantasize that he has just arisen from lovemaking, and looks tenderly down at a lover unseen to us.[9]

The slightly swaying pose and supple flesh of this Bacchus derive partly from prototypes in ancient sculpture and Pompeian fresco painting (on a journey to Italy in 1866–67 Solomon had studied Classical art, including the Pompeian artefacts in the Naples Museum). But the sensibility of Solomon's Bacchus, as well as of his Sappho and Erinna, is more complex than the impassive serenity conventionally ascribed to the Greek ideal, a point that Swinburne stressed in his article on Solomon, published in 1871:

> Modern rather than classical ... in sentiment and significance, [Solomon's designs] combine the fervent violence of feeling or faith which is peculiar to the Hebrews with the sensitive acuteness of desire, the sublime reserve and balance of passion, which is peculiar to the Greeks.

For Swinburne, then, Solomon's pictures of Classical subjects are *both* Hebraic and Hellenic; moreover this compound or double character also distinguishes them as 'modern'. He writes of the representations of Sappho and Bacchus respectively: "The wasted and weary beauty of the one, the faultless and fruitful beauty of the other, bear alike the stamp of sorrow; of perplexities unsolved and desires unsatisfied."[10]

Swinburne's article comes as close as possible, for a published text of its date, to open acknowledgement of same-sex desire in Solomon's work; this makes it the more disappointing that Swinburne was not brave enough to continue his critical support for Solomon after his arrest. The case is different with Walter Pater, the only writer to publish a sympathetic account of a work by Solomon in the years immediately following his disgrace. Moreover, Pater returns to the questions Swinburne had explored in his article of 1871, and perhaps offers a subtle correction to Swinburne's view of Solomon. The context is an essay of 1876 on the ancient myth of Dionysus (the Greek version of Bacchus), and Pater introduces Solomon's *Bacchus* partly to explore the post-Classical fortunes of the myth; it is not clear whether he is referring to the oil or the watercolour version, but his comments are equally apposite to both. He begins by agreeing with Swinburne that Solomon's characterization of Bacchus has a certain complexity that seems modern: "the god of the bitterness of wine, 'of things too sweet'; the sea-water of the Lesbian grape become somewhat brackish in the cup". This leads him to ask:

> Touched by the sentiment of this subtler, melancholy Dionysus, is anything similar in sentiment to be actually found, we ask, in the range of Greek ideas? – had some antitype of this fascinating figure any place in Greek religion?

Pater's answer is a resounding 'yes'. Swinburne sees Solomon's work as hybrid, androgynous, or even hermaphrodite, a mixture of Greek with Hebrew, and masculine with feminine; although this compound fascinates Swinburne, it is clear that he sees it as corrupt, impure, decadent. Pater shifts the terms, slightly but significantly; if the sensibility of Solomon's work is "subtler, melancholy", it is nonetheless pure Greek, pristinely so: "and discernible, not as a late after-thought, but as a tradition really primitive, congruous with the original motive of the idea of Dionysus".[11]

Thus Pater, in 1876, seems to redeem Solomon from the imputation of decadence. Yet we have seen that Solomon chose to align himself with Roman decadence, in his largest exhibited oils. A watercolour of 1866 is more modest in scale, yet more extreme in its implications: it shows

Heliogabalus, High Priest of the Sun (cat. 93), the most depraved of Roman emperors and an archetype of deviance, both sexual and religious; he reportedly took lovers of both sexes, and declared himself to be both a woman and the sun-god. In this, perhaps Solomon's most sumptuous watercolour, we see the languid voluptuary attired in jewels and silk, surrounded by gleaming black marble and the resplendent golden accessories of his unorthodox cult. Yet the figure is beautiful, and he stands in the pose, with crossed feet, of a sculpture famous for its special beauty, attributed to the ancient Greek sculptor Scopas and called *Pothos* or *Desire* (the same pose is used for Socrates' Agathodaemon, cat. 104). Is this Solomon's most outrageous representation of Roman decadence, a challenge to the spectator to recognize the compelling, or compulsive, beauty of supreme evil? Or does Solomon, in this work, ask us to abandon our moral preconceptions, to dissolve the tension Arnold criticized as unhealthy, between Hebraic rectitude and Hellenic beauty? To the right of Heliogabalus is an altar of golden cherubim, from the Jewish tradition; to his left is a branch of golden laurel, the symbol of the Greek Apollo; and the beautiful Heliogabalus wears what might be either a Christian halo or a sun disc. In either case, his head radiates the light that Arnold associated with Hellenism.

Perhaps we shall never be able to fathom Solomon's intentions in presenting Heliogabalus, ordinarily considered the supreme embodiment of Roman decadence, as the focus, instead, for the union of Hebraic and Hellenic religious ideas. Yet the special virtue of Solomon's Classicism may be precisely its potential to raise such questions. Solomon never presents us with a comfortable or conventional view of the Western Classical tradition; this helps to explain why many of his contemporaries found his Classicism disquieting or disturbing. Solomon's Classicism constantly asks us to question the customary divisions of the Western tradition, between Greek ideal beauty and Roman decadence, religious contemplation and erotic fervour, Hebraism and Hellenism.

I would like to thank Bob Fowler, Simon Goldhill and Charles Martindale for advice on Classical matters.

NOTES

1 Matthew Arnold, *Culture and Anarchy*, ed. J. Dover Wilson, Cambridge (Cambridge University Press) 1990, p. 130; the chapters, first published serially in the *Cornhill Magazine* (1867–68), appeared in book form in 1869, with 'Hebraism and Hellenism' as Chapter IV, 'Sweetness and Light' as Chapter I.

2 Sidney Colvin, 'English Painters of the Present Day: IV. Simeon Solomon', *Portfolio*, I, 3, 1870, p. 34.

3 Quoted in A.M.W. Stirling, *The Richmond Papers*, London (Heinemann) 1926, p. 161.

4 For a fuller account see Elizabeth Prettejohn, '"The monstrous diversion of a show of gladiators": Simeon Solomon's *Habet!*', in *Roman Presences: Receptions of Rome in European Culture, 1789–1945*, ed. Catharine Edwards, Cambridge (Cambridge University Press) 1999, pp. 157–72.

5 See Linda Dowling, *Hellenism and Homosexuality in Victorian Oxford*, Ithaca NY and London (Cornell University Press) 1994; and Richard Jenkyns, *The Victorians and Ancient Greece*, Cambridge MA (Harvard University Press) 1981, pp. 281–93.

6 The *Suda*, a Byzantine compilation of the late tenth century AD, is the first extant source to describe Sappho and Erinna as companions; modern scholars regard this as a misunderstanding, perhaps derived from an earlier habit of comparing Sappho and Erinna as celebrated female poets. It should be noted that there is virtually no secure biographical information on either poet; *Lemprière's Classical Dictionary*, a standard reference Solomon is known to have consulted, neatly resolves the discrepancy by proposing that there were *two* poets called Erinna, one the companion of Sappho, the other (of whose poetry fragments are extant) of later date.

7 See Joan DeJean, *Fictions of Sappho, 1546–1937*, Chicago and London (University of Chicago Press) 1989, pp. 265–76. For the parallel interest in Sappho in English literature see Yopie Prins, *Victorian Sappho*, Princeton NJ (Princeton University Press) 1999.

8 Fragment 31, preserved in Longinus' treatise *On the Sublime*. Briefer fragments were preserved in compilations and anthologies, and further fragments were found on papyri unearthed in Egyptian excavations from 1897 onwards.

9 I owe this observation to Whitney Davis, 'The Image in the Middle: John Addington Symonds and Homoerotic Art Criticism', in *After the Pre-Raphaelites: Art and Aestheticism in Victorian England*, ed. Elizabeth Prettejohn, Manchester (Manchester University Press) 1999, p. 204.

10 Algernon Charles Swinburne, 'Simeon Solomon: Notes on his "Vision of Love" and Other Studies', *The Dark Blue*, I, July 1871, p. 572.

11 Walter Pater, 'A Study of Dionysus', *The Fortnightly Review* (new series), XXVI, December 1876, p. 768.

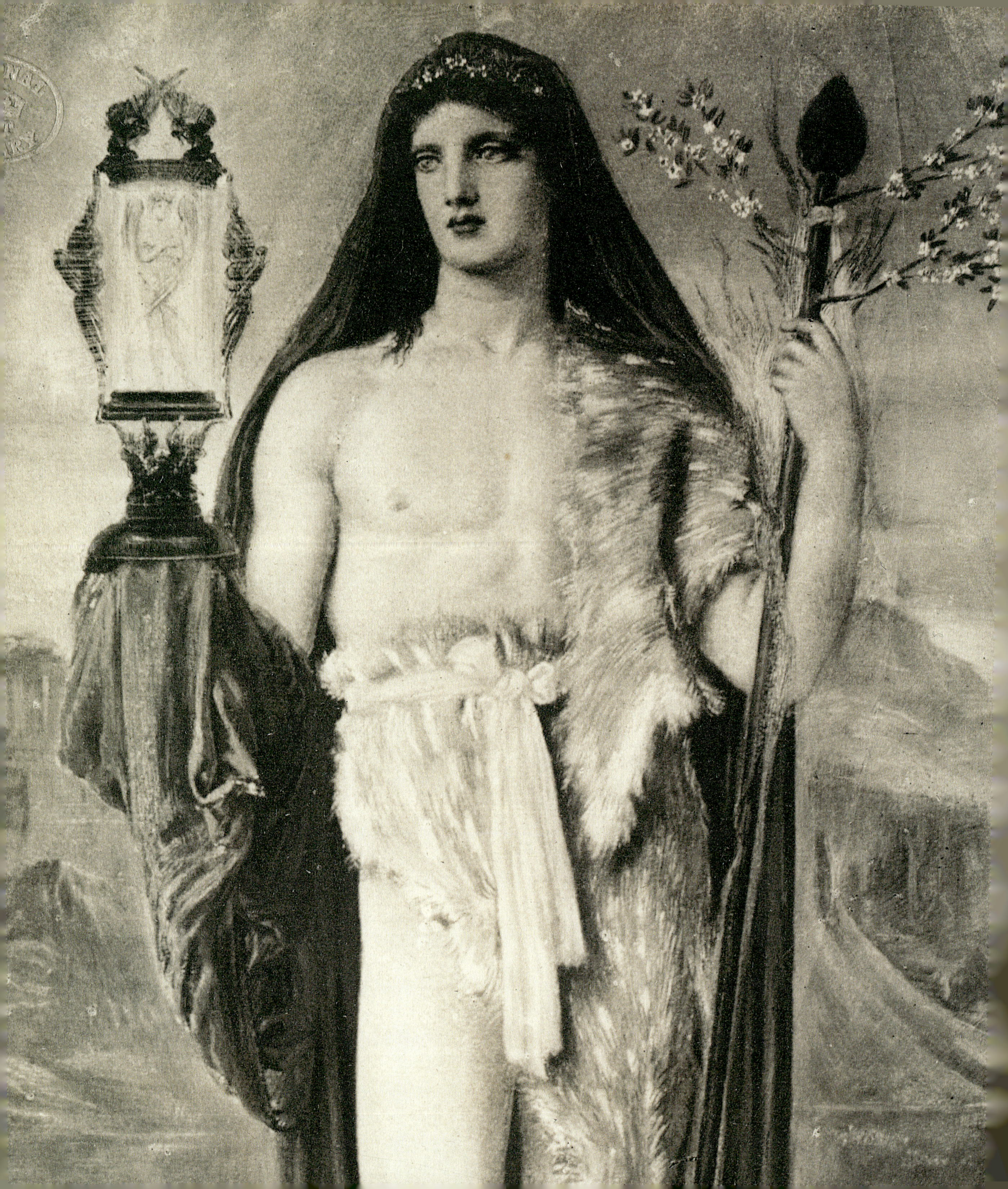

Roberto C. Ferrari

Pre-Raphaelite Patronage: Simeon Solomon's Letters to James Leathart and Frederick Leyland[1]

In the autumn of 1868 Simeon Solomon wrote to his patron, Frederick Leyland, "I have never had a patron whom I should be more anxious to please entirely than yourself for you have been kinder and more appreciative than any one else." Although written to Leyland, these sentiments could almost as easily describe Solomon's relationship with James Leathart and other supportive patrons and collectors. An examination of the correspondence between an artist and his patron provides us with an insight into the genesis of certain works. This artist/patron relationship also provides us with information about collecting practices and prices, among other things, for the rising Victorian middle classes. Solomon's letters to Leathart and Leyland are revealing; they provide background to his pictures as he describes his progress on them, his techniques and his reasons for choosing certain subjects. He also discusses payments, showing us his business acumen.

Little of Solomon's correspondence has survived compared to that of other Pre-Raphaelites.[2] Few, if any, letters written to Solomon are known to exist, ultimately leaving us with one-way conversations. Since there is no single public repository of Solomon's work, his letters have turned up among collections of letters by others, or as miscellaneous manuscripts in archives. Those letters that do survive are rarely dated, making their chronological ordering problematic. Because most of Solomon's letters have remained unpublished, it has been difficult for scholars to appreciate the extent of his contribution to Pre-Raphaelite art.[3]

Solomon was fortunate in his association with Edward Burne-Jones, Dante Gabriel Rossetti, James Abbott McNeill Whistler and others in the wider Pre-Raphaelite and Aesthetic circles, as they shared a group of patrons and collectors interested in purchasing what was seen as trendsetting contemporary art. Among these prominent collectors were the Glasgow MP William Graham, the Leeds stock-market speculator Thomas Plint, and the Liverpool merchant Philip Rathbone. All three owned work by Solomon, although no correspondence relating to their patronage of him has yet come to light.

There are, however, other Victorian patrons who collected Solomon's work and to whom he wrote letters that have survived. The artist engaged in a voluminous correspondence with the Eton tutor Oscar Browning, a particularly close friend. He detailed in letters his progress on the bookplate he designed for Browning (cat. 78) and a copy of *In the Summer Twilight* (1869, cat. 105), which he painted for Browning. With Eleanor Tong (later Mrs William Coltart), who owned numerous works by him, the artist had a close relationship, and he had no hesitation in asking for her assistance in marketing his pictures. With the Welsh squire George Powell, whom he had met through Swinburne, he wrote about the subject of *One Dreaming by the Sea* (1871, cat. 109). It is, however, in the letters to James Leathart and Frederick Leyland that we gain the best insight into Solomon's professional

Frederick Hollyer after Simeon Solomon
Sacramentum Amoris (detail)
Undated; original watercolour dated 1868
(see p. 157)

relationships. These letters tell us about both the artist's concern to please his patrons and his need to defend his techniques and subjects, an insistence that may in fact have ended his relationship with one of these patrons.[4]

James Leathart (1820–1895) lived in Newcastle and was a joint managing partner at the lead-processing firm of Locke, Blackett & Co. He was active in the arts, serving as secretary for the Art School in Newcastle and organizing art shows such as the Mechanics' Institute Exhibition in 1866, which highlighted much of the Pre-Raphaelite work in private collections in the Newcastle area at the time. He probably began to commission works by Solomon at the suggestion of Burne-Jones and/or Rossetti.[5]

Solomon's correspondence with Leathart must have begun before the first dated letter, although no such letters before 1863 are known. By the time he received Solomon's earliest dated letter, Leathart already owned two of the artist's ink drawings, both with Old Testament themes: *By the Waters of Babylon* (1858, untraced) and *Queen Esther Hearing the News of the Intended Massacre of the Jews* (1860, cat. 47). One of these early letters is dated 24 June 1863, and was sent to Leathart with the completed sepia and pencil drawing *Isaiah Reproving the Women of Jerusalem* (1861–63, untraced).

Two additional watercolours owned by Leathart are discussed in this correspondence. The two letters noted above were written from Solomon's studio address at 22 Charles Street. This return address appears on a subsequent undated letter that was probably written in February 1864. Here, Solomon lamented having foregone work on the commission:

> I am perfectly ashamed to write to you without sending the picture with the letter. I fear I can offer no better apology than that I have been up till within the last month very busy on other works that I sent into the Old Watercolor [*sic*] society of which I am *not* elected a member: your picture is within three days of completion and I trust will please you when it is entirely finished, I thought I would write to ask you to be kind enough to let me know when you are coming to town in order that I may finish the picture for you to see when you arrive.[6]

This commission was undoubtedly *Sappho and Erinna in a Garden at Mytilene* (cat. 64), which also dates from February 1864. This watercolour is unique in its subject, depicting the ancient Greek poetess and her lover Erinna in a garden setting (see Prettejohn's essay, pp. 42–43). It was one of Solomon's first Classically themed works, and distinctly different in subject from the Old Testament pictures Leathart had previously purchased from him.

Shortly thereafter, Leathart gave Solomon another commission, this time for a Christian work that would become the watercolour *St Michael of Good Children* (fig. 16). In an undated letter probably written in May 1864, when the picture was created, Solomon wrote:

> I have been working on the little picture of the Angel and children since you came and have today finished it, and as you said you would probably favour me with another visit before you left London, I thought I would ask you to do so tomorrow (Tuesday) when you would perhaps like to take the little picture away with you; but if you are unable to come, of course I will send it as usual to Newcastle.[7]

This work turned out to be the last thing Solomon did for his patron. Leathart apparently stopped commissioning works from Solomon after 1864, and there is no known reason why this happened or why their relationship waned. Their correspondence did continue until about 1868, although these remaining letters are sporadic and no longer discuss Leathart's commissions.[8]

Fig. 16
St Michael of Good Children
1864
(see p. 130)

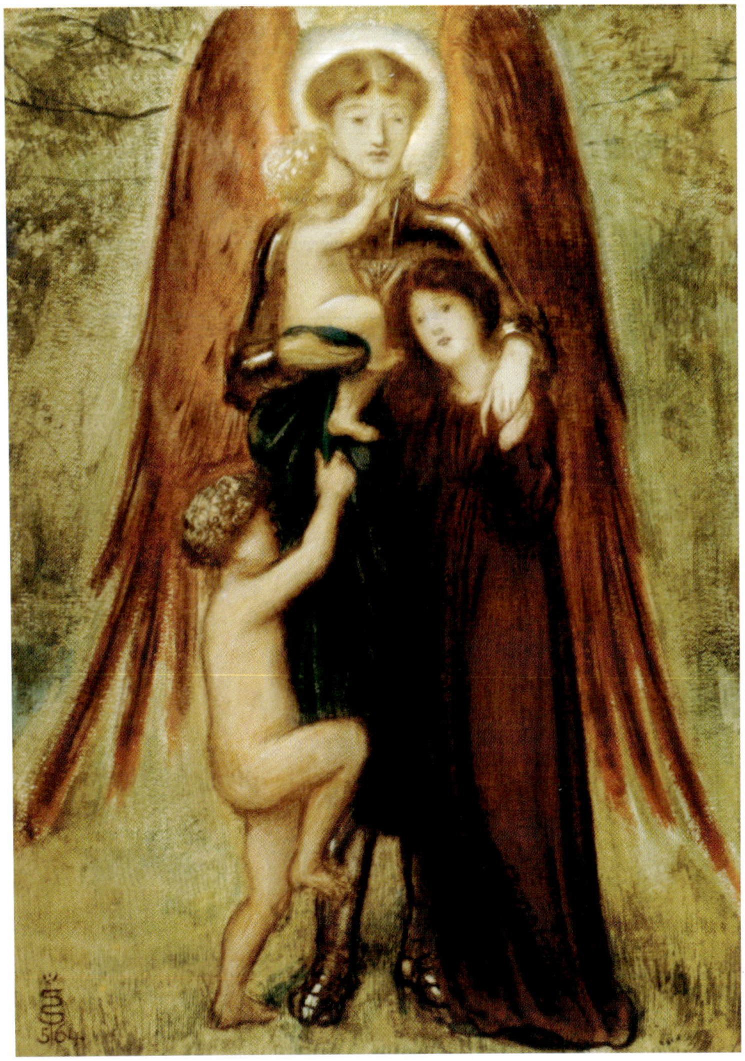

It was during this time that Solomon began corresponding with Frederick Richards Leyland (1831–1892). Leyland's story was one of rags to riches: having grown up supposedly fatherless in Liverpool, he worked his way up to become owner of one of the largest shipping companies of the day. His residences in London and Liverpool became shrines to Pre-Raphaelitism and Aestheticism, with every piece of art acquired for a specific location or purpose.[9] Leyland may have begun to commission works by Solomon at the suggestion of Rossetti, with whom he had first established contact in December 1865. However, it is also possible that Leyland commissioned works from Solomon after he had purchased his *Isaac and Rebekah* (Tel Aviv Museum of Art), an oil painting exhibited at the Royal Academy in 1863.[10]

Some of Solomon's correspondence with Leyland is missing, although at twenty-six extant letters it is one of the largest surviving collections of Solomon's correspondence and includes references to each work he painted for him. The watercolour *Heliogabalus, High Priest of the Sun* (1866, cat. 93) is discussed in seven of these letters, the first of which was written from Leghorn (Livorno) in September 1866 at the beginning of Solomon's year-long tour of Italy (see Cruise's essay, p. 57).[11]

Heliogabalus, known for his decadent lifestyle, was a third-century Roman emperor. Solomon depicted him as an androgynous figure in vibrant colours resting beside a black marble altar and

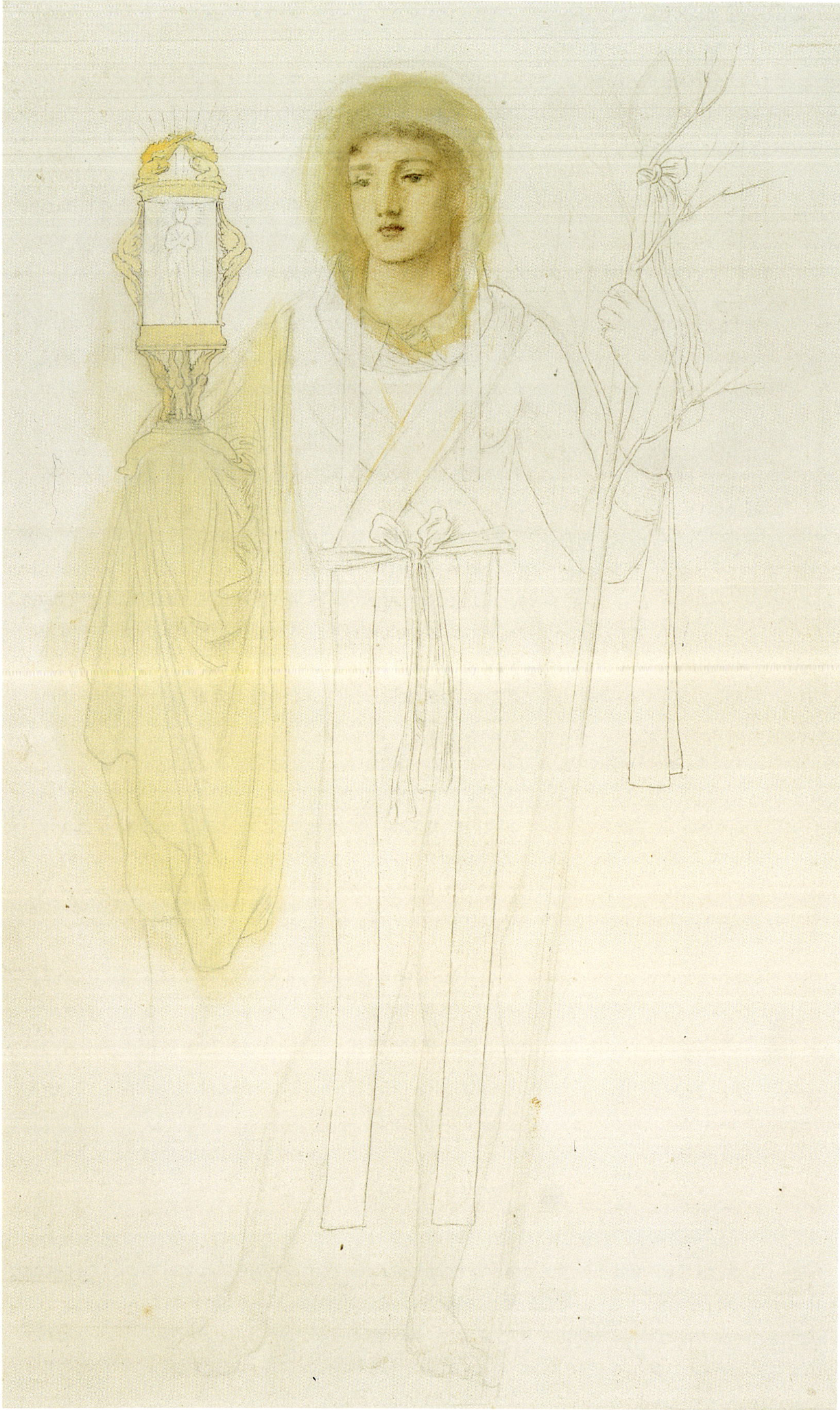

Fig. 17
Study for **Sacramentum Amoris**
1868
(see p. 157)

surrounded by religious symbols (see Prettejohn's essay, pp. 44–45). Solomon explains briefly in the letter his amalgamation of pagan and Judaeo-Christian imagery.[12]

Painting *Heliogabalus* turned out to be difficult, as Solomon wrote in a subsequent letter from Florence: "I feared that I should not have made the drawing as satisfactory as it might have been as I finished it at Leghorn where it was so very hot and the flies worried the very paint brush out of my hand, and as they generally were crawling over both eyes at once." Writing from Rome in March 1867, Solomon lamented that he had missed the opportunity to exhibit *Heliogabalus* at the Dudley Gallery that year. He suggested the possibility that he might exhibit it in the future, and later that year he asked if he could do so. On receiving the picture from Leyland, Solomon wrote:

> Many thanks for your kind letter and also for the picture which I got Agnews to send to me. It was packed with the most tremendous care. it certainly looks better than I expected to have found it: owing to my having no medium at Leghorn. I fancied it would have been too dull in certain parts from others.[13]

Heliogabalus was exhibited at the Dudley Gallery in February 1868, along with the watercolours *Bacchus* (1867, cat. 92) and *A Patriarch of the Eastern Church* (1867, private collection).

In addition to the seven pictures that Solomon had painted for Leyland, there was another work Leyland commissioned from him. *Sacramentum Amoris* (1868) is discussed at length in many of these letters, and probably led to the end of Leyland's patronage. No evidence of the picture having been sold has come to light, and its current whereabouts are unknown. What does survive is a study for the painting located at the British Museum (fig. 17) and a Frederick Hollyer photograph of the work that was published in Percy Bate's study of Pre-Raphaelitism (cat. 114).[14] The androgynous semi-nude figure is draped in fabric and animal-skin, and holds in one hand a flowering thyrsus and in the other hand a glowing lantern.

This missing picture is the subject of some of Solomon's most detailed remarks regarding his choice of subject-matter. The first mention of the picture is in a letter that can best be dated to around April 1868. Solomon wrote, "I worked hard yesterday on the flesh of the 'Sacramentum Amoris' and I think I have much improved it." This implies that Leyland was apparently familiar with the work and had seen its initial composition. By the end of spring, Solomon wrote:

> May I take the liberty of asking you to let me have a cheque for the 'Sacramentum' as it will just now be of service to me. it is at the point of completion, but I wish to keep it a short time here for people to see that is, Rossetti, Brown, Ned Jones and one or two others.

Solomon's desire to show the work to his Pre-Raphaelite colleagues suggests his awareness both of its significant subject-matter and its originality of design.

Leyland received the picture during the summer of 1868. However, by that autumn, he had informed Solomon that he was dissatisfied with it, and was considering selling it. Solomon wrote back:

> With regard to the 'Sacramentum Amoris' I can only say that I am certain you would do nothing that I would not approve, and I am deeply sorry that, since you knew the idea I wished to convey, your feelings should have so changed towards the picture. ... It has always been my aim in art to keep my work as free as lay in my power from indelicacy which quality I consider the worst treason against art, I cannot think of any approach to indelicacy in that picture; the

> sentiment in it appears, in kind, at least, if not in degree, precisely the same as that of Plato's 'Symposium', Dante's 'Vita Nuova', Shakespeare's Sonnets, and Tennyson's 'In Memoriam'. Pardon my having said so much. I have never had a patron whom I should be more anxious to please entirely than yourself for you have been kinder and more appreciative than any one else. I am therefore the more grieved that you feel as you do about what, I sincerely think, is the most *beautiful* picture I have painted.

Solomon used references to Plato, Dante, Shakespeare and Tennyson to defend his work because the texts he names deal with spiritual love, within which both androgyny and homosexuality are either discussed or intimated. Androgyny becomes the union of the masculine and feminine aspects of spiritual love, and the love between two men is perceived as a superior form of love. Solomon's words imply that Leyland's disfavour was based on the figure's "indelicacy", the androgyny and homoeroticism that Solomon claimed were merely a spiritual union of genders. But neither did this subject fit with what M. Susan Duval has noted as Leyland's usual "preference for non-narrative scenes of a woman, a solitary figure, in an intimate setting with her designated attributes", female 'stunners' like the redheaded Alexa Wilding in Rossetti's *Lady Lilith* (1868, Delaware Art Museum) and the nude *A Venus* (1868, York Art Gallery) by Albert Moore.[15] The study for *Sacramentum Amoris* (fig. 17) depicts a more feminine face. One wonders if Leyland had seen this study early on, mistook the figure for a woman, and was unaware of Solomon's intention to further increase the androgynous quality of the finished figure.

In a postscript to this same letter, Solomon asked if he could exhibit the picture at the upcoming Dudley Gallery exhibition in 1869. This letter was presumably followed by one in which Leyland agreed but requested alterations to the work, specifically to make the figure appear less feminine. His request might not have been surprising because, as Gayle M. Seymour has noted, Leyland often "made a point of discussing the subject and composition of works he commissioned, and took an active interest in the works as they progressed".[16] Solomon refused, however, noting how Leyland had given him "so much greater a compliment in admiring it as a *picture* and not as a sermon in paint", implying that Leyland was requesting a change because of its suggestive appearance and not appreciating its overall aesthetics. Solomon's continued response gives not only an explanation regarding the meaning behind the work, but ultimately provides insight into his artistic intentions at a time when he was painting other Greco-Roman subjects with androgynous or homoerotic male figures:

> I mean the whole thing to represent Love in its very highest and most spiritual form, it is therefore sexless; I have mingled the sexes, or endeavoured to do so, in an equal proportion, but I have not made it hermaphrodite in the usual artistic way. the head although not that of a male is not female as you may see by the form of the jaw. Love in it's [*sic*] highest form is above and beyond consideration of sex, which would at once limit and animalise it, the saffron colored marriage veil covering both the Bridegroom and the Bride mingled in one spiritual form, the Sacrament an outward and visible sign, as the holy things contained in the ark is, like it, covered with cherubim hiding the face. The Thyrsus; like the bush that was burnt but not consumed, has a flame round it and running up it to symbolise that Love which is forever ardent but which can have no end or consummation: the dead stick, blossoming into myrtle flowers, like Aaron's rod that budded, symbolises that what was thought dead is ever freshly blooming; the wings of light to the feet show the spiritual nature of the Love which has little of the earth in it, but, when it

> touches it, makes flowers spring up at it's [*sic*] steps; the figure especially the Sacrament, being glowing against a dull background, enjoys the "Light which showeth in darkness" but that the darkness "comprehendeth it not" or has no sympathy with it. the Acropolis in ruins at the back, expresses that although the body has passed away the spirit is still living in the figures. the faunskin and girdle have an import of a similar character ...

These specific explanations of the symbolism of the androgyny, the clothing, the lantern, and the thyrsus all serve Solomon's purpose in defining *Sacramentum Amoris* as a pictorial paean to spiritual love. But it did not seem to convince Leyland. The autograph letter appears to be fragmentary, and we do not know if Leyland replied.

The next letter in their correspondence dates from about December 1868, when Solomon wrote to Leyland, again requesting the picture for the upcoming exhibition. He added, "if it be still your intention to part with it ... let me know if you would like the price to be appended to the title in the catalogue?" *Sacramentum Amoris* was exhibited at the Dudley Gallery in February 1869 along with the watercolours *A Prelude by Bach* (shown with the title *A Song*, 1868, cat. 69) and *A Saint of the Eastern Church* (1867–68, cat. 90). Despite Leyland's desire to sell the picture, the work was not priced and was not for sale during the exhibition. It is not known if the picture was ever sold, because it subsequently disappeared from Leyland's collection.

In April 1869 Solomon accompanied Oscar Browning to Italy. On his return, he received a letter from Charles Augustus Howell, the self-proclaimed art dealer and secretary to John Ruskin. Howell wrote to him that *Sacramentum Amoris* had never made its way back to Leyland. Solomon wrote back to Howell:

> I have only just seen your letter enclosing Leyland's or I should have answered before; I am extremely sorry and surprised to hear that the picture has never reached Leyland and cannot understand it; before I went to Italy in April I called upon Bourlet and gave him directions to send the three pictures in the Dudley to their owners. The 'Song' and the 'Sac. Am.' to Leyland and the other to Palmers, and never until now having heard further, I thought all was right; I will go off at once to Bourlet and enquire about it and of course I shall at once have it sent to you; I am really very anxious for I don't at all understand how the one can have been sent without the other, however, it *must* be all right.[17]

After this letter Solomon pursued the matter with Bourlet and wrote Howell a second letter:

> I hope that the picture has arrived at your house. I went immediately to the idiotic Bourlet and found the picture there. *Why* he did not send it at the same time as the other he didn't seem to know and certainly I didn't – I was very angry for I don't know what Leyland could have thought, but it was useless bullying the man; I believe Leyland wishes to sell the picture – the reason for so doing is certainly better known to himself and Mrs Leyland (I believe) than to me, as he originally seemed to like it better than my others.[18]

From this point on, there is no further mention of *Sacramentum Amoris* in Solomon's letters to either Leyland or Howell. The letter above suggests that Howell acted as an intermediary between Leyland and Solomon and received the picture on Leyland's behalf. Howell often acted in this role for artists and their patrons, so it seems reasonable that Howell might have agreed to take the picture off Leyland's hands and find a buyer for it. However, no evidence has come to light that he succeeded or, in fact, did anything with the picture. Indeed, he might have kept it for himself.[19] Howell gained a reputation among the Pre-Raphaelites as someone not to be trusted and ultimately alienated himself from Burne-Jones, Whistler and others following disputes over prices and other matters.

Solomon's professional relationship with Leyland ceased towards the end of 1869, with a final letter in which he wrote:

> You will possibly be astonished in receiving a letter from me after so long an interval has passed without our seeing each other, but I am emboldened to do so by something that Ned said to me the other day when I was dining with him. I imagined, and I fear not without foundation, that you have for a long time past been offended with me about something, which I have always regretted for many reasons; I unburdened myself to Ned on the subject and he assured me, as far as he could, that such was not the case. I hope it is so – but I am afraid it is otherwise.

Solomon's fears turned out to be true. In an intriguing connection between Leathart and Leyland, the artist William Bell Scott wrote to Leathart on 11 February 1870 that "Howell has all the Solomons' Leland [*sic*] had purchased from year to year from Simeon, something or somebody having put L. against our little friend. They are very fine, three or four of them at least."

If Leyland never received *Sacramentum Amoris* back from Solomon, he might have held this against him thereafter. Worse, Howell might have assisted in this alienation, leading Leyland to sell the rest of Solomon's works. If the loss of *Sacramentum Amoris* was not the reason for the end of their relationship, there may be other explanations. Seymour believes that Solomon's refusal to alter the work angered Leyland and ended his patronage. Solomon's persistent requests for money for commissions could be another reason for the end of their relationship. In the same final letter to Leyland, Solomon continued by writing, "I must frankly tell you that I am at this moment in some little difficulty with regard to a small money affair ...". Another reason for the split might be related to Solomon's homosexuality, which by this time was presumably more publicly acknowledged than before. It has been speculated that his 1870 trip to Italy, his second with Browning, was predicated on a homosexual scandal that forced him to leave London.[20] Whatever the reason for the rupture in the relationship between Solomon and Leyland, it was permanent.

NOTES

1 The following institutions granted permission to publish Simeon Solomon's letters from their collections: Harry Ransom Humanities Research Center at the University of Texas at Austin; University of British Columbia Library, Rare Books and Special Collections; the Director and University Librarian, John Rylands University Library of Manchester. I have retained Solomon's original spelling and grammar, although hyphenation has been altered for publication. Research for this essay was funded in part by awards from the ARLIS/NA H.W. Wilson Foundation and the Division of Research and Graduate Studies, Florida Atlantic University. My thanks to Gayle M. Seymour for her helpful comments on an early version of this essay, and to Angela Graven and Valerie Hoyt at Christie's New York Library for their research assistance.

2 To date, I have transcribed approximately 200 extant letters by Solomon. This is a very small number compared to the thousands of letters by Dante Gabriel Rossetti, currently being published in a multivolume set (*The Correspondence of Dante Gabriel Rossetti*, ed. William Fredeman *et al.*, Cambridge [D.S. Brewer] 2002–).

3 Until recently, the largest set of Solomon's letters ever published was the dozen in *The Swinburne Letters*, ed. Cecil Y. Lang, New Haven CT (Yale University Press) 1959–62, II, pp. 32–35 *et al.* Jean Overton Fuller subsequently published three additional Solomon letters to Swinburne; *Swinburne: A Biography*, London (Chatto & Windus) 1968; New York (Schocken) 1971, pp. 175–88. For more on Solomon's letters published in the past, and those now being published for the first time, see Roberto C. Ferrari, 'The Unknown Correspondence of Simeon Solomon', *The Journal of Pre-Raphaelite Studies*, XII, Spring 2003, pp. 23–34, and 'To the Rossettis, From the Solomons: Five Unpublished Letters', *Notes and Queries*, LII, 1, March 2005.

4 Solomon's letters to these individuals are located in the following repositories: King's College, University of Cambridge (Browning), University of Rochester (Tong), University of Wales, Aberystwyth (Powell), University of British Columbia (Leathart) and the Library of Congress, Washington, DC (Leyland).

5 According to Dianne Sachko Macleod, Leathart's motivation for patronizing the Pre-Raphaelites was based on his desire to retreat from problems at work and the death of one of his children. She writes, "It was disappointment and loss, then, which caused him to insulate himself from the disturbing realities of everyday life by turning his home into a place where he could retrench and recoup his energy. ... Leathart accordingly created an art-filled panacea at Bracken Dene [his Newcastle home]"

(*Art and the Victorian Middle Class: Money and the Making of Cultural Identity*, Cambridge [Cambridge University Press] 1996, pp. 274–75). Leathart's Pre-Raphaelite art collection included Ford Madox Brown's replica of *Work* (1863), Burne-Jones's *The Merciful Knight* (1863, cat. 121), William Holman Hunt's *The Hireling Shepherd* (1851) and other important works. The 1896 Goupil Gallery catalogue identifies seven sepia and watercolour drawings by Solomon in Leathart's collection: *By the Waters of Babylon* (1858, untraced), *Queen Esther Hearing the News of the Intended Massacre of the Jews* (1860, cat. 47), *Isaiah Reproving the Women of Jerusalem* (1861–63, untraced), *'Who is he that cometh from Edom with dyed garments from Bozrah?'* (1862, untraced), *Judith Going to the Assyrian Camp* (1863, private collection), *St Michael of Good Children* (1864, cat. 87), and *Sappho and Erinna in a Garden at Mytilene* (1864, cat. 64). Leathart's collection was for sale at the Goupil Gallery exhibition, where presumably *Babylon* and *Isaiah* must have sold since the remaining five works were auctioned by Christie's on 19 June 1897 with most of his remaining art collection.

6 Solomon's reference in the letter to the Old Watercolour Society also assists in dating the letter to February 1864 because it coincides with a contemporary letter from George du Maurier to Thomas Armstrong, in which he wrote, "Jones, Boyce, Walker and Lohengrin [Lundgrun] elected members of the old water colours – S. Solomon ejected" (*The Young George du Maurier: A Selection of his Letters, 1860–1867*, ed. Daphne du Maurier, New York [Doubleday & Co.] 1952, p. 227).

7 Solomon had moved to 26 Howland Street around April 1864 and remained there for less than a year. This return address appears on the letter and thus also helps to date it.

8 Two letters mention Leathart's intervention regarding a payment dispute over Solomon's work *Antinous Dionysiacus* (c. 1865, untraced). The names of other northern collectors of Solomon's work, such as Thomas Emerson Crawhall and William Watson Pattinson, also appear in these letters, suggesting Leathart's influence on his neighbours regarding their art collections and patronage of Solomon.

9 Macleod describes Leyland's approach to art as "fetishistic" and his London residence as "a temple of Aestheticism". She writes, "Leyland did not try to disguise the fact that he venerated art when he metamorphosed his home into a secular shrine … with rooms specifically designed as mood chambers to induce meditation." His interiors were "intended to fulfil Leyland's affective needs and because money was no object, his efforts to escape the tyranny of loneliness, frustration, and despair knew no bounds" (Macleod, *op. cit.*, pp. 284, 286). Leyland's contemporary art collection included works such as Albert Moore's *A Venus* (1868), Rossetti's *Lady Lilith* (1868) and *The Blessed Damozel* (1875–78), and the Peacock Room by Whistler and Thomas Jeckyll (1876–77), a subject of acrimonious disagreement between artist and patron. It is unknown exactly how many works Solomon painted for Leyland, but the auction of some of Leyland's collection on 9 March 1872 included a significant number of his works. The pictures sold were the six watercolours *A Priestess of Diana Offering Poppies* (c. 1866, private collection), *Vanozza Borgia* (c. 1866, untraced), *Heliogabalus, High Priest of the Sun* (1866, cat. 93), *Bacchus* (1867, cat. 92), *A Greek Priest* (1867, private collection) and *A Song* (or *A Prelude by Bach*, 1868, cat. 69), and the oil painting *Isaac and Rebekah* (1863, Tel Aviv Museum of Art). All of these pictures were purchased at the auction by the art dealer Arthur Tooth for just over £184.

10 *Isaac and Rebekah* is discussed in at least five of Solomon's letters to Leyland, mostly discussing the artist's having borrowed it in order to paint a copy in oil for William Graham. Graham's 1868 copy is untraced.

11 Shortly before Solomon had departed for Italy, Rossetti wrote to Leyland on 3 August 1866, "I heard Burne Jones speak yesterday of Solomon's Heliogabalus as one of his very finest drawings. I have not yet seen it myself" (*Correspondence*, III, *op. cit.*, p. 458; and *The Rossetti–Leyland Letters: The Correspondence of an Artist and his Patron*, ed. Francis L. Fennell, Jr, Athens OH [Ohio University Press] 1978, p. 3). Rossetti's letter suggests that Leyland was familiar with Solomon's work and was contemplating commissioning this picture based on an original sketch, possibly described here, although no such sketch has been discovered. It is also possible that Leyland may have seen *Heliogabalus* after it had been begun in London and had decided to purchase it once it was completed during Solomon's stay in Italy.

12 This letter also ends with Solomon asking Leyland to send final payment for the picture to his sister Rebecca, who was acting as his agent in London. In a single surviving letter dated 26 October 1866, Rebecca Solomon wrote to Leyland:

> Having recd the enclosed from my brother to forward to you, I take the opportunity of mentioning a thing I omitted doing before I sent the picture to you, that is, that if I remember rightly the back of the picture was not covered with paper to prevent dust from entering between that and the frame therefore will you kindly pardon my neglect and have it attended to as soon as possible, if it escaped your notice until now.

Like her brother, Rebecca often sought to market her own work as an artist and added at the end of her letter, "If you should be visiting London and the Winter Exhibition of Mr. Gambarts may I take the liberty of directing your attention to some of my works that will be exhibiting there." No evidence has come to light suggesting that Leyland was a patron of Rebecca as he was of her brother. It is unknown what works Rebecca had on exhibit at Gambart's that year, but her brother was represented by the picture *During the Gloria* (1866, untraced).

13 Agnews refers to the Manchester- and London-based art selling company that was run by William Agnew at the time. According to Geoffrey Agnew, Leyland was a regular buyer of theirs (*Agnew's 1817–1967*, London [Bradbury Agnew Press] 1967, p. 26).

14 Percy Bate, *The English Pre-Raphaelite Painters: Their Associates and Successors*, London (George Bell & Sons) 1899.

15 M. Susan Duval, 'F.R. Leyland: A Maecenas from Liverpool', *Apollo*, CXXIV, August 1986, p. 111.

16 Gayle M. Seymour, 'The Life and Work of Simeon Solomon, 1840–1905', PhD diss., University of California at Santa Barbara, 1986, p. 126.

17 Bourlet refers to James Bourlet & Sons, a fine-art packing company. Solomon's handwriting regarding "Palmers", who would have been the owner of *A Saint of the Eastern Church*, is illegible and a guess on my part. This letter by Solomon to Howell is located at the Harry Ransom Humanities Research Center at the University of Texas at Austin.

18 This letter by Solomon to Howell is part of the Fairfax Murray Papers, MS 1280/173, at the John Rylands Library, University of Manchester.

19 The picture did not appear in Howell's collection when it went up for auction on 13 November 1890 after his death. This auction was eagerly attended by many of the surviving Pre-Raphaelites who had been swindled by Howell and were curious to see what would turn up at the auction. See Helen Rossetti Angeli, *Pre-Raphaelite Twilight: The Story of Charles Augustus Howell*, London (Richards Press) 1954, pp. 15–22. One unknown work by Solomon that did appear was a picture entitled *A Bacchante and Faun*. It sold for one guinea.

20 In February 1870 Solomon wrote to Eliza Solomon, his sister-in-law: "My behaviour has been perfectly disgraceful. I can hardly ask you to forgive me, but I hope you will do so without" (quoted in Bernard Falk, *Five Years Dead: A Postscript to 'He Laughed in Fleet Street'*, London [Hutchinson] 1937, p. 326). While in Italy, Browning and he went their separate ways but kept in touch through letters. Solomon travelled with a young man named 'Willie', whose identity is unknown, frequently fawning over him in these letters.

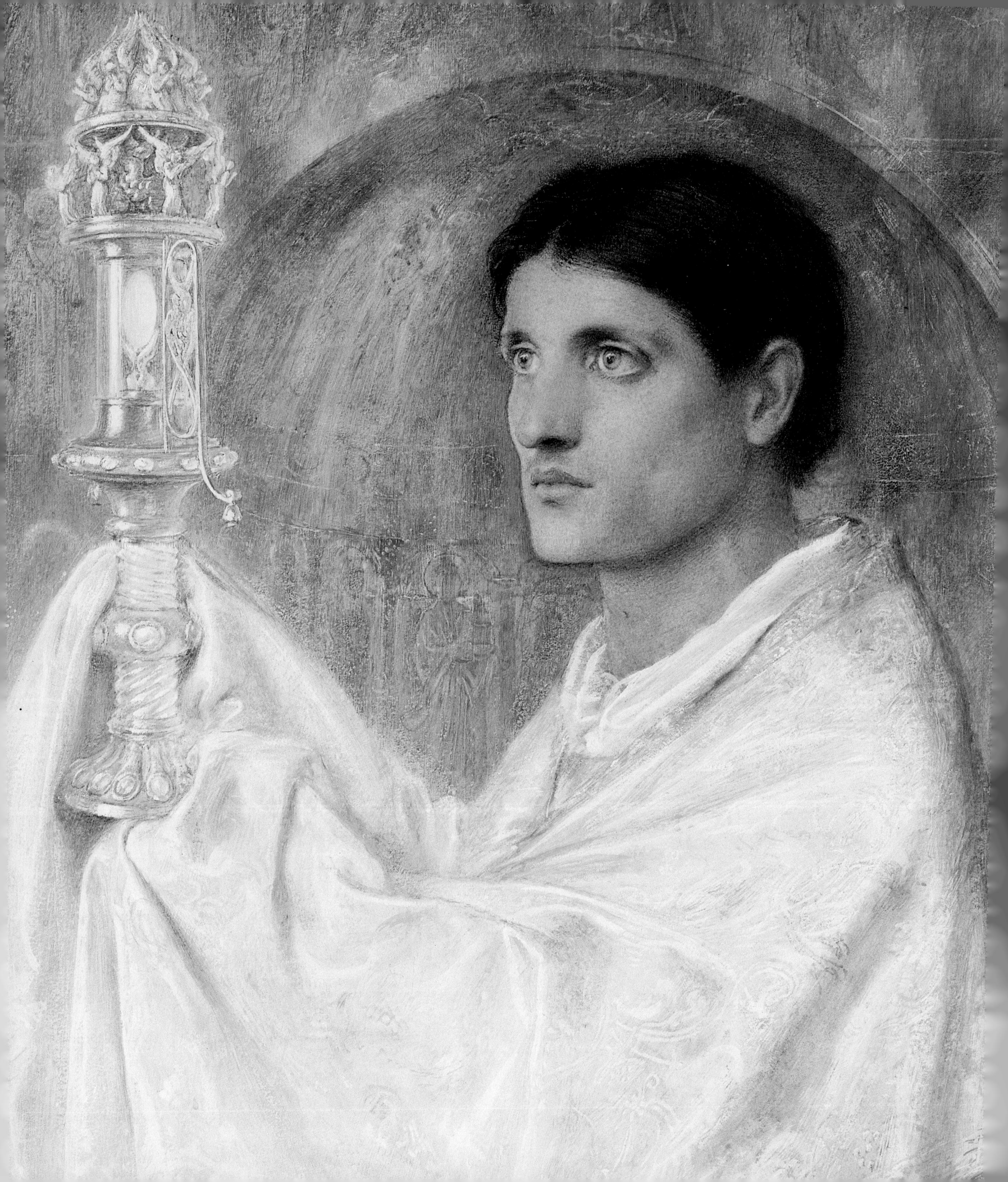

Colin Cruise

"Pressing all religions into his service": Solomon's Ritual Paintings and Their Contexts

In 1866 Simeon Solomon wrote from Leghorn to his patron Frederick Leyland about the progress of his painting *Heliogabalus, High Priest of the Sun* (1866, cat. 93) in which the emperor is depicted leaning against an altar, languidly censing it with a smoking incense-burner.

> I hope you do not object to the black marble. I thought it would be a better setting to the figure than any other color [*sic*]. The altar of incense I have designed of Cherubim taken from the Jewish idea [of] the Emperor pressing all religions into his service. The golden laurel bough in the amphora is sacred to Apollo, and to his divinity under the name of Elagabalus.[1]

The painting represents Solomon's experiments with religion, ritual and ceremony, which are usefully summed up in his own statement about Heliogabalus's intent in "pressing all religions into his service". It is hard to ignore the religious subject-matter of many of Simeon Solomon's paintings, yet also hard to define either the nature of the religious experience they outline or the precise denominational position they indicate. Religious painting, while being part of the Academic ideal, had not been popular in England in the first half of the nineteenth century; relatively few religious paintings were shown at the Royal Academy because denominational divides and debates militated against a consistent or centralized iconography for British art. Thus, although early Victorian Britain was ostensibly pious and God-fearing, artists based their careers on producing domestic scenes or on illustrating in paint works of literature or popular history rather than the Scriptures. With interests in both medieval literature and art and a desire to produce modern paintings, Pre-Raphaelitism offered an alternative to the *status quo*. In paintings as diverse as *The Light of the World* (1853, Keble College, Oxford), *The Awakening Conscience* (1853, Tate) and *The Finding of the Saviour in the Temple* (fig. 18), Holman Hunt produced paintings relevant to contemporary debates around religious faith. Yet again, Millais's *The Return of the Dove to the Ark* (1851, The Ashmolean Museum, Oxford) and *The Blind Girl* (1854–56, Birmingham Museums & Art Gallery) recast scriptural texts and their dramas in a new pictorial mode, often using a simple confrontation of two figures or, in the case of *Autumn Leaves* (1855–56, Manchester Art Gallery), a group of expressionless figures, to carry the import of the story.

Critics opposed to Pre-Raphaelitism on religious grounds saw it as linked to a religious movement in mid-nineteenth-century England, Ritualism, which was dedicated to reviving the ceremonies and rituals, vestments and practices, of a pre-Reformation English church. Such an influence can be detected only – and then only partially – in the works of Rossetti, whose earliest paintings of incidents in the life of the Virgin Mary were, broadly speaking, Catholic, and in those of James Collinson (cat. 26).[2] Other works by members of the original Brotherhood had pictorial

Simeon Solomon
The Mystery of Faith (detail)
1870
(see p. 131)

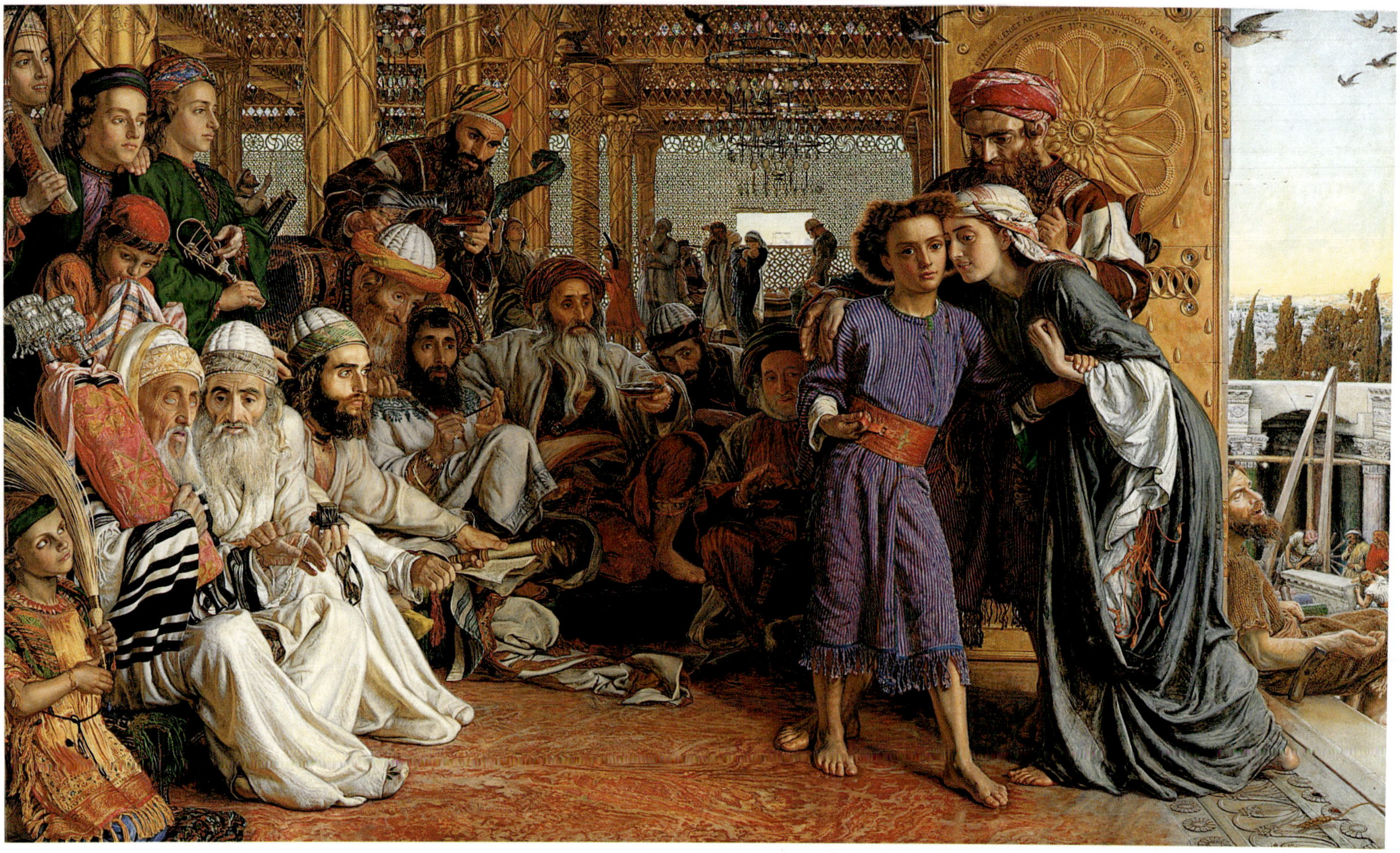

Fig. 18
William Holman Hunt (1827–1910)
The Finding of the Saviour in the Temple
1854–60
Oil on canvas
85.7 × 141 cm (33¾ × 55½ in.)
Birmingham Museums & Art Gallery

elements of a revived 'early Christian' style that was often identified variously with Catholicism, Tractarianism and Ritualism. The rise of Pre-Raphaelitism coincided with developments in debates and disputes within the Church of England about the function of ritual objects, vestments, furniture and ceremony in religious practice. The Gothic Revival of the early nineteenth century was extended into a significantly religious culture, with an extraordinary emphasis on the visual arts and particularly on the 'applied arts', as they were known, that contributed to the accessories of ritual – embroidery, gilding, carving and other crafts. The formation of the Cambridge Camden Society in 1839 was further evidence of the importance of a new role for art and architecture in contemporary ecclesiology.[3]

Solomon, identified early in his career as a Pre-Raphaelite, became famous, even notorious, for works on Anglican or Catholic themes such as *The Mystery of Faith* (1870, cat. 88). In the first survey of his work to date, Sidney Colvin observed: "For the last five years the Dudley Gallery exhibition has seldom been without a ceremonial piece, whether of one figure or many, done with [his] unique splendour and lustre of imitative colour."[4] However, Solomon's early works draw on the young artist's Jewish background and the contemporary conditions of middle-class Jewish culture in England, as Gayle Seymour points out in her essay (see pp. 13–21). The set of drawings now belonging to the Jewish Museum, London, for example, depicts ceremonies that show a Jewish life otherwise unrepresented in English visual culture. They remind us of the background of Jewish emancipation steadily progressing throughout Europe in the latter half of the eighteenth century and the first half of the nineteenth.[5] Solomon's rituals are not as cosy and homely as those enacted in works by

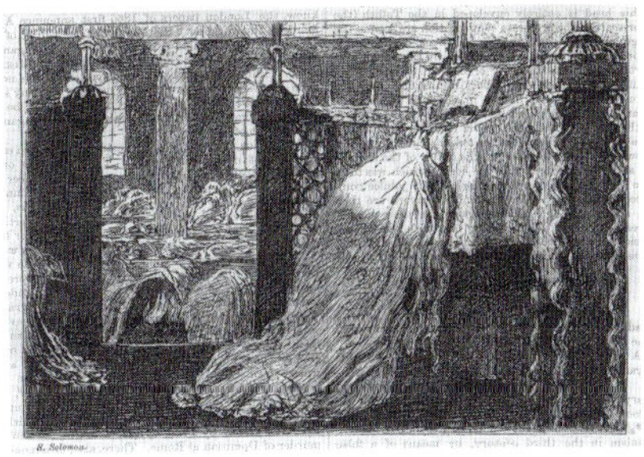

Fig. 19
The Day of Atonement
1866
Wood engraving from a design by Solomon
9.8 × 13.6 cm (3⅞ × 5⅜ in.)
Published in *The Leisure Hour*, 1866, p. 540
Birmingham Libraries

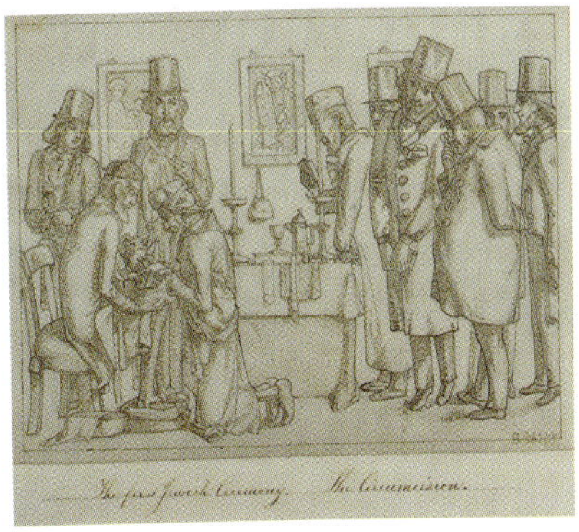

Fig. 20
The first Jewish Ceremony.
The Circumcision
1854
(see p. 72)

Central European artists such as Moritz Oppenheim; rather, they anticipate the darker view of Jewish life in industrial societies in the last decade of the century. At the same time they represent ideas of continuity of tradition and mystery (see, for example, cat. 8 and 9). Solomon's images were given wide currency when in 1862 they were issued both in a popular periodical form in *Once a Week* (VII, 1862, cat. 83), for the article 'Jews in England', and in photographic form by Coundall, Downes & Co. (fig. 37). Four years later a series of engravings representing Jewish customs was published in *The Leisure Hour* throughout 1866 (see, for example, figs. 19 and 38). These are not simply genre scenes; the domestic rituals depicted here illustrate the co-existence of the sacred and the everyday, and they are, as a consequence, dark, numinous and glowing all at the same time. In presenting them in engraved form to a wide audience the editor of *The Leisure Hour* explained:

> We propose to present our readers from time to time with pictures (after drawings executed by Mr Simeon Solomon) of various rites and ceremonies observed by the Jews at the present day in their synagogues and homes. We believe that such illustrations will not be without interest, as they will serve to show in what manner several commandments of the Bible are carried out in practice by this ancient people.[6]

Sidney Colvin, in his overview of Solomon's art up to 1870, saw the illustrations as marking a different phase both for the artist and Jews in general and noted that they had a particular contemporary context in Jewish culture:

> The phase of the historical past which first occupied the imagination of Mr Solomon was the history, legends, and ceremonial traditions of his race, – that marvellous race which, by its law in prohibition of the making of images, has in great part prevented the splendid materials that its legends and ceremonies offer to art from being put to the service of art. With the universal loosening of dogmatic restrictions in our time has come, I understand, the relaxing of Jewish practice and Jewish prejudice in this matter. ...[7]

The depiction of a circumcision (fig. 20) shows the ways in which a culture values its rituals and ceremonies in a modern society, so that here the operation is accompanied by a panoply of vessels and objects. The simple domestic table becomes an altar. There is, too, an interesting representation of the male figures, who are all – but for the baby – aged. The traditional depiction of rabbis in paintings by artists as diverse as Rembrandt and Solomon Hart shows the subject as old and bearded, weary yet noble, a correlation being made between the 'ancient' Jewish law and its existence as a religion, and the age of the sitter. A kind of Orientalism is evident in these works, too, and there is a sense of reportage of the exotic lives of the young artist's fellow Jews transported from distant lands to London, the centre of the modern, industrial world. The turbaned figures who feature in several of the artist's depictions of contemporary Jewish life in the London of the 1860s appear as characters in a biblical drama, as Boaz or Isaiah (see cat. 45, for example). They are, by implication, survivors of an older culture, although it is not clear how many such figures the artist would actually have seen in the London of his childhood and youth.

The world depicted by Solomon in his *Jewish Ceremonies* is not 'timeless'; it was just about to change. In part, this change was to be brought about as a response to industrial modernity reflected by debates in the Jewish communities in Britain and the USA. There would be an expressed desire in some parts of these communities for a religious practice less ceremonially elaborate. In an argument between two characters in Israel Zangwill's *Children of the Ghetto* (1892), the divide is made apparent:

"Orthodoxy is inextricably entangled with ritual observance; and ceremonial religion is of the ancient world, not the modern."

"But our ceremonialism is pregnant with sublime symbolism and its discipline is most salutary. Ceremony is the casket of religion."

"More often its coffin," said Strelitski drily. "Ceremonial religion is so apt to stiffen in a *rigor mortis*. It is all too dangerous an element; it creates hypocrites and Pharisees ... much of our so-called ceremonialism is merely the primitive mix-up of everything with religion in a theocracy. ..."[8]

Emancipation, however, informs both Solomon's earliest Jewish ceremonial works and those that represent Christian, often Catholic, ceremonial. The years 1829 and 1845 are among the key dates of Christian denominational history in England. The former was the year of the emancipation of Catholics, the second the year of John Henry Newman's conversion – or 'perversion', as it was commonly called – to Roman Catholicism. Both events are important for the cultural identity of English Christians and had a huge impact on the arts, not the least in extending the life and significance of the Gothic revival by encouraging an interest in ecclesiology, ceremony, church art and architecture particularly, as well as art history and iconology generally. Solomon was surrounded by the evidence of the, often heated, religious debates that ensued from such events. Their repercussions lasted throughout the 1850s and 60s and well into the 70s, culminating in the passing of the Public Worship Regulation Act in 1874.[9] In 1858, for instance, the Bishop of London, Archibald Tait (later Archbishop of Canterbury), forbade the use of ritual objects in worship. During the years that followed, 'Ritualism', as it became known, was one of the most hotly debated topics of modern life, as satirized in the popular press as Pre-Raphaelitism and, later, Aestheticism were to be. Indeed, they might be linked as cultural phenomena that dealt with the visual representation of controversial ideas about identity and belief.

It is in his representation of priests that Solomon unites both Judaism and Christianity. If we consider some of the Aaronic imagery of the artist's illustrations for the Dalziel Bible project, such as *The Burnt Offering* or *The First Offering of Aaron* (cat. 46c), we can see that two of the traditions of sacrifice outlined in the Old Testament were being represented – the bullock as a sin offering and the ram as a burnt offering representing surrender to God's will. But the offices of a priest – offering sacrifice, burning incense, teaching the Law, communicating divine will and blessing the people in the name of the Lord – are all fulfilled in the idea of a Christian, perhaps, particularly for a mid-nineteenth-century English audience, a Catholic, priesthood. The functions of priesthood are largely shared between an Aaronic and a Petrine concept, having their roots in Levitical commands. Swinburne united the two different 'ritualisms' – Jewish and Christian – in his overview of the artist's work, observing:

As the Hebrew love of vast atmosphere and infinite spiritual range without foothold on earth or resting-place in nature is perceptible in the mystic and symbolic cast of so many sketches and studies, so is a certain loving interest in the old sacred forms, in the very body of historic tradition, made manifest in various more literal designs of actual religious offices.[10]

The Mystery of Faith (1870, cat. 88) is perhaps the most coherent of images about Christian ritual, although the subject is, in effect, one of the most obscure. It depicts the elevation of the Host in a crystal monstrance and thus deals with the complex Christian doctrine of the 'Real Presence', a subject that vexed Anglicans in relation to their own eucharistic belief but which was central and unquestioned by 'Roman' Catholics. There was a relatively current public context for the work: Solomon's painting was exhibited a decade after the settlement of the 'Denison Case', named after Archdeacon Denison, who had been prosecuted for his teachings on the Real Presence of the Eucharist.[11] Timothy I, 3:9–11, might have been an inspiration for this work – and for *A Deacon* (cat. 85) also – and might explain the gravity of these priests. The text may have caused, too, in the instance of *The Mystery of Faith*, a visual pun to have been created by the artist concerning Timothy's advice about 'holding the faith'. Timothy, advising his listeners that those following the religious life must adopt certain behaviour and foster certain virtues, stated that "Deacons in like manner must be grave, not double-tongued, not given to much wine, not greedy of filthy lucre; holding the mystery of faith in a pure conscience. And let them serve as deacons, if they be blameless." 'Holding the faith' is illustrated most vividly here as well as controversially. For non-Catholics – and others for whom the doctrinal nuances were unimportant or irrelevant – there were the colour harmonies and the subtlety of close tones as well as the sheer virtuosic handling of the medium to commend the work. Certainly the painting illustrates an obscure religious point in an advanced style; the whiteness of the eucharistic wafer provides the key for the entire white and yellow harmony of the whole. It is a kind of Whistlerian 'symphony in white' with a controversial religious narrative lying beneath the abstract beauty. The *Art Journal* reviewed it in a way that covered both doctrinal and aesthetic readings:

> Mr. Simeon Solomon is never so at home as in the Dudley Gallery, and to our mind has seldom shown himself so well as on the present occasion. Once again his genius oscillates between medievalism and classicism. *The Mystery of Faith* pertains to the religion and ritual of the Romish Church. A priest, robed richly, elevates the Eucharist; his eye fixed as in a trance, his countenance that of an ascetic, reveal a soul steadfastly set on 'the mystery of faith' – the Real Presence. The execution is worthy of the conception; the artist has achieved a triumph.[12]

Solomon's focus was on priests rather than the usual subjects of Christian religious painting – Christ's ministry or death, the life of the Virgin Mary, the lives of saints or martyrs. His pictorial solution, as it were, is also one with a religious dimension; it helps to sidestep the problem of depictions of sanctity and particularly the problematical 'Mariolatry' that had fixated Protestant thinkers throughout the first half of the nineteenth century. Instead – although arguably just as controversially – he depicts priests in the act of celebrating the Mass or performing other duties at the altar. Such activities were controversial precisely because of their emphasis on the sacraments, particularly the sacrament of the Eucharist or Holy Communion. Other practices, including the decoration of the altar, the incense, the vestments and vessels, as well as the ritual observances, had led to court cases and legal struggles throughout the 1860s and 70s, at the time when Solomon was exhibiting pictures on these subjects. Even the presence of a stone altar in a church might point to transgressive ritualistic practices; its appearance in a painting might be deemed subversive and provocative.

A characteristic of both *The Mystery of Faith* and *Carrying the Scrolls of the Law* (1867, cat. 94) is the youthfulness of the bearers of their sacred responsibilities; the emphasis on the externals of religion serves to point to that element which is invisible to the viewer, the spiritual. There is no denying the poignancy of the juxtaposition of youth with tradition and of masculinity with mystery. Solomon's iconography identifies mystery and tradition in the unchanging nature of religious ritual while the transitory nature of mere human endeavours is represented by the bearer of the vessel or object. This is plainly the case in what is arguably the most famous of Solomon's paintings, *Carrying the Scrolls of the Law*, in which the young man embraces the Torah, his head bent, eyes closed. His

Fig. 21
Height of Fashion
1866
Wood engraving
Published in *Punch*, 22 December 1866, p. 258

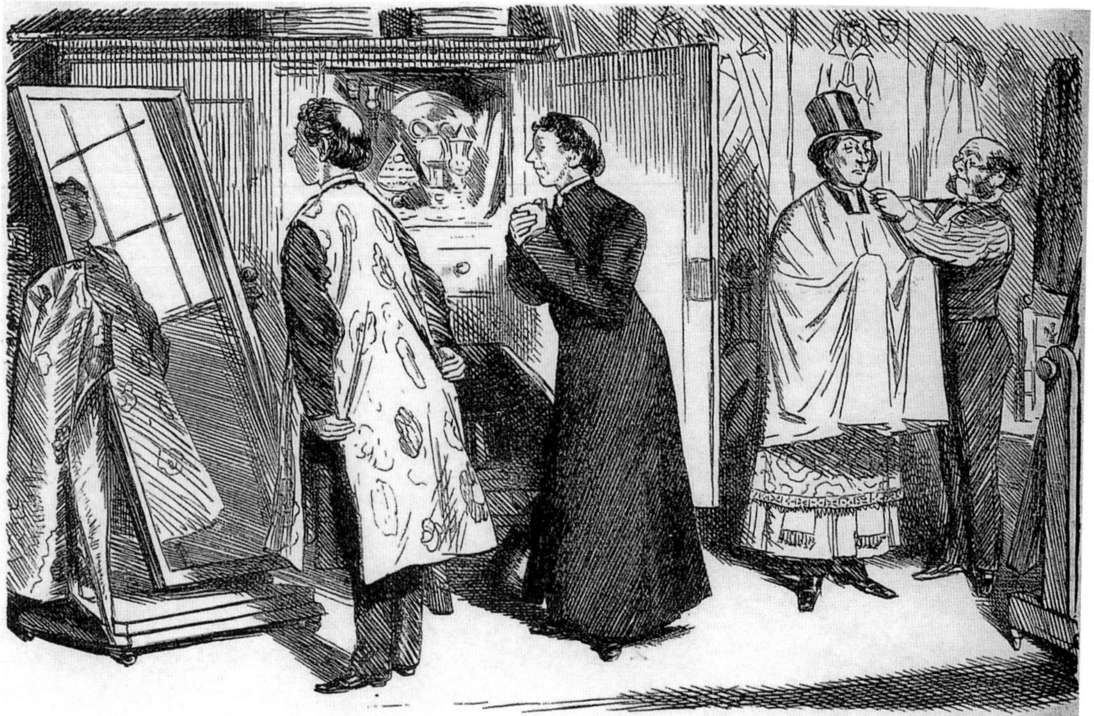

HEIGHT OF FASHION.
Ardent Ritualist. "OH, ATHANASIUS, IT'S CHARMINGLY BECOMING!"

reverence is palpable. The painting operates as a way of juxtaposing a personal reverence with an enduring common cultural one. Thus the sensitivity of the facial features is offset by the specific details of the Torah-shield or the *rimonim* (the silver crown-like finials on top of the Torah scrolls). Such details cannot be faked; the existence of traditions and functions of religious objects must be observed in order for the painting to make sense. Both the functions of the objects and their decorative forms must be observed accurately by the artist.

We can link both of these depictions of young religious men to Solomon's most controversial painting, *Sacramentum Amoris* (see cat. 114). The pictorial connections are many – ritual robes, ritual objects, intensity of expression – but they coalesce in the concept of mystery in religion; they draw attention to the limits of scientific reasoning and the primacy of pictorial symbols in understanding religious truths. Solomon's is an obscure symbolism, sometimes personal.

Ultimately we might see other intentions behind Solomon's subject paintings – the advancement of a religion of beauty and the declaration of his sexuality. The first of these – Aestheticism – might be characterized by several formal qualities of the works: the colour combinations and the references to musical or other non-visual sensations, like the sound of the harp or the smell of incense. But there were popular perceptions of links between Aestheticism as an art practice, Ritualism as a religious practice, and sexual preference. The ritual wing of the Anglican Church was often dismissed in periodical literature and cartoons; *Punch* regularly satirized Ritualist priests in terms that made clear their apparent 'effeminacy' (fig. 21), and contemporary literature, when not characterizing Ritualist priests as ascetic and threatening, characterized them as 'odd', while several scandals in the period incriminated Anglican or Anglo-Catholic priests in homosexual activities.[13] The association of Ritualism with the religious vocation and particular sexual behaviour was acted out at least until the end of the nineteenth century in works like 'The Priest and the

Acolyte' (often wrongly attributed to Oscar Wilde), which appeared in the student magazine *The Chameleon*. The story ends with the Consecration of the Eucharist and the suicide of a priest and his beloved friend. The priest has confessed that his "delight is in the aesthetic beauty of the services, the ecstasy of devotion, the passionate fervor that comes with long fasting and meditation".[14]

There is a Blakean sense that 'all religions are one' in Solomon's pictorial argument. His experiment with a new kind of religious painting might have some of the same roots in Philo's promulgation of an allegorical reading of the scriptures. It might, like Blake, have a radical purpose – of undermining religion altogether, of evaporating the materialism of religion. Solomon uses religious ritual and its objects, vessels and vestments as a way of focusing on the externals of religion, but, in doing so, shifts attention away from the surface to the interior, from the visible to the invisible, from stuff and things to beliefs and desires, from the visible to the visionary. His comprehensiveness in the matter of religious ceremony anticipates the tendency in comparative religious studies of our own times to what William James was to describe succinctly, in the title of his work on religion, as "varieties of religious experience".[15] Solomon's religious works, particularly those of the 1860s, point to a further innovation: an interest in ritual and ceremony for itself, not bound by the usual Christian denominational restrictions. His work embraces a variety of religions, not only Judaism, the religion of his birth, but also Anglicanism, Greek Orthodoxy and Catholicism. In his religious paintings Solomon suggests that, for him, the future of religion might be in that "pressing all religions into his service" that he assigns to Heliogabalus and, further, that religion can illuminate areas of the personal life, like sexuality, and, rather than conceal them, celebrate them.

My thanks are due to the British Art Center at the University of Yale, where much of the research for this paper was undertaken. I would like, too, to thank the staff of St Deiniol's Library, Hawarden, Flintshire, Patsy Williams and Gregory Morris and the Warden, Peter Francis, for various kinds of help in preparing this essay; thanks also to Victoria Osborne for her helpful comments on an earlier draft.

NOTES

1 Unpublished letter from Solomon to Leyland, not dated but probably 1866 (Library of Congress, Washington, DC). The black altar is not entirely Solomon's invention but is based on the *baetyl*, a sacred black stone, brought from Syria to Rome by the emperor to be the focus of the establishment of sun worship as the official Roman religion, c. AD 218.

2 See Alastair Grieve, 'The Pre-Raphaelite Brotherhood and the Anglican High Church', *The Burlington Magazine*, XI, May 1969, pp. 294–95.

3 For an account of the role of the Cambridge Camden Society, see James F. White, *The Cambridge Movement: The Ecclesiologists and the Gothic Revival* [1962], Cambridge (Cambridge University Press) 1979. For the context of English ecclesiology before the advent of Ritualism, see Nigel Yates, *Buildings, Faith and Worship: The Liturgical Arrangement of Anglican Churches 1600–1900*, Oxford (Oxford University Press) 1991.

4 Sidney Colvin, 'English Painters of the Present Day: IV. Simeon Solomon', *Portfolio*, I, 3, 1870, p. 34.

5 For a discussion of the impact of Jewish emancipation on art, see Susan Tumarkin Goodman (ed.), *The Emergence of Jewish Artists in Nineteenth-Century Europe*, London (Merrell) 2001.

6 Quoted in Paul Goldman and Brian Taylor (eds.), *Retrospective Adventures: Forrest Reid, Author and Collector*, Aldershot (Scolar Press) 1998, p. 61.

7 Colvin, *op. cit.*, p. 33.

8 Israel Zangwill, *Children of the Ghetto*, Leicester (Leicester University Press) 1977, II, XV, p. 380.

9 For an account of the impact of Ritualism on the Church of England and the reactions against it, see Nigel Yates, *Anglican Ritualism in Victorian Britain 1830–1910*, Oxford (Oxford University Press) 1999. For the passing of the Public Worship Regulation Act (1874) and its consequences, see James Bentley, *Ritualism and Politics in Victorian Britain: The Attempt to Legislate for Belief*, Oxford (Oxford University Press) 1978.

10 Algernon Charles Swinburne, 'Simeon Solomon: Notes on his "Vision of Love" and Other Studies', *The Dark Blue*, I, July 1871, p. 572.

11 The 'Denison Case' (1853–58) concerned the controversial teaching of Archdeacon Denison on the Real Presence; for a brief account of the case see Horton Davies, *Worship and Theology in England*, Grand Rapids MI and Cambridge (Eerdmans) 1996, IV, 5, p. 116.

12 *Art Journal*, March 1871, p. 85.

13 For literary depictions of priests in nineteenth-century literature, see Robert Lee-Wolff, *Gains and Losses*, New York and London (Garland Publishing) 1977. For a discussion of homosexual scandals and other gendered aspects of Ritualism, see David Hilliard, 'UnEnglish and Unmanly: Anglo-Catholicism and Homosexuality', *Victorian Studies*, XXV, 2, 1982, pp. 181–210.

14 Reprinted in *The Columbia Anthology of Gay Literature: Readings from Western Antiquity to the Present Day*, ed. Bryne R.S. Fone, New York (Columbia University Press) 1998, pp. 322–28. Wilde was challenged with authorship of 'The Priest and the Acolyte' in cross-examination by Edward Carson in his first trial in 1895. For an account of the trial, see Richard Ellmann, *Oscar Wilde*, London (Hamish Hamilton) 1987. The author of the offending story, which had been published anonymously, was John Francis Bloxam (1873–1928).

15 William James's *Varieties of Religious Experience* was first published in 1902 in London (Longmans, Green). It is not a study of denominational variety but is, as its subtitle indicates, 'a study of human nature'.

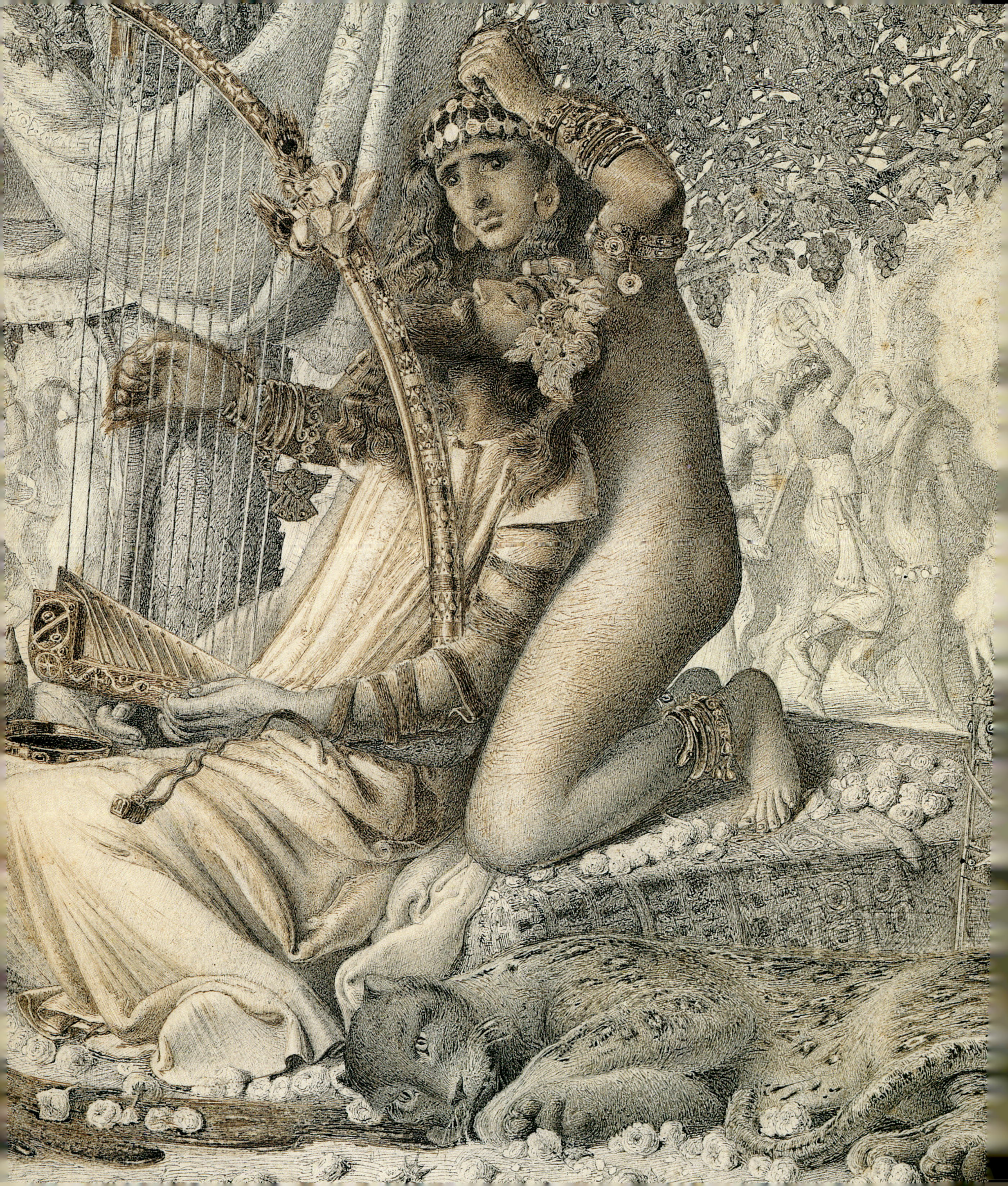

Juvenilia and First Exhibitions

"That singular young genius"
William Michael Rossetti, *The Spectator*, 6 November 1858

Some of Solomon's earliest work has been preserved in drawings and sketchbooks showing his prodigious talent for imaginative composition. A group of works now at the Jewish Museum, London, from around 1854–55, when the artist was aged between thirteen and fifteen, demonstrates his inventiveness and his interest in subjects derived from the Hebrew Scriptures (the Old Testament) as well as Jewish ceremonies. A related sketchbook now at the Mishkan Le'Omanut Museum, Ein Harod, Israel (to which some of the London sheets appear to have belonged originally), bears the inscription '1855' on the cover, although some of the sheets are dated 1854. It contains drawings illustrating Shakespeare, Dickens and contemporary novels.

The London drawings are often mounted in pairs (once in a group of three, in cat. 6) and inscribed with titles in the young artist's best copperplate handwriting. Although several of the sheets show pencil markings under the ink, the bold confidence of the line is impressive, as is the inventiveness of the compositions.

Some of the drawings exhibited here are likely to be among those referred to by members of the Pre-Raphaelite Brotherhood who were shown them in April 1857 and February 1858, as recorded by George Price Boyce (1980) in his diaries:

> (7 April 1857): "Went to Solomon's. He has a grand picture, 'Waiting for the Verdict'. Saw some remarkable designs by his young brother (Simeon) showing much Rossetti-like feeling."
> (19 February 1858): "Solomon's weekly reunion. Tea and fish, wine and cake. Much interested with a book of sketches by young Simeon."

As both his brother Abraham (1823–1862) and his sister Rebecca (1832–1886) were painters, the young Simeon probably had informal training as well as encouragement. He began his formal training in his brother's studio and then at F.S. Cary's Academy until his admission to the Royal Academy Schools on 24 April 1856. Within two years Solomon was showing his work in public. Many of the motifs invented at this time were to be explored and developed in his mature works.

17
Babylon Hath Been a Golden Cup (detail)
1859
Pen with black and brown ink over traces of pencil on paper
26.6 × 28.3 cm (10½ × 11⅛ in.)
Signed and dated *SS/9/59* lower left
Birmingham Museums & Art Gallery. Purchased (Alfred Leadbeater Bequest Fund) 1925

1
Ahasuerus
Undated
Pen and ink on paper
17 × 20.5 cm (6½ × 8¼ in.)
Courtesy of The Jewish Museum, London

This drawing shows King Ahasuerus (Xerxes) enthroned and surrounded by slaves and courtiers, one of whom might be Haman. The 'Esther' in the inscription refers to the Book of Esther; Ahasuerus was king of the Persians and Esther's husband.

2
The Sacrifice of Isaac
Undated
Pen and ink over pencil on paper
21 × 23 cm (8¼ × 9 in.)
Courtesy of The Jewish Museum, London

The story is told in Genesis 22:9–14. This is Solomon's earliest version of a subject that, like the earlier stage of Abraham's journey with Isaac (cat. 5b), was attempted several times. Solomon extemporizes on the biblical text by having Abraham turn to the angel and say "Hallelujah!", which is written in Hebrew script.

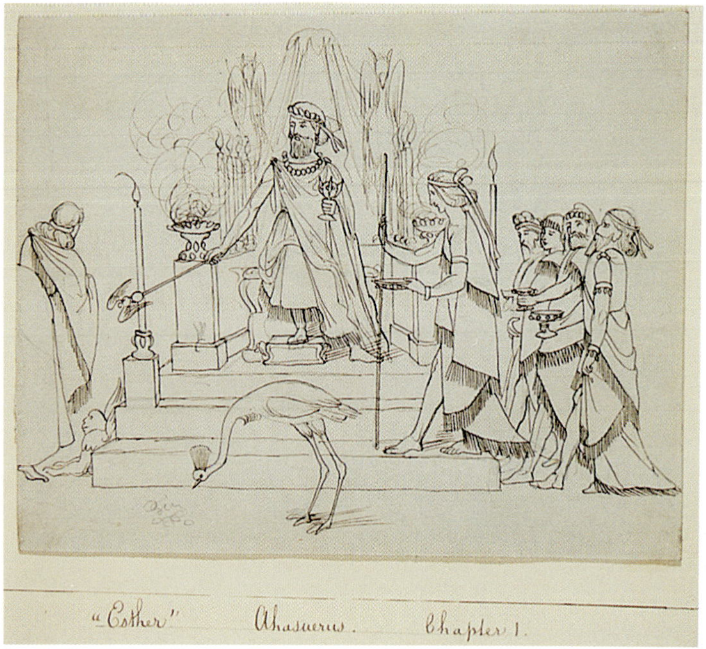

1

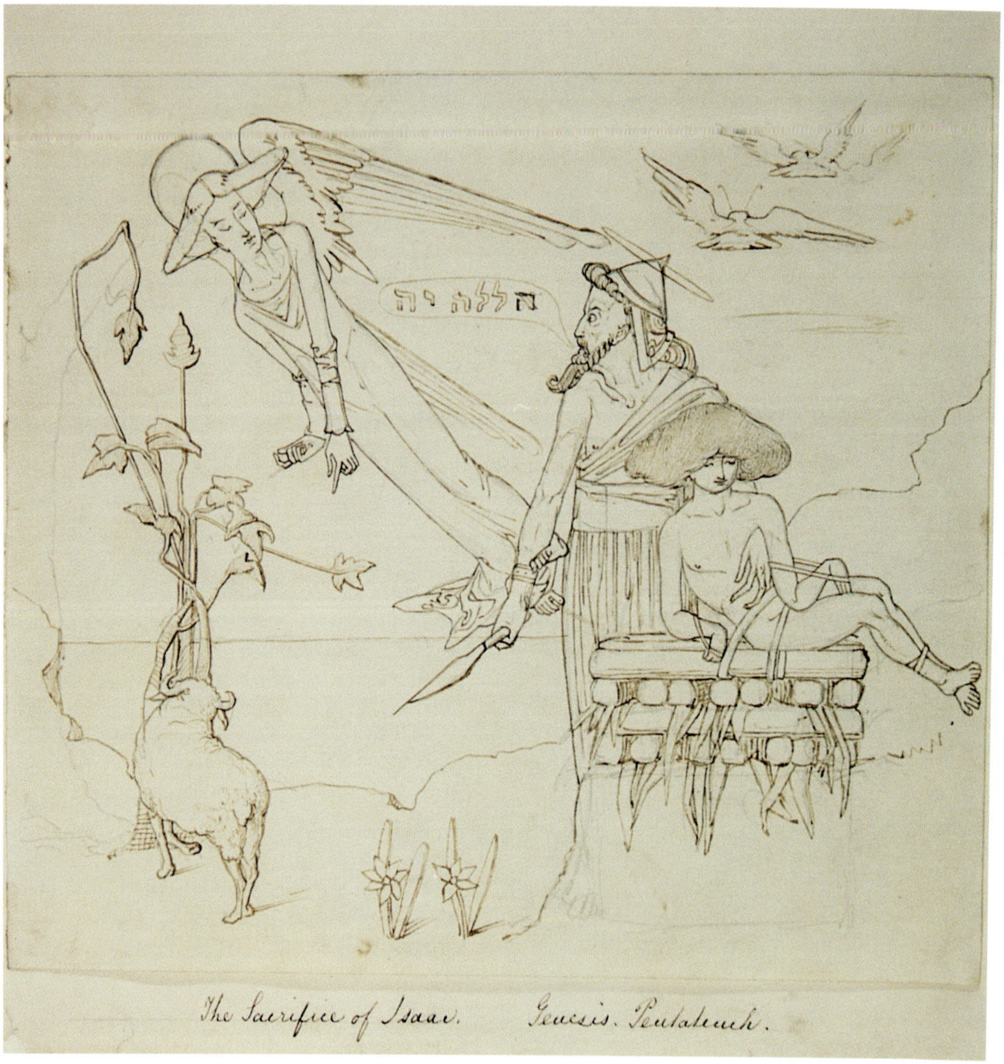

2

3a
The Meeting of Joseph and Jacob
Undated
Pen and ink over pencil on paper
16.5 × 21 cm (6½ × 8¼ in.)
Courtesy of The Jewish Museum, London

The moment when the aged Jacob meets his son Joseph, whom he thought dead, in Egypt, where Joseph had grown rich and powerful, is recorded in Genesis 46:29–31. In Solomon's depiction the greeting is dignified and solemn, yet touching. Joseph is wearing a "long robe with sleeves" decorated with figures, perhaps a reference to the robe his father had given him (37:3) and which had been smeared with blood by his brothers to convince Jacob of the boy's death. The brothers look on with their wives and children in tow, still, to judge by their expressions, a little stand-offish and jealous.

3b
Abraham and the Angels
Undated
Pen and ink on paper
17 × 22 cm (6½ × 8¾ in.)
Signed in full lower right
Courtesy of The Jewish Museum, London

The story of the appearance of God in the form of three angelic strangers, who inform Abraham that his wife Sarah shall have a son despite her advanced age, is recorded in Genesis 18:1–15. Abraham shows hospitality to the three strangers; he offers them *challot*, plaited and glazed bread, but fails to notice that they are angels. Sarah – whose reaction is to laugh at the news of her unlikely pregnancy – is seen peering out of a tent to the right.

Nos. 3a and 3b are mounted on one sheet with the added title *Illustrations from the Scriptures: The ~~New~~ Old Testament*. The correction perhaps indicates the young artist's unfamiliarity with Christian terminology. The heading is flanked with drawings representing Moses (left) and Jesus (right), both depicted peering over clouds and stars.

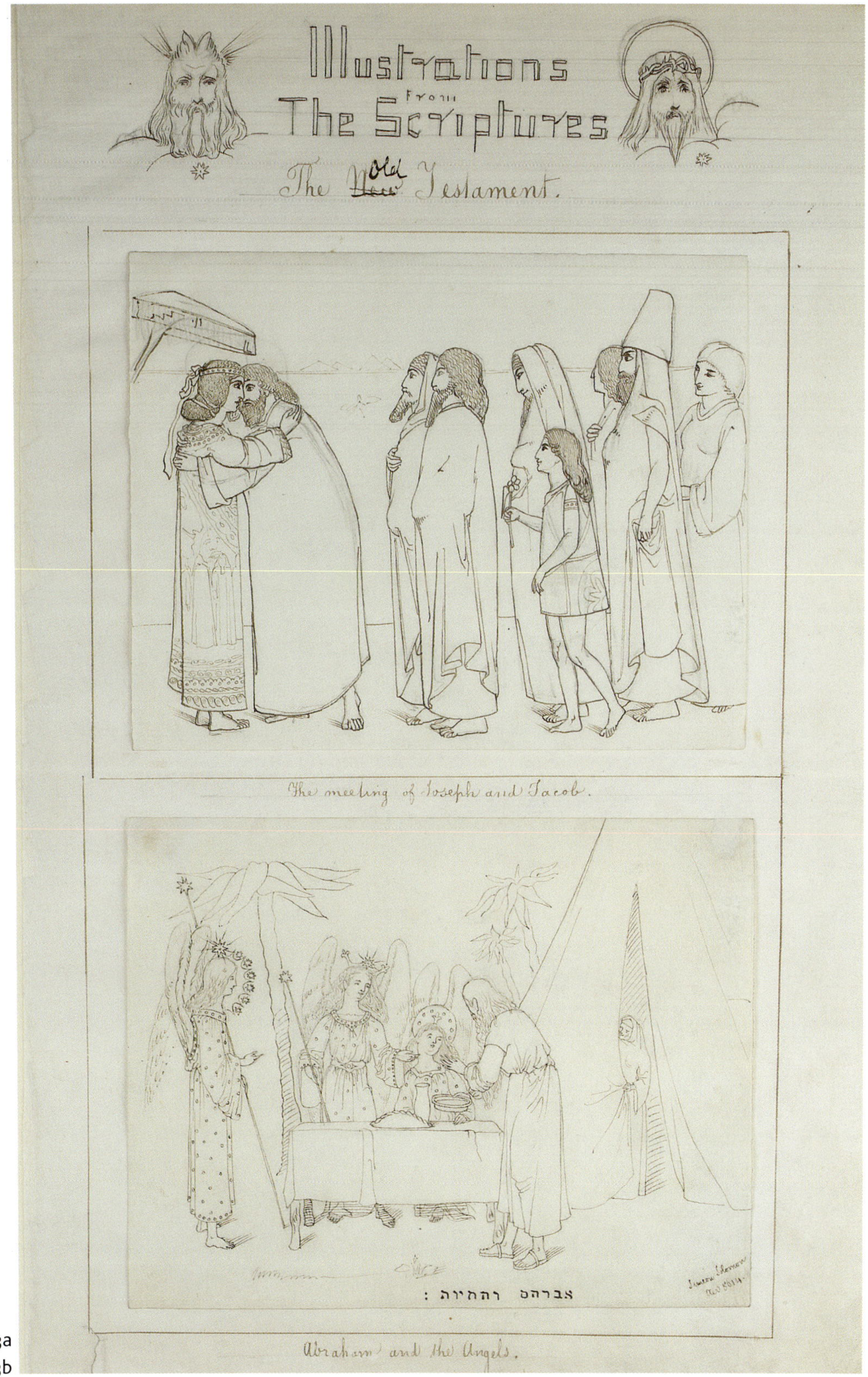

3a
3b

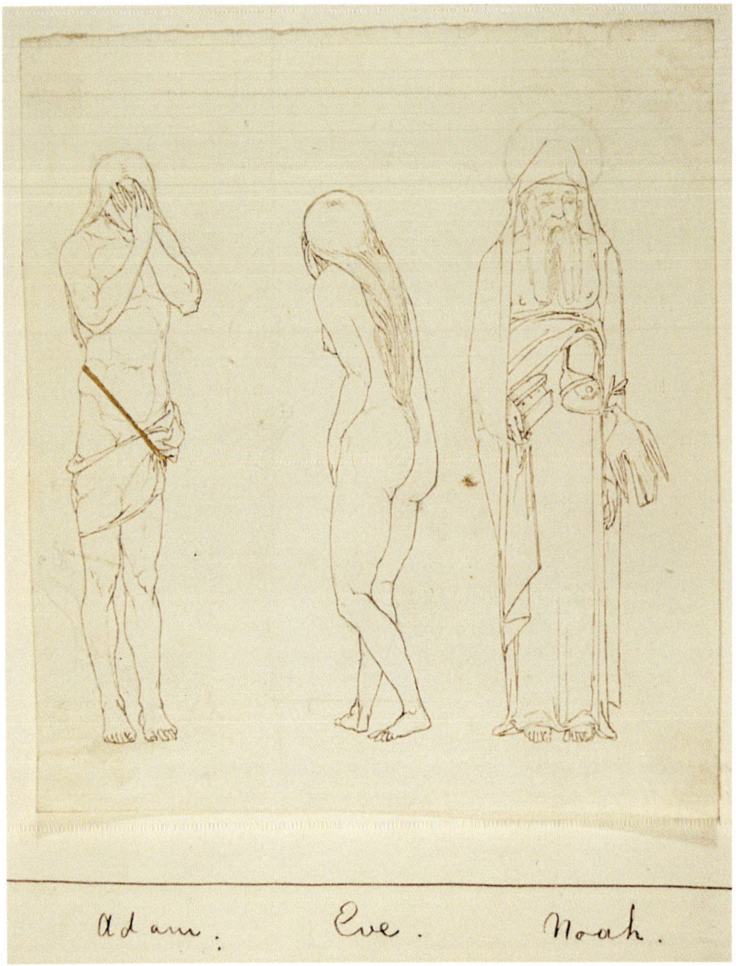

4a

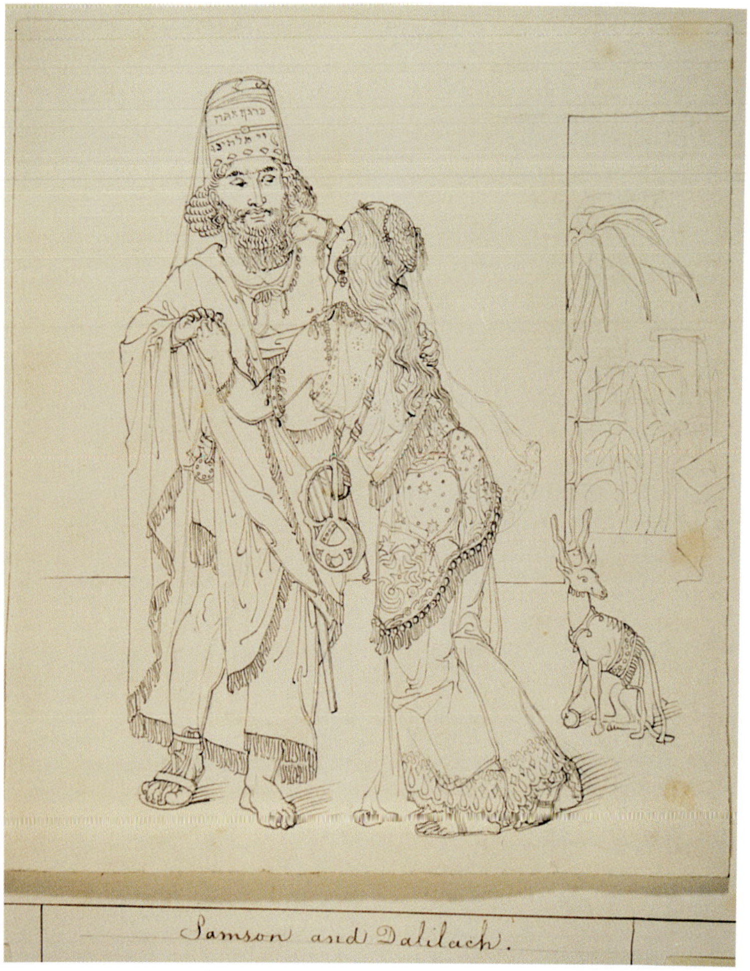

4b

4a
Adam, Eve, Noah
Undated
Pen and ink with touches of gold paint and pencil on paper
13 × 12 cm (5¼ × 4½ in.)
Courtesy of The Jewish Museum, London

Cat. 4a is a significant sheet of studies for its treatment of the nude figure. In both cases the musculature is drawn as a series of sharply defined and highly stylized marks, yet still conveys Solomon's intense interest in form. The figure of Noah, haloed, is bare-breasted and is accompanied by the dove bearing the olive branch.

4b
Samson and Dalilach
Undated
Pen and ink over pencil on paper
22.5 × 19 cm (8¾ × 7½ in.)
Courtesy of The Jewish Museum, London

No specific event seems to be illustrated here, although the arrangement of the figures summarizes the passionate relationship between the characters; the moment, however, might be that when Samson finally tells Delilah the secret of his strength because he is wearied by her nagging and pestering (Judg. 16:15–18).

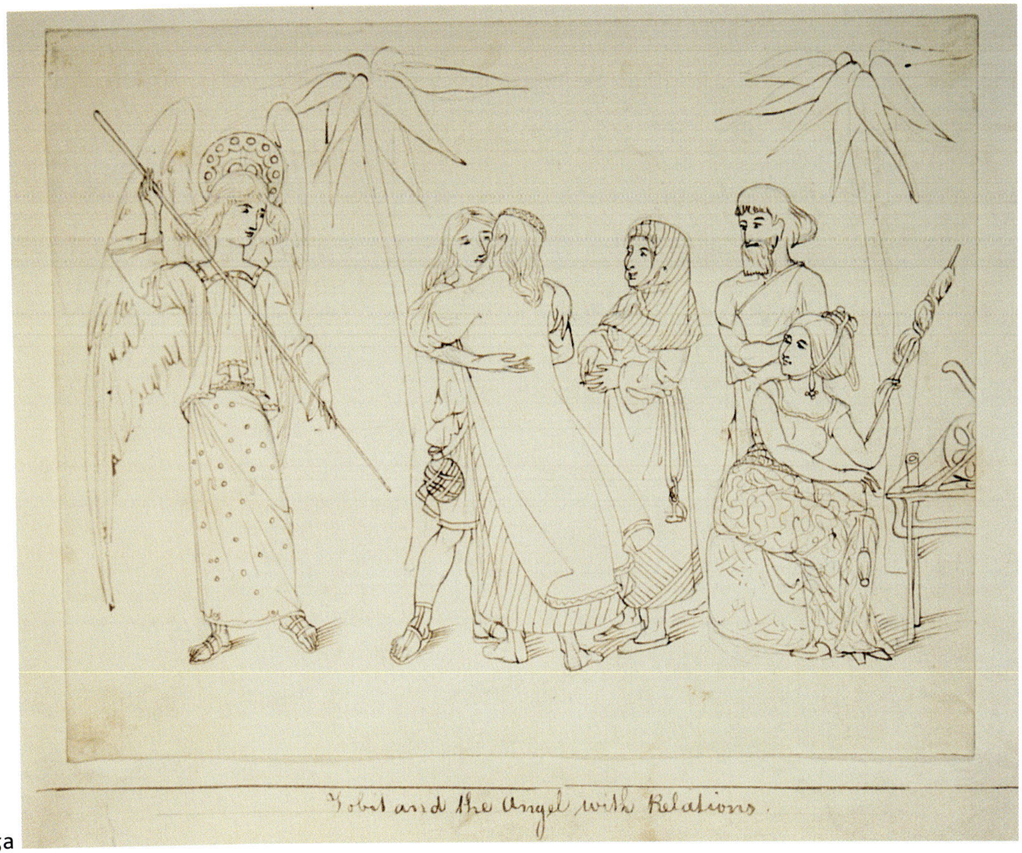

5a

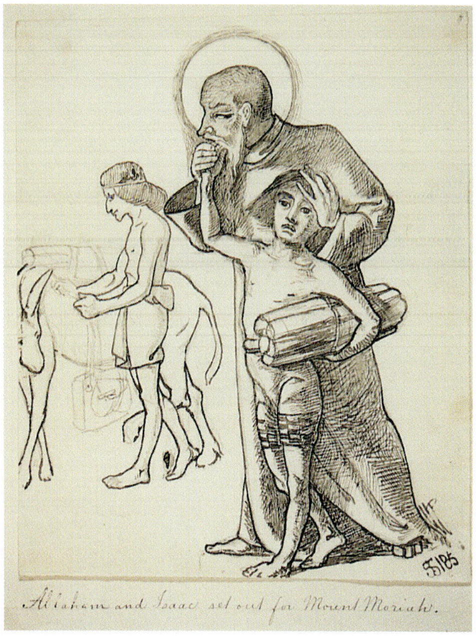

5b

5a
Tobit and the Angel with Relations
Undated
Pen and ink over pencil on paper
17 × 20.5 cm (6½ × 8 in.)
Courtesy of The Jewish Museum, London

Cat. 5a illustrates the meeting of Tobias and his father's kinsman Raguel, his wife Edna and their daughter Sarah in Ecbatana, recorded in Tobit 7:1–9. It is tempting to see resemblances to the artist and his family in the various characters. Solomon's inscription confuses Tobit, the father, with his son Tobias.

5b
Abraham and Isaac set out for Mount Moriah
c. 1855?
Pen and ink over pencil on paper
21 × 17 cm (8¼ × 6¾ in.)
Signed *SS* and dated *185* lower right
Courtesy of The Jewish Museum, London

Cat. 5a is Solomon's first attempt at the subject from Genesis 22:1–3; he was to treat it in both oil (RA 1858) and watercolour (*c.* 1858) paintings, which formed the basis of his illustration for the Dalziel Brothers' Bible project (fig. 22). This version is cruder yet more tender, emphasizing both Abraham's fear and his son's innocence. The motif of Abraham kissing Isaac's hand is a common feature of all four versions.

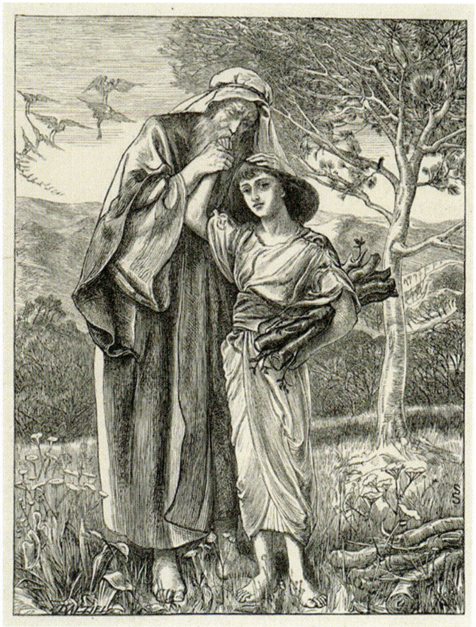

Fig. 22
Dalziel Brothers after Simeon Solomon
Abraham and Isaac
c. 1862
Wood engraving
17.9 × 13.5 cm ($7\frac{1}{16} \times 5\frac{5}{16}$ in.)
Published in *Dalziels' Bible Gallery*, 1881
Birmingham Museums & Art Gallery

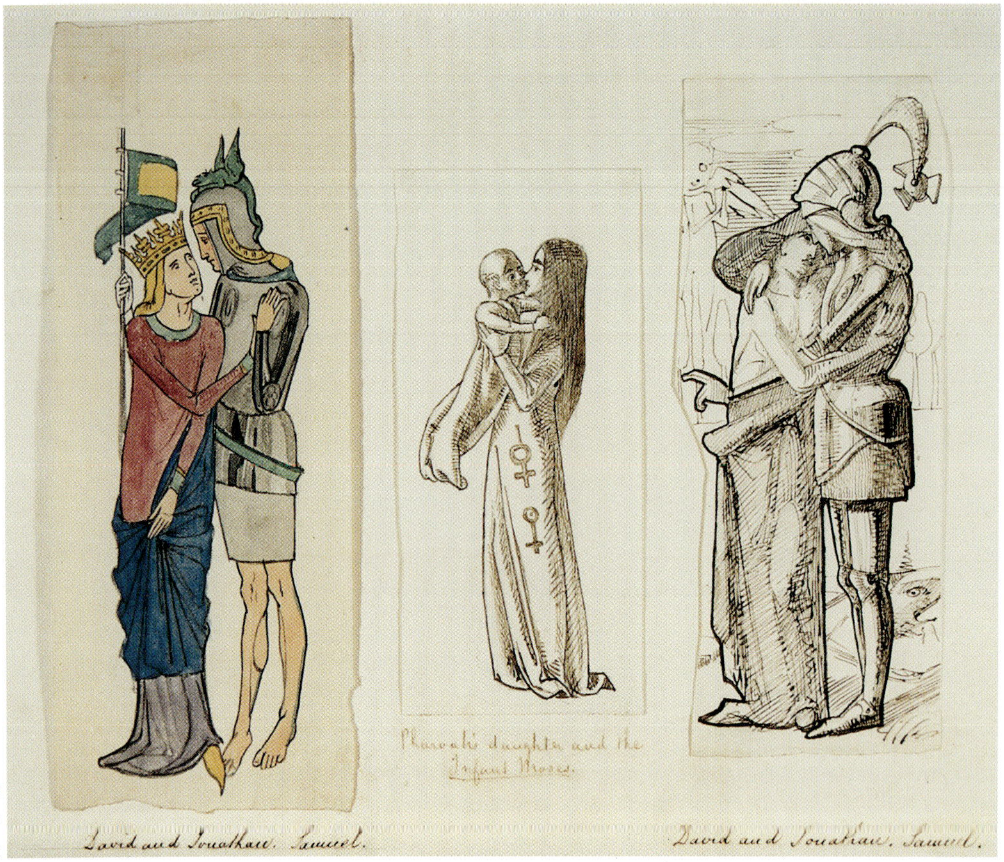

6a
6b
6c

7
King David dancing before the Ark
Undated
Pen and ink over pencil on paper
14.5 × 8.5 cm (5½ × 3¼ in.)
Courtesy of The Jewish Museum, London

Cat. 7 is an extraordinary subject for the young artist, which was to be worked up into a complex, highly finished drawing (formerly in the collection of Lord Houghton, untraced) completed in 1860. The subject is a fragment of a complex incident in the life of David related in II Samuel 6 in which he ordered the bringing of the Ark from Baale-Judah to Jerusalem. On its arrival in the city David danced before it wearing only a linen *ephod*, a short apron-like skirt. His "nakedness" displeased his wife, and her subsequent criticism of him caused a breach in their relationship. Solomon has daringly shown David's genitals as they would have been exposed in a vigorous dance in a short garment; his depiction of the king, angular and awkward, owes a little to his understanding of the formal qualities of Assyrian sculpture developed further in works such as cat. 47.

6a
David and Jonathan
Undated
Watercolour with pen and ink on paper
24 × 9 cm (9¾ × 3 9/16 in.)
Courtesy of The Jewish Museum, London

With cat. 6c this is among the first of Solomon's attempts to depict the friendship of David and Jonathan, which was, according to David's lament on the deaths of Saul and Jonathan, "passing the love of women" (II Sam. 1:26). The moment depicted could be either that conveyed in I Samuel 18:1–5, "the soul of Jonathan was knit to the soul of David, and Jonathan loved him ...", or the later scene relating the flight of David from Saul's court, the last meeting of the two friends before Jonathan's death in battle (I Sam. 20:17).

Both drawings are highly stylized in a version of the medieval illuminated style adopted by the Pre-Raphaelite Brotherhood in its earliest phase, yet they have an overlay of an earlier Romantic style of the 1820s.

6b
Pharaoh's Daughter and the Infant Moses
Undated
Pen and ink over pencil on paper
17 × 7.5 cm (6¾ × 3 in.)
Courtesy of The Jewish Museum, London

Cat. 6b is an almost comic rendering of the scene from Exodus 2:5–7, yet curiously touching, emphasizing the baby Moses's surprise at the stranger's embrace and the girl's rather stiff delight in finding him. Thermuthis's dress is decorated with made-up hieroglyphs resembling astrological symbols, perhaps Solomon's fanciful version of Egyptian design.

6c
David and Jonathan
Undated
Pen and ink on paper
20 × 7.5 cm (8 × 3 in.)
Courtesy of The Jewish Museum, London

David is represented as effeminate; his hair is long, his figure slender, and he is stripped to the waist, while Jonathan, tall and protective, is in full armour.

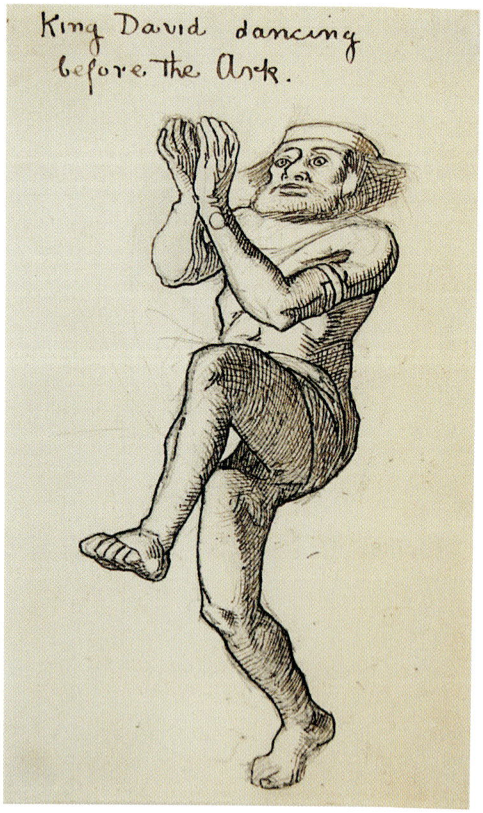

7

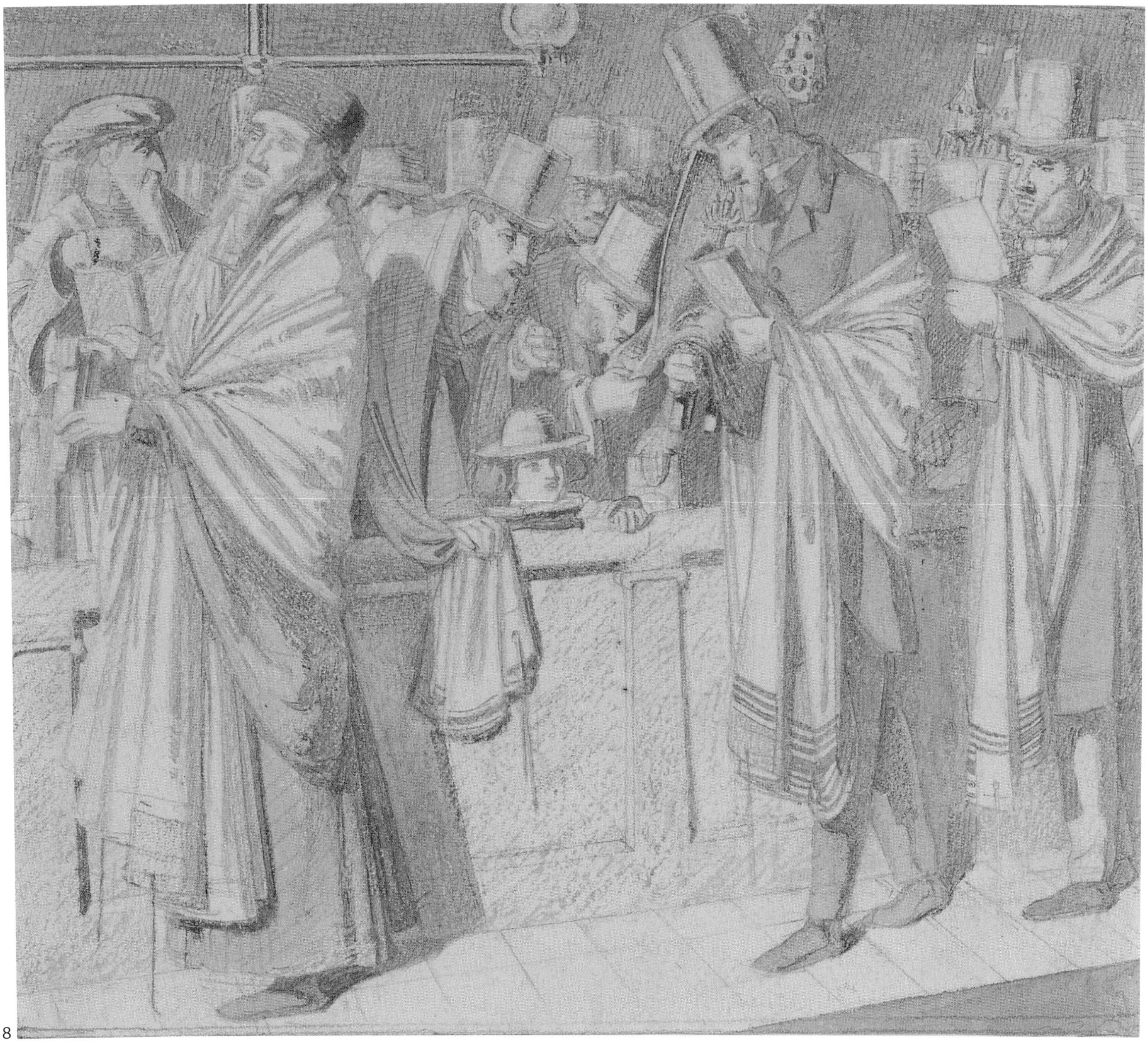

8

8
Procession with the Scrolls of the Law
Undated
Pen and sepia ink with wash over pencil on paper
13 × 15 cm (5¼ × 5¾ in.)
Courtesy of The Jewish Museum, London

Compared with cat. 94, this scene is a type of reportage noting a variety of dress and demeanour in a relatively humble setting. The piety and respect of the two men at the centre of the congregation, one of whom bends to kiss the covering of the Torah scrolls, is offset by the frank curiosity of the little boy at the front who stares at the procession.

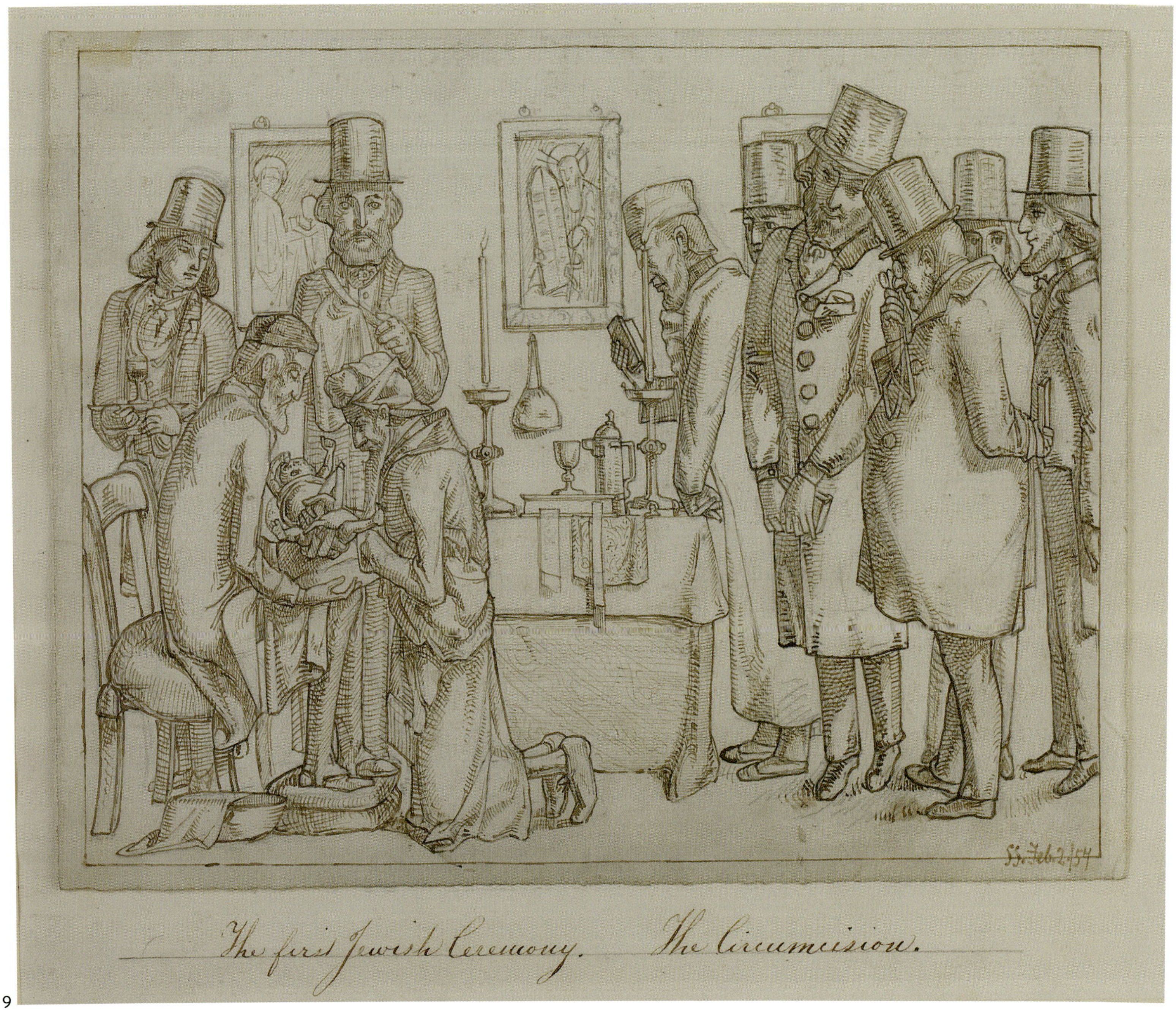

9

9
The first Jewish Ceremony. The Circumcision
1854
Pen and ink over pencil on paper
17 × 21 cm (6½ × 8¼ in.)
Signed *SS* and dated *Feb 2/54* lower right
Courtesy of The Jewish Museum, London

Cat. 9 is a piece of reportage of contemporary Jewish life, rendered in a highly stylized linear style with much cross-hatching and a slight attenuation of the figures. The style allows a clarity of vision so that, although the composition is crowded, all the separate parts of the ceremony and the reactions of the men can be seen and understood. Pictures hung on the wall in the background include a prominent depiction of Moses with the tablets of stone.

The inscription underlines the importance of the ritual of circumcision for the Jewish religion, affirming and reconsecrating the *brit milah*, the 'everlasting covenant' made by God with Abraham, giving the land of Canaan in perpetuity to a people who observe circumcision as a ritual (Gen. 17:7–14). The operation, performed by a *mohel*, is fairly graphically portrayed. One figure wipes a knife; another, a young attendant with long hair, looks on.

Cat. 9 was originally mounted with a scene representing a *barmitzvah*, inscribed *The Confirmation*, now missing.

10
Eight Scenes from the Story of David and Jonathan
1856
Pencil with gold leaf on paper
25.5 × 36.6 cm (10 1/16 × 14 7/16 in.)
Signed and dated *22/7/1856* lower right
Tate. Bequeathed by Alfred M.H. Solomon and the estate of Marguerite I.R. Solomon, 1993

Showing almost divergent influences, both stylistic and religious, on the young artist, cat. 10 combines Solomon's interest in the emotionally highly charged story of David, Saul and Jonathan with Gothic-revival pointed architecture and the 'Early Christian' outline drawing style made popular by the German Romantic artists, the Nazarenes, and later adopted by the Pre-Raphaelite Brotherhood.

Eight scenes tell the life story of David from his summons to appear before Samuel to his death, with various key episodes, such as the slaying of Goliath (scene 4), occupying the intervening compositions.

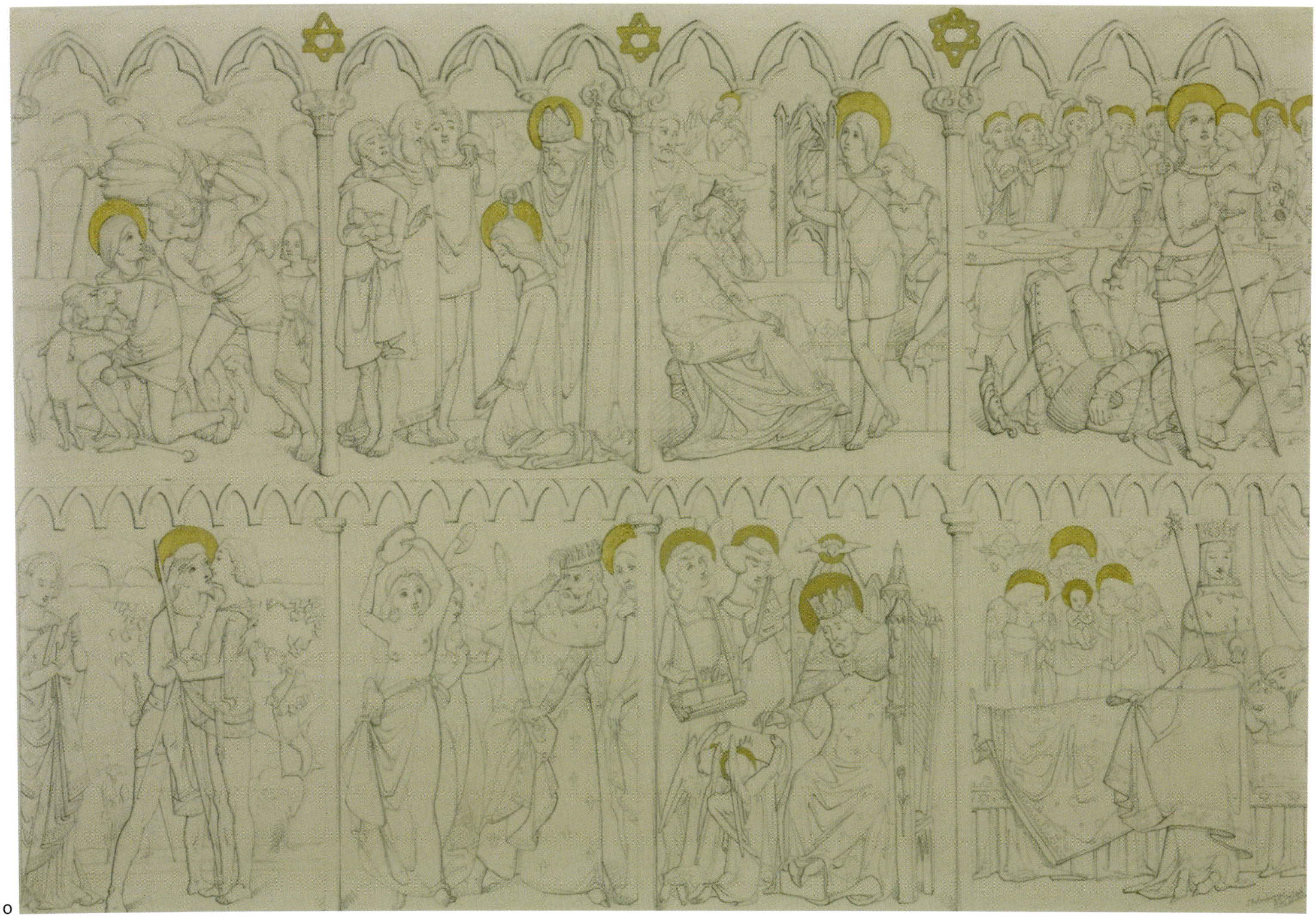

10

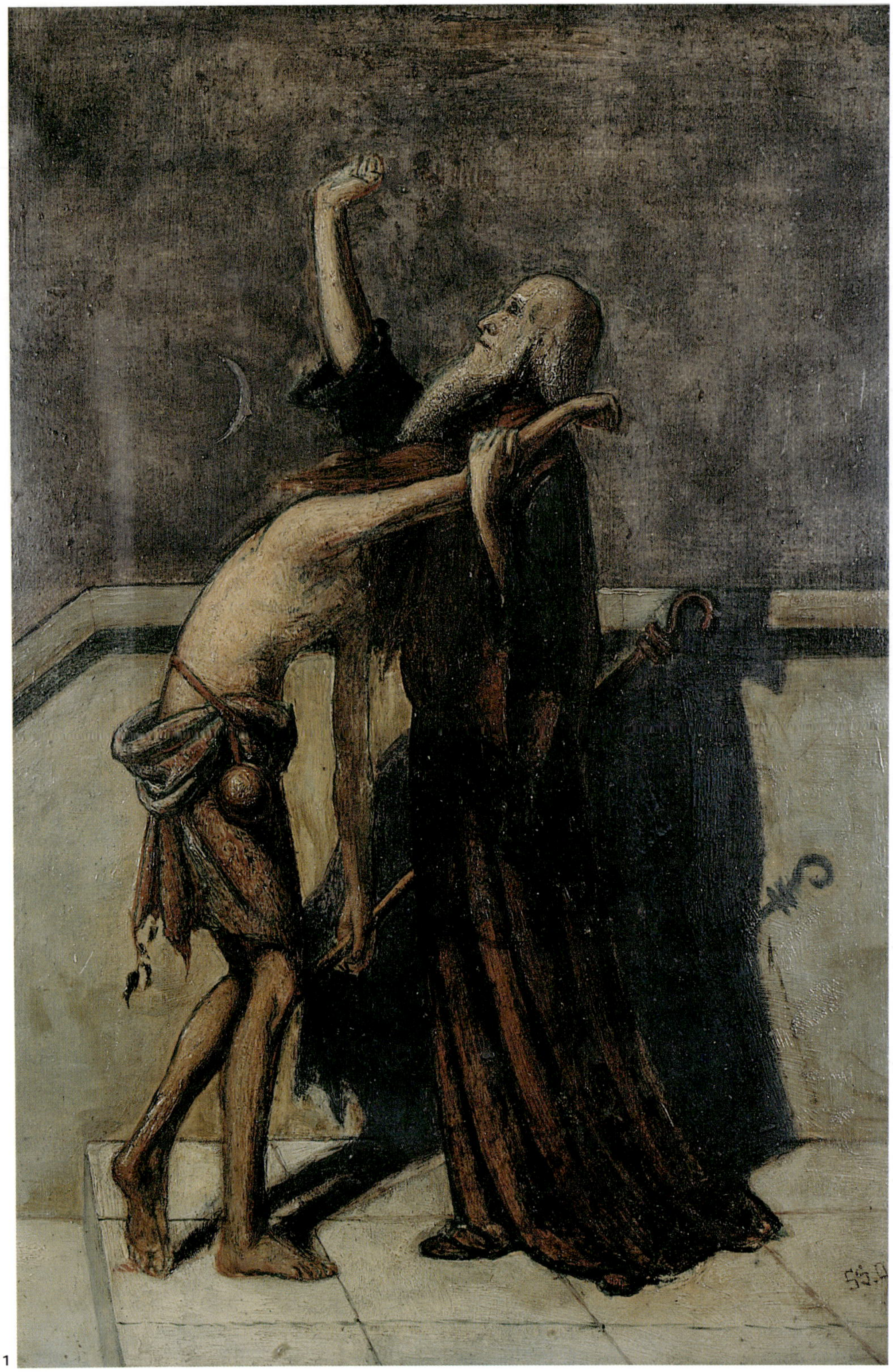

11

11

The Prodigal Son

1857

Oil on card

26 × 18.2 cm (10¼ × 7³⁄₁₆ in.)

Signed *SS* and dated *9.6.57* lower right

William Morris Gallery, London

The story of the prodigal son is found in the Gospel of St Luke 15, the incident of the welcoming of the son by the father in verse 20.

Solomon's realization of the story is angular and simplified yet powerfully dramatic, rejecting some of the already familiar characteristics of truth to nature and precise historical detail. Cat. 11 concentrates on the contrast between the abjection of the youth and the quiet beneficence of the old man.

12

The Soul Released from the Body

1857

Sepia ink with wash on paper

26 × 20.6 cm (10¼ × 8⅛ in.)

Dated 17/3/57 lower left

Lionel Lambourne

The subject of cat. 12 is obscure, although it reflects Solomon's early interest in Rossetti, particularly his short story 'Hand and Soul' (first published in the Pre-Raphaelite journal *The Germ* in 1849), which Solomon illustrated in a sketchbook around this time (Mishkan Le'Omanut Museum, Ein Harod, Israel). The two

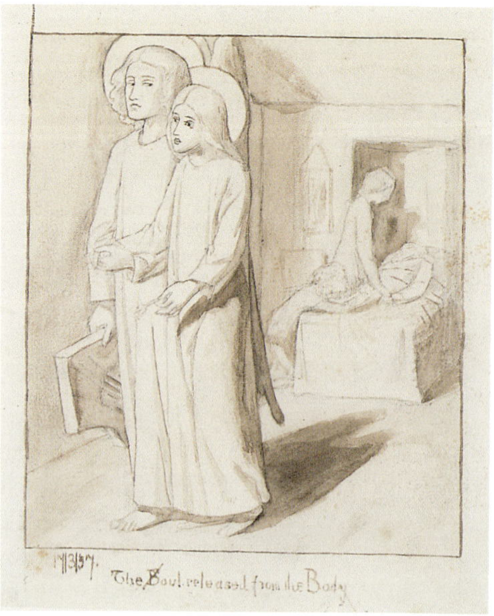

12

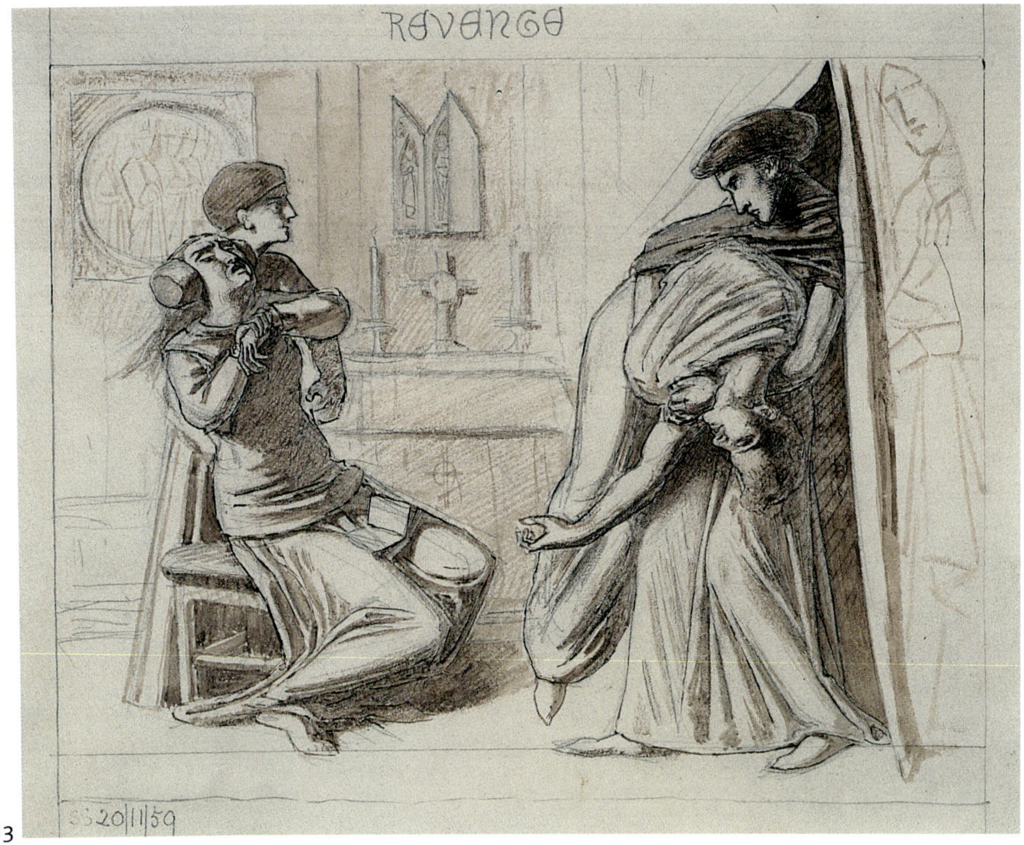

13

main figures, both with haloes, are reminiscent of Rossetti's Angel Gabriel and the Virgin Mary in *Ecce Ancilla Domini! (The Annunciation)* (1849–50, Tate). In the background is a deathbed scene; in the foreground a soul, depicted as a female figure, is led away by a watchful male figure who carries a stringed musical instrument. Lionel Lambourne notes that cat. 12 is evidence of the artist's "lifelong preoccupation with the theme of metamorphosis of the human soul, which was to achieve its fullest expression in his prose poem *A Vision of Love Revealed in Sleep*" (*Solomon: A Family of Painters*, 1985, p. 65).

13
Revenge
1859
Pen and sepia ink and wash over pencil on paper
20.6 × 26.5 cm (8⅛ × 10¾ in.)
Signed *SS* and dated *20/11/59* lower left
Dr Dennis T. Lanigan collection, Canada

The origin of the subject is now obscure, although it might relate to one of the Border ballads that enjoyed a vogue among the early Pre-Raphaelite Brotherhood and which were often bloody and ghastly in their imagery. There is something of a parody of Pre-Raphaelite 'intensity' about the dramatic postures, the shadowy modelling of the figures and the setting, a chamber with a tapestry hanging and an altar.

14
Love
1858
Pen and sepia ink and wash over pencil on paper
26.7 × 21 cm (10½ × 8¼ in.)
Dated *21/4/58* lower left
Private collection

Cat. 14 is a fine drawing of an obscure subject, perhaps – because of the 9 inscribed lower right – part of a series of drawings of medieval subjects that includes cat. 13. Some fanciful 'intense' medieval flourishes, such as the decoration of the recessed bed, might be derived from Rossetti, whose watercolours on medieval subjects, like *Fra Pace* (1856, private collection) or *Dante's Dream at the Time of the Death of Beatrice* (1856, Tate), contain such details. However, in composition and feeling, cat. 14 is closer to another, but unfinished, work of Rossetti's, *The Ballad of Fair Annie* (*c*. 1855, private collection) and, in the awkwardness of the male figure, to Holman Hunt's *Claudio and Isabella* (1850, Tate).

Both cat. 13 and cat. 14 relate to two designs of Solomon's, one inscribed *Peace*, dated 26 May 1858 (private collection), the other *Triumph*, dated 10 November 1858 (private collection); see Seymour (1986), figs. 32 and 34.

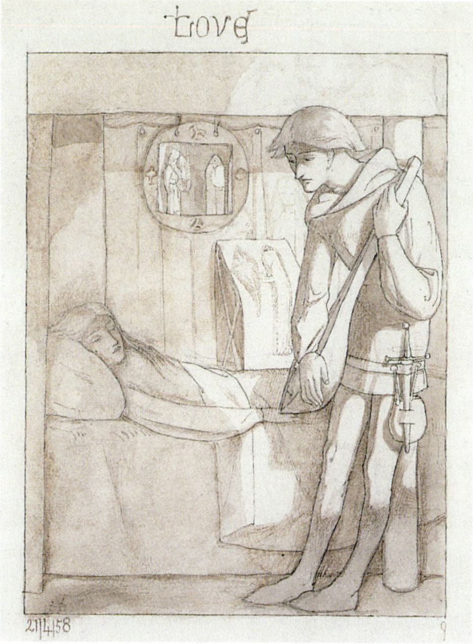

14

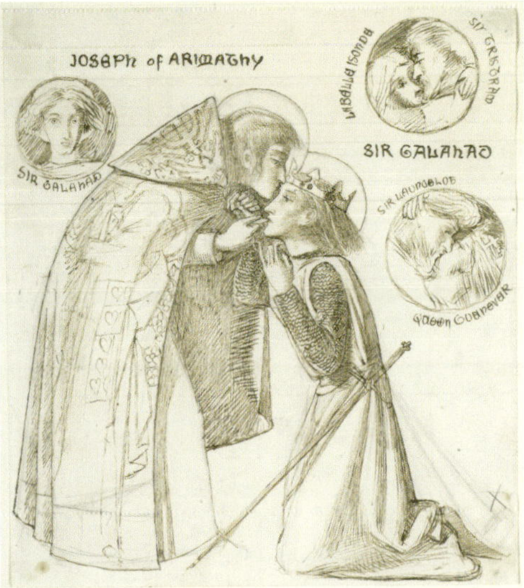

15

15
The Death of Sir Galahad While Taking a Portion of the Holy Grail Administered by Joseph of Arimathea
Undated; *c.* 1857–59
Pen and ink over pencil on paper
18.5 × 16.6 cm (7⁵⁄₁₆ × 6⁹⁄₁₆ in.)
Birmingham Museums & Art Gallery. Presented by Mr A.E. Anderson, 1922

A gaunt and youthful Galahad receives both the kiss of peace and the eucharistic wafer from Joseph of Arimathea, who is dressed in a richly embroidered and hooded chasuble; both men are haloed. Around the main figures roundels contain love scenes involving Tristan and Iseult (Sir Tristram and La Belle Isonde) and Launcelot and Guinevere. Arthurian subjects were enormously popular within the later Pre-Raphaelite circle. Rossetti had instigated the mural scheme based on Malory's *Morte d'Arthur* for the Debating Hall at the Oxford Union in the summer of 1857. Although undated, this drawing can be stylistically dated to the years 1857–59 and thus might be directly influenced by Rossetti's scheme.

16
Dante's First Meeting with Beatrice
1859–63
Pen and ink on paper
19.4 × 22.9 cm (7⅝ × 9 in.)
Signed with monogram and dated *12/9/5963* lower right
Tate. Bequeathed by Robert Ross through the National Art Collections Fund, 1919

Cat. 16 was first shown at the Seventh Annual Winter Exhibition of Cabinet Pictures organized by the Belgian picture dealer Gambart at the French Gallery with cat. 17 and a version of cat. 18. A date was attached to the title in the Winter Exhibition catalogue: 1 May 1275.

Cat. 16 indicates a knowledge of Rossetti's Dante watercolours, such as *Beatrice Denying the Salutation of Dante* (1851, private collection), although this is no slavish copy but an original interpretation of an original subject. However, the young artist appears to have been influenced by Rossetti's illustrations for the Moxon edition of Tennyson's poems (1856–57, published in 1857), especially that of St Cecilia for 'The Palace of Art' (cat. 53), where irrelevant, naturalistic detail helps to heighten the emotion of the central subject; a guard bites into an apple in the foreground of Rossetti's design, while a little girl in the background of Solomon's drawing idly eats grapes.

The *Times* review was provocative, not sparing the young man's sensitivities: "For an illustration ... of the extreme length to which quaint ugliness can be carried, we must go to works of a very young pre-Raffaelite – nay almost pre-historical artist – Mr. Simeon Solomon, whose rare facility in designing accessories and whose determined pursuit of the Ninevitish in local colour give his drawings and pictures a character absolutely their own, in spite of Mr. Solomon's obvious debt to the influence of Mr. Rosetti [*sic*]. Nothing uglier was surely ever conceived than the drawing in which Mr. Solomon has recorded the first introduction of the boy Dante to the child Beatrice" (24 May 1859, p. 9).

The odd dating of the drawing, 12/9/5963, indicates that it was amended between its first showing in 1859 and 1863.

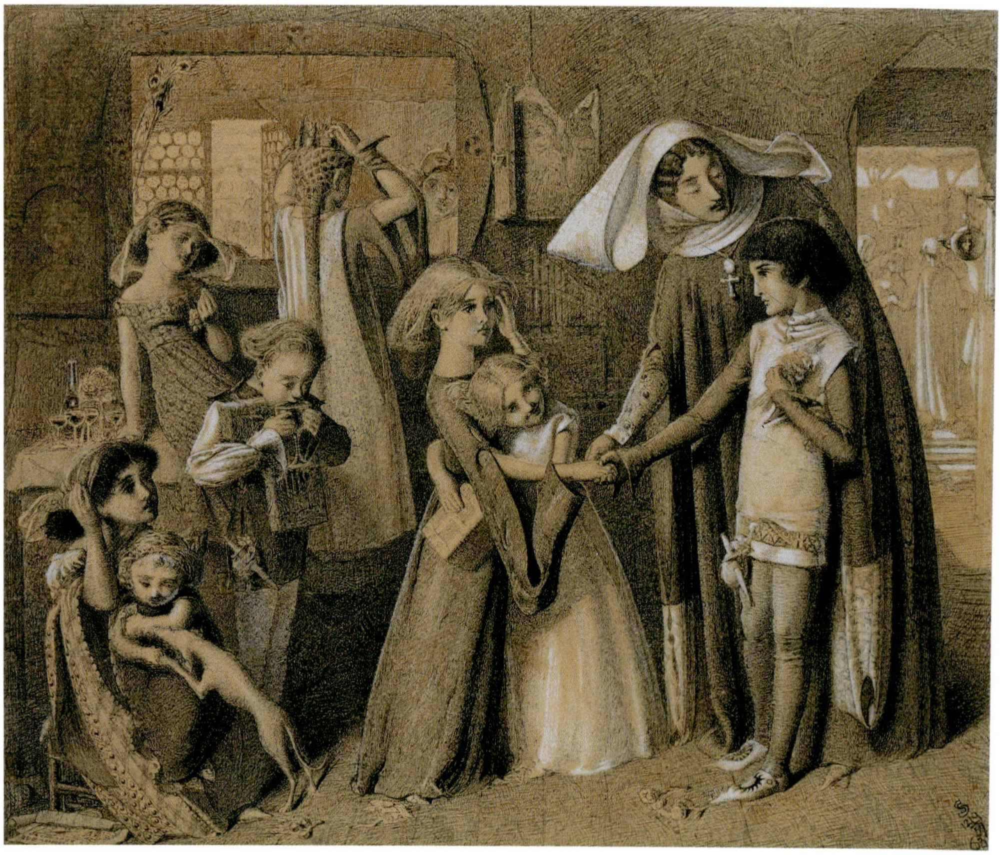

16

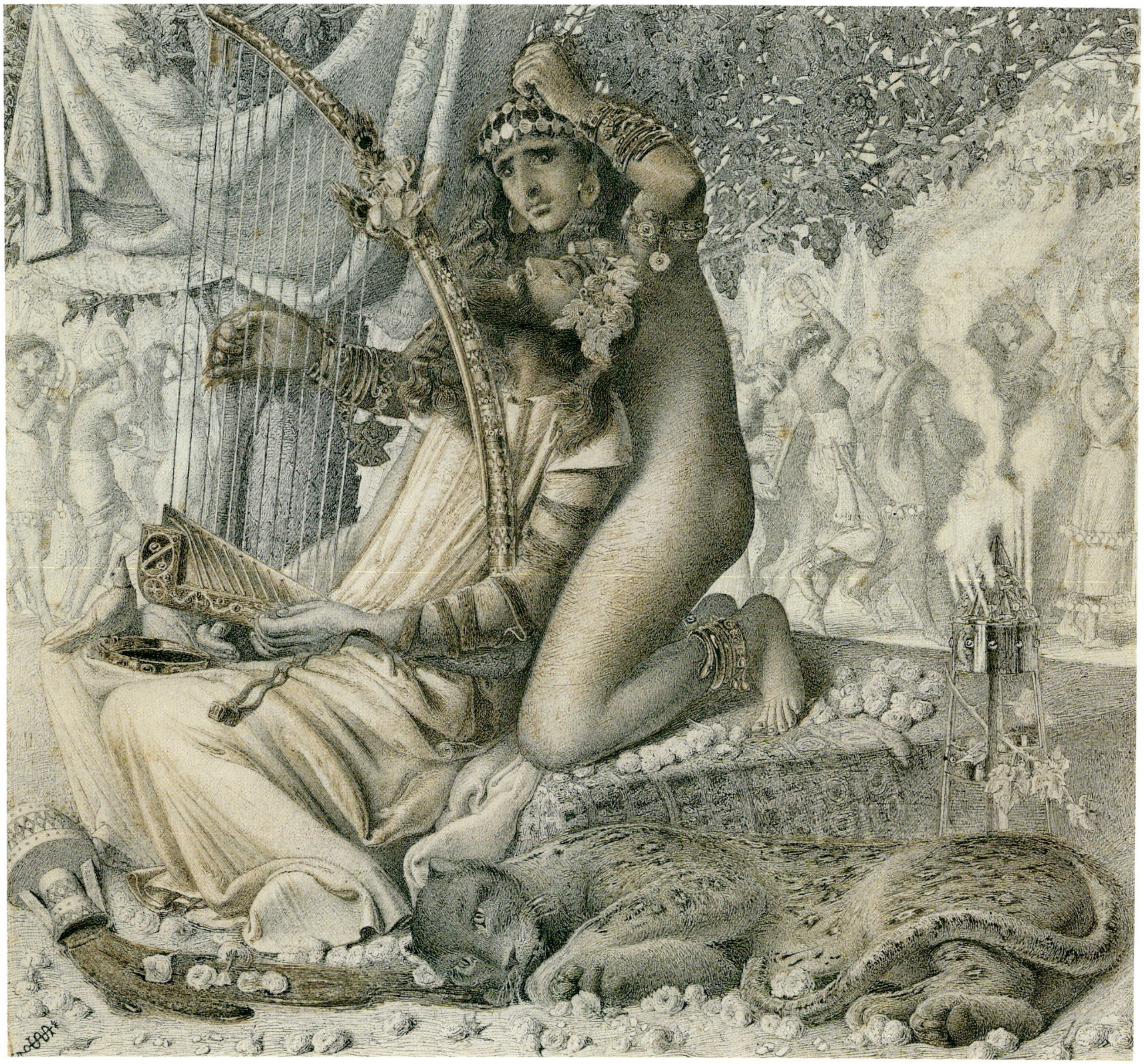

17

17
Babylon Hath Been a Golden Cup
1859
Pen with black and brown ink over traces of pencil on paper
26.6 × 28.3 cm (10½ × 11⅛ in.)
Signed and dated *SS/9/59* lower left
Birmingham Museums & Art Gallery. Purchased (Alfred Leadbeater Bequest Fund) 1925

Cat. 17 was listed in the Winter Exhibition catalogue with the text: "Babylon hath been a golden cup in the hand of God, which hath made all the earth drunken: the nations have drunken of her wine, therefore the nations are mad" (Jer. 51:7).

The drawing is extraordinary in several ways: in its original vision of an unusual subject, its highly charged eroticism, and its assured and yet unconventional handling of drawing media. The treatment of the detail is minute and the finish meticulous, while at the same time some details are awkward and clumsy. In many ways the drawing can be seen as an exemplar of Pre-Raphaelite draughtsmanship, although the subject was entirely original.

The *Athenaeum* was ambiguous in its review and offered the young artist advice: "Young Mr. Solomon, with all the tarnish of the absence of common sense, imitativeness, and gross affectation, is yet so astonishingly clever that he deserves a paragraph to himself for his two pictures – *David Playing before Saul* [see cat. 18] and *Babylon*, both surprisingly daring and imaginative for a youth, or indeed anyone, but both spoiled by ludicrous blots and sectarian imperfections ... 'Babylon' is less extravagant, and there is a weird, oriental feeling about it highly commendable [*sic*]. Avoid the ridiculous, unwise but clever Mr. Solomon, work hard at geometric drawing, curb your Pegasus, and you must do great things" (*Athenaeum*, 1673, 19 November 1859, p. 673).
For a discussion of the drawing's meanings, see Gayle Seymour's essay, pp. 17–18.

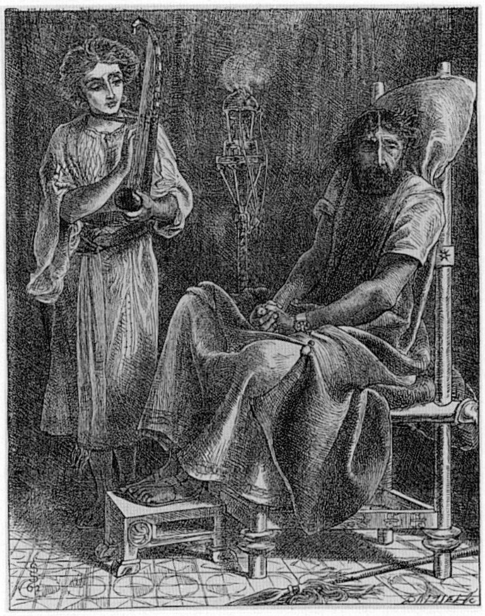
18a

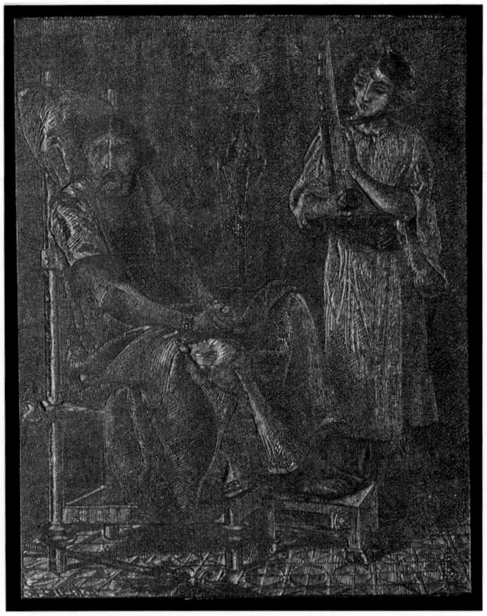
18b

18b
Dalziel Brothers after Simeon Solomon
'And David took an harp'
c. 1862
Woodblock
16.3 × 12.5 × 2.4 cm (6⅜ × 4⅞ × 1 in.)
Birmingham Museums & Art Gallery

19
The Sacrifice of Isaac
c. 1858
Pen and brown ink over pencil on paper
16.5 × 19 cm (6½ × 7½ in.)
The Ashmolean Museum, Oxford

The story of Abraham and Isaac was to concern the artist in these years, and it was the subject of Solomon's Royal Academy painting of 1859 (see cat. 2 and 5b).

The ornate Gothic vestments of the angel indicate the artist's concern with ecclesiological detail; their voluminousness contrasts with the nakedness of Isaac. The style of the drawing belongs to one of the artist's earliest modes – a version of medieval illumination, part decorative, part naturalistic. The flat composition and angular treatment of the human form anticipate later nineteenth-century draughtsmanship such as that of Charles Ricketts or the Dutch Art Nouveau artist Jan Toorop.

Solomon later illustrated the subject for the Dalziel Bible project (fig. 23).

20
Hagar and Ishmael
1857
Pen and ink on paper
17.7 × 12 cm (6$^{15}/_{16}$ × 4¾ in.)
Signed with monogram and dated *57* lower left
Lionel Lambourne

The drawing illustrates the moment in the history of Abraham when he banishes his concubine Hagar and their son Ishmael at the request of his wife Sarah, who has given birth to Isaac: "And Abraham rose up early in the morning and took bread, and a bottle of water, and gave it to Hagar, putting it on her shoulder, and the child, and sent her away: and she departed, and wandered in the wilderness of Beersheba" (Gen. 21:14).

Solomon has captured the mixed emotions of the scene: the resentment of Hagar, the

18a
Dalziel Brothers after Simeon Solomon
'And David took an harp'
1862
Wood engraving
16.3 × 12.7 cm (6⅜ × 5 in.)
Signed with monogram *SS* and dated *1862* in block lower left with *Dalziel SC* at lower right
Private collection

Cat. 18a is the engraving published in 1894 in *Art Pictures from the Old Testament and Our Lord's Parables*, p. 149. The text (on p. 148) is by Aley Fox.

The story of David had preoccupied Solomon from childhood (see, for example, cat. 6 and 10), and he seems to have been aware at an early age of its homoerotic potential.

The incident in the life of David, recorded in the Book of Samuel (I Sam. 16:23), has been used by Solomon to contrast the figure of the youthful David with King Saul. The older man is possessed by melancholy and self-doubt while the younger attempts to soothe him by playing sweet music. The accessories are particularly striking – the chair, footstool, incense-burner and musical instrument.

Cat. 18a is based on Solomon's oil painting *David Playing before Saul* (1859, untraced), exhibited with cat. 16 and 17 at the Seventh Annual Winter Exhibition of Cabinet Pictures in 1859.

When the painting was exhibited three years earlier, it was the subject of interesting discussion in the press: "Saul is gloomy and grand, but then it is too evident that he has eaten too many of those grapes, or that the smoke of that queer smoking extinguisher has affected his stomach; it is also painful to see that the small stove he sets his feet on has just scorched his toes. David is surprisingly lank and spindley [*sic*]" (*Athenaeum*, 1673, 19 November 1859, p. 673).

The *Times* reviewer noted the artist's inventiveness: "Mr. Solomon's large picture of David playing before Saul sins less egregiously in this respect, especially as we have no right to look for beauty in the Israelitish monarch possessed by his raging demon. Here, too, we have an admirable illustration of the determined precision of Mr. Solomon's invention in architecture, furniture, and dress, based doubtless on archaic reading, but rising from books and stones to a height of realism to which no reading could have carried any but a very original and singularly constituted mind. Mr. Solomon is of course a Jew, and it is satisfactory to note his marked national bent at a time when national bents in art are hardly traceable. If Mr. Solomon can conquer his besetting sins of ugliness, and if his nationalism be more than affectation, he may educate into a power a gift which at present produces little beyond singularity" (24 May 1859, p. 9).

The subject of a youthful Jewish musician was to feature in several of Solomon's works of the 1860s; see, for example, cat. 36.

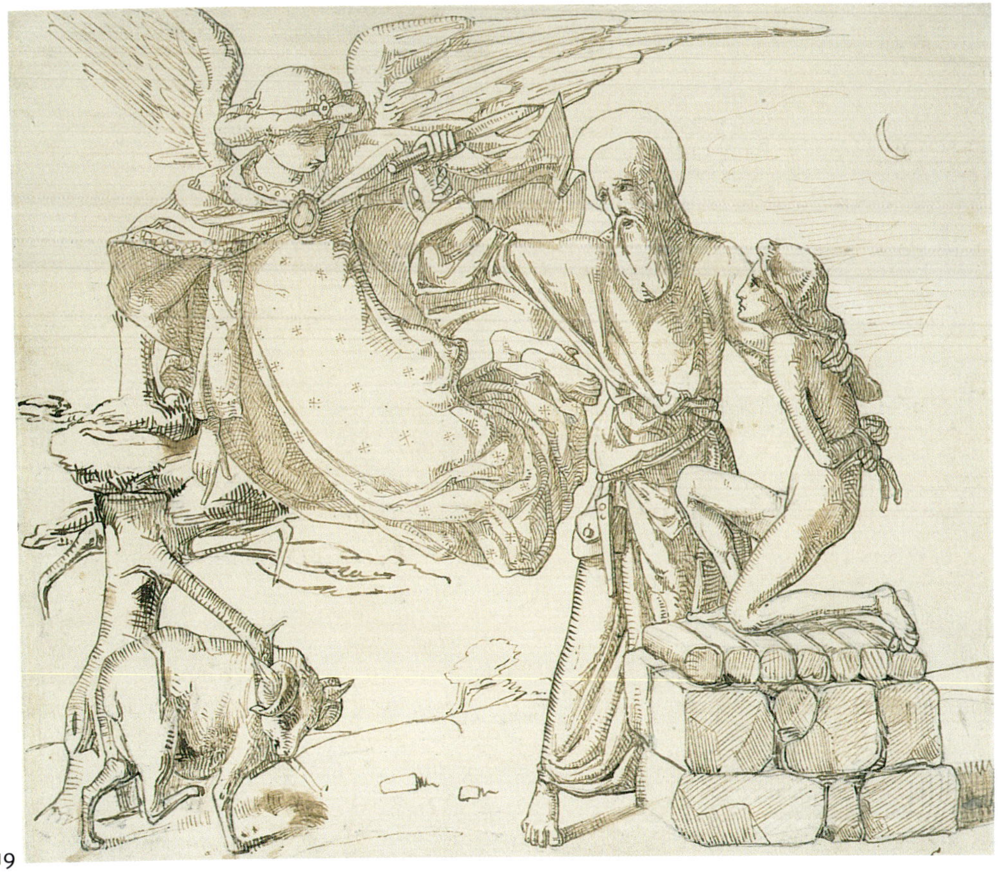

19

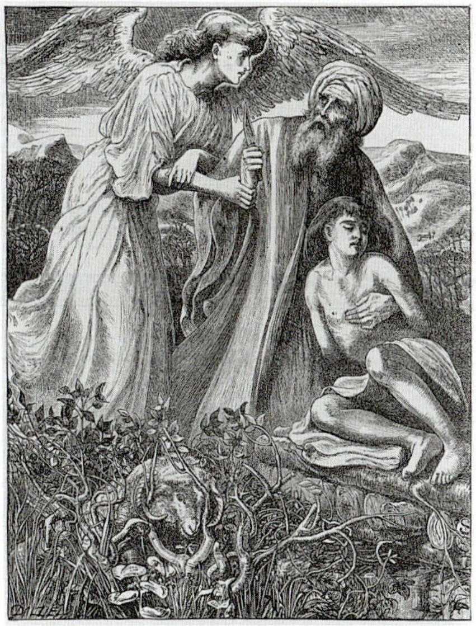

Fig. 23
Dalziel Brothers after Simeon Solomon
Abraham's Sacrifice
c. 1862
Wood engraving
17.7 × 13.6 cm ($6\frac{15}{16} \times 5\frac{3}{8}$ in.)
Published in *Art Pictures from the Old Testament and Our Lord's Parables*, London (Edwin Dalton) 1894
Private collection

insouciance of her son. A characteristic of the work is the vivid treatment of objects, the water-bottle, the staff decorated with peacock feathers, the broken bracelets (signifying slavery or concubinage and their end), all of which are seen in the low light of the rising sun.

Cat. 20 differs significantly from the subject as treated in the illustration for the Dalziel Bible (*c.* 1862, fig. 24) and in a drawing (dated 20 May 1863) in the Victoria and Albert Museum, London, both of which feature the figure of Abraham and in which Hagar's expression is more conventionally sad, sweet and accepting. The version of the story of Hagar commissioned by the Dalziel Brothers for their Bible project appeared in the 1894 edition. It shows some conventionalities adopted from Pre-Raphaelite drawing and illustration and some moderation of the force of the artist's inventiveness.

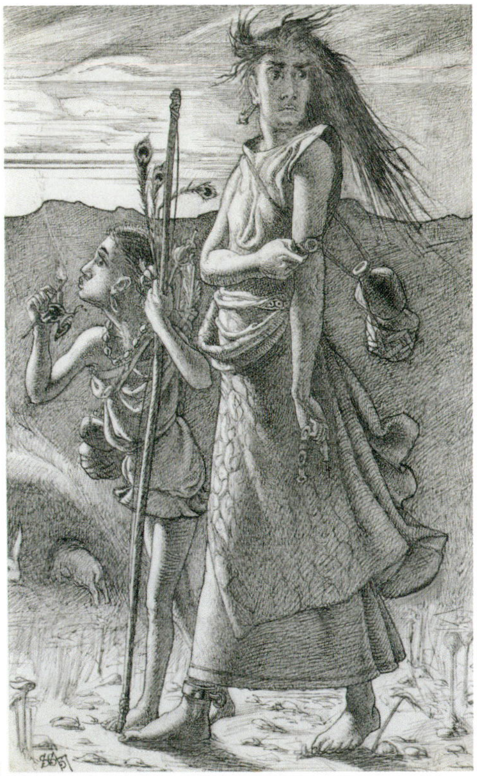

20

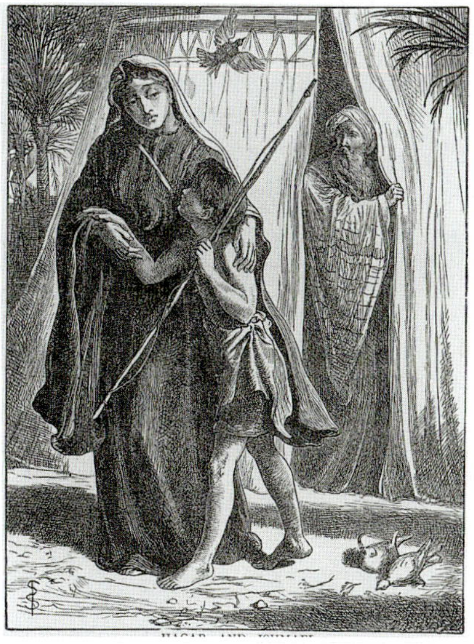

Fig. 24
Dalziel Brothers after Simeon Solomon
Hagar and Ishmael
c. 1862
Wood engraving
16.5 × 12.1 cm ($6\frac{1}{2} \times 4\frac{3}{4}$ in.)
Published in *Art Pictures from the Old Testament and Our Lord's Parables*, London (Edwin Dalton) 1894
Private collection

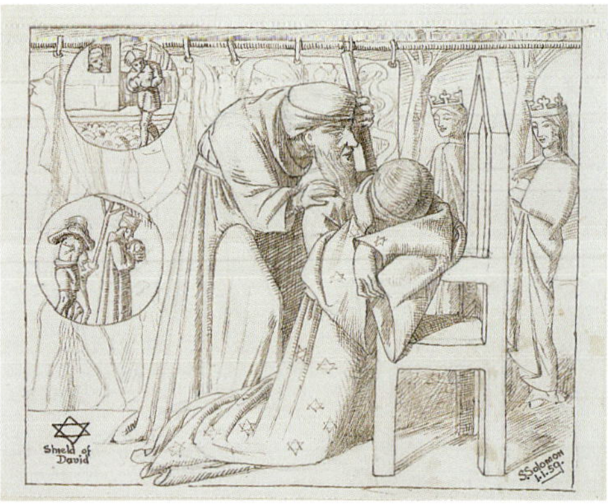

21

21
Nathan Reproving David
1859
Pen and ink over pencil on paper
14.9 × 17.6 cm (5⅞ × 6⅞ in.)
Signed *S. Solomon 1.1.59*
Victoria and Albert Museum

In II Samuel 12, Nathan the prophet tells David of a divine message in the form of the parable of the rich and the poor man and of the ewe lamb. David had seduced Bathsheba and impregnated her, and had arranged the death of her husband, Uriah the Hittite. Here, forced to recognize his wrongdoing by the parable, the king gives way to his feelings of guilt. The prophet continues to reprove him while laying a hand on his shoulder as a sign of conciliation.

A tapestry depicting Adam and Eve expelled from Paradise hangs behind the figures of Nathan and David, pointing to the consequences of temptation and the origin of human failings. The artist has inserted roundels, after the fashion of recent Pre-Raphaelite art, to illustrate the parable without losing focus on the central story. A six-pointed star is inscribed at lower left with the words 'Shield of David'; the device is scattered over the king's robe.

22
Portrait of Kate Solomon
1861
Black chalk on paper
19.4 × 14.2 cm (7⅝ × 5⅞ in.), oval
Signed and dated *28/9/61* lower right
Private collection

Simeon Solomon was the youngest of the eight children of Michael (also known as Meyer) and Catherine Solomon. His father had inherited a hat-importing business but had started a paper-embossing firm in 1840, the year of Simeon's birth. The family was wealthy and well-known within the Jewish community in London.

Cat. 22 shows Kate Solomon (*née* Levy) to be a lively personality; accounts of the family stress their wealth and their sense of fun (see, for example, Lionel Lambourne, 'The Solomon Family', in *Solomon: A Family of Painters*, 1985, pp. 6–7). Kate's ringlets and dress are a little old-fashioned, and she wears a locket with a portrait, perhaps that of her husband.

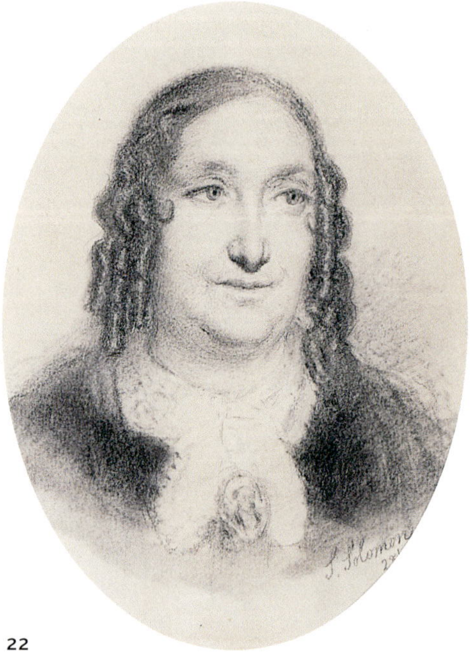

22

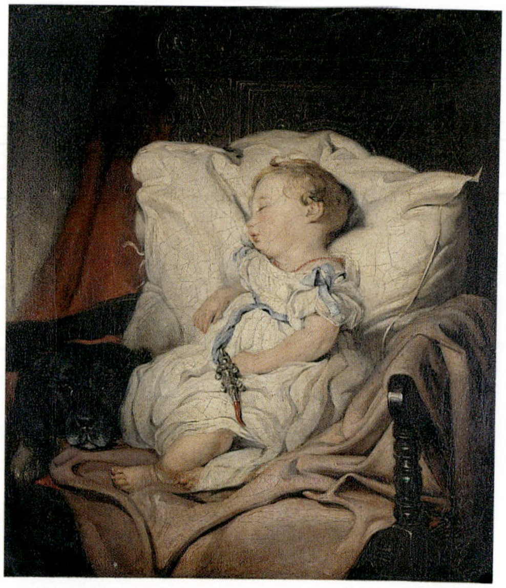

23

23
Abraham Solomon (1823–1862)
Simeon Solomon as a Baby
1841
Oil on canvas
33.5 × 29 cm (13³⁄₁₆ × 11⁷⁄₁₆ in.)
Private collection

This affectionate family portrait depicts Simeon Solomon as a baby asleep, watched over by a pet dog. The object lying in the baby's lap is a soother and rattle although, given its prominence, its similarity to a *yad*, a pointer used to trace the words when reading the Torah, might be a deliberate reference to the centrality of the Jewish religion for the family.

At this time Abraham Solomon was at the beginning of a successful career that was cut short by his death aged thirty-nine. He had been enrolled at the Royal Academy for two years and was to exhibit there for the first time in this year. He specialized in genre and costume pieces. His most famous paintings depicted modern subjects, typically the two-part drama of railway culture, *First Class: the Meeting* (1854) and *Second Class: the Parting* (1855), versions of which are at the National Railway Museum, York.

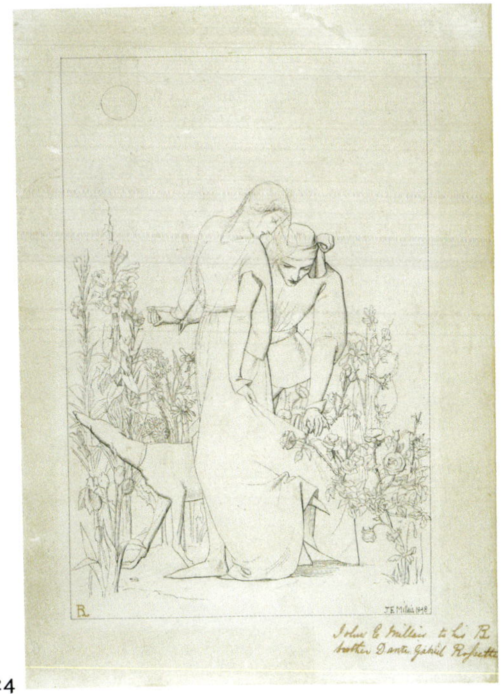

24

24
John Everett Millais (1829–1896)
Lovers by a Rosebush ('My Beautiful Lady')
1848
Pen and ink over traces of pencil on paper
25.4 × 16.5 cm (10 × 6½ in.)
Signed and dated in black ink, lower right; inscribed in brown ink with dedication to D.G. Rossetti
Birmingham Museums & Art Gallery. Purchased 1920

Drawn in the earliest Pre-Raphaelite graphic style, which was based on various models – Nazarene drawings and engraved copies of early Italian paintings, among others – the drawing is notable for its angularity and romantic atmosphere.

The fanciful medievalism of cat. 24 is typical of the revivalism associated with the Pre-Raphaelites that helped to formulate Solomon's early pen-and-ink drawings such as cat. 13.

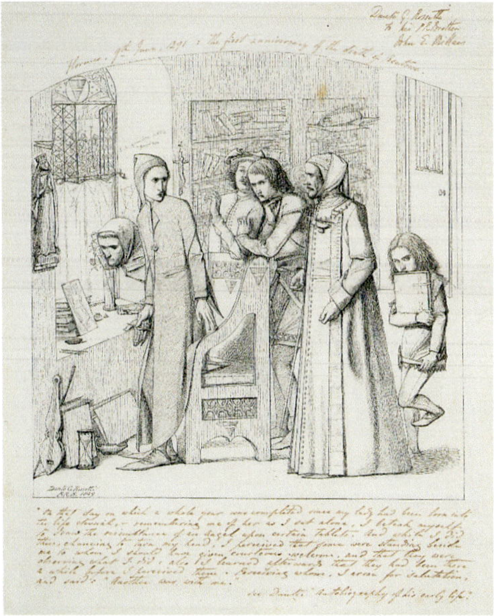

25

25
Dante Gabriel Rossetti (1828–1882)
The First Anniversary of the Death of Beatrice
1849
Pen and ink on paper
39.8 × 32 cm (15¾ × 12⅞ in.)
Signed and dated in black ink, lower left; inscribed in brown ink with dedication to J.E. Millais, upper right
Birmingham Museums & Art Gallery. Presented by subscribers, 1904

Rossetti's first important Dante subject is notable for its proliferation of detail and its high degree of stylization, its figures drawn in a hard-edged, 'spiky' outline style that provided Solomon with a model for his earliest 'medieval' drawings, such as cat. 14, as well as his own extraordinary venture into Dante subjects, cat. 16.

26
James Collinson (1825–1881)
An Incident in the Life of Saint Elizabeth of Hungary
1850
Pen and black and brown ink over traces of pencil on paper
40 × 54.6 cm (15¾ × 21½ in.)
Signed with monogram and dated *1850* lower left
Birmingham Museums & Art Gallery. Purchased (Christina Feeney Bequest Fund) 1929

A detailed study for Collinson's oil painting shown at the Portland Gallery in 1851 (now in Johannesburg Art Gallery), cat. 26 records an obscure, if dramatic, incident in the life of St Elizabeth in which she humbles herself before a crucifix. The incident occurred before her renunciation of worldly goods, her subsequent embracing of the religious life and her work with the poor and sick.

Both the painting and drawing depict the scene as taking place during the Mass. A priest accompanied by two acolytes can be seen approaching the altar in the background. Collinson's work can be seen as an extreme version of the kind of Catholic imagery that led to accusations of Pre-Raphaelitism as 'popish'. The altar, the priest and the procession all became important elements in Solomon's work in the 1860s.

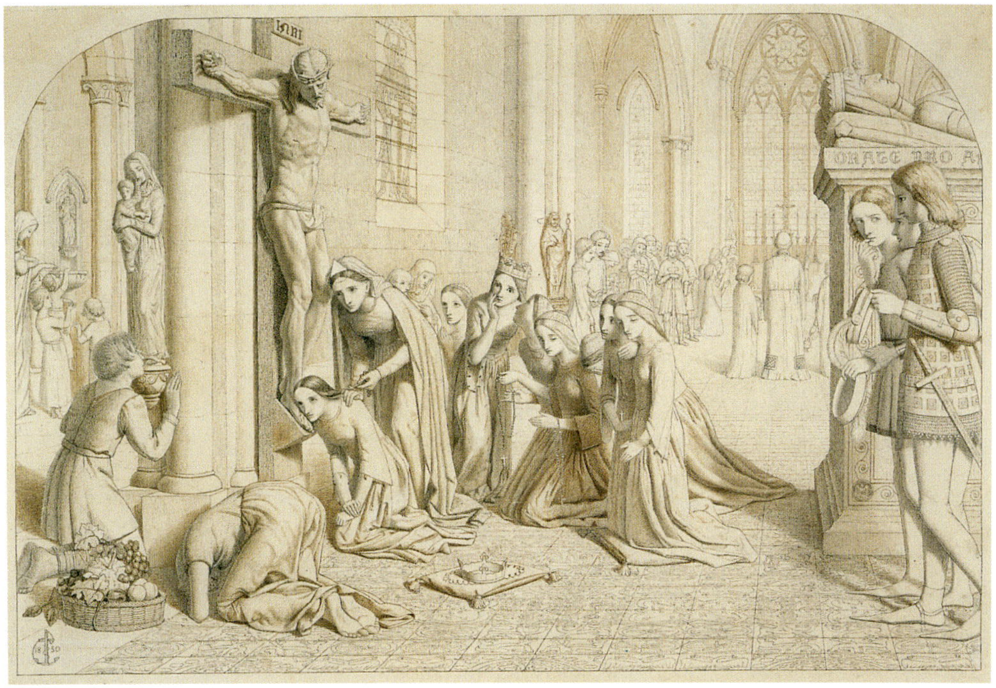

26

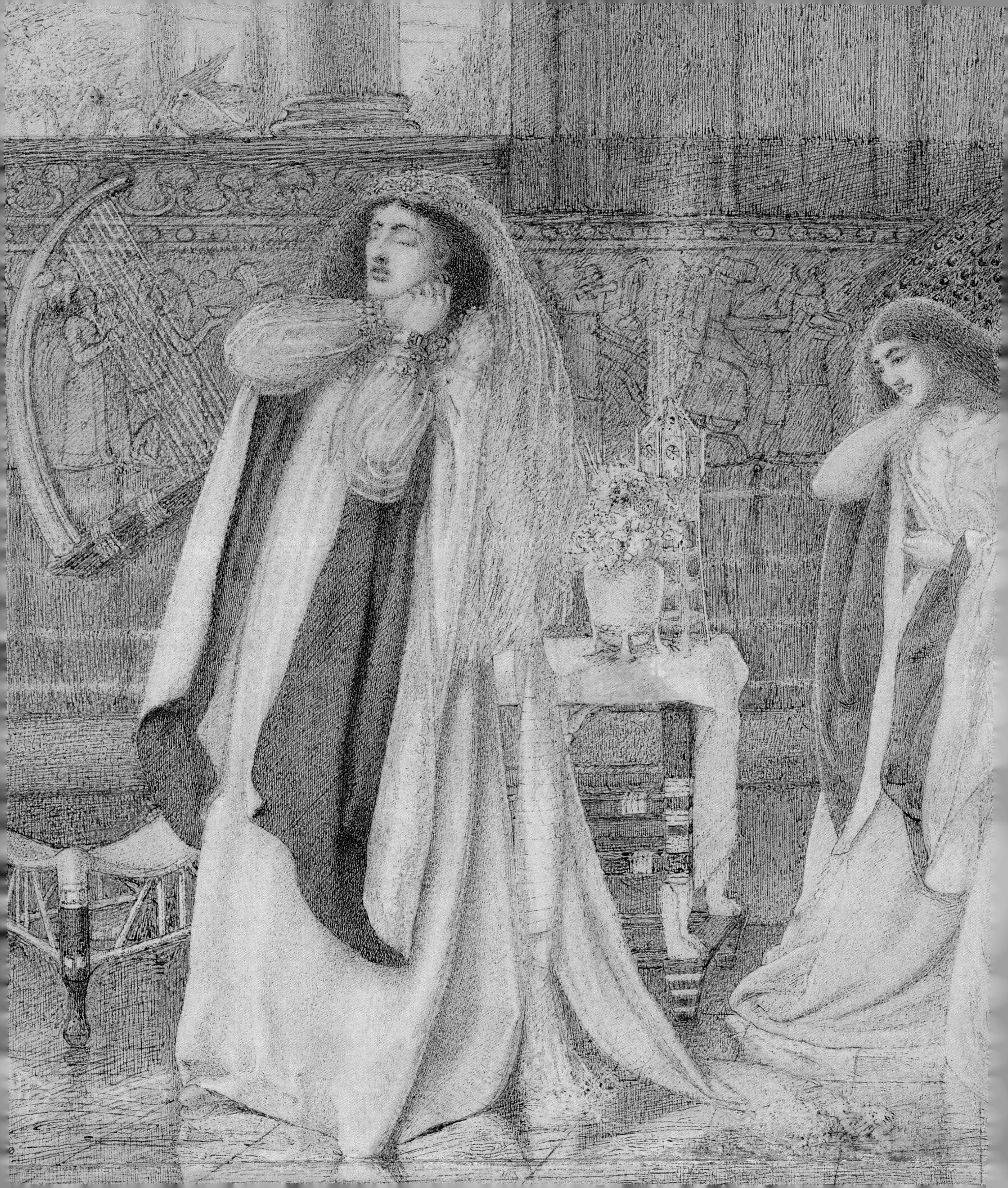

Pre-Raphaelitism and Early Success

"A genius entirely unique"

Sir William Blake Richmond, *The Richmond Papers*, 1926

Solomon's debut in 1858, although greeted with scant praise, was followed by a success at the Royal Academy with *The Mother of Moses* (not available for this exhibition but see cat. 31 and fig. 25).

It is significant, however, that Solomon continued to exhibit at smaller venues, most importantly at the Dudley Gallery, where he served briefly on the selection committee.

Although Solomon had been identified as a "pre-Raffaelite" as early as 1859 (see cat. 16), his earliest successes were of biblical subjects with a particularly Jewish interpretative emphasis, which can be seen in several illustration projects of this period.

However, Solomon's friendships with members of the Pre-Raphaelite circle of artists were formative; he became an intimate friend of Burne-Jones. His friendship with other leading figures, including Swinburne (see cat. 29), was to introduce him to a wider range of literature, including De Sade.

Evidence of Solomon's involvement with the wider aims of the Pre-Raphaelites can be found in his contributions to the Dalziel Bible project, which involved William Holman Hunt, Ford Madox Brown and other artists, in his painted decorations for a cabinet designed by William Burges (1859–62) involving the participation of younger Pre-Raphaelites such as Burne-Jones and Holiday (fig. 34), and his designs for stained-glass windows at Middleton Cheney in Northamptonshire, a project that involved William Morris and Burne-Jones (see cat. 51).

47
Queen Esther Hearing the News of the Intended Massacre of the Jews (detail)
1860
Brown and black ink on paper
28.6 × 33.6 cm (11¼ × 13¼ in.)
Signed with monogram and dated 60 lower left
Private collection

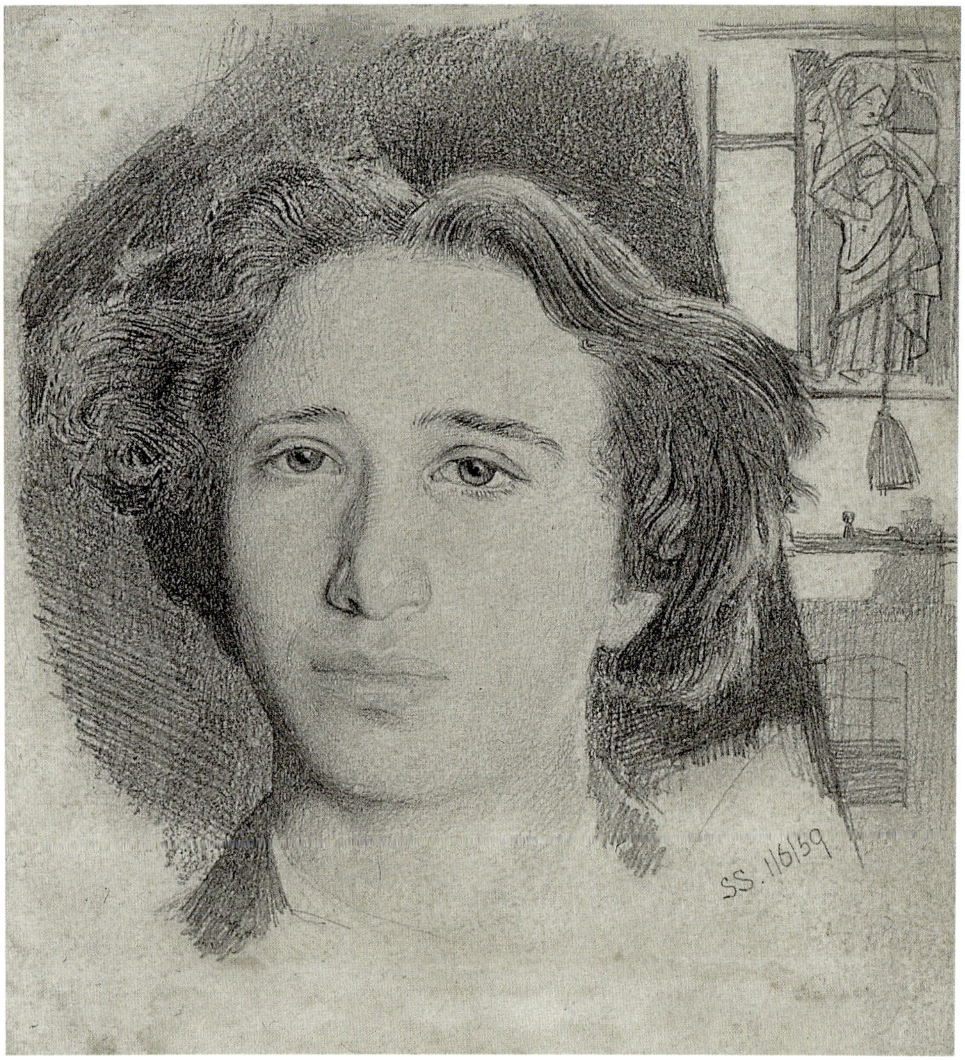

27

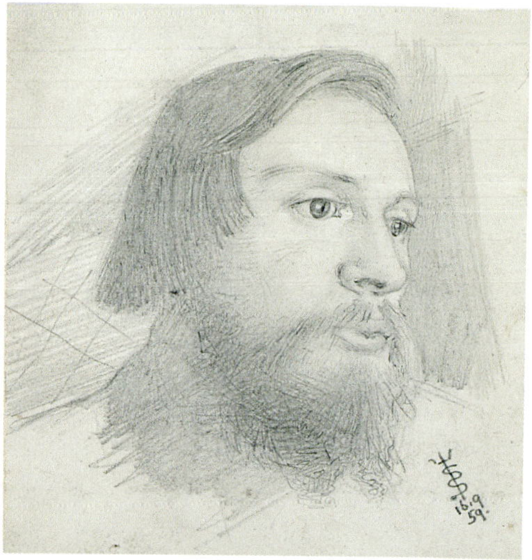

28

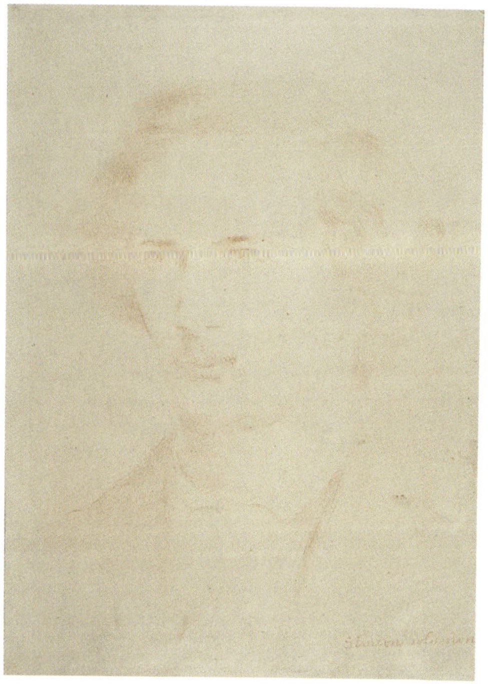

29

27
Self-portrait
1859
Pencil on paper
16.5×14.6 cm ($6\frac{9}{16} \times 5\frac{13}{16}$ in.)
Signed *SS* and dated *1/6/59*
Tate. Presented anonymously, 1919

The artist was eighteen years old when he drew this self-portrait, which is notable for its finesse and sensitivity. Although full-faced, the image is sad rather than confrontational. The treatment of the hair particularly follows the Pre-Raphaelite style of meticulous observation. The stained-glass detail in the background also shows Solomon's concern with Pre-Raphaelitism, both in its interests in ritual and ecclesiology and in the earliest phase of the Arts and Crafts movement. He went on to design for Morris & Company (see cat. 51).

28
Portrait of Edward Burne-Jones
1859
Pencil on paper
11.8×7 cm ($4\frac{5}{8} \times 2\frac{3}{4}$ in.)
Signed with monogram and dated *16.9.59* lower right
The Ashmolean Museum, Oxford

29
Portrait of Algernon Charles Swinburne
c. 1863
Red chalk on tinted paper
20.9×14.5 cm ($8\frac{1}{4} \times 5\frac{11}{16}$ in.)
Lent by the Syndics of the Fitzwilliam Museum, Cambridge

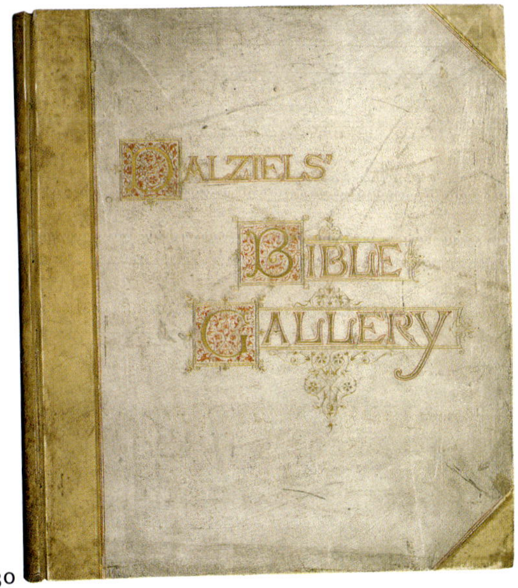

30

30
Dalziels' Bible Gallery
1881
Book, India paper proofs edition; no. 256 of 1000
43 × 36 × 4.3 cm (17 × 14⅛ × 1¾ in.) when closed
Volume of subjects from the Old Testament, engraved on wood by the Dalziel Brothers from designs by various artists and published by George Routledge & Sons, London, 1881
Birmingham Museums & Art Gallery. Presented by Wilfred L. Phillips, 1920

The Dalziel Brothers, the most well-known Victorian commercial company of engravers, approached Solomon in 1862 to contribute to their venture of publishing an illustrated Bible, possibly having seen the artist's painting of *The Mother of Moses* at the Royal Academy (fig. 25) and the illustrations he had contributed to *Good Words* and *Once a Week* that year (see fig. 28 and cat. 83). The publication was much delayed, and the volume *Dalziels' Bible Gallery* was not published by Routledge until 1881. Leighton, Holman Hunt, Brown (see cat. 59) and Watts were among the established artists commissioned for the project, while Poynter and Sandys were among those of Solomon's wide group of friends who also produced designs. Cat. 30 contains six engravings after Solomon: *Melchizedek Blesses Abram* (cat. 84), *Hagar and Ishmael* (fig. 24), *Abraham and Isaac* (fig. 22), *The Infant Moses* (cat. 31a), *Naomi and the Child Obed* (cat. 35) and *Hosannah!* (cat. 37). For examples from a later edition of the project, much expanded (*Art Pictures from the Old Testament and Our Lord's Parables*, 1894), see cat. 41 and 43.

In addition to cat. 30, Birmingham Museums & Art Gallery holds a second example of the volume, an unnumbered press copy presented to the editor of the *Art Journal*.

31a
Dalziel Brothers after Simeon Solomon
The Infant Moses
c. 1862
Wood engraving on India paper, in bound volume
14.2 × 11.4 cm (6 × 4 in.)
Signed in the block, lower left
Birmingham Museums & Art Gallery

31b
Dalziel Brothers after Simeon Solomon
The Infant Moses
c. 1862
14.1 × 11.4 × 2.3 cm (6 × 4 × 15⁄16 in.)
Woodblock
Birmingham Museums & Art Gallery. Presented by Wilfred L. Phillips, 1920

Solomon's second major oil painting (fig. 25), unavailable for this exhibition, was first shown at the Royal Academy in 1860 (as no. 346). Solomon had exhibited another Old Testament subject at the RA in 1859 (see cat. 19). It is significant that he did not treat the subject with academic conventionalities but stressed the emotional moment before Jochabed abandons her child in the bulrushes. *Punch* praised the "novel and admirable treatment of an old subject" (16 June 1860, p. 246). Solomon's treatment is not so novel; it might derive from the narrative approach advanced by Millais in *The Return of the Dove to the Ark* (1851, The Ashmolean Museum, Oxford) where a new kind of biblical subject painting was heralded, one that rejected gesture and facial expression in favour of an atmospheric intensity; the viewer must do some work to read the emotions that are obscured or withheld.

Some of the novelty of the treatment might have been due to the perception of a stylistic innovation in the treatment of the heads of the two female figures, the mother, Jochabed, and the sister, Miriam. *The Guardian* found the work a "clever Egyptianesque version of Moses" (16 May 1860, p. 449), and *The Times* described the women as "Coptic in their crisp hair and the cast of their features" (17 May 1860, p. 11). For studies of the heads, see cat. 32 and 33.

However, such originality was objected to by some critics, notably that of the *Art Journal*: "There is an oppressive influence in this work that sinks the spirits; there is no ray of hope to point to a glorious future for the infant, whom his mother is about to commit to the thin basket held by his sister. The heads are rather Egyptian than Jewish; they appear to have been painted from the same model. Being mother and daughter, a certain degree of likeness is allowable, but they are too distinctly identical. Joshebed [*sic*] is too poorly clad; every credit, however, is due to the artist for the style of the apparel of both figures" (June 1860, p. 169).

For the critic of the *Illustrated London News* such racial and other particularities were the

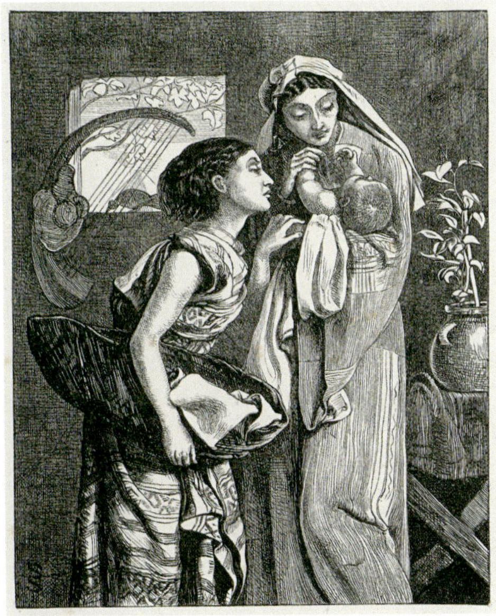

31a

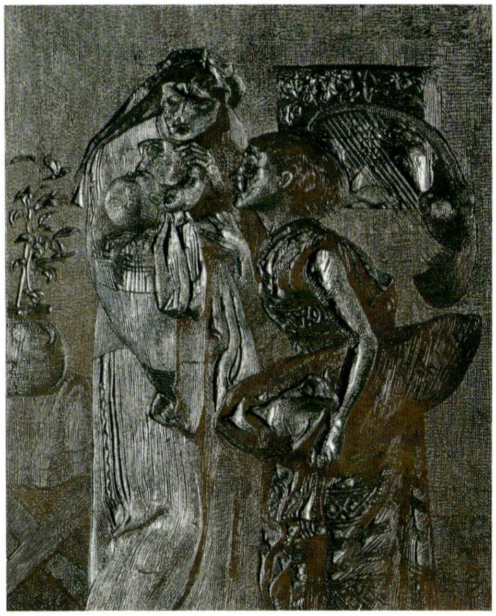

31b

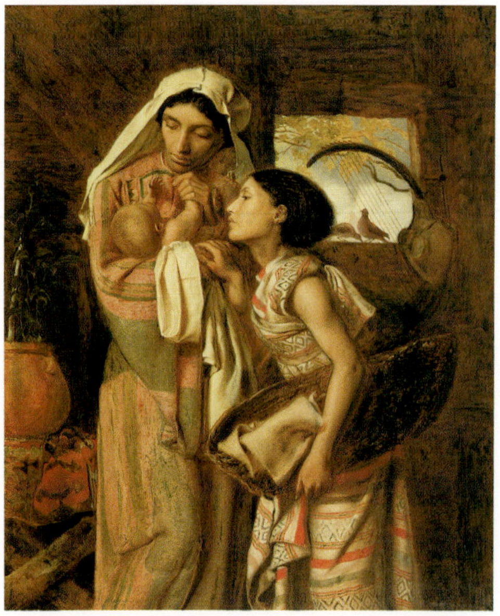

Fig. 25
The Mother of Moses
1860
Oil on canvas
56.6 × 48.2 cm (23 × 19 in.)
Signed with monogram lower right
Delaware Art Museum, Wilmington, USA, Bequest of Robert Louis Isaacson:/Bridgeman Art Library

painting's strengths: "It is gratifying, after forcing one's way through crowds listlessly staring at mediocrities, to light occasionally upon a work which one may pronounce of undoubted and eminent merit – one displaying promise as well as achievement, thought as well as executive skill; and of such character unquestionably is the little picture of 'Moses'. ... The scene is supposed to pass in the humble dwelling of the persecuted Israelite, and through the small unglazed window is seen one of the pyramids, the supposed product of the labour of God's people, now enslaved and suffering. The spectator on first stopping before the picture may be startled, as we were, at the boldness of the artist in representing the family of Moses as of the peculiar type of feature and complexion which the Jewish nation may be supposed to have displayed at that early period – prominent nose; large, oval shaped, dark eyes; strongly-marked mouth; black hair with a natural wave in it, &c: but after a little reflection he will become reconciled to a peculiarity which was almost rendered necessary by the occasion, and which fixes the identity of the subject in a way which would not have been possible with any other materials. And when we come to look further into those sad, expressive faces of the mother and the younger sister beside her, as they hang over the little innocent whom they are about to intrust to the mercy of Providence upon the waters, – when we dwell upon the pent-up agony depicted in that last fond look – we are compelled to admit that under no other selection of features, real or conventional, could so much have been done. Even the little brown-headed child but partially seen in a back view appeals to our sympathy as he lifts his tiny hands imploringly to his mother. Beside stands the younger sister already mentioned, with a rude wicker basket and a coarse blanket in her hand, in which in another instant the helpless child will be deposited. A more touching, a more impressive domestic group it would almost be impossible to imagine; and how is its interest heightened and increased when we contemplate it in association with the grand historical event of which it was an incident. It remains to be added that the technical performance is of the highest order; and the rounding and relief of the figures, the flesh-modelling, the colour, the textural surfaces in every part, all excellent" (*Illustrated London News*, 23 June 1860, p. 595).

32
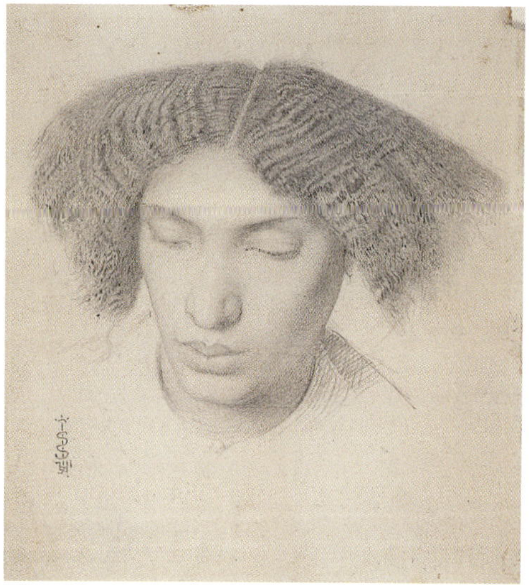

33
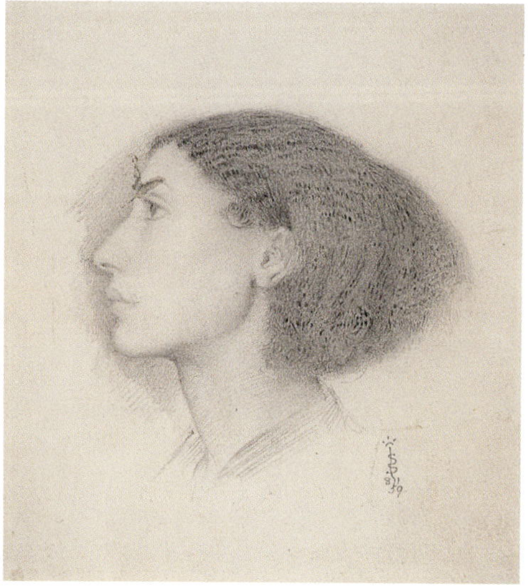

32
Head of Jochabed
1859
Pencil on paper
14.9 × 13.3 cm (5⅞ × 5¼ in.)
Signed and dated *7/11/59* lower left
Lent by the Syndics of the Fitzwilliam Museum, Cambridge

A study for the oil painting *The Mother of Moses* (1860, see fig. 25). See also cat. 58.

33
Head of Miriam
1859
Pencil on paper
14.9 × 13.3 cm (5⅞ × 5¼ in.)
Signed and dated *8/11/59* lower right
Lent by the Syndics of the Fitzwilliam Museum, Cambridge

A study for the head of Moses's sister, Miriam, for *The Mother of Moses* (1860, see fig. 25).

34
Ruth, Naomi and the Child Obed
1860
Pen and brown ink over pencil on paper
29.2 × 22.9 cm (11½ × 9 in.)
Signed with monogram and dated *19/9/60* lower right
Birmingham Museums & Art Gallery. Presented by the Trustees of the Public Picture Gallery Fund, 1911

Cat. 34 is the first of several versions of this subject, later engraved for the Dalziel Bible (see cat. 35). It depicts Ruth with her mother-in-law, Naomi, who holds her baby, Obed, the subject of their rapt and loving attention. It acts as a kind of companion piece to *The Mother of Moses* (fig. 25). Certainly both pictures represent two female characters with a child whose historical significance will overshadow theirs; in this case

Obed, as the final verses of the Book of Ruth tell us, is the father of Jesse and the grandfather of David. Thus, Solomon's picture might remind us of the importance of the female line for Judaism as well as the persistence of the male forebears.

Cat. 34 is particularly striking in its suggestion of bright sunlight and heat offset by the dark interior space that is glimpsed behind Ruth's right shoulder. Ruth's abstracted expression and her proximity to Naomi recall Rossetti's *The Girlhood of Mary Virgin* (1849, Tate) and its many Renaissance prototypes. The resemblance may be a deliberate reminder of the continuance of the House of David in Jesus.

An oil version of the subject exists (private collection).

35
Dalziel Brothers after Simeon Solomon
Naomi and the Child Obed
c. 1863
Wood engraving on India paper, in bound volume
15.9 × 12.6 cm (6¼ × 5 in.)
Birmingham Museums & Art Gallery. Presented by Wilfred I. Phillips, 1920

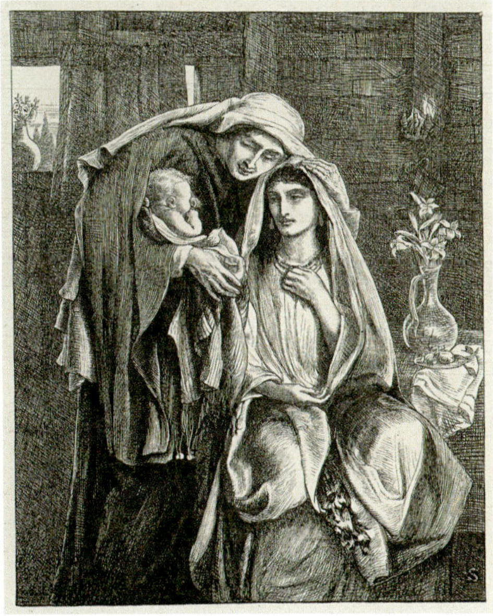

35

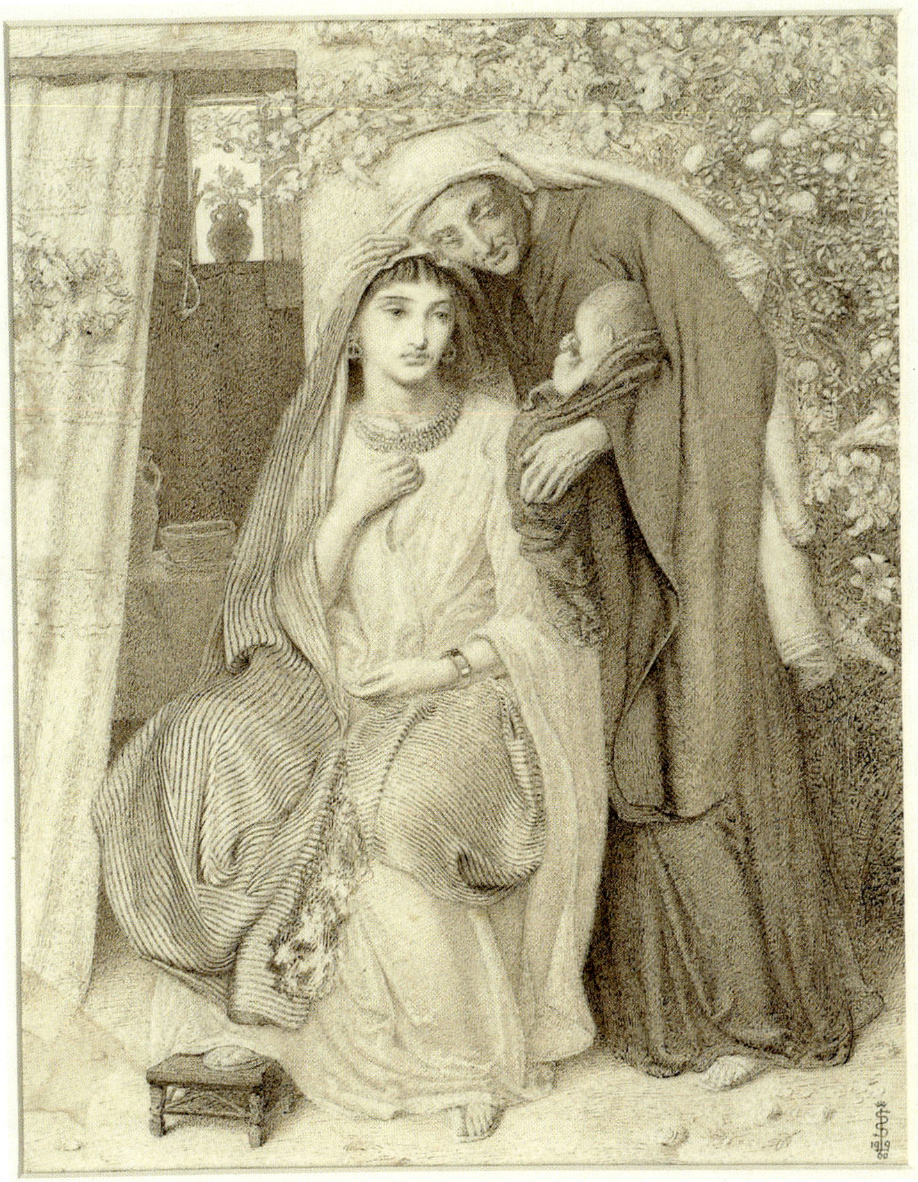

34

36
A Young Musician Employed in the Temple Service During the Feast of Tabernacles
1861
Oil on canvas
59.7 × 45.7 cm (23½ × 18 in.)
Signed with monogram and dated *3/61* lower left
Private collection

Now known as *Hosannah!*, cat. 36 was first shown at the Royal Academy in 1861 (as no. 493). It is a historical reconstruction of a kind to be made popular slightly later, towards the end of the decade, by the artist's contemporaries but with significant differences; here the figure is male and Jewish, while Alma-Tadema, for example, chose mainly Classical subjects with central female figures (see fig. 35). As a non-specific, non-biblical yet Jewish subject, cat. 36 has little precedent in English academic painting.

The *Times* critic commented: "We commend Mr. Solomon for his hearty nationality. He paints Jewish subjects, as a Jew should, with evident reverence and delight in recalling the mystery and greatness of the chosen people. This is a very impressive and noble figure, not marred by the ugliness in which Mr. Solomon has sometimes appeared to revel" (12 May 1861, p. 6).

F.G. Stephens's review in the *Athenaeum* was couched in similar terms but noted the musical suggestiveness of the painting: "A youth of the highest Jewish type, is seen bearing the immemorial ten-stringed harp, such as we find sculptured on the Ninevite bas-reliefs. From its construction not allowing strength against a high

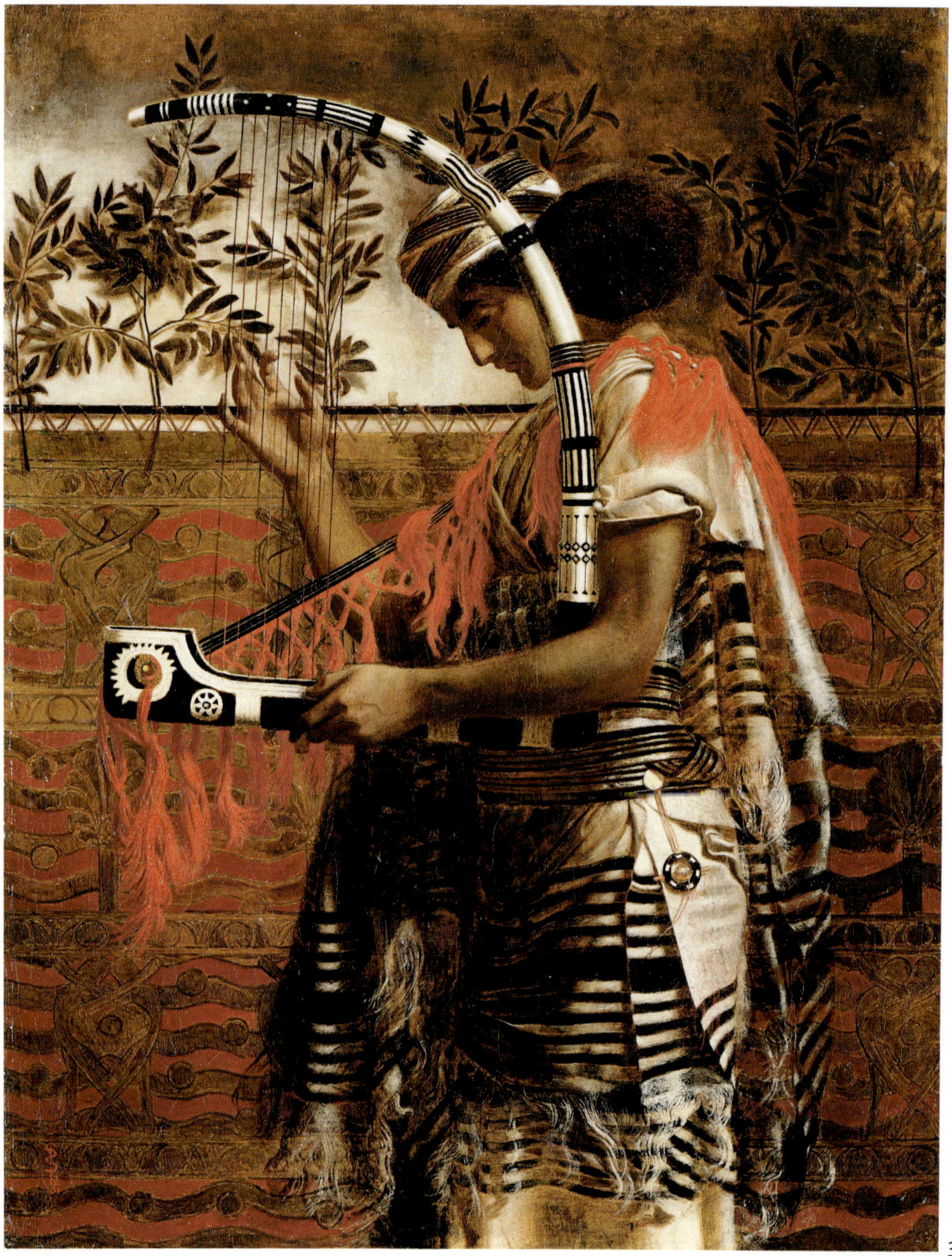

36

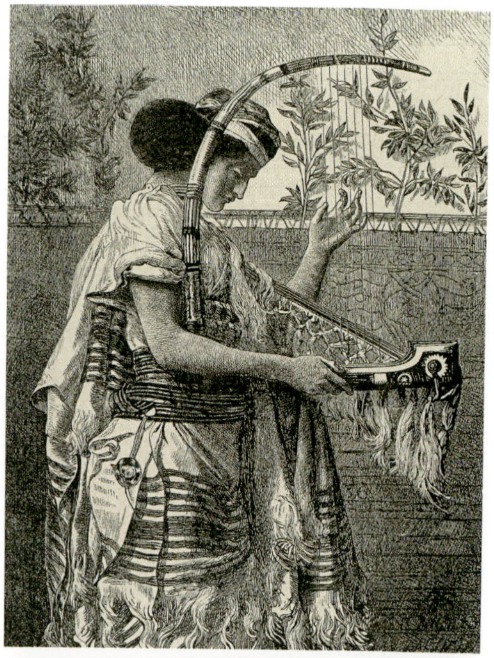

37a

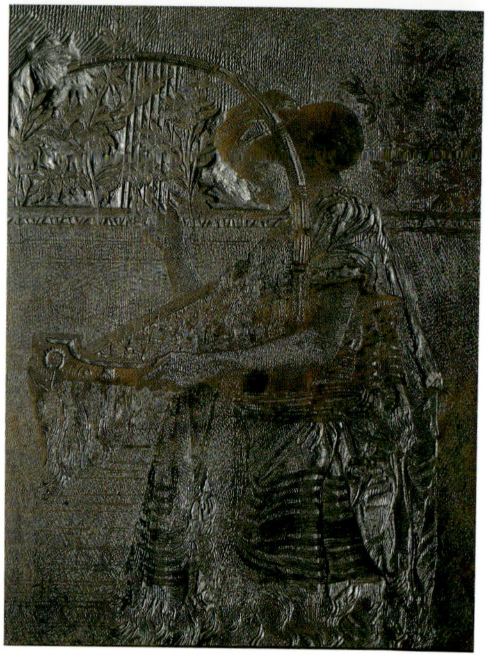

37b

tension of the chords, this must have been a low-noted instrument. We may imagine the sweet pulsings of the music as the player's slender fingers draw the strings" (25 May 1861, p. 698).

The image of a musician playing a stringed instrument forms a part of the composition (at the extreme right) of F.R. Pickersgill's *Delilah Asking Forgiveness of Samson* shown at the RA in 1859 (engraved in the *Illustrated London News*, 23 July 1859). The musician motif was to become part of Solomon's repertoire for the next decade, featuring in several works, including cat. 69.

Solomon was one of the first artists to make a pictorial point about the relationship between music and painting that was to become such an important part of Aesthetic Movement practice in works by Whistler, Rossetti and Burne-Jones and in the critical writings of Walter Pater, particularly in the *Fortnightly Review* article 'The School of Giorgione' (1877), which was to appear in the 1888 edition of his *The Renaissance*.

37a
Dalziel Brothers after Simeon Solomon
Hosannah!
c. 1862
Wood engraving
16.6 × 12.2 cm (6⅜ × 4¾ in.)
Collection Laurin Federlein

A version of Solomon's painting of the young musician in the Temple (cat. 36) was used as the basis for a design in the Dalziels' illustrated Bible, although it does not refer to a specific subject.

The illustration is appended with the inscription (on the contents page of the 1894 edition) "Chron. 25:1–7, Chron. 8:14", although the Dalziel touched proof (The British Museum, not in exhibition) is inscribed "Psalm 149", which indicates that the psalm 'Praise for God's goodness to Israel' was the intended text.

37b
Dalziel Brothers after Simeon Solomon
Hosannah!
c. 1862
Woodblock for *Dalziels' Bible Gallery*, London (Routledge) 1881
16.4 × 12 × 2.3 cm (6½ × 4¾ × 15⁄16 in.)
Birmingham Museums & Art Gallery

38
The Child Jeremiah
1862
Oil on canvas
35 × 24 cm (13¾ × 9⁷⁄16 in.)
Signed and dated *12/61* lower right
Private collection

First shown at the Royal Academy in 1862 (as no. 487), cat. 38 was not reviewed widely, perhaps because of its small scale. The artist's brother, Abraham, showed *The Lost Found*, a dramatic domestic genre scene, at the same exhibition, giving the *Times* critic the chance to reflect on the racial origins of the brothers: "Another of the Solomon family is Mr. Simeon Solomon, the painter of 'the Child Jeremiah' – a dreamy young Israelite, with his harp, in one of the Temple passages, under an effect of reflected light, and profoundly imbued with that nationality the seal of which is set strongly on everything this young painter does. Mr. A. Solomon is Jewish as Wilkie was Scotch, and though the nationalism in the one case appeals to a narrower public than in the other, it gives Mr. Simeon Solomon's work a value of its own, which is enhanced by his power of intense imaginative conception. He has only to eschew grotesqueness and superfluous ugliness to paint pictures which will give him a high place of his own among our painters. The Jews have the credit of cherishing their nationality. Let the rich and exalted of the nation see to the future of this young painter, who seems to work under the inspiration of the Prophets and Psalmists of the Holy Land" (26 May 1862, p. 10).

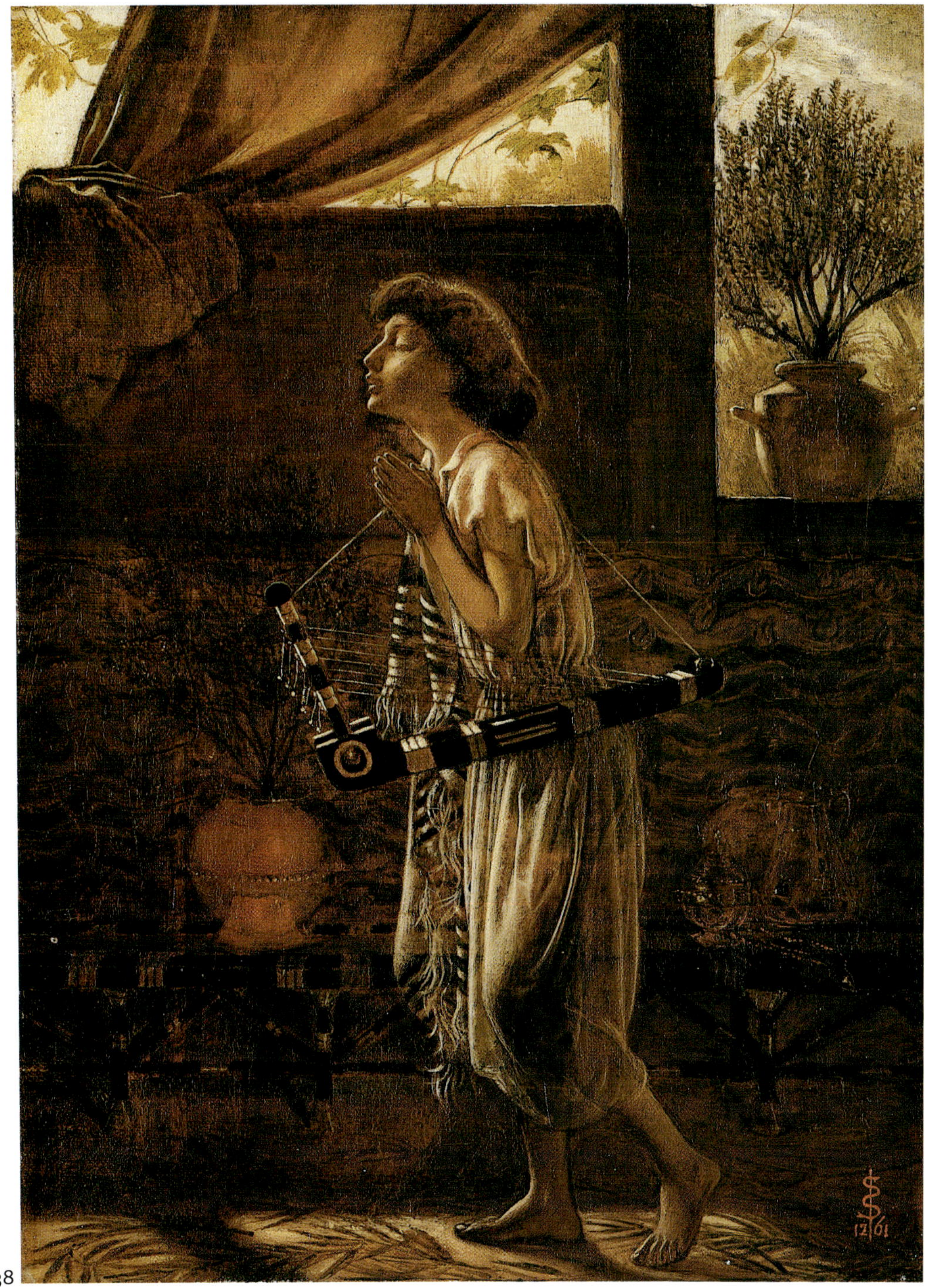

38

Although cat. 38 concerns a historical figure, the prophet Jeremiah, it does not record a significant event in his life. It illustrates the kind of communion with God recorded at the start of the Book of Jeremiah 1:4–9, in which the prophet recalls God speaking to him as a boy. The child objects: "Ah, Lord GOD! Behold, I do not know how to speak, for I am only a youth." God rebukes him, telling him that he has put His words into the boy's mouth. With *Hosannah!* (cat. 36 and 37) the work conveys its deep religious feeling in the use of closed eyes, a motif that was to find its fullest expression in *Carrying the Scrolls of the Law* (cat. 94).

For a discussion of the work's Jewish context, see Gayle Seymour's essay, pp. 14–15.

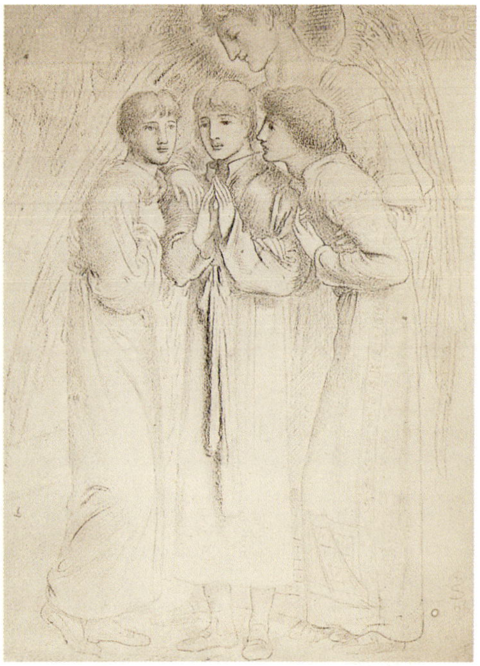

39

39
Frederick Hollyer after Simeon Solomon
Shadrach, Meshach and Abednego
Undated
Photographic print
22.1 × 16 cm (8⁷⁄₁₆ × 6³⁄₁₆ in.)
Private collection

Cat. 39 is probably Solomon's first exploration of this important subject. The original drawing is now lost, and this platinotype, perhaps unique, provides a record of the original composition. Several other versions were undertaken in various media; see cat. 40 and 41.

40
Shadrach, Meshach and Abednego
1863
Watercolour on paper
33 × 23 cm (13 × 9¹⁄₁₆ in.)
Signed with monogram and dated *10/63* lower left
The Hearn Family Trust

First shown in the Winter Exhibition of 1863, where W.M. Rossetti found it "especially remarkable" (*Fine Art Quarterly Review*, I, May 1863, p. 195), cat. 40 was reshown at the Sixth General Exhibition of Water-Colour Drawings held at the Dudley Gallery in January 1870 (as no. 45).

The subject is one of the artist's most ardently Jewish subjects, representing the protection granted by God to the Jewish heroes Shadrach, Meshach and Abednego from the fiery furnace as recorded in Daniel 3. In this episode the Jewish faith is vindicated and visibly triumphant. The three heroes have refused to worship the golden statue put up by King Nebuchadnezzar and refuse to defend themselves, offering instead to be thrown into a furnace of blazing fire: "Then Nebuchadnezzar was so filled with rage ... that his face was distorted. He ordered the furnace to be heated up seven times more than was customary, and ordered some of the strongest guards to bind Shadrach, Meshach and Abednego" (Dan. 3:19).

When he checked the furnace the king saw four unbound rather than three bound figures, the fourth being an angel (with "the appearance of a god") who had rescued them. Astonished, Nebuchadnezzar proclaims: "I make a decree: any people, nation, or language that utters a blasphemy against the God of Shadrach, Meshach, and Abednego shall be torn limb from limb, and their houses laid in ruins; for there is no other god who is able to deliver in this way" (Dan. 3:29).

Although depicting a specific biblical story, cat. 40 is a suggestive picture for much of Solomon's subsequent development as an artist. The image of a protective figure can be found in *The Sleepers and the One who Watcheth* (cat. 106 and 107) and the numerous angelic images of Love as a winged adolescent male, for example, cat. 100.

A supposition, often repeated, that the picture represents Swinburne, Rebecca Solomon and the artist himself cannot be verified.

The critical reception of cat. 40 on its re-exhibition in 1870, when Solomon was a notable figure on the London art scene, was mixed, although most critics recognized the technical achievement of the work. The critic of the *Athenaeum* wrote: "We cannot praise more highly certain technical qualities of his pictures which are here, but if the student looks at *The Three Holy Children in the Fiery Furnace* he will wonder why they resemble fools" (12 February 1870, p. 234).

The Spectator was even more dismissive: "A certain strange beauty of colour in the same artist's *Three Holy Children in the Fiery Furnace* does not compensate for its total want of expression. The lugubrious aspect and protruded chins of these figures are at least not indicative of any appropriate ideas. Think how William Blake would have treated the subject. Mr. Solomon only reminds us of the old school-trick of a big boy knocking together the heads of three little ones. The subject is apparently 'beyond the reaches of his soul'" (19 February 1870, p. 237).

Only the *Illustrated London News* was generally approving: "Mr. Solomon has also wrought out some original colour effects from combinations of gold and black and grey, which give his work distinctive value, and this year (more than on any previous occasion) entitle him to rank high as a colourist. His 'Three Holy Children in the Fiery Furnace' is really a rare triumph of colouring as well as a finely imaginative design. The great angel-wings which screen the three figures; the flame-coloured tongues which enframe them, and the floor of molten gold on which they stand, are thoroughly artistic in execution" (12 February 1870, pp. 181–82).

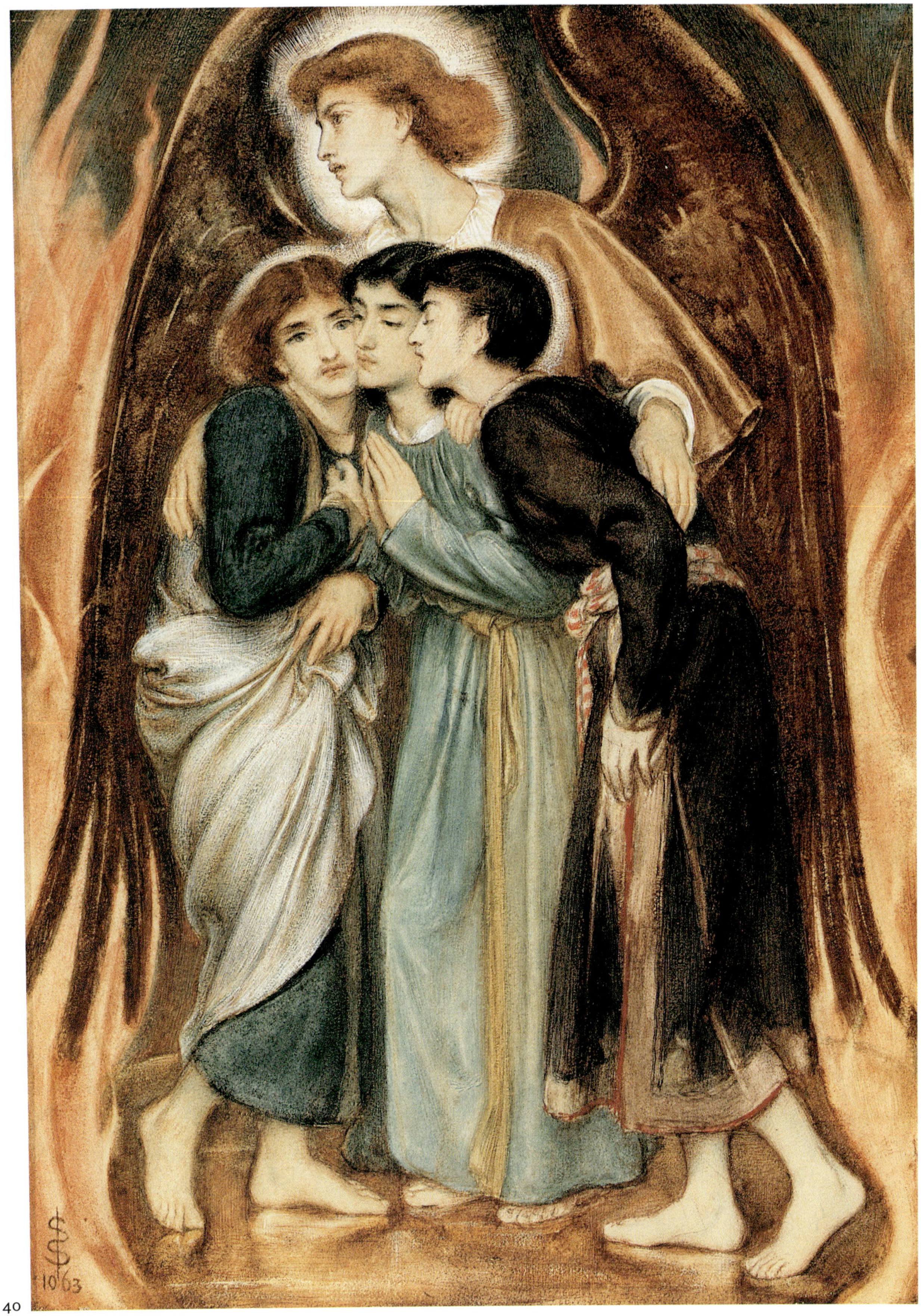

40

41
Dalziel Brothers after Simeon Solomon
Shadrach, Meshach and Abednego
c. 1863
Woodblock
16.4 × 12 × 2.2 cm (6¼ × 4¾ × ⅞ in.)
Birmingham Museums & Art Gallery

Although one of the first of Solomon's drawings to be commissioned for *Dalziels' Bible Gallery*, the design for *Shadrach, Meshach and Abednego* was unused in the publication when it was finally issued in 1881 but appeared in the expanded and cheaper 1894 version (see fig. 26).

The composition of cat. 41 differs from the watercolour version of the same subject (cat. 40), presenting the central angelic figure as bolder and the joined hands as a more fearless and defiant gesture. The central pose is hieratic, and the artist combines the appearance of the angel with that of Christ as depicted in Orthodox Christian icons. This is perhaps the earliest suggestion of the artist's interest in Greek Orthodoxy, which was to form the subject of several paintings later in the 1860s (for example, cat. 89 and 90).

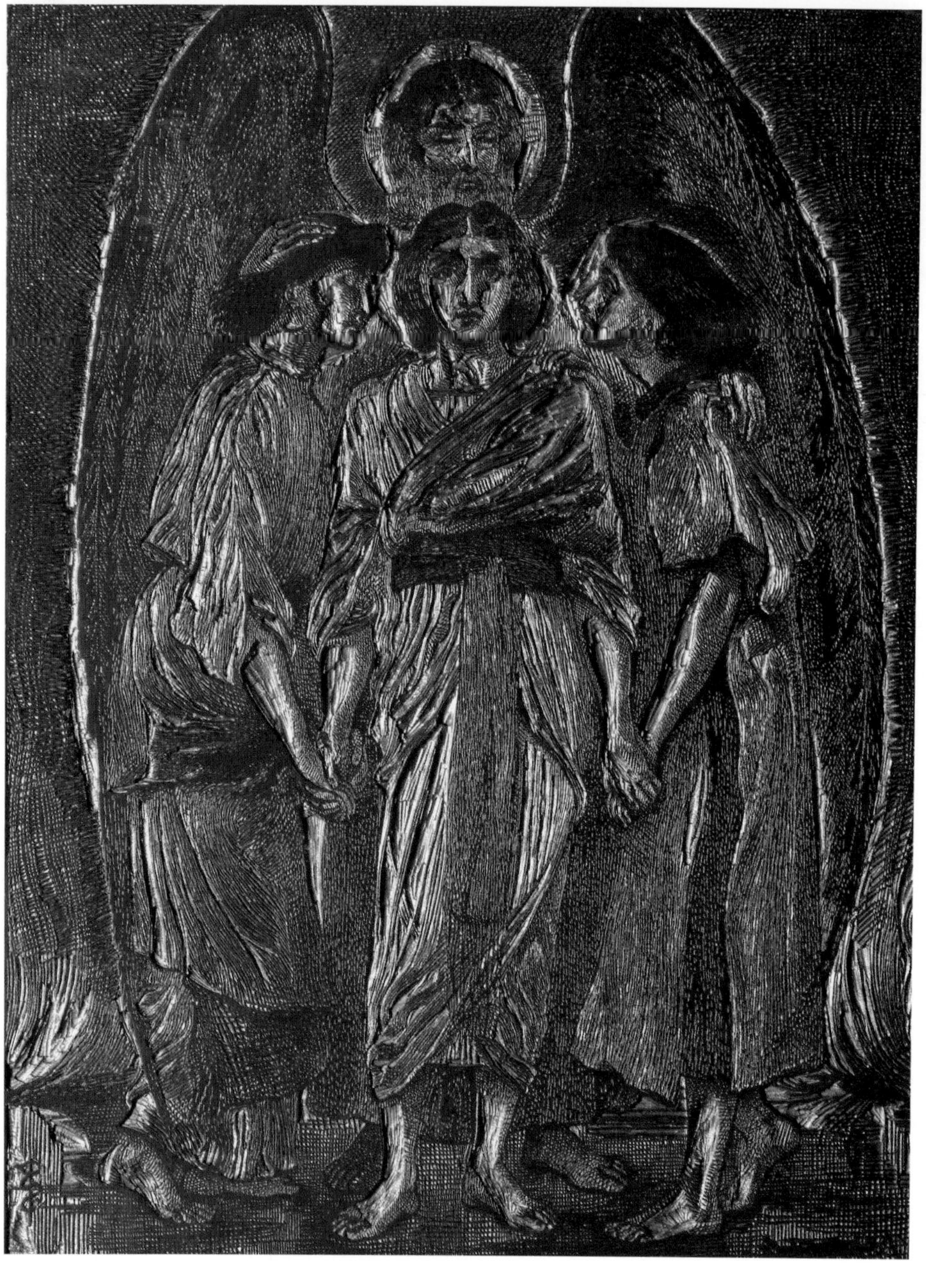

41

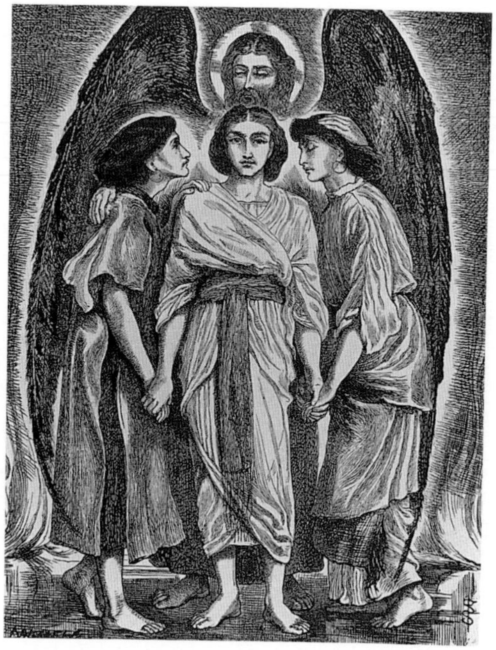

Fig. 26
Dalziel Brothers after Simeon Solomon
Shadrach, Meshach and Abednego
c. 1863
Wood engraving
16.5 × 12 cm (6½ × 4¾ in.)
Published in *Art Pictures from the Old Testament and Our Lord's Parables*, London (Edwin Dalton) 1894

42
Offering the First-Fruits of the Harvest
1864
Watercolour and bodycolour with scratching-out on paper
38.8 × 28.5 cm (15¼ × 11¼ in.)
Signed with monogram and dated *64* lower left
Private collection

This work follows the design made for *Dalziels' Bible Gallery* and published in the 1894 edition (see cat. 43).

The subject represents the sacrifice of fruits in accordance with instructions found in the Books of Exodus (22:29) and Leviticus (2:14) and other biblical texts. There is a certain ambiguity in these texts between a literal meaning of fruit as the produce of the earth and a more metaphoric meaning, that the 'first-fruits' are, in fact, the choice offspring and that they should be 'given' (rather than sacrificed) to the Lord. This second reading might account for the prominence of the attendant youths.

In recent years the work has been known as *The Bringers of Gifts*.

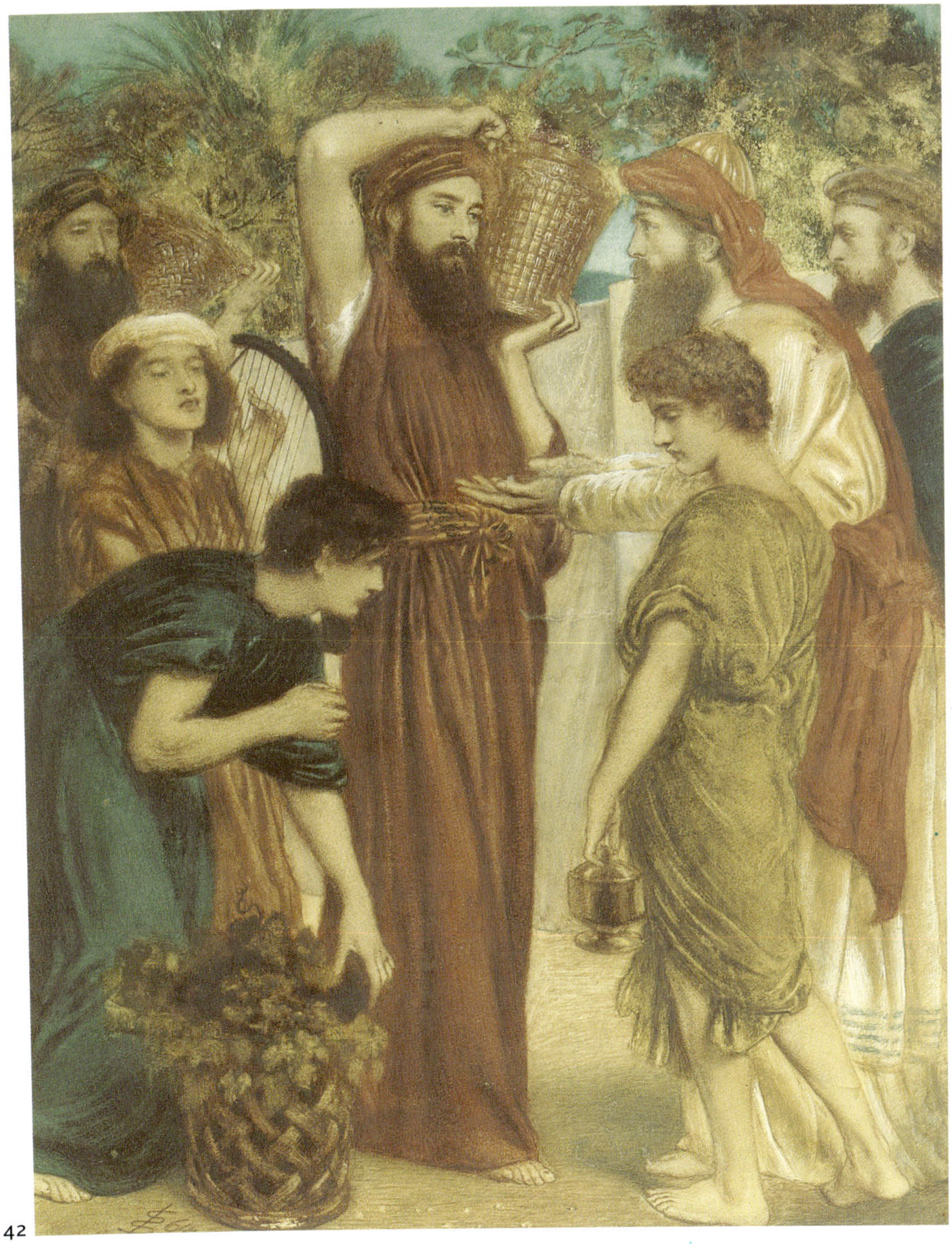

42

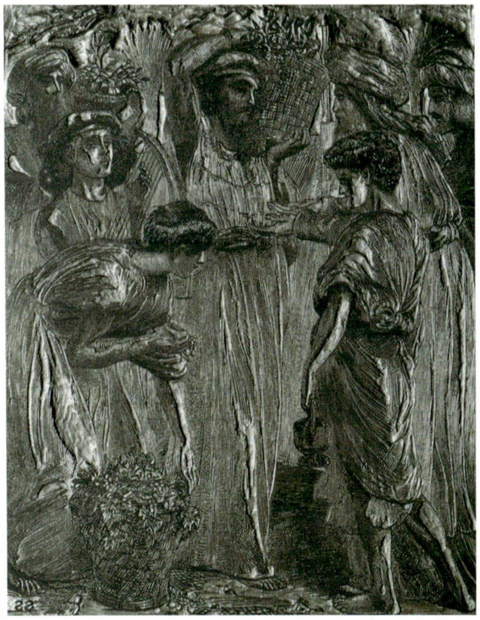

43

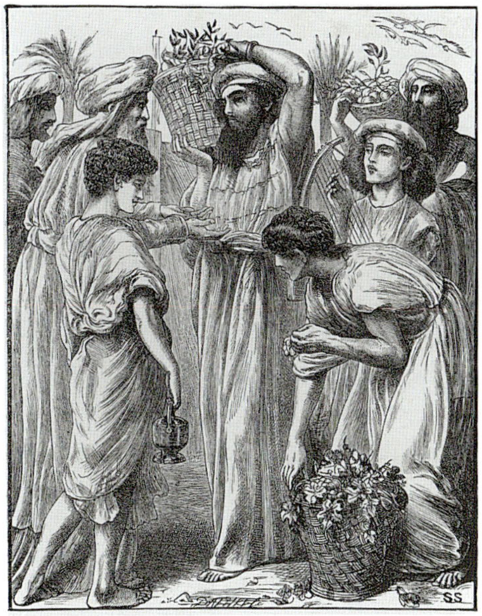

43
Dalziel Brothers after Simeon Solomon
Offering the First-Fruits of the Harvest
c. 1862–63
Woodblock
17.7 × 13.5 × 2.3 cm (7 × 5¼ × 1 in.)
Birmingham Museums & Art Gallery

Cat. 43 was one of the 'new' subjects that appeared in the 1894 version of the Dalziel Bible (see fig. 27); the others were *Abraham and the Three Angels*; *Abraham's Sacrifice* (fig. 23); *'And David took an harp'* (cat. 18); *The Burnt Offering*; *The Feast of Tabernacles*; *The First Offering of Aaron* (cat. 46c); *Hagar and Ishmael* (fig. 24); *'He shall order the lamps'*; *Hosannah!* (cat. 37); *Jewish Women Burning Incense* (cat. 46b); *Jeremiah*; *Naomi and the Child Obed* (cat. 35); *Offering Incense*; *The Passover*; *Righteousness and Peace Have Kissed Each Other* (cat. 46a); *Ruth and Naomi*; *Shadrach, Meshach and Abednego* (cat. 41).

Fig. 27
Dalziel Brothers after Simeon Solomon
Offering the First-Fruits of the Harvest
c. 1862–63
Wood engraving
17.8 × 13.6 cm (7 × 5⅜ in.)
Published in *Art Pictures from the Old Testament and Our Lord's Parables*, London (Edwin Dalton) 1894

44 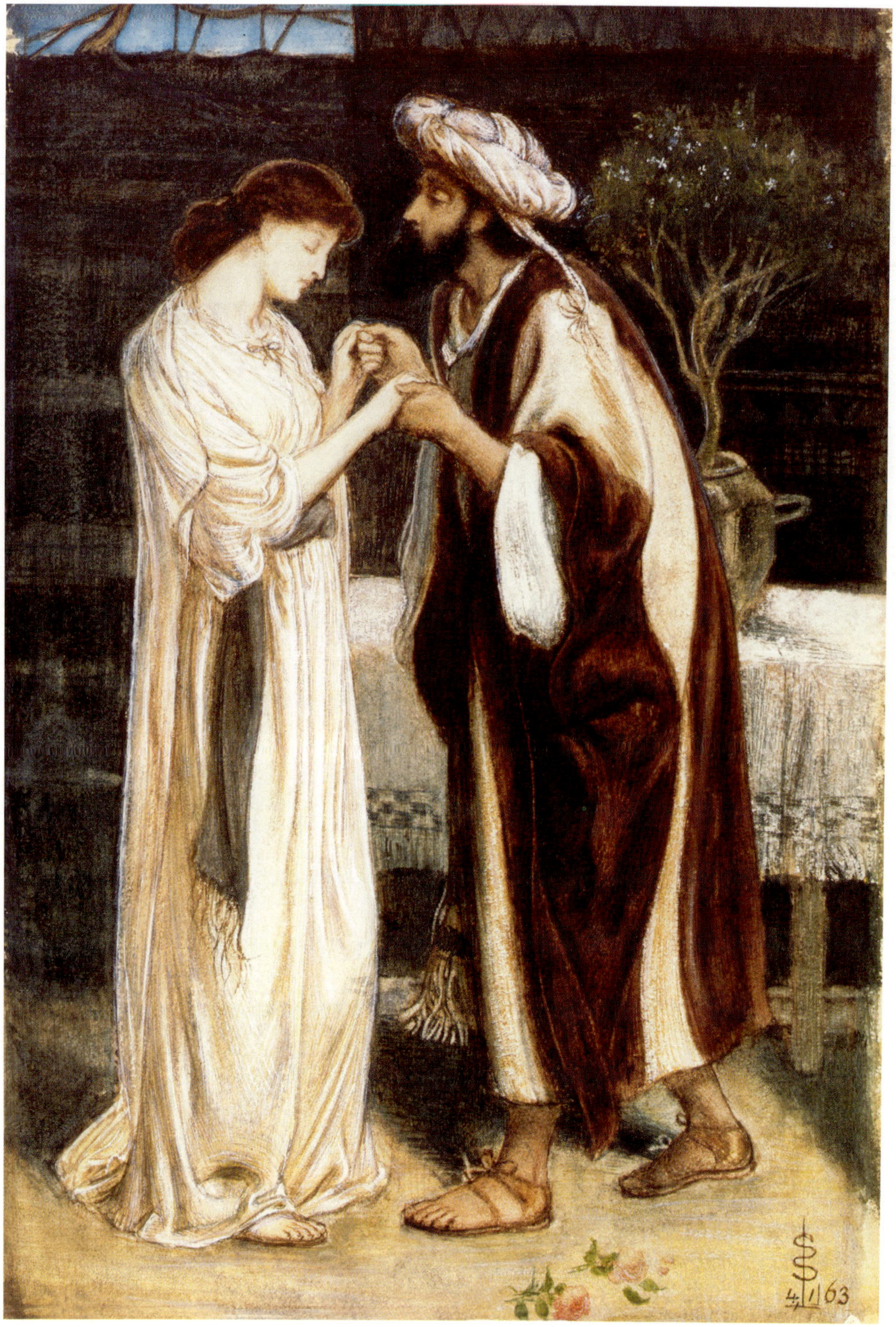

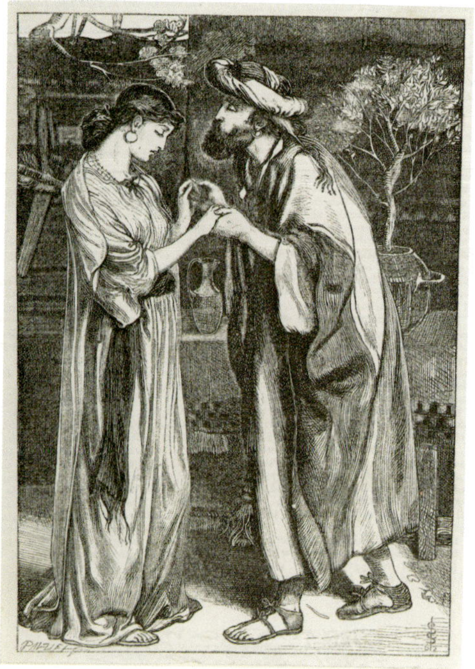

Fig. 28
Dalziel Brothers after Simeon Solomon
The Veiled Bride
1862
Wood engraving
14.9 × 10.3 cm ($5\frac{7}{8} \times 4\frac{1}{16}$ in.)
Illustration to the poem 'The Veiled Bride' by William Robertson, published in *Good Words*, III, 1862, p. 592
Birmingham Museums & Art Gallery

44
Isaac and Rebekah
1863
Watercolour on paper
29.1 × 20.3 cm ($11\frac{7}{16} \times 8$ in.)
Signed with monogram and dated *4/1/63* lower right
Victoria and Albert Museum

Another of the designs that found its way into the Dalziel Bible project, this subject was first represented by Solomon in an illustration for *Good Words*, III, 1862, p. 592, as *The Veiled Bride* (also engraved by the Dalziel Brothers; see fig. 28). An oil version (also from 1863) is in the Tel Aviv Museum of Art, Israel.

The subject is based on Genesis 24:62–67, when Rebekah veils herself to meet her future husband. Solomon develops his scene from very scant details and imbues it with great tenderness; the veil has fallen around Rebekah's shoulders, revealing her to Isaac's enraptured gaze. Cat. 44 was shown at the Winter Exhibition of 1863 with cat. 40.

45
Ruth and Boaz
1862
Watercolour with bodycolour on paper
23 × 17.5 cm (9 × 7 in.)
Signed with monogram and dated *5 62* lower left
Private collection

Stylistically cat. 45 relates to the two versions of *The Painter's Pleasaunce* (cat. 49 and 50); although it is one of Solomon's biblical designs, it shares with them the mixture of close detail and loose handling of the medium. Cat. 45 is independent of the Dalziel illustrations and unusual in presenting a distant landscape, rather English in appearance, in the background. The composition might derive from, or have originated at the same time as, the illustration *The Veiled Bride* (fig. 28). The furniture has similarities to that depicted in cat. 47 and 57, and shows a Pre-Raphaelite concern with the accurate reconstruction of historical details.

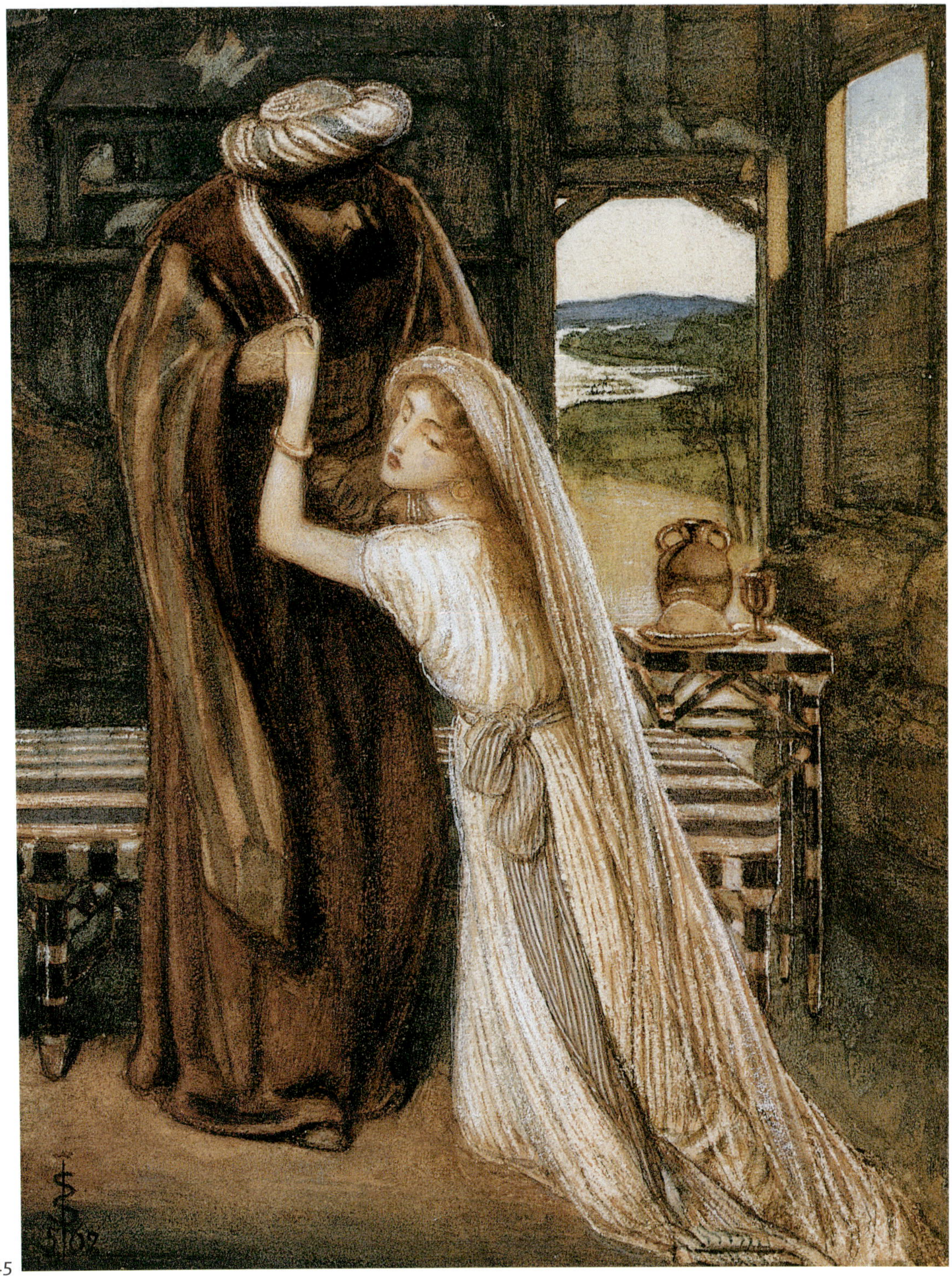
45

46
Dalziel Brothers after Simeon Solomon
Woodblocks for Solomon's illustrations for the Bible project
1862–*c.* 1870

a) **Righteousness and Peace Have Kissed Each Other**
16.3 × 11.9 × 2.3 cm (6½ × 4¾ × 1 in.)
b) **Jewish Women Burning Incense**
16.3 × 11.9 × 2.3 cm (6½ × 4¾ × 1 in.)

c) **The First Offering of Aaron**
14.3 × 18.2 × 2.3 cm (5⅝ × 7⅛ × 1 in.)

Birmingham Museums & Art Gallery

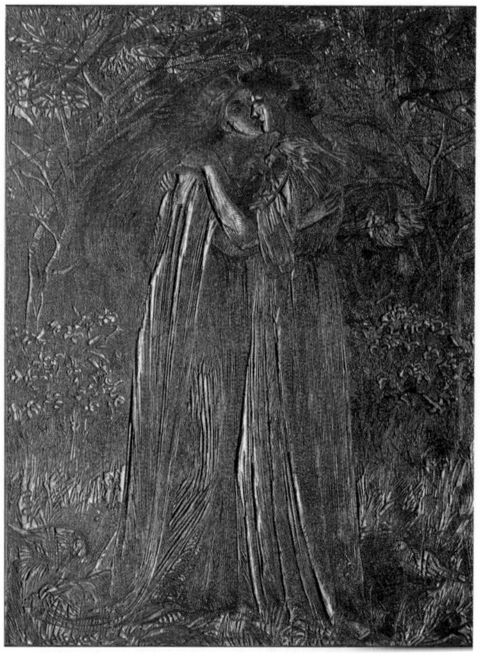
46a

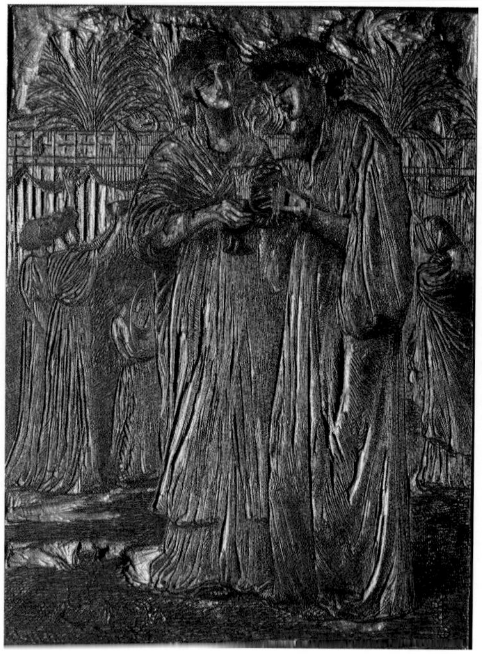
46b

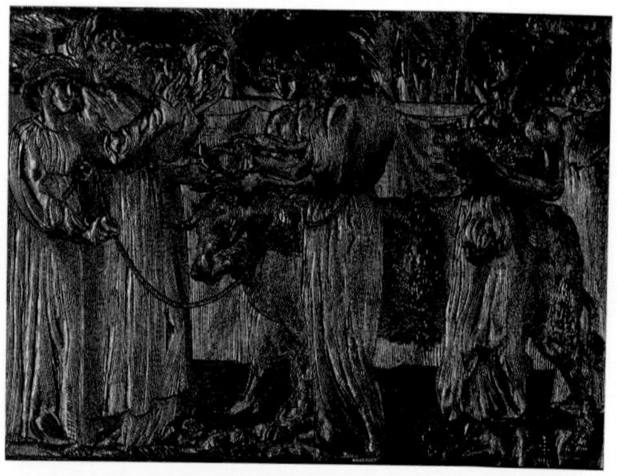
46c

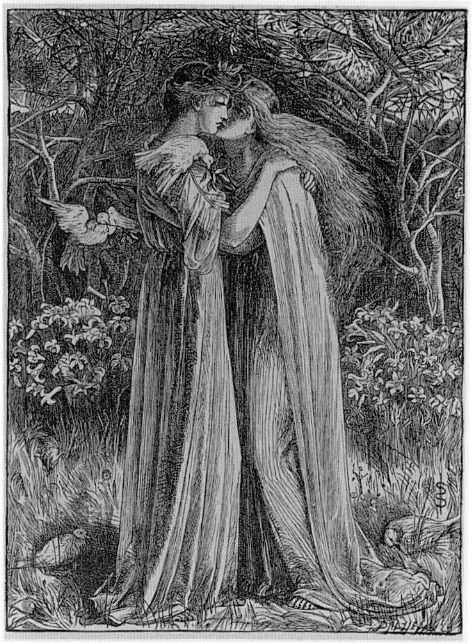

Fig. 29
Dalziel Brothers after Simeon Solomon
Righteousness and Peace Have Kissed Each Other
Wood engraving
16.3 × 11.9 cm (6½ × 4¾ in.)
Published in *Art Pictures from the Old Testament and Our Lord's Parables*, London (Edwin Dalton) 1894

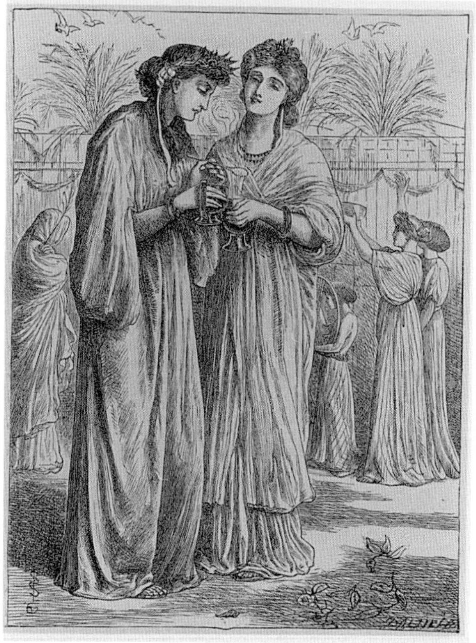

Fig. 30
Dalziel Brothers after Simeon Solomon
Jewish Women Burning Incense
Wood engraving
16.3 × 11.9 cm (6½ × 4¾ in.)
Published in *Art Pictures from the Old Testament and Our Lord's Parables*, London (Edwin Dalton) 1894

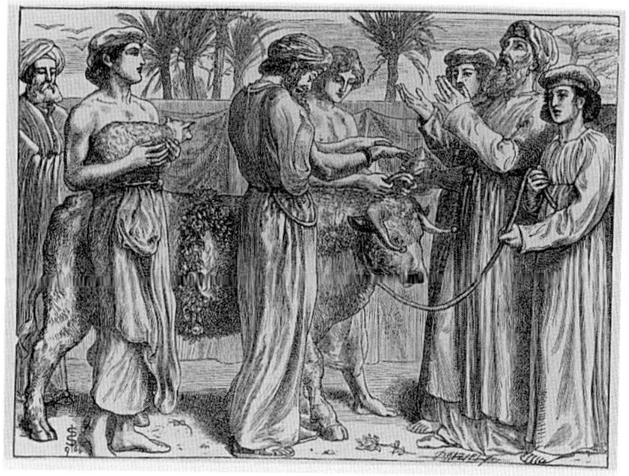

Fig. 31
Dalziel Brothers after Simeon Solomon
The First Offering of Aaron
Wood engraving
14.3 × 18.2 cm (5⅝ × 7⅛ in.)
Published in *Art Pictures from the Old Testament and Our Lord's Parables*, London (Edwin Dalton) 1894

47
Queen Esther Hearing the News of the Intended Massacre of the Jews
1860
Brown and black ink on paper
28.6 × 33.6 cm (11¼ × 13¼ in.)
Signed with monogram and dated *60* lower left
Private collection

Sometimes referred to as *The Anguish of Miriam* (e.g. in Reynolds, 1985, plate 20), cat. 47 depicts the emotions of Esther as she contemplates the news that her husband King Ahasuerus (possibly a corruption of the name Xerxes I, King of Persia), plans to exterminate the Jews living in his kingdom. Esther had kept her religion a secret. Her husband acts on the advice of Haman, her enemy, who had discovered that she was Jewish and knew that she could not escape the decree. Esther's anxiety is both for her own safety and that of her race.

The elaborate interior, while no doubt a response to the description of the king's palace in the Book of Esther (1:16), is also inspired by the excavations at Nineveh and the current vogue for Pre-Raphaelite historical fidelity first put forward by Ford Madox Brown in his essay 'On the Mechanism of a Historical Picture', published in *The Germ* in February 1850. The furniture appears to have been derived from William Holman Hunt's designs of *c.* 1855, made by Crace (fig. 32).

The rather operatic representation of Esther might reflect the elaboration of her plight and the literary exploration of it by Grace Aguilar in her *The Women of Israel* (third edition, 1853): "Clothed in unwonted gorgeousness, and radiant in her extraordinary beauty" (II, p. 113). Aguilar emphasizes, however, not beauty or earthly power but the effectiveness of prayer: "Surely we may picture the young queen wrapt in earnest and fervent prayer, still for strength and grace for the pursuance of her entreaty; was she not a weak and trembling woman, whose only strength was PRAYER?" (p. 115; Aguilar's emphasis).

The scene might well represent the occasion of Esther's prayer, the queen with her eyes closed, her hands joined.

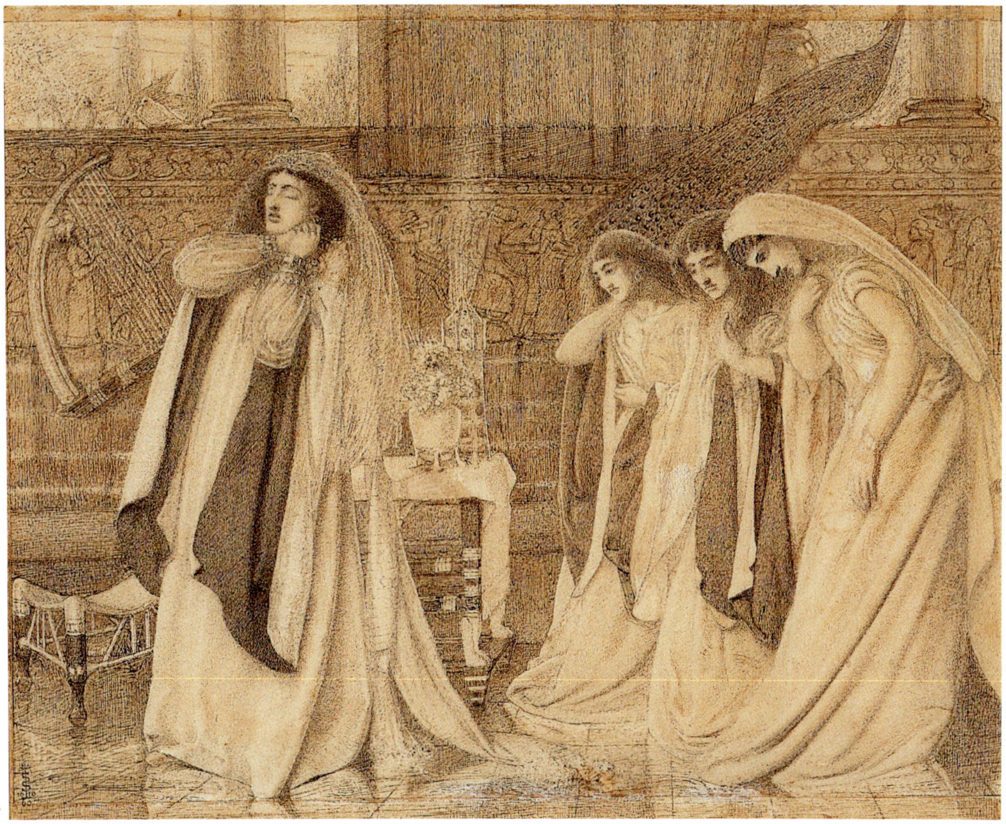
47

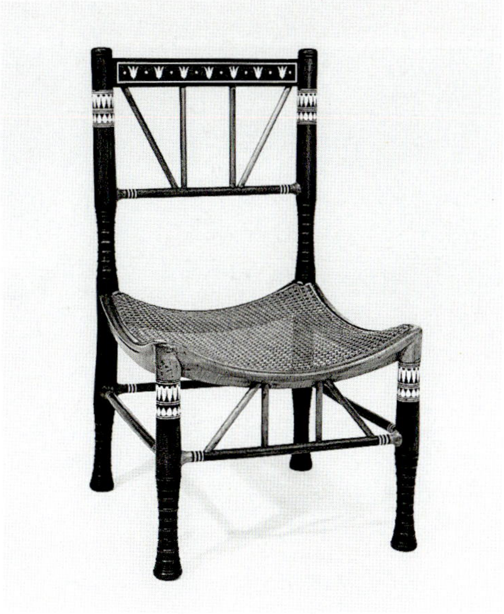
Fig. 32
Chair
1856–57, one of a pair
Designed by William Holman Hunt (1827–1910)
Made by J.G. Crace, London
Mahogany and sycamore, inlaid with ebony and ivory
Birmingham Museums & Art Gallery

48
Angels and Babies Going to a Pic-nic
1862
Watercolour with gold paint on paper
12.5 × 22 cm (5 × 8⅝ in.)
Private collection

This drawing, given to Georgiana Burne-Jones, is a reminder not only of the closeness of the artist to the Burne-Joneses at this period of their lives but also of their light-heartedness. Georgiana and Edward were married in 1860, and their first child, Philip, was born in 1861.

The subject, invented by Solomon, might refer to the presence of babies in Georgie's life, and it mixes them with some of his more solemn motifs – musicians and winged figures – seeming to send them up gently. Both Burne-Jones and Solomon, and on occasion Rossetti, indulged in comic drawing and caricature (a skill inherited by Philip Burne-Jones) and illustrated their letters with satirical, nonsensical or ribald drawings.

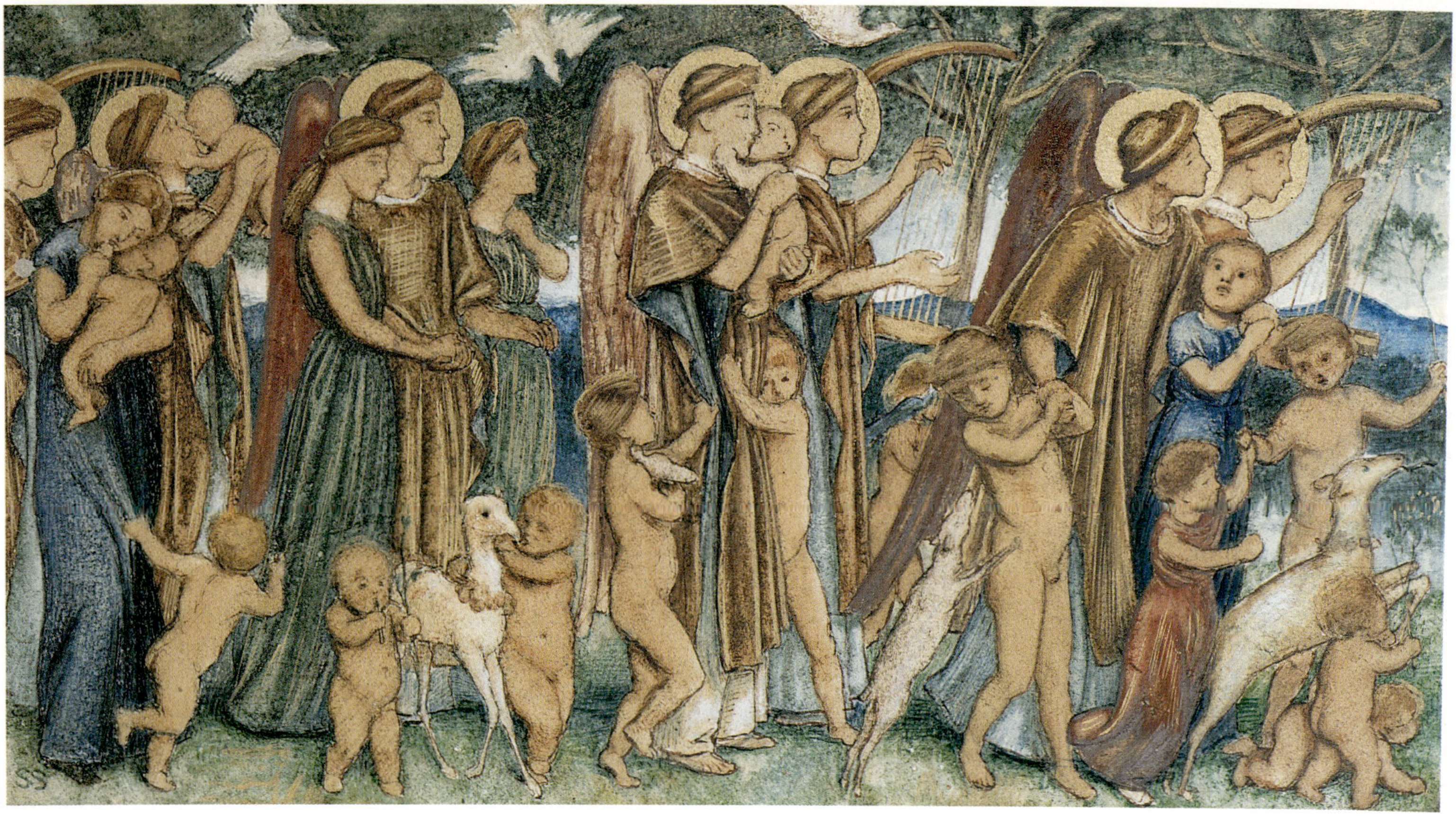
48

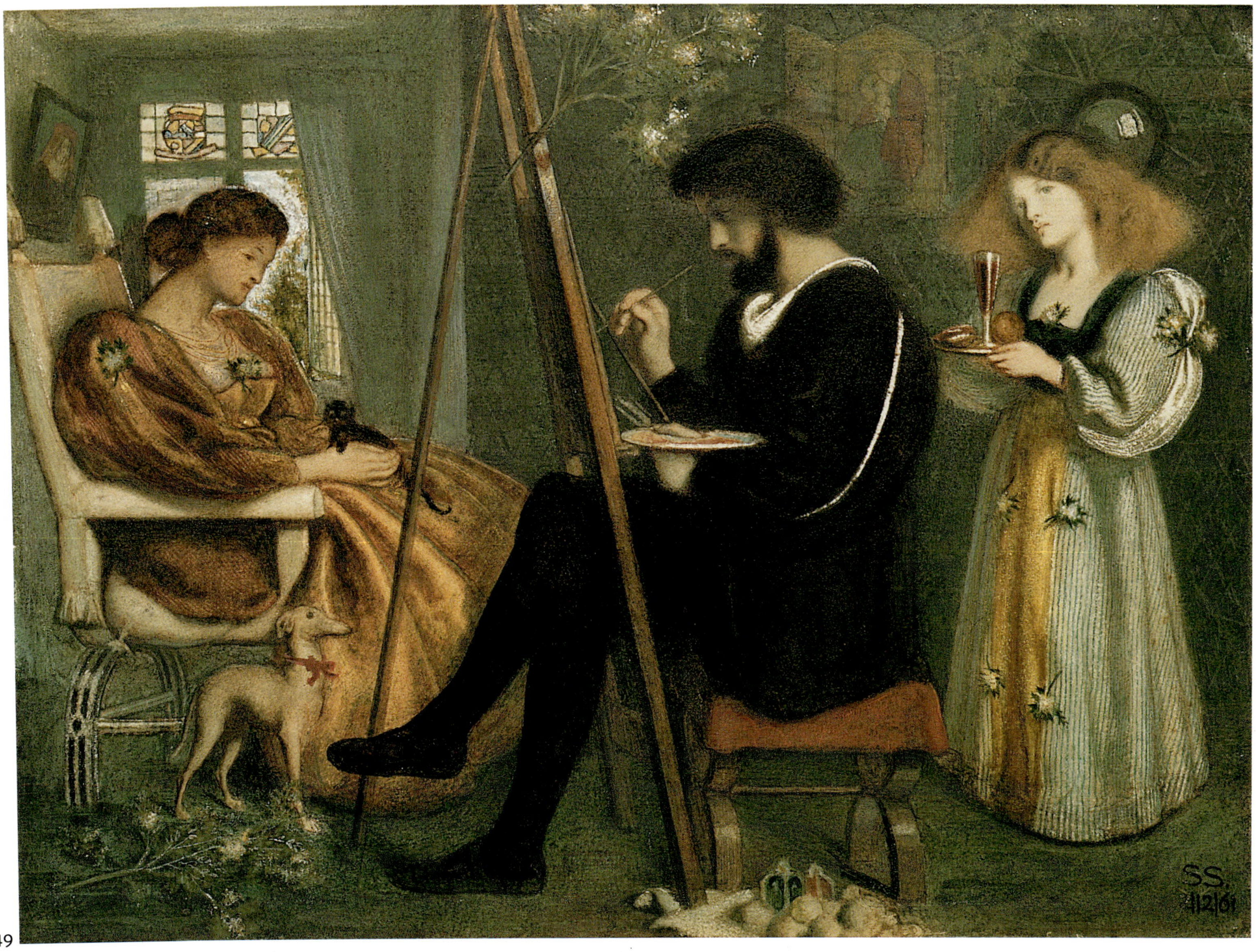

49

49
The Painter's Pleasaunce
1861
Watercolour and bodycolour with scratching-out on paper
25.6 × 33.1 cm (10 × 13⅛ in.)
Signed and dated lower right, *SS/2/12/61*
The Whitworth Art Gallery, University of Manchester

The subject seems entirely fanciful but relates to similar depictions of artists and models by several Pre-Raphaelites, such as Millais's etching to illustrate Rossetti's *St Agnes of Intercession* (1850, fig. 33). Rossetti was particularly drawn to the theme, producing *Giotto Painting the Portrait of Dante* (1852, Tate). There are strong similarities between cat. 49 and Rossetti's drawings of *Fra Angelico Painting* (*c.* 1853), particularly in the open lattice motif, and *Giorgione Painting* (cat. 54), particularly in the inclusion of incidental details (both Birmingham Museums & Art Gallery).

The disparity between the foreground finish and detail and the relatively hasty execution of the model in the background might indicate that cat. 49 was undertaken during a period of stylistic transition.

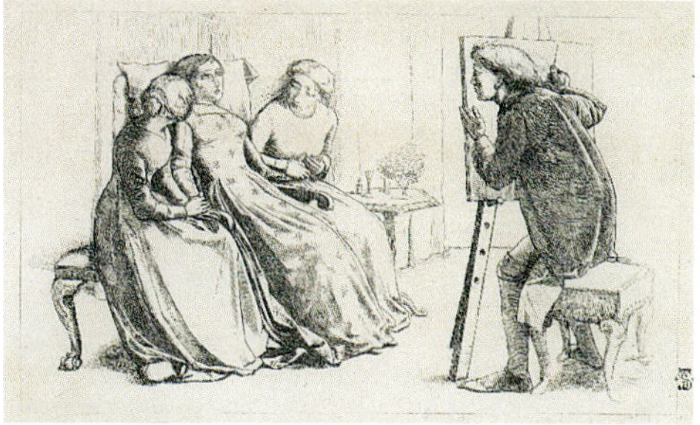

Fig. 33
John Everett Millais (1829–1896)
St Agnes of Intercession
1850
Etching
11.7 × 18.8 cm (4½ × 7¼ in.)
Birmingham Museums & Art Gallery

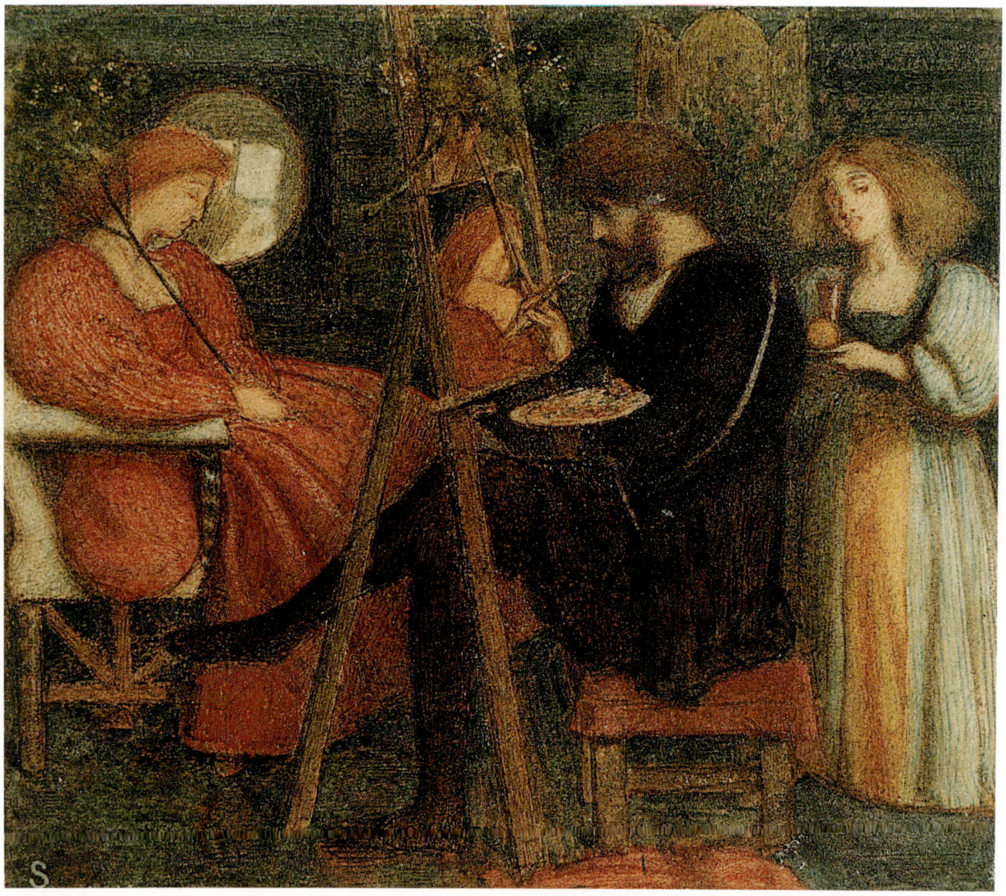

50

50
The Painter's Pleasaunce
c. 1862
Watercolour on paper
11.9 × 13.3 cm (4 11/16 × 5 1/4 in.)
Signed with initial *S* lower left
The British Museum, London

Cat. 50 is a replica of cat. 49, although lacking fine detail and departing from it in some compositional flourishes – the greyhound, the open windows, for example. The overall finish, however, is consistent across the surface of the painting. In cat. 50 the painting on the easel is visible: a head and shoulders portrait of the sitter, linking the work to Rossetti's innovative 'stunner' pictures of the period. The window has been replaced by a round mirror.

51
Two designs for stained-glass windows
1864
Photographic prints of cartoons by Simeon Solomon for the east window at All Saints Church, Middleton Cheney, Northamptonshire, mounted in showroom volume

a) **Abraham and Moses**
10.6 × 6.9 cm (4 1/4 × 2 11/16 in.)
b) **David and Isaiah**
10.9 × 7.2 cm (4 5/16 × 2 7/8 in.)
Birmingham Museums & Art Gallery.
Presented anonymously, 1940

Cat. 51 a and b are photographic records of studies for the east window at All Saints, Middleton Cheney, Northamptonshire undertaken by Morris, Marshall, Faulkner & Co. in 1865. The upper section of the scheme contains figures designed by Solomon described variously as a 'Procession of Saints and Martyrs' or as 'The Twelve Tribes of Israel' who carry banners that were designed separately by Philip Webb. For the second tier Solomon supplied designs for the figures of David and Isaiah, and for the third Abraham and Moses. The window also has panels by Burne-Jones, Brown and Morris.

Solomon's designs of 1864 are shown here in one of four showroom books from Morris & Company now held at Birmingham Museum & Art Gallery, three of them containing photographic records of stained-glass cartoons and one of completed windows.

While Solomon showed promise as a designer, his career was brief. He had many contacts with young designers and architects; he was close friends with the architect William Eden Nesfield and with the artist-designers of the earliest phase of Pre-Raphaelite design but did not exploit these contacts. However, he worked on one of the most important pieces of painted furniture of the period, the 'Great Bookcase', designed by William Burges (fig. 34). He designed and executed three panels for Burges, *Architecture* (St John and the Angel measuring the Heavenly Jerusalem) (fig. 7), *Sculpture* (Pygmalion) and *Philosophy* (St Augustine).

The first meeting of the two men is recorded by Boyce: "Miss Cooke came to sit for me. Little Simeon Solomon called and stayed a long while and jawed and bored us considerably. Burges came up and I introduced them" (Boyce, 1980, p. 21, entry for 15 February 1858).

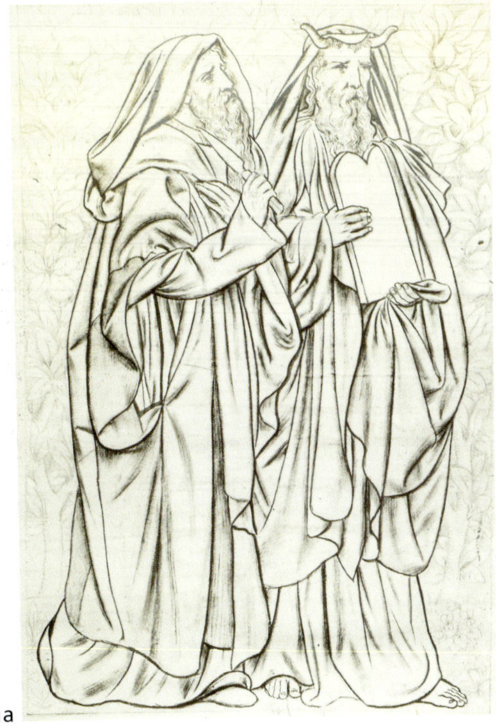

51a

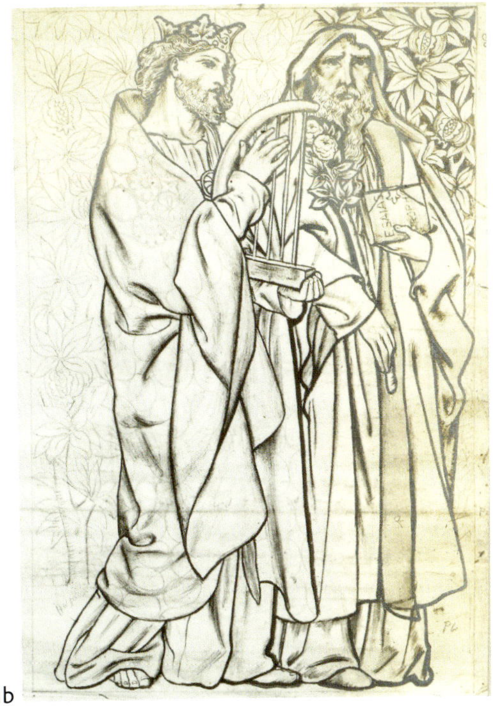

51b

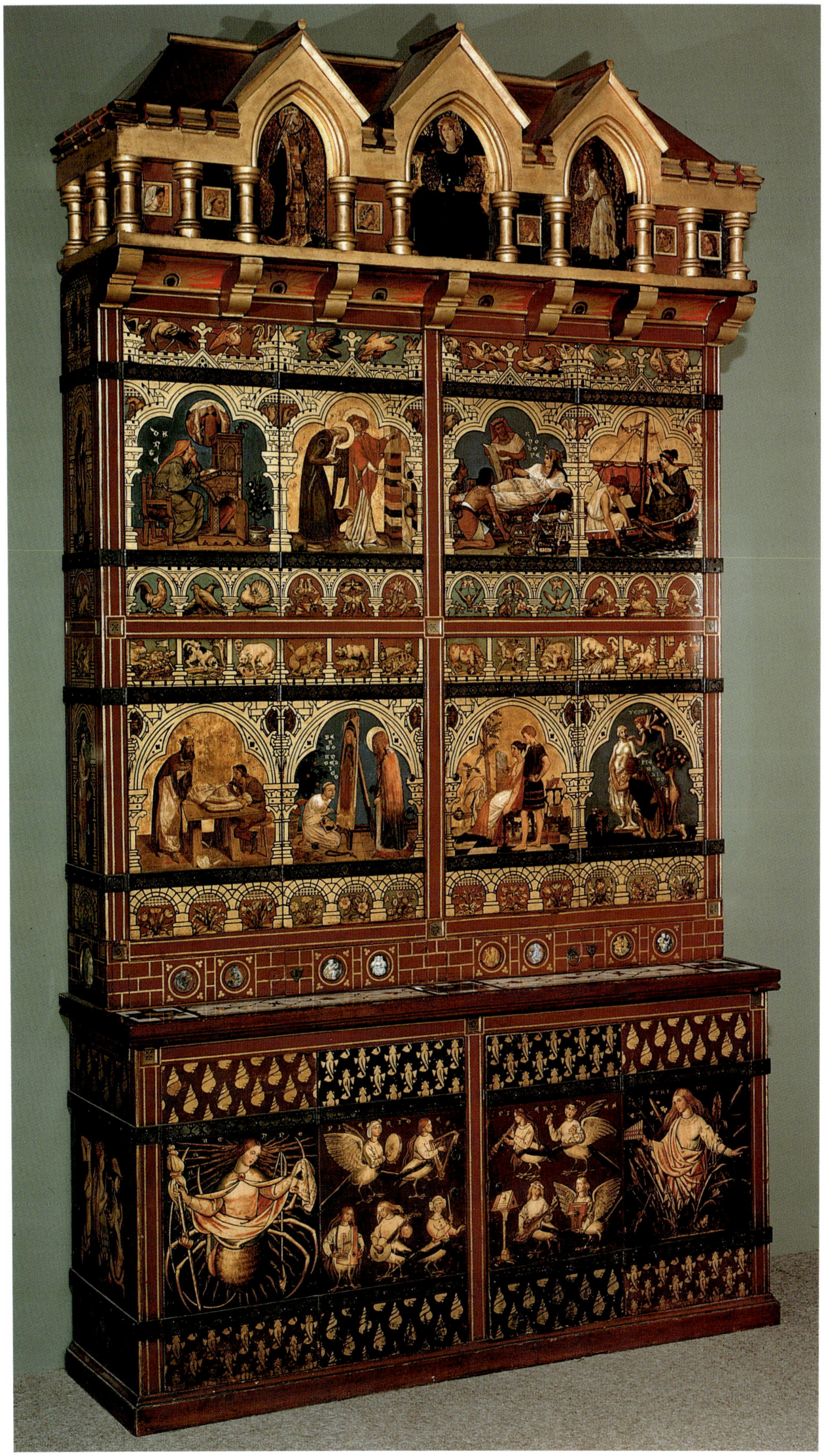

Fig. 34
William Burges (1827–1881)
The 'Great Bookcase'
1859–62
Carved, painted and gilded wood
317.1 × 173.8 × 49.5 cm (125 × 68½ × 19½ in.)
The Ashmolean Museum, Oxford

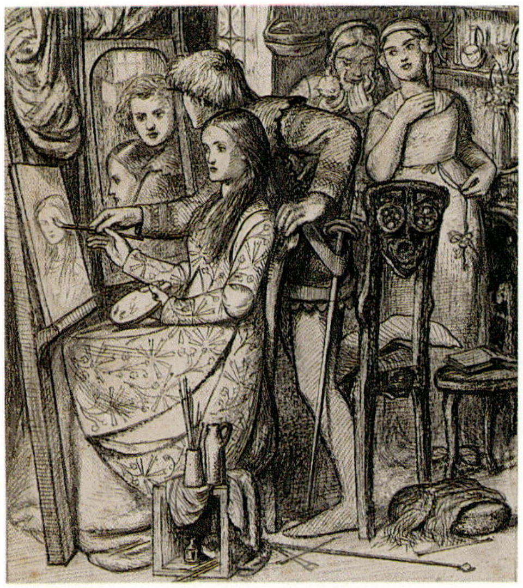

52

52
Dante Gabriel Rossetti (1828–1882)
Love's Mirror
1849–50
Pen and ink with wash on paper
19.3 × 17.5 cm (7⅝ × 6⅞ in.)
Birmingham Museums & Art Gallery. Presented by subscribers, 1904

Also known as *A Parable of Love*, this complex narrative drawing introduces the artist-and-model subject to Pre-Raphaelite art at an early stage in the movement's history. It is a theme developed by Solomon in his two versions of *The Painter's Pleasaunce* (cat. 49 and 50).

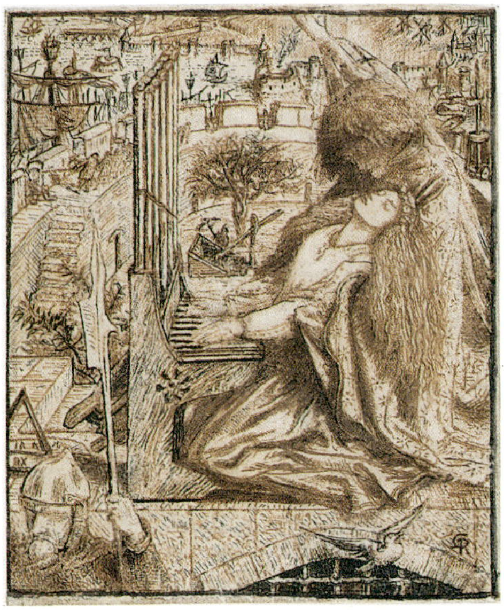

53

53
Dante Gabriel Rossetti (1828–1882)
Saint Cecilia
1856–57
Pen and brown ink on paper
9.9 × 8.3 cm (3⅞ × 3¼ in.)
Signed with monogram lower right
Birmingham Museums & Art Gallery. Presented by subscribers, 1904

Rossetti's illustrations for the Moxon Tennyson of 1857 set a standard for inventiveness and, in their inclusion of intricate detail, challenged the technical abilities of engravers. Their impact on Solomon, among others, can be seen in several works, including cat. 16 and 98. This drawing is for the most controversial of the designs, illustrating an incident from the poem 'The Palace of Art' but in a highly elaborated and idiosyncratic way. St Cecilia is on the ramparts of a castle, her body embraced from behind by an angel who regards her fixedly. She has fallen backwards, eyes closed as if in death. The intensity of emotion, ambiguously sexual, is offset by the details of mundane daily life that go on around her.

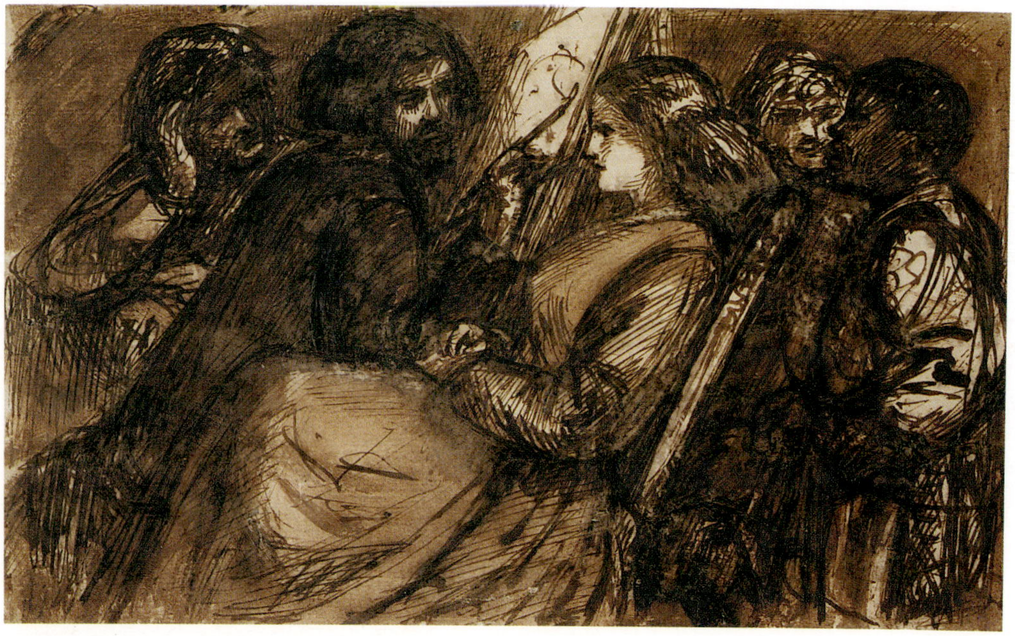

54

54
Dante Gabriel Rossetti (1828–1882)
Giorgione Painting
c. 1853
Brown ink and wash on paper
11 × 17.6 cm (4⅜ × $6\frac{15}{16}$ in.)
Birmingham Museums & Art Gallery. Presented by subscribers, 1904

Rossetti's enthusiasm for Giorgione dated back to the earliest phase of the Pre-Raphaelite Brotherhood but communicated itself best to his younger followers; compare, for example, Solomon's treatment of a similar scene (cat. 49 and 50).

Cat. 54 imagines the interior of the artist's studio; the artist works concertedly from a model while friends, or servants or patrons – perhaps all three – stand around talking. The relationship between artist and model is as intense as love.

55
Edward Poynter (1836–1919)
Study for a Garden Scene in the 'Decameron'
1859
Pen and ink and wash with white bodycolour on paper laid on card
18.4 × 22.8 cm (7⅛ × 8⅞ in.)
Signed and dated lower left
Birmingham Museums & Art Gallery. Presented by Sir Ambrose Poynter, Bart., 1921

Poynter was one of Solomon's closest student friends; the two shared studio accommodation and, for a short time, lived at the same address. The two artists' careers ran in parallel throughout the 1860s. Poynter's earliest work was often as experimental and diverse as his friend's, although he was later to become an establishment figure, famed for his rather dry drawing style and classical subjects. Cat. 55, drawn with great assurance and invention, represents an essay in the Italianate style reminiscent of Rossetti's 'Borgia' watercolours (begun c. 1858) and anticipating the great Academy successes of Leighton. It is based on the most famous work of Giovanni Boccaccio (1313–1375), *The Decameron* (1349–53). The theme is poetry, music and love, all represented in Solomon's work by the early 1860s, although Poynter's treatment of them is more conventional. Indeed, it was common for reviewers of the Dudley Gallery exhibitions to contrast the two artists; for example, the critic of *The Spectator* observed that, at the Dudley Gallery Winter Exhibition, "Passing from Mr. Solomon's pictures to the manly and accomplished work of Mr. E.J. Poynter is like emerging from an atmosphere heavy with oppressive scents into the free air of heaven" (19 February 1870, p. 237).

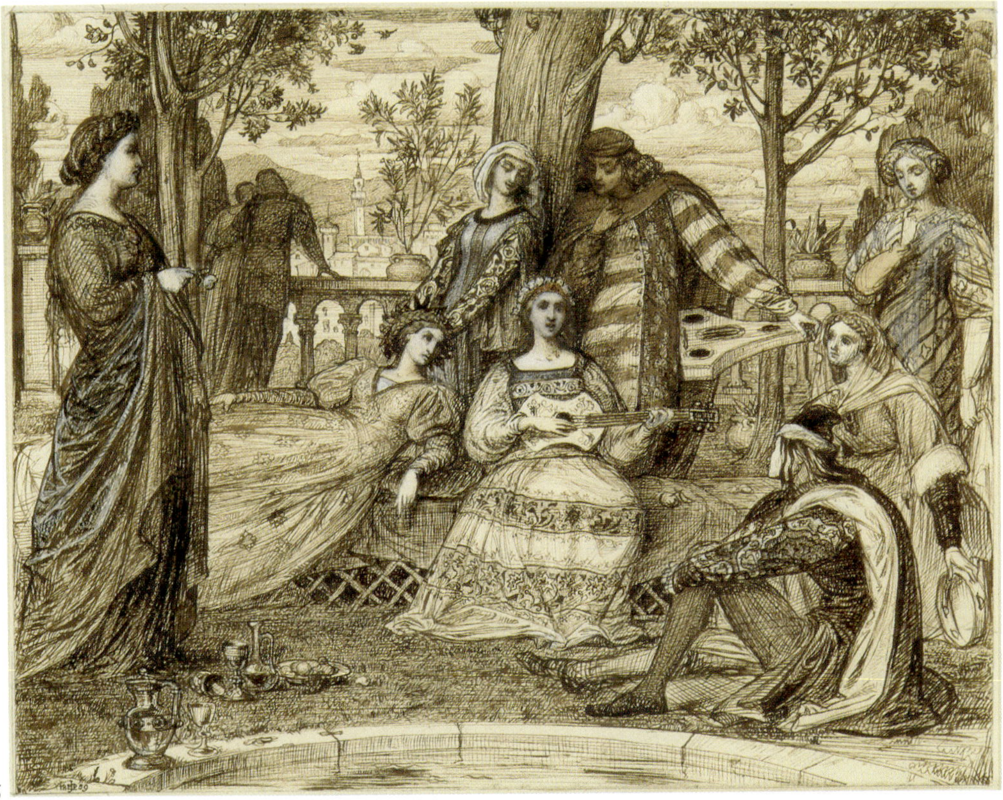
55

56
Edward Burne-Jones (1833–1898)
An Idyll
1862
Watercolour, bodycolour and gum on paper laid on canvas
30.5 × 28 cm (12 × 11 in.)
Signed with monogram lower right
Birmingham Museums & Art Gallery. Presented by Mrs G.F. Watts, 1924

This scene of lovers in a meadow anticipates some of Burne-Jones's more elaborate watercolours like *Chant d'Amour* (1865, Museum of Fine Art, Boston), and demonstrates well some of the characteristics of new watercolour technique developed initially by Rossetti (see cat. 119) and perfected by Solomon (for example, in cat. 49).

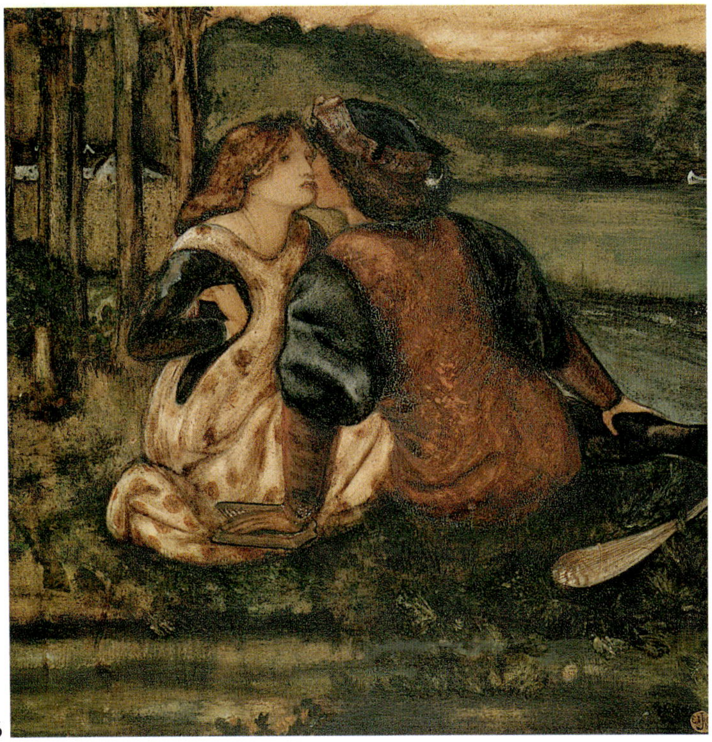
56

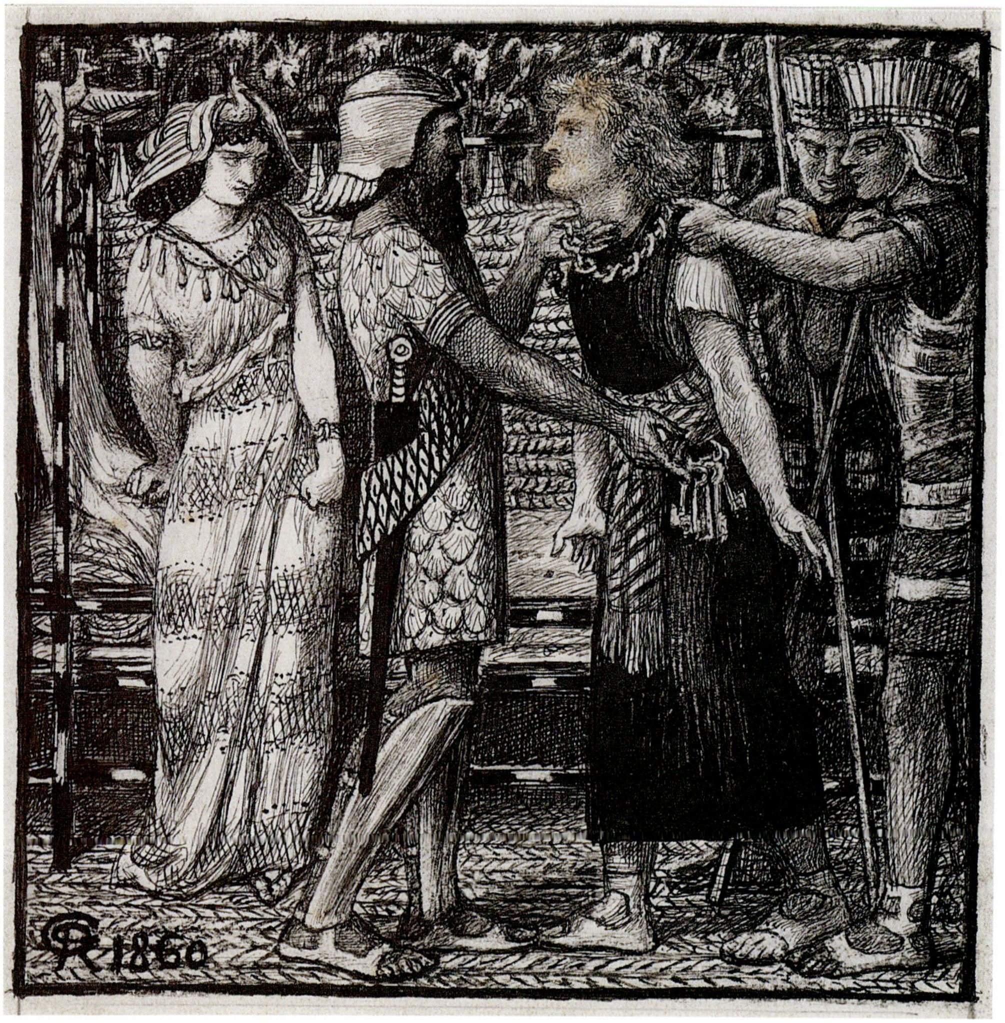

57

57
Dante Gabriel Rossetti (1828–1882)
Joseph Accused before Potiphar
1860
Pen and ink on paper
15.1 × 14.7 cm ($5\frac{15}{16} \times 5\frac{13}{16}$ in.)
Signed with monogram and dated lower left
Birmingham Museums & Art Gallery. Presented by subscribers, 1904

The story of Joseph's entrapment by the wife of Potiphar is found in Genesis 39. It is a tale of female sexual desire thwarted and good triumphing over evil. Rossetti has depicted the unnamed wife as a brooding and provocative femme fatale and Joseph as a Pre-Raphaelite hero with curling lip and long waving hair. The other figures are rendered almost in caricature.

Cat. 57 is not characteristic of Rossetti's other subjects at this stage of his career but relates closely to Solomon's Old Testament pictures, particularly in its attempt to realize the story through costumes and accessories fanciful in design but loosely based on historical examples. The design of the sofa that occupies much of the background has similarities to the furniture in several of Solomon's biblical illustrations, for example cat. 47.

58
Albert Moore (1841–1893)
Study for the Head of Elijah
c. 1861
Pencil on paper
26.6 × 20.3 cm (10½ × 8 in.)
Birmingham Museums & Art Gallery. Bequeathed by J.R. Holliday, 1927

Moore's large finished drawing *Elijah Running to Jezreel before Ahab's Chariot* (1861, private collection) had some of the archaisms derived from Assyrian relief sculpture that can be traced in Solomon's *Queen Esther Hearing the News of the Intended Massacre of the Jews* (cat. 47). This study, however, shows the proficiency of Moore's naturalistic drawing (see Asleson, 2000, p. 30).

Moore was close to Solomon at this early stage in both their careers, and they shared models. The sitter for Moore's *The Mother of Sisera Looked Out at a Window* (1861, Tullie House Museum & Art Gallery, Carlisle) was Mrs Eaton. She modelled for Jochabed in Solomon's *The Mother of Moses* (see cat. 31 and 32) and for the servant in *Habet!* (cat. 75) as well as for Joanna Boyce's *A Sibyl* (now lost; oil study, 1861, Yale Center for British Art, New Haven).

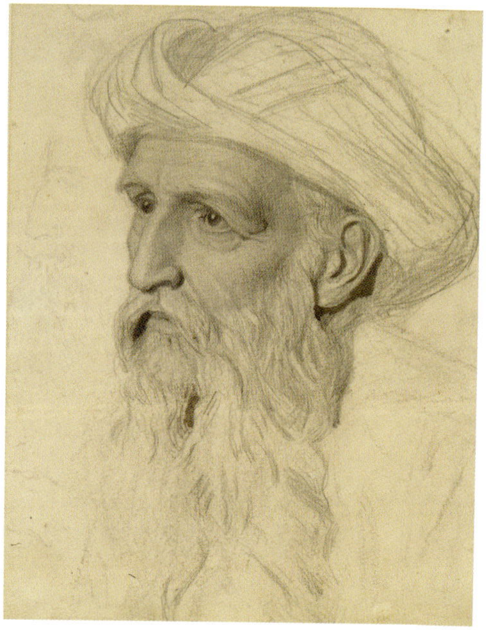

58

59
Ford Madox Brown (1821–1893)
Elijah and the Widow's Son
1864
Oil on wood
52.5 × 34.3 cm (20¾ × 13½ in.)
Signed with monogram and dated *64*
centre right
Birmingham Museums & Art Gallery. Presented by Sir John Middlemore, Bart., 1912

Brown was one of the artists chosen by the Dalziel Brothers to illustrate scenes for their Bible project. He undertook three designs.

The story of Elijah's instructions to visit Zarephath, his stay with the widow and his bringing back to life her dead son is recorded in I Kings 17. This image and one of Brown's other designs, that illustrating the story of Joseph's coat brought to his father, are among the most striking of the entire project. Cat. 59 follows the illustration faithfully but conveys the effect of hot, strong light contrasting with the cool gloom of the interiors; a similar effect can be seen in Solomon's oil paintings, for example, the oil version of cat. 34. Here, however, there is some narrative intent: the warmth of life triumphs over the coldness of the tomb.

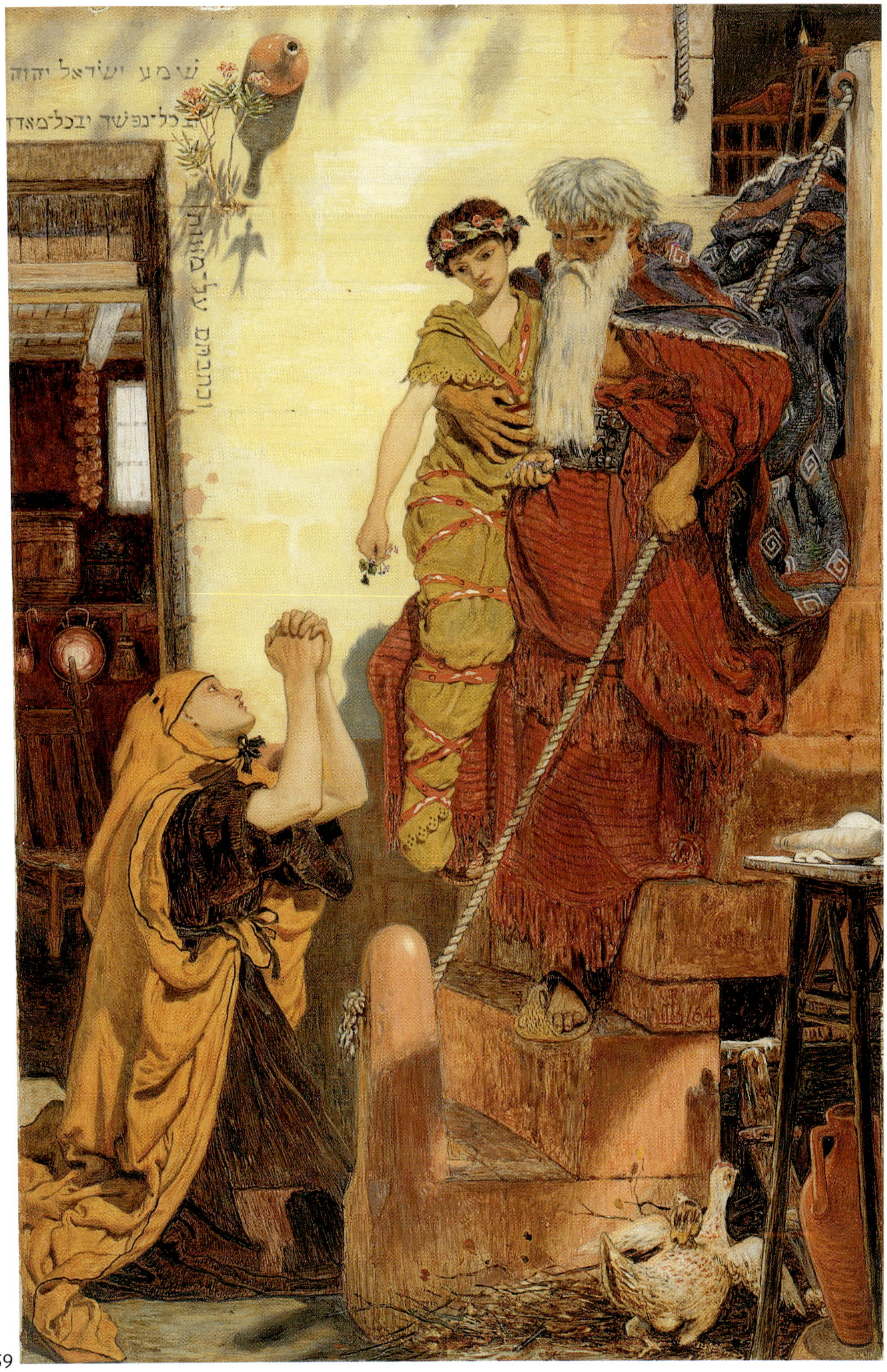

59

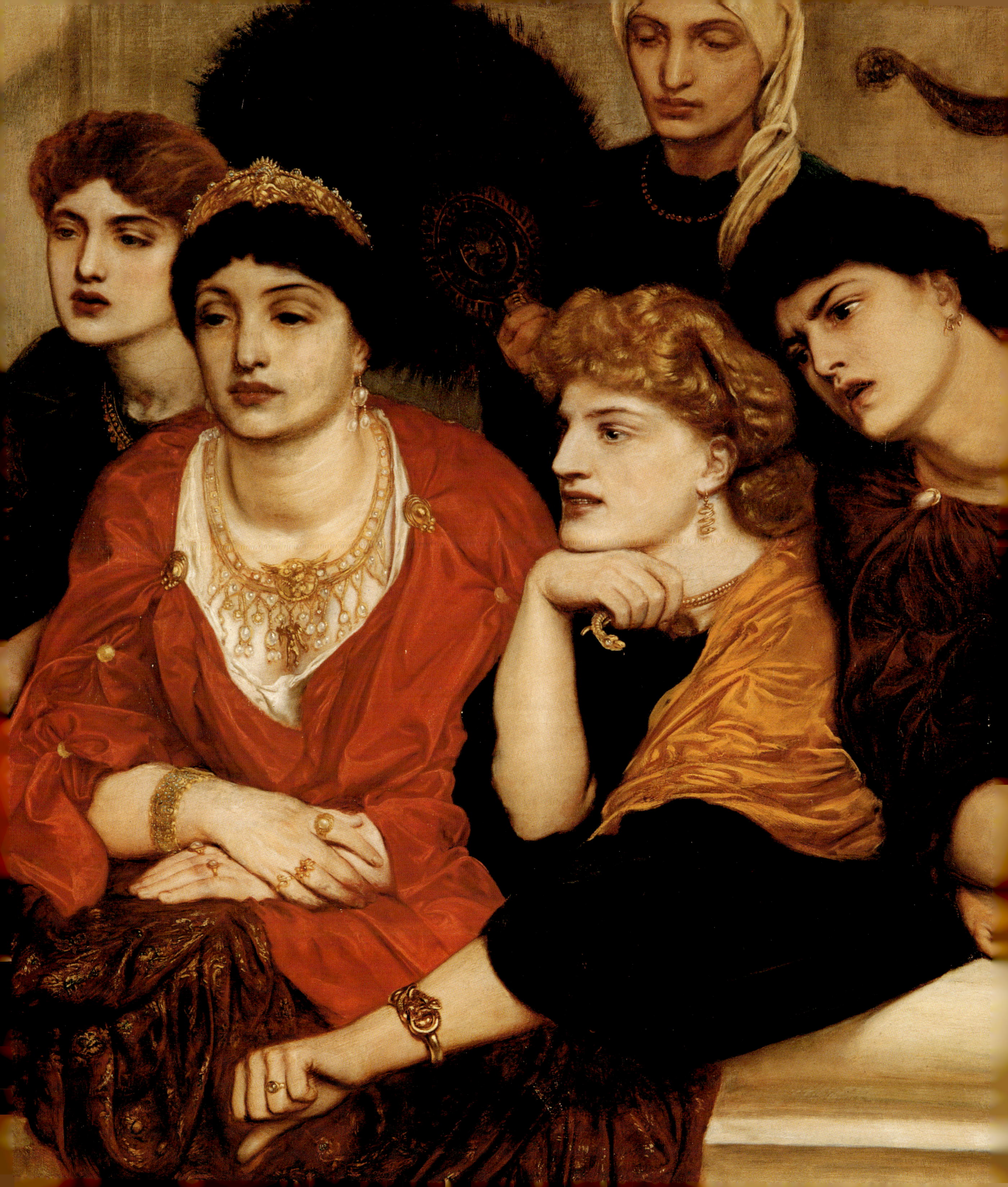

Experiments in Beauty

"The aberrant eccentricities of genius"
Art Journal, 1867, p. 269

In the 1860s Solomon was extremely prolific, and his work became extraordinarily diverse. This section of the exhibition deals chiefly with his representation of the female figure, often, although not always, classically draped. The temporary shift to depictions of the Classical female figure anticipates by several years the works of Lawrence Alma-Tadema, whose fame resides on such subjects.

However, Solomon was also experimenting with some of the new non-narrative or even anti-narrative aspects of contemporary painting practice found in Whistler's work. Whistler, like Solomon, showed at the Dudley Gallery, which had become associated with the exhibition of new and challenging works (see the next section). Whistler was a particularly strong presence at the Dudley in 1871, showing two much-reviewed pictures there, *Variations in Violet and Green* and *Harmony in Blue-Green – Moonlight*.

Rossetti's version of Pre-Raphaelitism changed the movement from within. Eschewing detail and historical accessory and costume, it concentrated on the female subject, often dreamy, ill-fated or fateful, with flowers, exotic objects and clothing and an oblique approach to narrative. It is clear that Solomon was not only aware of the changes in the direction of Pre-Raphaelitism but was prepared to take the lead. Thus *Poetry* (cat. 60) anticipates the motif of the dreamy woman with an open book, later exploited by Rossetti in several works including his wedding portrait of Jane Burden, *The Blue Silk Dress* (1866–68, National Trust, Kelmscott Manor, Oxfordshire).

In 1865 Solomon exhibited his most ambitious work at the Royal Academy, *Habet!* (cat. 75), which was widely reviewed and, generally, well received. His reputation was built, however, on smaller works, often in watercolour, a medium that allowed him a kind of graphic flexibility that was a characteristic of his early drawing style, incorporating a subtlety and richness of colour that became his trademark.

75
Habet! (detail)
1865
Oil on canvas
101.5 × 122 cm (39⅞ × 48 in.)
Signed *SS* and dated *IIII.LXV*
Private collection (on loan to Bradford Museums, Galleries & Heritage)

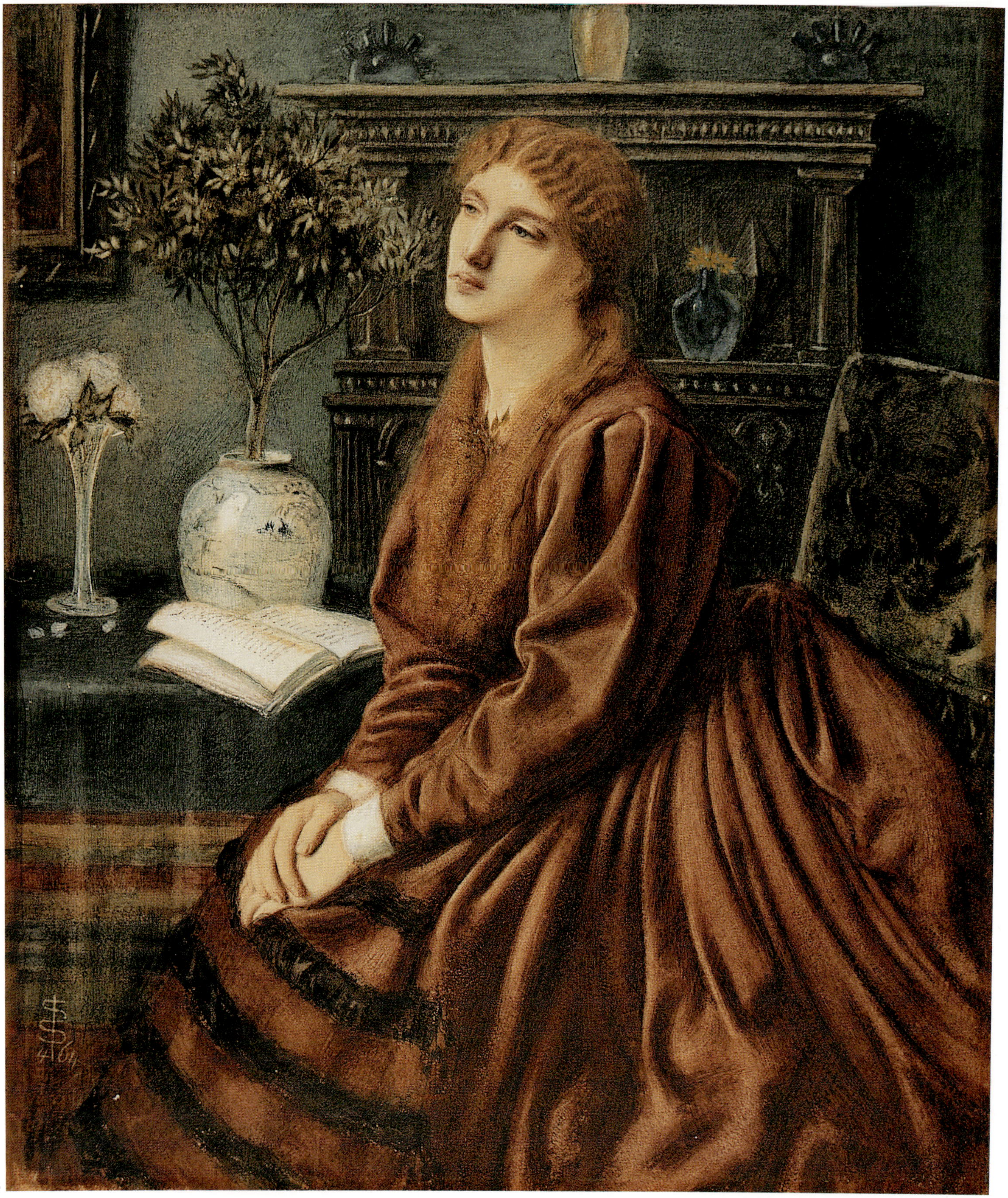

60

60
Poetry
1864
Watercolour on paper
39.3 × 32.1 cm (15½ × 12⅝ in.)
Signed with monogram and dated *4/64* lower left
Grosvenor Museum, Chester City Council

Cat. 60 is one of Solomon's strongest images of this period. A woman sits staring into space, neglecting her book. The subject is similar to Solomon's brother's work depicting Marie Antoinette, *A Study* (untraced, RA, 1859; see Cruise, 2003, pp. 1–13). Cat. 60 departs from the usual historicized genre and fancy pictures by introducing diverse decorative objects that speak of the emerging Aesthetic Movement taste for collecting odd and exotic objects for home decoration. Cat. 60 was owned by Eleanor Tong Coltart, who collected Solomon paintings, including cat. 61; the two might have been regarded as a pair.

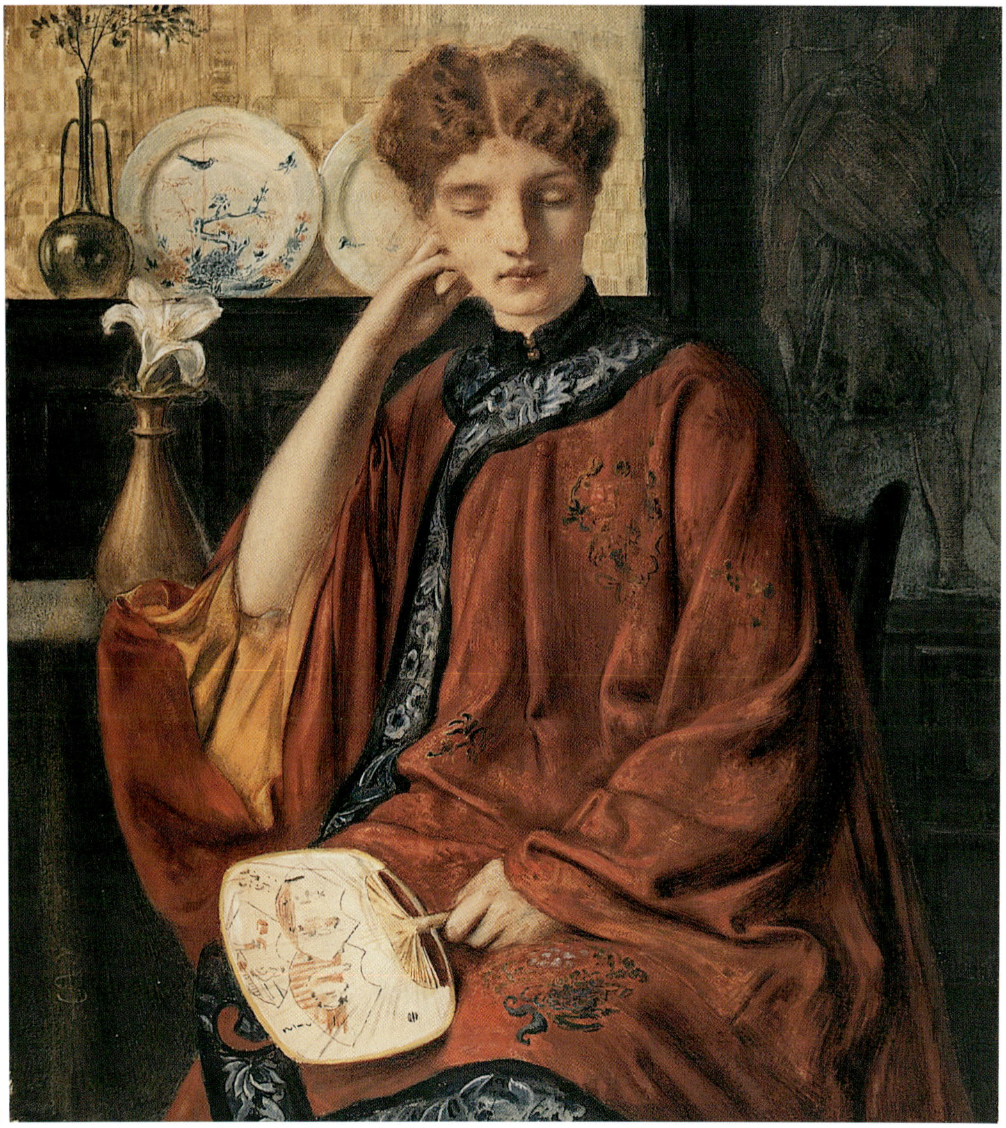

61

61
Lady in a Chinese Dress
1865
Watercolour on paper
41 × 35.5 cm (16⅛ × 14 in.)
Signed with monogram and dated lower left
Grosvenor Museum, Chester City Council

Cat. 61 might have been seen as a companion piece to cat. 60, with which it shares the dreamy, abstracted female subject. They were both owned by Eleanor Tong Coltart of Birkenhead, an important Pre-Raphaelite collector; as there is no record of either being shown at exhibition, it might be that Mrs Coltart commissioned them directly from the artist. Solomon shows his advanced taste in posing the fair-haired European model in oriental dress, although a similar idea lies behind two of Rossetti's most important oil paintings of this time, *The Blue Bower* (1865, Barber Institute, University of Birmingham), in which Fanny Cornforth is posed in a Chinese robe, and *The Beloved* (1865–66, Tate), in which 'the bride' wears a Japanese kimono and a Chinese headdress.

A work with the same title appears as Plate 33 in Reynolds (1985), and there are strong similarities with Rebecca Solomon's *The Wounded Dove* (1866, cat. 79). There are similarities, too, with Solomon's *Marguerite* (cat. 62), painted the following year, in the use of Chinese *objets d'art* and the red robe.

62 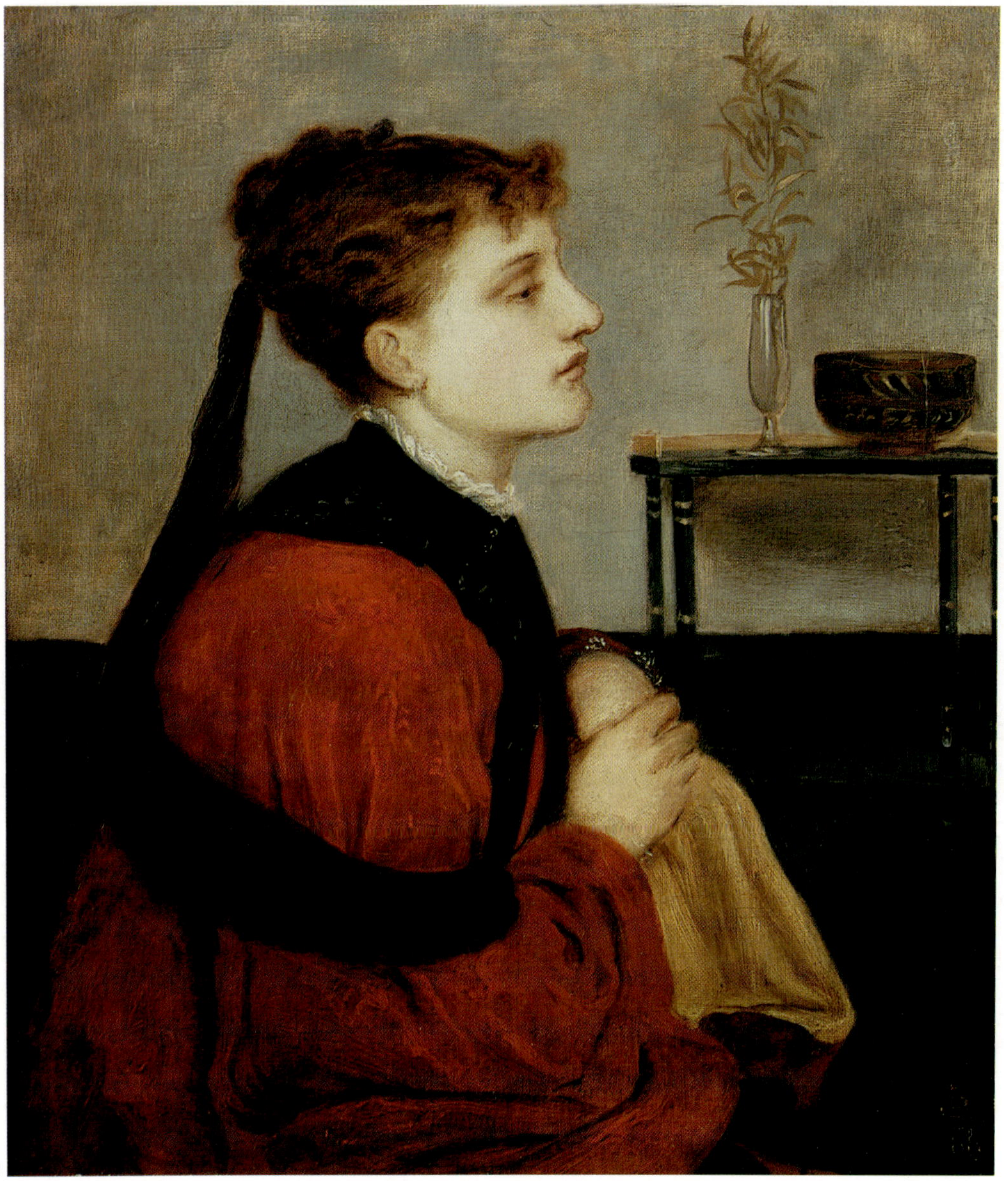

62
Marguerite
1866
Oil on canvas
39.3 × 34.2 cm (15½ × 13½ in.)
Signed with monogram and dated lower right
Private collection

Exhibited at the Fifth Winter Exhibition of Cabinet Pictures in Oil, Dudley Gallery, 1871 (as no. 217), this Whistlerian compositional exercise, a kind of Whistler's-mother-in-reverse, has a bold rather than a subtle colour arrangement, with a very un-Whistlerian red dominating the picture. The sitter in cat. 62, who appears to be wearing a Chinese robe, sports an Aesthetic Movement hairstyle, the bun tied with a black ribbon that hangs from the back of the head on to the shoulder and forms an elegant black curve counteracting the geometric design of the cabinet at the back of the composition. The hairstyle appears in Sandys's *Helen and Cassandra* (1866, Birmingham Museums & Art Gallery), as well as in many of du Maurier's illustrations for *Punch* of fashionable women in 'artistic' circles and, later, in designs by Walter Crane and Henry Holiday. The furniture resembles that of E.W. Godwin, whose first ebonized mahogany or deal furniture was designed *c.* 1866 (see Seymour, 1986, fig. 128).

The title of cat. 62 might suggest that Solomon was depicting the heroine of Goethe's *Faust*, Gretchen, known in England by the French version of her name following the success of Gounod's operatic version of the story (1859). The *Art Journal* suggested this connection: "Had Mr. Solomon named his 'Marguerite' 'A Reverie', we should have been better satisfied, but as the title stands we feel there is something lacking to complete our ideal of Goethe's Marguerite. Nevertheless, the modelling of the face is very beautiful, and the half-shut eye is tender and full of love" (1871, p. 285). There is a possibility, however, that the artist intended Marguerite to represent the tragic central figure in Dumas's *La Dame aux camélias* (1848). The image is an extraordinary predecessor to Beardsley's design for Oscar Wilde's *Salomé* (1894), *The Toilette of Salomé*, in which French Rococo, Japanese and Victorian elements are combined.

Cat. 62 is inscribed on the back, 'Given to me / by Andrew Lang / about 1878 / H. Rider Haggard'. Neither man would be the obvious owner of the picture. Lang (1844–1912) was something of an anti-Aesthetic Movement satirist, famous for his fairy- and folklore stories and his prodigious scholarship; Rider Haggard (1856–1925), celebrated author of adventure stories, was otherwise more 'muscular' in his tastes.

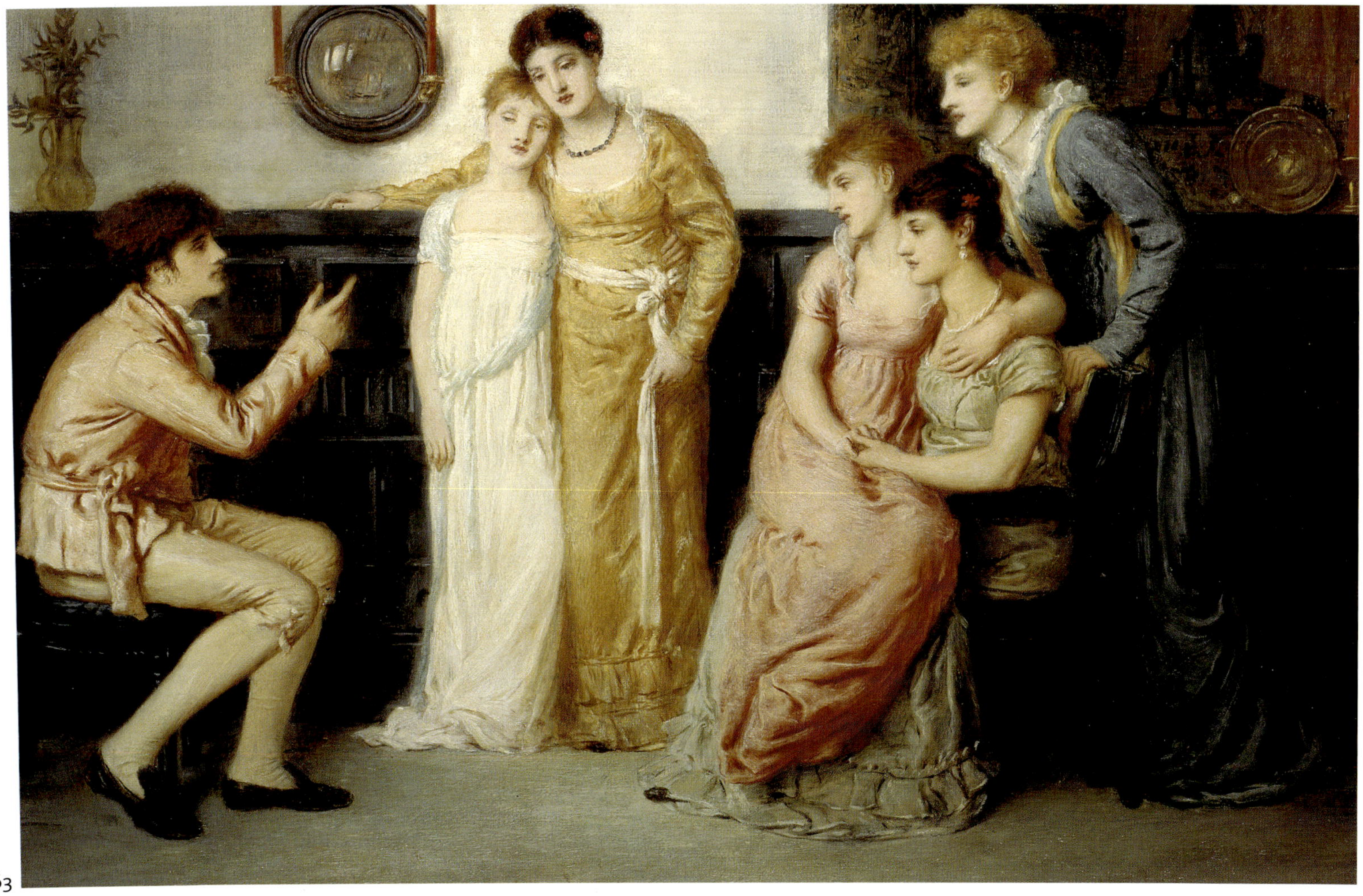

63

63
A Youth Relating Tales to Ladies
1870
Oil on canvas
35.5 × 53.4 cm (14 × 21 in.)
Signed and dated, right
Tate. Presented by the Kretschmer family in accordance with the wishes of William Kretschmer, 1983

The literary salon of eighteenth-century France is here translated into a sapphic group who listen intently to a young man. The subject perhaps owes something to Swinburne's enthusiasm for eighteenth-century French culture, to De Sade in particular. The atmosphere is of a barely suppressed eroticism. Some of the female heads resemble those chosen for *Habet!* (cat. 75) and for the illustrations to Swinburne's *Lesbia Brandon* (*c.* 1877, published 1952).

64
Sappho and Erinna in a Garden at Mytilene
1864
Watercolour on paper
33 × 38.1 cm (13 × 15 in.)
Signed with a double sigma and dated *2.64*
Tate. Purchased 1980

Painted for the industrialist James Leathart, who most probably knew of Solomon through his patronage of D.G. Rossetti (see *The Leathart Collection*, 1968, p. 34); when shown at the Goupil Gallery in 1896 as part of 'A Pre-Raphaelite Collection' (as no. 48), it was catalogued as having the title *Sappho and Erinna* with a subtitle, or alternative title, in brackets, *In a Garden at Mytilene*.

Sappho, described as 'the Tenth Muse', was one of the most famous poets of the ancient world. She was born on the island of Lesbos in the mid-seventh century BC. Mytilene was one of the island's chief towns. Among Sappho's lovers was, supposedly, the poet Erinna, although modern scholarship has proved that Erinna was living at a later date. Sappho's verse, known only in fragments, was of deep importance to many nineteenth-century writers including Swinburne, who particularly identified with her; his 'Anactoria' is an impersonation of her.

Cat. 64 is one of several works of Solomon's depicting Sappho (see cat. 65, 66 and 67); she appears to represent all same-sex desire and Solomon's own sexual feelings. Cat. 64 is charged with passion and intensity, poetry abandoned momentarily for passion; the stillness of the scene contrasts with the turbulence of the

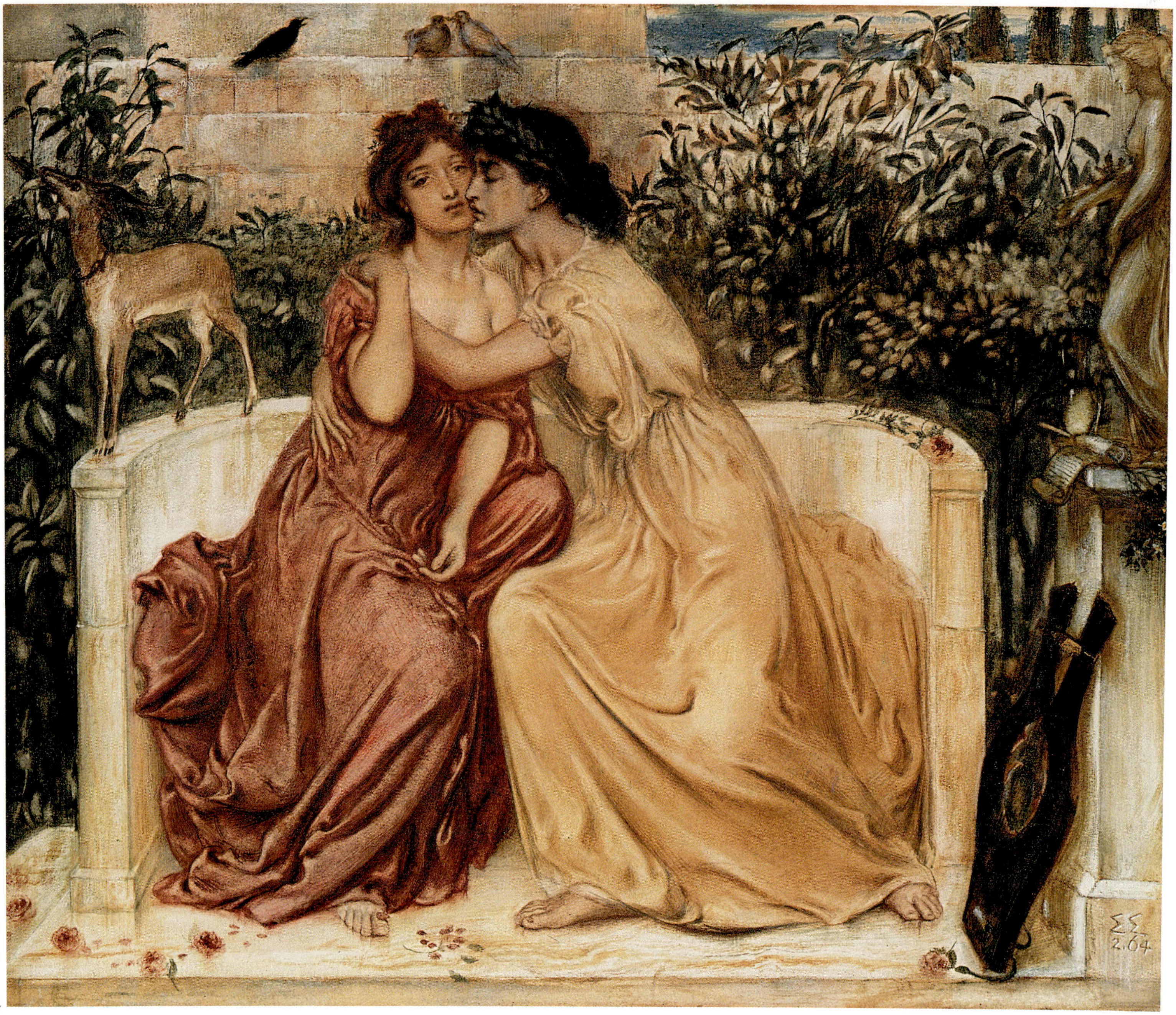

64

emotions; so still are the lovers that a rose petal that has fallen on to Erinna's foot remains undisturbed. The little deer is similar to that in Rossetti's *Mary Magdalene at the Door of Simon the Pharisee* (1858–59, Fitzwilliam Museum, Cambridge).

The theme of women embracing was taken up in one of the artist's designs for the Dalziel Bible project, *Righteousness and Peace Have Kissed Each Other* (c. 1863, see cat. 46a), and several 'aesthetic' works, including *A Prelude by Bach* (cat. 69) and *A Youth Relating Tales to Ladies* (cat. 63).

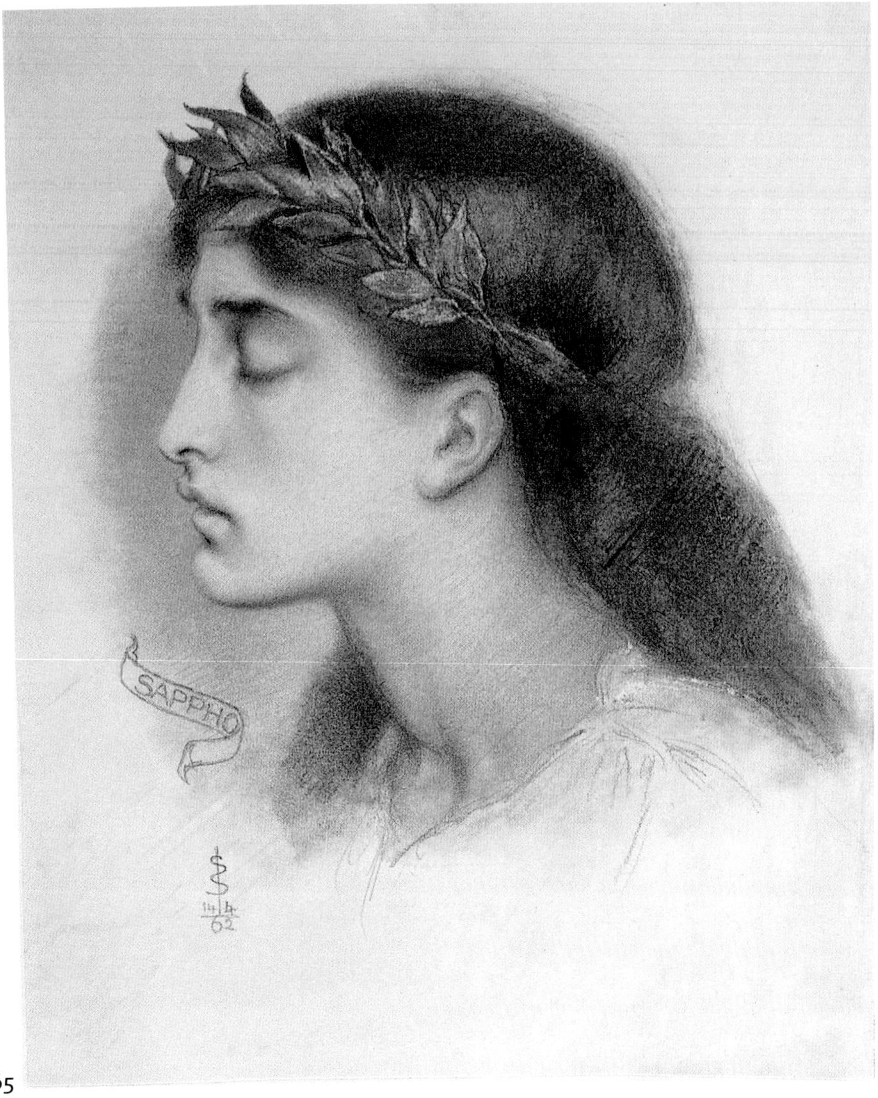

65

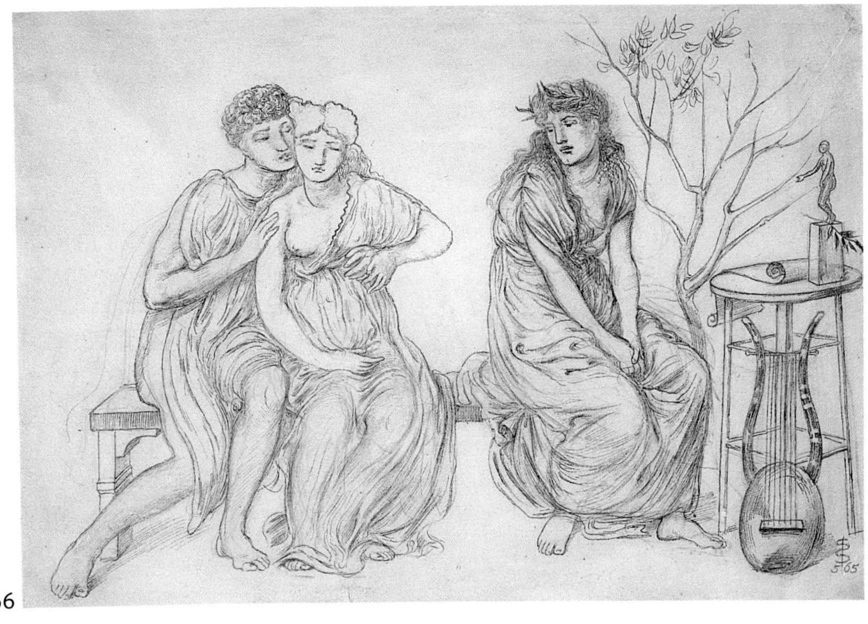

66

65
Study of Sappho
1862
Pencil on paper
26.7 × 20.9 cm (10½ × 8¼ in.)
Signed with monogram and dated *14 4 62* with title inscribed in scroll, lower left
Tate. Purchased 1980

Although cat. 65 appears to be a study for cat. 64, it may have originated as an independent work that suggested the later watercolour. The likeness of the sitter to Jane Morris is striking, although the sitter might have been Keomi, a dark-haired, strong-featured model who sat for Frederick Sandys at this time (see Elzea, 2001, pp. 170–75); there is some similarity between cat. 65 and the painting by Sandys for which Keomi is known to have sat, *Cassandra* (c. 1863–64, Ulster Museum, Belfast).

66
Erinna Taken from Sappho
1865
Pen and ink on paper
23.2 × 32.3 cm (9⅛ × 12¹¹⁄₁₆ in.)
Signed with monogram and dated *5 65* lower right
Dr Dennis T. Lanigan collection, Canada

The event depicted in cat. 66 is entirely imaginary, although Solomon is at pains to depict it as sharply and clearly as his pen will allow. Dennis T. Lanigan identifies the statue on the table (to the right of the composition) as "most likely representing Aphrodite the goddess of Love whom Sappho and her followers worshipped" (*A Dream of the Past*, 2000, p. 205). The pain of Sappho's position might echo that of all those desirous of same-sex love who involve themselves with bisexuals: from the unrequited emotion arises a disappointment that momentarily heightens desire.

67
Frederick Hollyer after Simeon Solomon
Sappho, Atthis and Eros
1865
Photographic print
21.9 × 14 cm (8⅝ × 5½ in.)
Signed with a double sigma and dated *5.65* lower centre right
Private collection

The original drawing for cat. 67 is untraced, and the title is conjectural. This work is a variation on cat. 66, although, in this instance, Solomon shows Sappho staring fixedly at Atthis, who smiles secretly without taking notice of her attentions. Eros, a version of the 'sad Love' motif that appears in several works of around this date (see cat. 111, for example), clings to Atthis, perhaps expressing the hopelessness of Sappho's fixation. Cat. 67 is notable for showing Solomon's acquaintance with Sappho's romantic history; she addressed Atthis by name in several poetic works, now only existing in fragmentary form. The best-known fragment is no. 49, "I loved you, Atthis, once long ago", although Solomon might have had Fragment 131 in mind in designing cat. 67: "Atthis, the thought of me has grown hateful to you, and you fly off to Andromeda" (see Campbell, 1982).

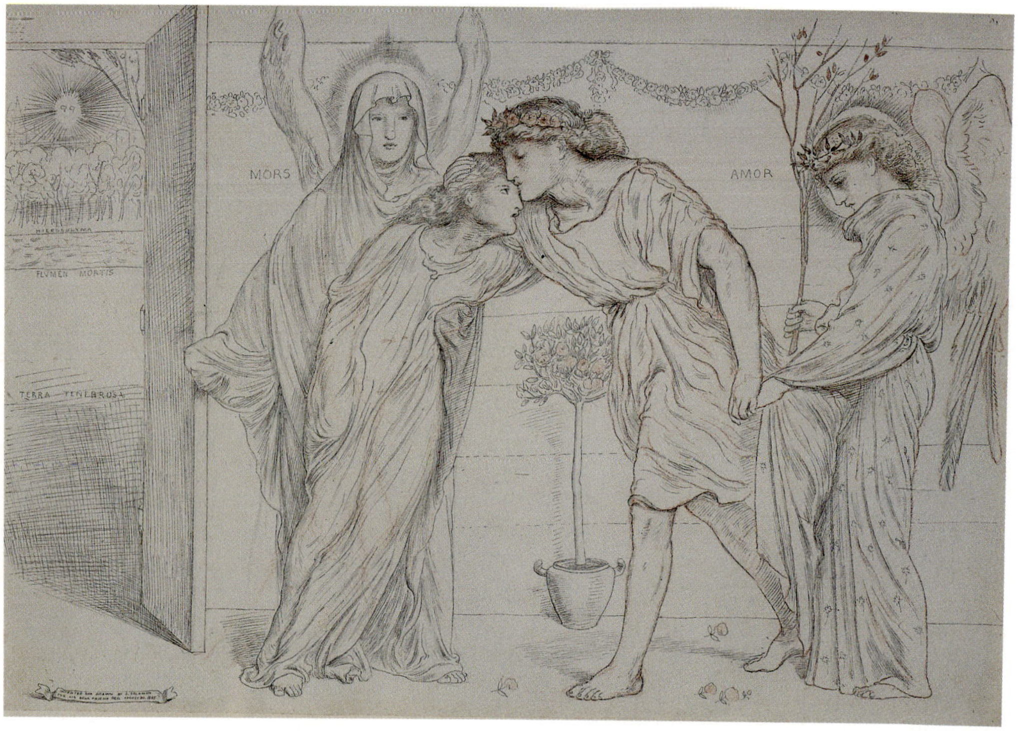

68

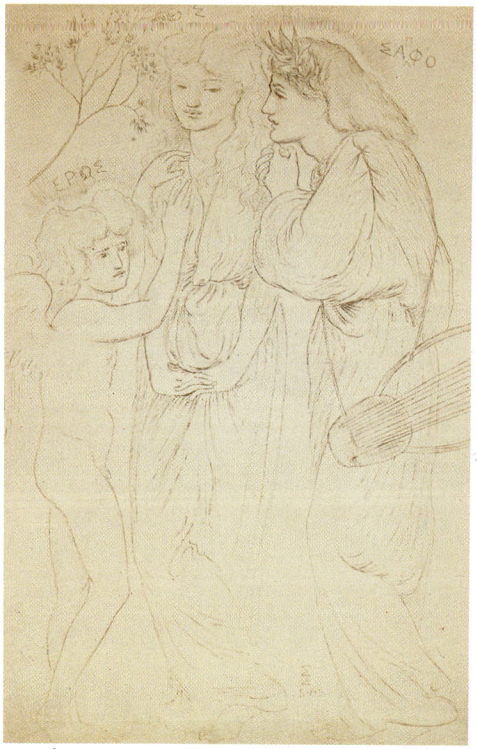
67

68
Mors et Amor (Death and love)
1865
Pen and ink with red crayon on paper
25.3 × 35.4 cm (9¹⁵⁄₁₆ × 13¹⁵⁄₁₆ in.)
Signed and inscribed lower left: *Invented and drawn by S. Solomon for his dear friend Ned August 30, 1865*
Dr Dennis T. Lanigan collection, Canada

The Angel of Death holds open the door to the Land of Shadow for a young woman who is being kissed by her husband while the Angel of Love, head bowed, holds his hand. The subject bears a strong resemblance to Rossetti's *Dante's Dream at the Time of the Death of Beatrice* (1856, Tate); its precise relevance to the recipient of this presentation drawing, Burne-Jones, the 'Ned' of the inscription, is obscure.

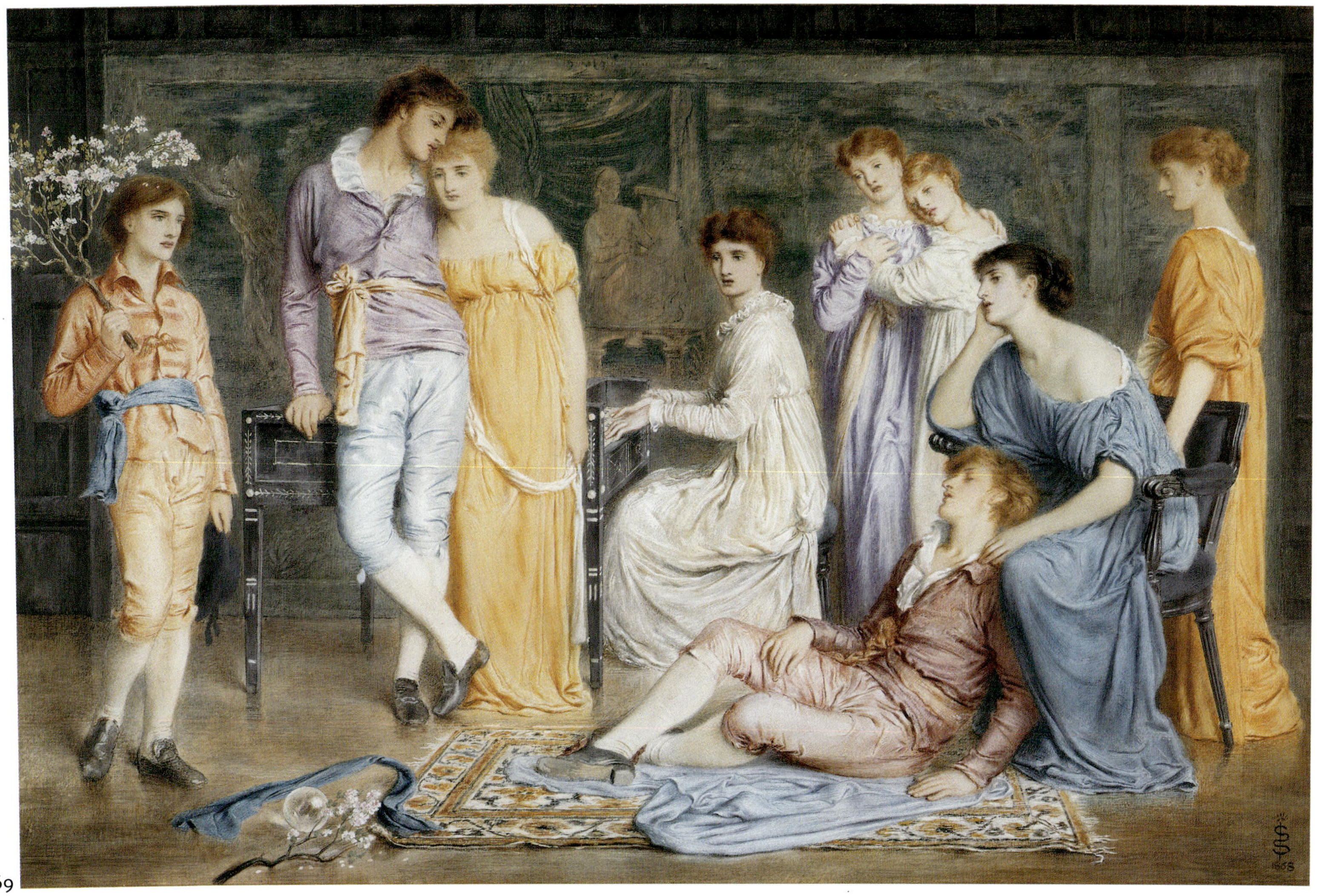

69

69
A Prelude by Bach
1868
Watercolour on paper
41.6 × 63.5 cm (16⅜ × 25 in.)
Signed with monogram and dated lower right
Private collection

Solomon called cat. 69 *A Song of Spring* while he was painting it, and it was exhibited at the Fifth General Exhibition of Water-Colour Drawings at the Dudley Gallery in February 1869 (as no. 111) with the title *A Song*.

The Times dismissed the work as "a bevy of young men and maidens in the Watteauish costumes, in which Cosway and Battoni used to dress their sitters, grouped round a lady at the piano, with the title, 'A Song'" (15 February 1869, p. 4). However, the work is more daring than it seems superficially; not only does it publicly advertise the existence of lesbian desire in its depiction of embracing female couples, but these figures might symbolize, or stand in for, male same-sex desire for Solomon and his circle of friends. The subject of an audience listening to performers as a motif of Aesthetic Movement art has some of its origins in Rossetti's works of the 1850s and 60s; it was taken up by Albert Moore in works like *A Quartet: A Painter's Tribute to the Art of Music*, AD *1868* (1868, private collection).

The pictorial origin of cat. 69 can be found in Botticelli's *Primavera* (c. 1478, Uffizi, Florence), a work that the artist is most likely to have seen on his trip to Florence in 1866–67. The composition echoes Botticelli's, with the central figure taking the place of Venus and the young man at the left Mercury. The work is one of the first public recognitions of Botticelli's genius; previously his work had been overlooked by artists and critics alike (see also cat. 100). Following the 1860s Botticelli's art enjoyed a revival, particularly after the publication of Walter Pater's essay in *The Fortnightly Review* in August 1870, which was to appear in the 1873 and subsequent editions of *Studies in the History of the Renaissance*.

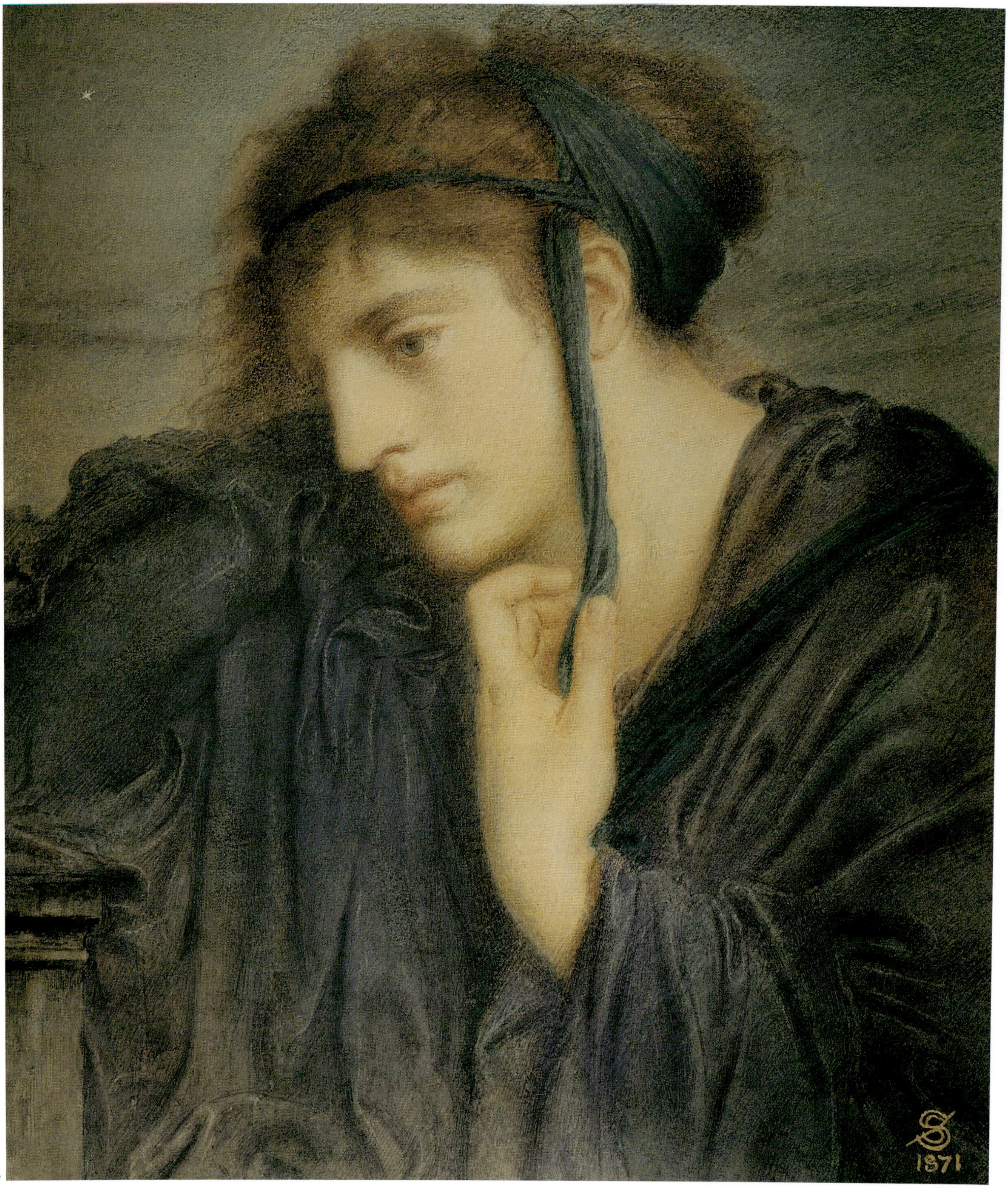

70

70
The Evening Star
1871
Watercolour on paper
30.5 × 24.2 cm (12 × 9½ in.)
Signed with monogram and dated *1871* lower right
The Hearn Family Trust

Also known as *Melencolia*, this might be a depiction of Sappho – the dark hair and strong, firm features correspond to ancient descriptions of the poet; as such, cat. 70 bears a close resemblance to Alma-Tadema's *Sappho* (1881, Walters Art Gallery, Baltimore), which draws on those descriptions.

The title of cat. 70 might be an allusion to one of Sappho's most famous fragments apostrophizing evening. Byron appropriated it in *Don Juan*: "O Hesperus, thou bringest all good things ...". Tennyson, Symonds and Edwin Arnold, among others, borrowed the same lines. However, the expression is more mournful than one might expect from the tone of the fragment, and the painter might be developing another line of thought about Sappho's feelings of loss of her love Erinna, as depicted in cat. 64. The painting's harmonious greys and blacks reflect the melancholic subject.

A pencil drawing and an oil painting of the head depicted in cat. 70 are entitled *A Hebrew Maid* (both private collections).

71
In the Temple of Vesta
1862
Watercolour, bodycolour, graphite and scratching-out on paper
27.6 × 16.7 cm (10⅞ × 6$\frac{9}{16}$ in.)
Signed and dated lower left
Dr Dennis T. Lanigan collection, Canada

Based on Solomon's illustration for *Dalziels' Bible Gallery*, *Jewish Women Burning Incense* (cat. 46b), this watercolour is significant for its classicizing tendency, translating a Jewish subject into a Roman one and marking a change in the narrative intent of Solomon's paintings.

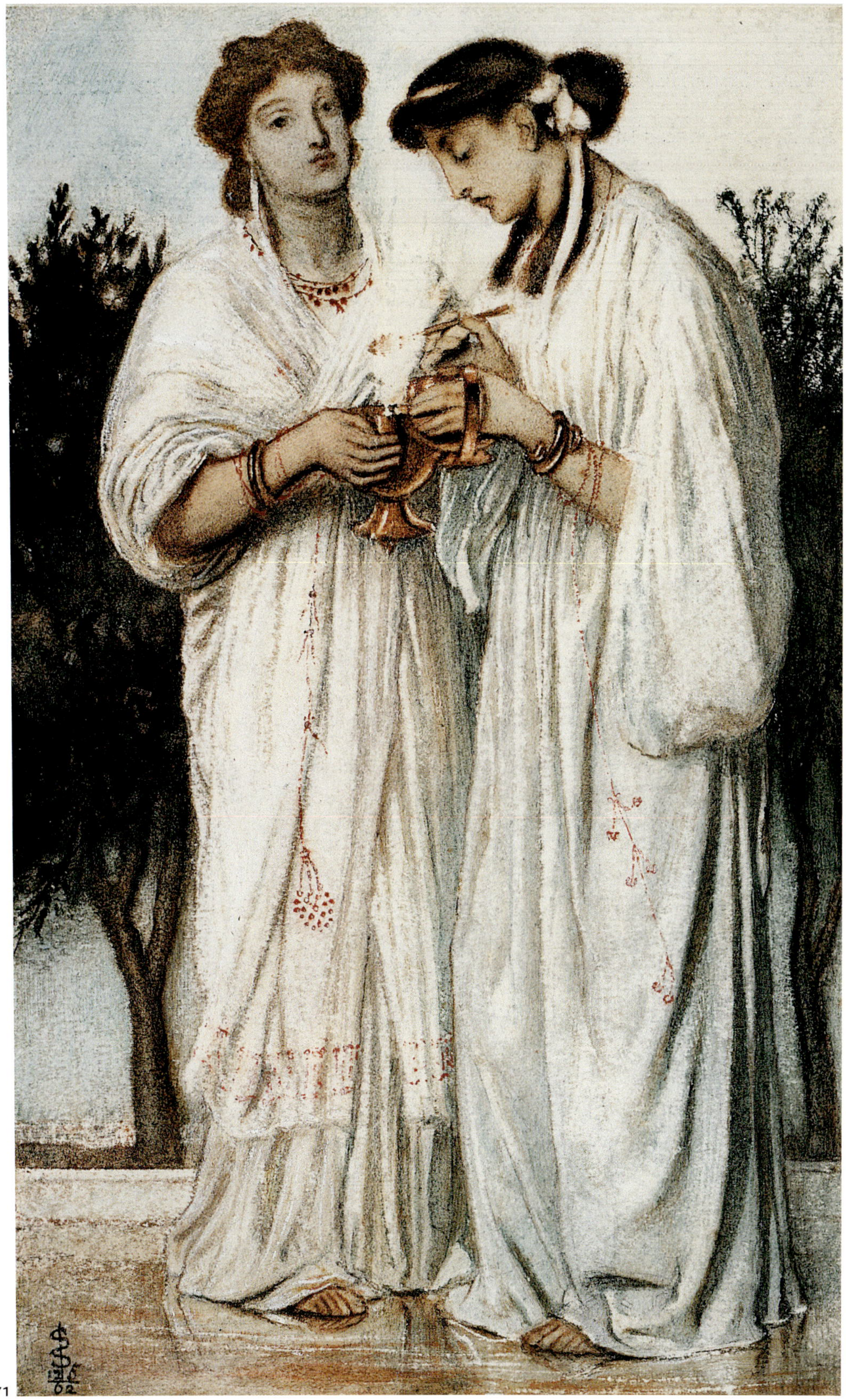

71

72
In the Temple of Venus
1863
Oil on canvas
24 × 17 cm (9½ × 6 11⁄16 in.)
Private collection

This kind of subject became famous in works by Solomon's friend Edward Poynter and, perhaps even more so, in those by the Dutch artist Lawrence Alma-Tadema, resident in London from 1870, whose classical temple and recreation scenes became a key part of late Victorian Royal Academy exhibitions (see fig. 35). Solomon is more modest in his technical range, although this painting has some of the same mixture of historical reconstruction, sentiment and eroticism. The subject stares slightly upwards, as if in prayer, and beyond the viewer, chaste in expression yet tantalizingly revealing her right breast.

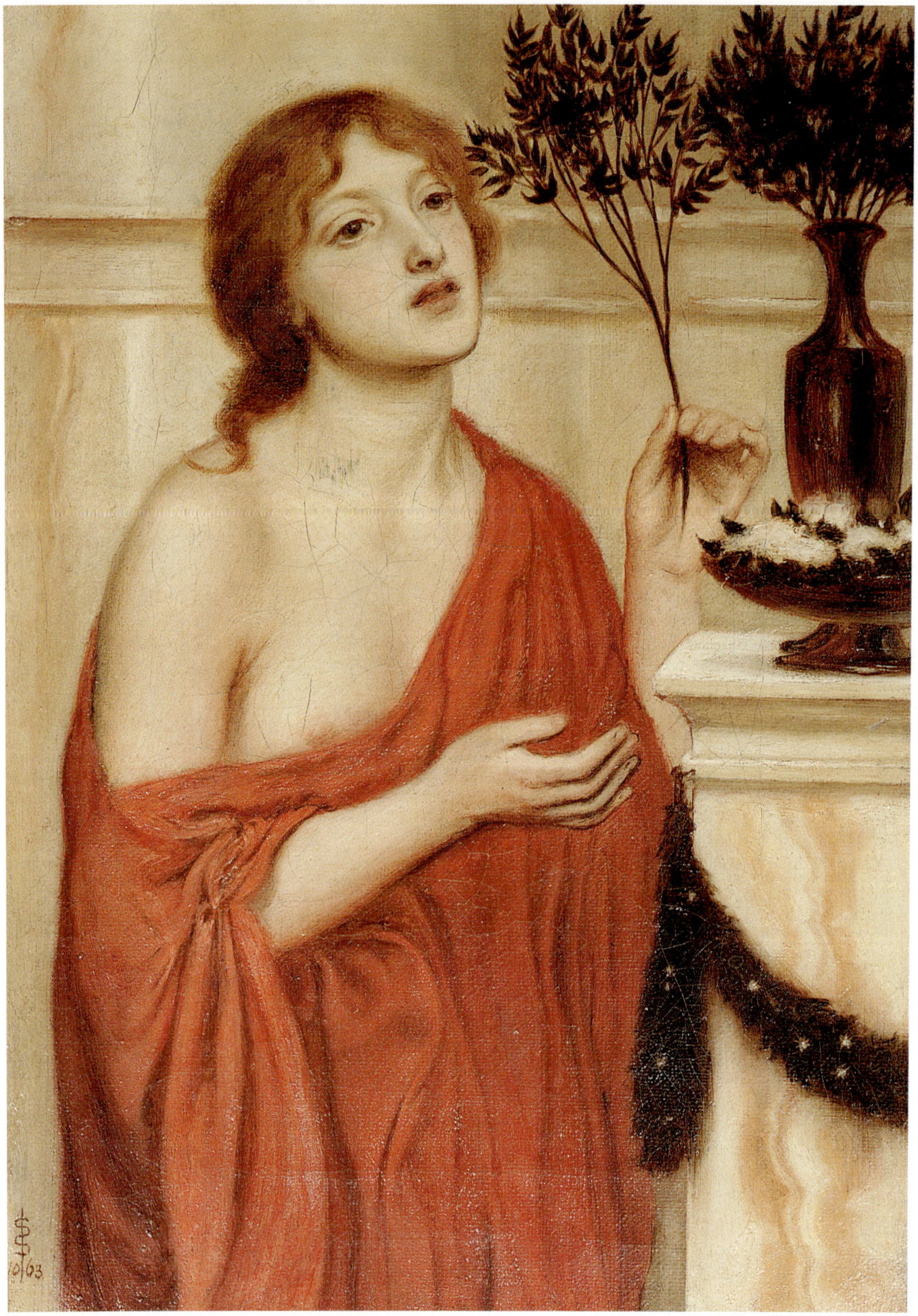

72

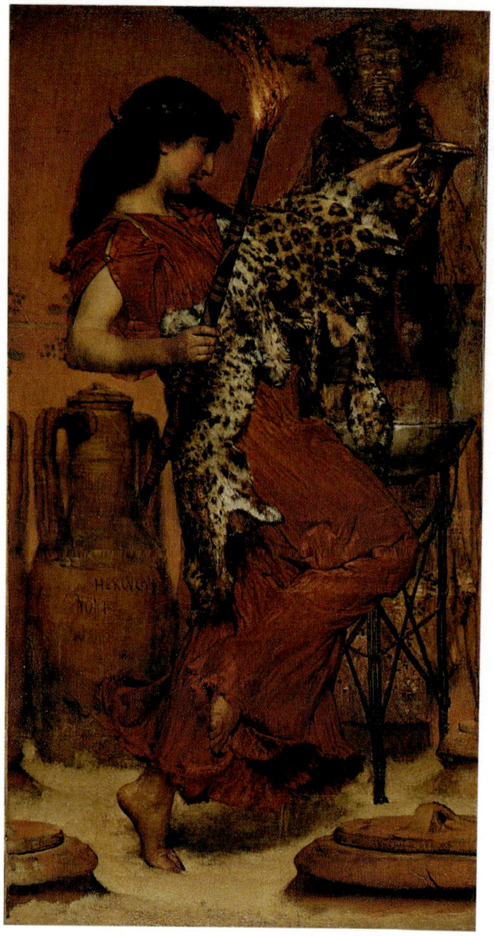

Fig. 35
Lawrence Alma-Tadema (1836–1912)
Autumn Vintage
1877
Oil on canvas
75.3 × 38.1 cm (29⅝ × 15 in.)
Birmingham Museums & Art Gallery

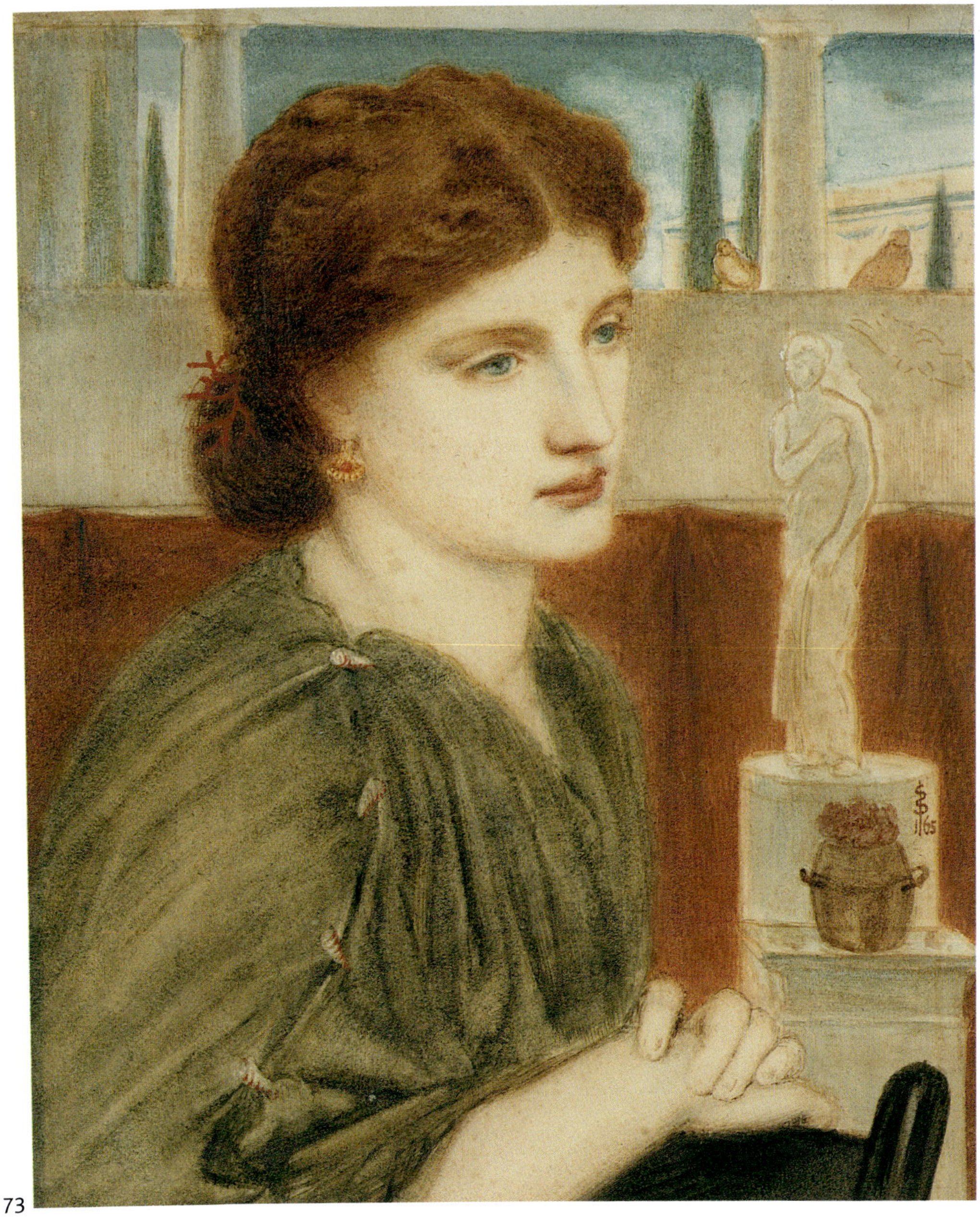

73

73
In the Temple of Venus
1865
Watercolour on paper
25.4 × 19.1 cm (10 × 7½ in.)
Signed with monogram and dated *1/65* lower right
Victoria and Albert Museum

Like cat. 74, this demonstrates the artist's eye for a fancy picture subject, part Rossettian, part *Keepsake* illustration, a mixture that depends on an ambiguous facial expression that mingles sadness and sweetness. As with Rossetti, however, such a subject could help the painter concentrate on colour combinations and harmonies.

74
Girl at a Fountain
1865
Watercolour on paper
33 × 25.5cm (13 × 10¹⁄₁₆ in.)
Signed with monogram and dated *65* lower left
National Museums Liverpool, Lady Lever Art Gallery

F.G. Stephens described cat. 74 as "one of the best instances of [the] artist's powers. It is the figure of a sweet faced damsel in classical draperies, filling a vase of pale opal colour with water at a fountain flowing on our left from a wall of stone. Her pale and passion-worn features retain their sculpturesque character and choice forms; her hazel eyes and full lips seem charged with memories of happiness. Their expression is in keeping with the motives of the design, the colour, and the soft low tones of the picture as a whole" ('The Private Collections of England. No. LXXXI: Mr. W. Coltart's, Woodleigh, Birkenhead', *Athenaeum*, 26 September 1885, pp. 407–408).

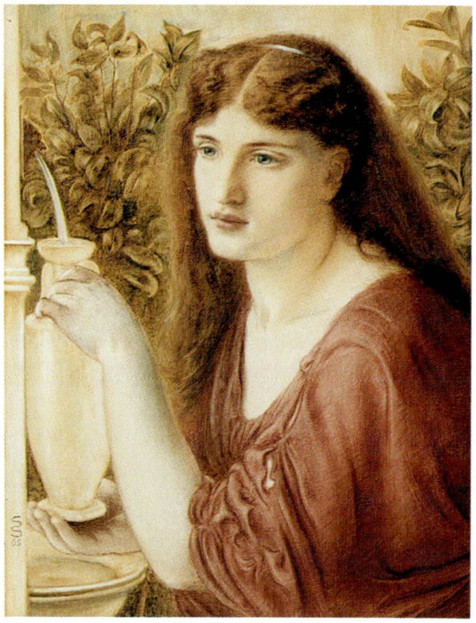

74

75
Habet!
1865
Oil on canvas
101.5 × 122 cm (39⅞ × 48 in.)
Signed *SS* and dated *IIII.LXV* lower right
Private collection (on loan to Bradford Museums, Galleries & Heritage)

Solomon's largest and most ambitious work created a huge amount of press interest when shown at the Royal Academy (as no. 431) in 1865. The subject ostensibly concerns gladiatorial contests in Ancient Rome, but the artist, most probably under the influence of Swinburne (see cat. 29), focuses on the reactions of the viewers, a group comprising aristocrats, a servant and a child. While the facial expressions and reactions are individualized, the overall impression is of impassivity, boredom or perverse sexual enjoyment of death, almost the quintessence of decadence. The central figure of the empress is particularly ambiguous. Similar themes were treated by Swinburne in several poems in his notorious *Poems and Ballads* ('First series', 1866), for example 'Dolores' or 'Faustine', with their images of decadent females addicted to sensuality, bringers of death. Many of these poems had been written several years previously, and Solomon knew them. In his review for *Fraser's Magazine* W.M. Rossetti, describing cat. 75 as "the most conspicuously successful picture, whether classical or otherwise", reminded his readers of Swinburne's Althaea:

> She set her face as a bride's –
> truly a bride of death and of the pit.

The emphasis on the feminine is certainly notable, although the motif of women of various complexions clustering around a central female figure had been explored by D.G. Rossetti in his *The Beloved* (1865–66, Tate).

The *Athenaeum* (1958, 6 May 1865, p. 627) devoted much space to describing and analysing the scene with great enthusiasm, while many other reviewers took the opportunity to reflect on the immorality of Ancient Rome; many believed it to be the artist's strongest work to date. Francis Turner Palgrave, for example, commented in the *Saturday Review*: "A striking scene from the Roman Amphitheatre by Mr Solomon has attracted an attention which its original power well deserves, although some portion of its effect is, we think, due to quaintness – indeed, perhaps, even to that incompleteness in the drawing, and that conventional monotone prevalent in the colouring, which assist in giving the whole a character unlike ordinary work. The heads of the women are too much alike, and one does not distinctly see where the light comes from; perhaps the diffused daylight produced by the 'velarium' is here intended. Allowing, however, for some deficiencies which a strong and conscientious painter will correct as he advances, enough remains to leave an impression of real power" (review reprinted in Palgrave, 1866, p. 111).

A significant number of periodicals expressed dislike for cat. 75, however, among them the *Builder*, whose reviewer noted: "Mr Solomon's fish-blooded monstrous nonentities are horrid mistakes, and all alike; – their apathy quite incompatible with the excitement such savage spectacles entirely owed their popularity to; and he has worked to little end beyond that of immortalizing about the ugliest mode of dressing hair modern European ladies ever adopted. He is a clever artist for all that" (13 May 1865, p. 330: 'The Royal Academy Exhibition').

Four years later Solomon was to exhibit a similar, although less controversial, Ancient Roman subject, *The Toilette of a Roman Lady* (unavailable for this exhibition, see fig. 36). This picture also used the device of a noble woman surrounded or framed by others, contrasting her beauty to theirs (see Elizabeth Prettejohn's essay, p. 41).

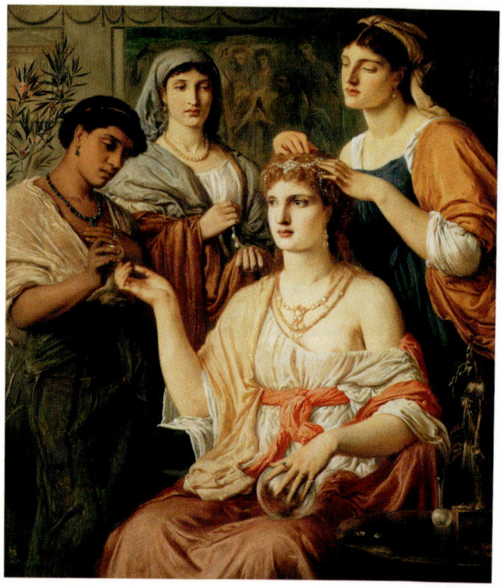

Fig. 36
The Toilette of a Roman Lady
1869
Oil on canvas
111.7 × 96.5 cm (44 × 38 in.)
Delaware Art Museum, Wilmington, USA, F.V. DuPont Acquisition Fund;/Bridgeman Art Library

75
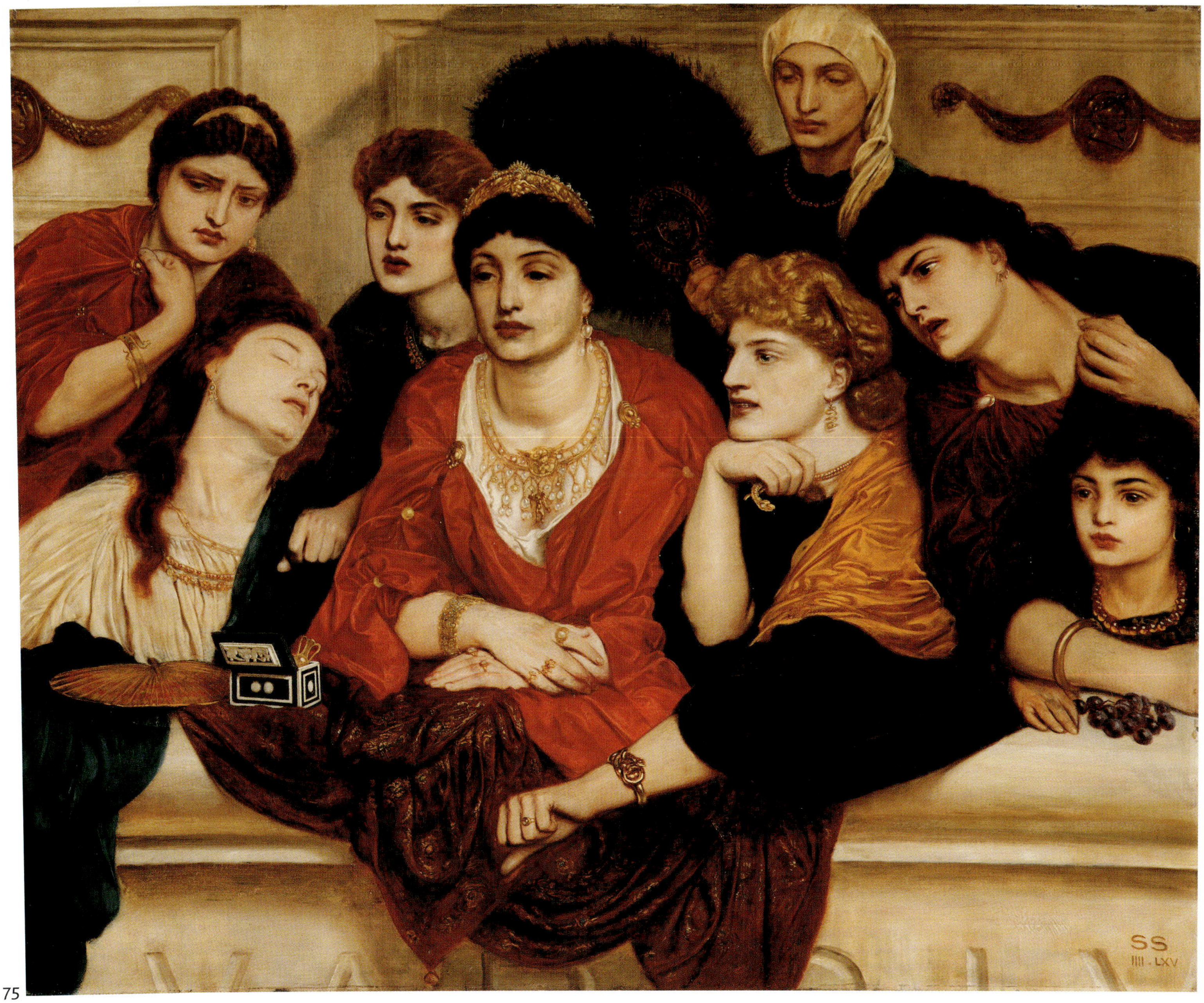

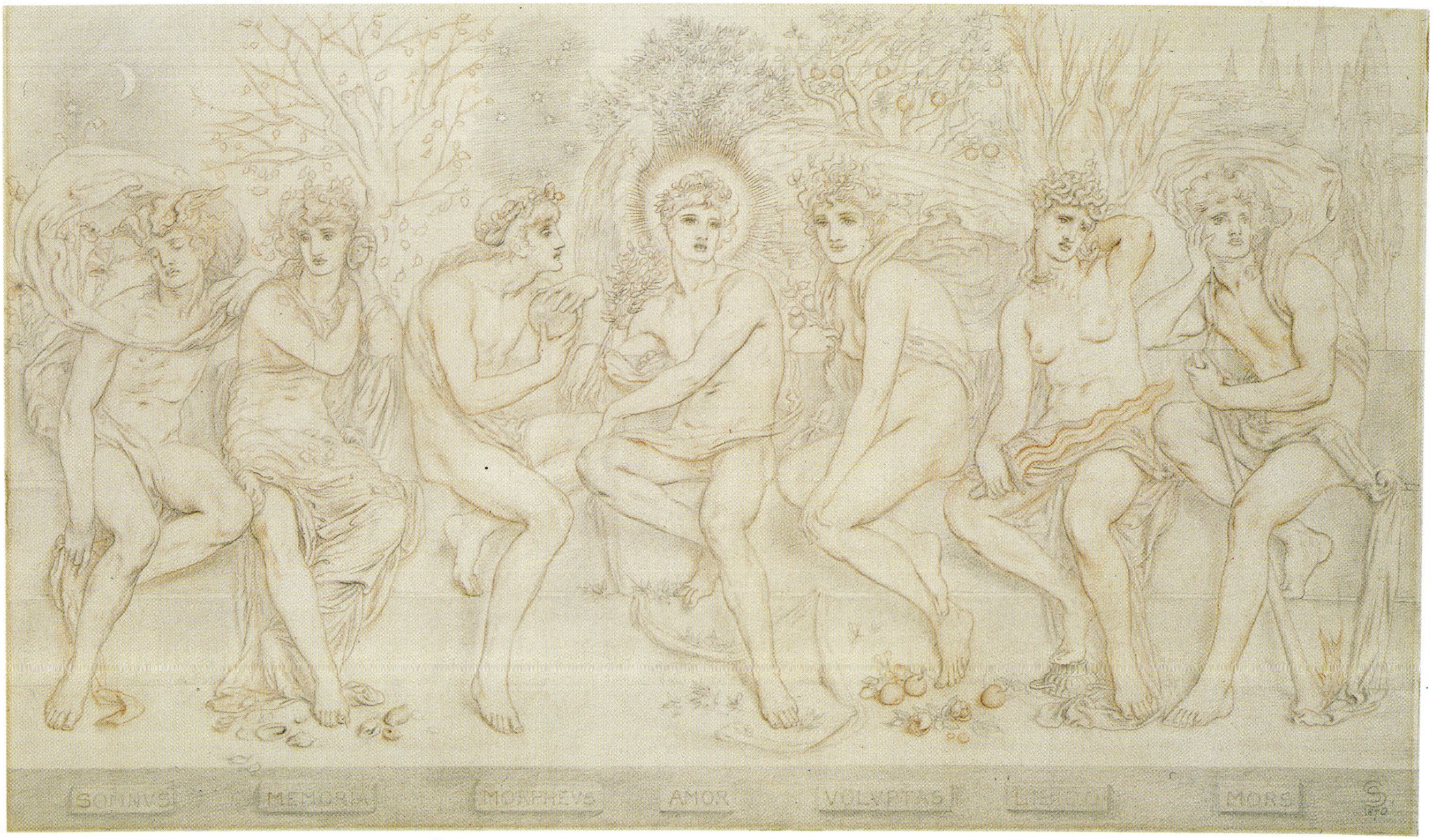

76

76
The Singing of Love
1870
Pencil and red crayon on paper
48.9 × 75 cm (19¼ × 29½ in.)
Signed with monogram and dated *1870* lower right
Birmingham Museums & Art Gallery. Purchased (Alfred Leadbeater Bequest Fund) 1928

Cat. 76 was shown at the Seventh General Exhibition of Water-Colour Drawings, Dudley Gallery, 1871 (as no. 496), oddly juxtaposed with *The Mystery of Faith* (cat. 88), demonstrating the versatility of the artist and his diverging interests. Cat. 76 is an allegory with four male figures and three female representing Somnus, Memoria, Morpheus, Amor, Voluptas, Libido and Mors; their titles are inscribed below their feet. In the centre the winged figure of Love (Amor) is posed holding a branch and, mouth open, appears to be singing.

The *Times* critic disliked the work: "A large pencil drawing by [Solomon], 'The Singing of Love' (496) with Amor for central figure, and on either side an attendant row of genii, ranging from that of dreamless sleep on one side to that of death on the other, has … all the characteristic 'notes' of the painter – the uniformity of feature and expression in the heads, an unpleasant and unmanly suggestiveness in the choice of personifications and their attributes" (11 February 1871, p. 4).

77
Noon
c. 1865
Watercolour on paper
20.7 × 26 cm (8 3⁄16 × 10 1⁄8 in.)
University of Wales, Aberystwyth

Cat. 77 was owned by Solomon's friend and patron, the Welsh landowner George Powell (1842–1882), who also commissioned cat. 101 and 109 from Solomon and cat. 79 from Rebecca Solomon. Cat. 77 is unusual in Solomon's work in its use of the female nude. Three semi-naked female figures stand or sit around a sculpture of Minerva. The atmosphere is one of intense heat.

Cat. 77 strives for the effects of a Whistler harmony or a subjectless idyll by Albert Moore, with whom Solomon was acquainted; it seems deliberately to eschew 'finish', both in academic and Pre-Raphaelite applications, to create its pictorial effects through informality and sketchiness in a manner perfected by Whistler in canvases exhibited from the 1860s onwards.

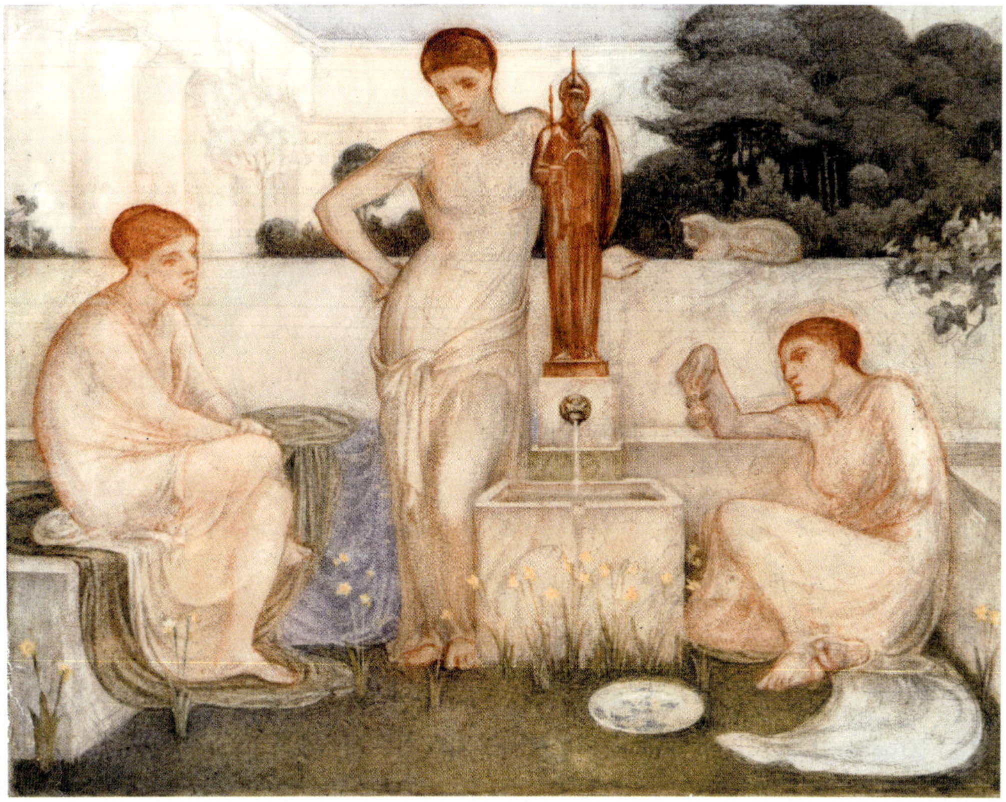

77

78
Swain and Co. after Simeon Solomon
Bookplate for Oscar Browning
1870
Wood engraving
8.5 × 5.7 cm (3 3⁄8 × 2 1⁄4 in.)
Original design signed with monogram and dated, lower left
Private collection

Cat. 78 shows two female figures, one pruning a tree, the other sitting reading a volume with an antique binding; above their heads are scrolls bearing the Latin words *Labor* and *Theoria*, while, in French, a scroll bears the legend *Content Ailleurs*, top right.

Although this is rather crude in drawing, Solomon deliberately kept the design in outline to avoid the alteration of any details by the engraver. His intention was to illustrate "two opposing conditions of mind by only two figures", although he was disappointed by the cutting of the block (undated, unpublished letter to Oscar Browning).

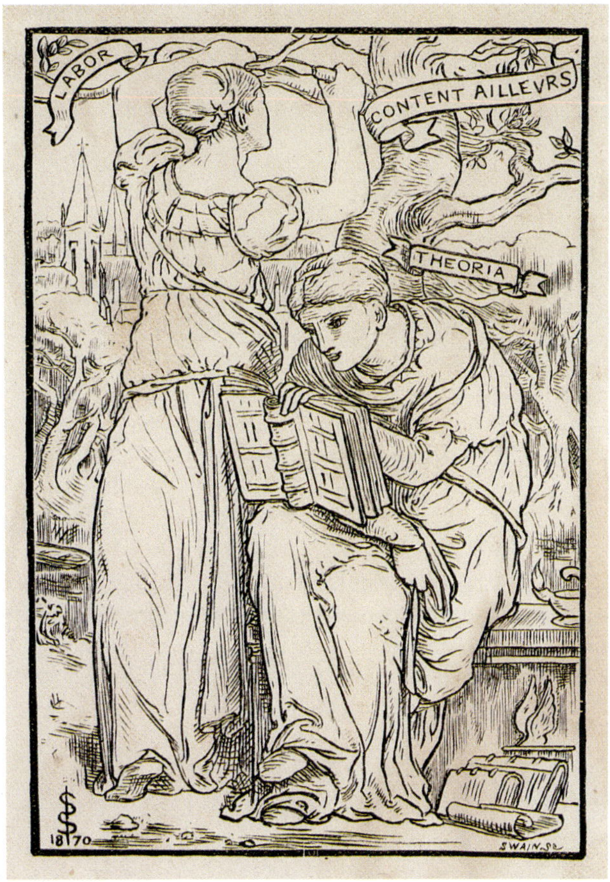

78

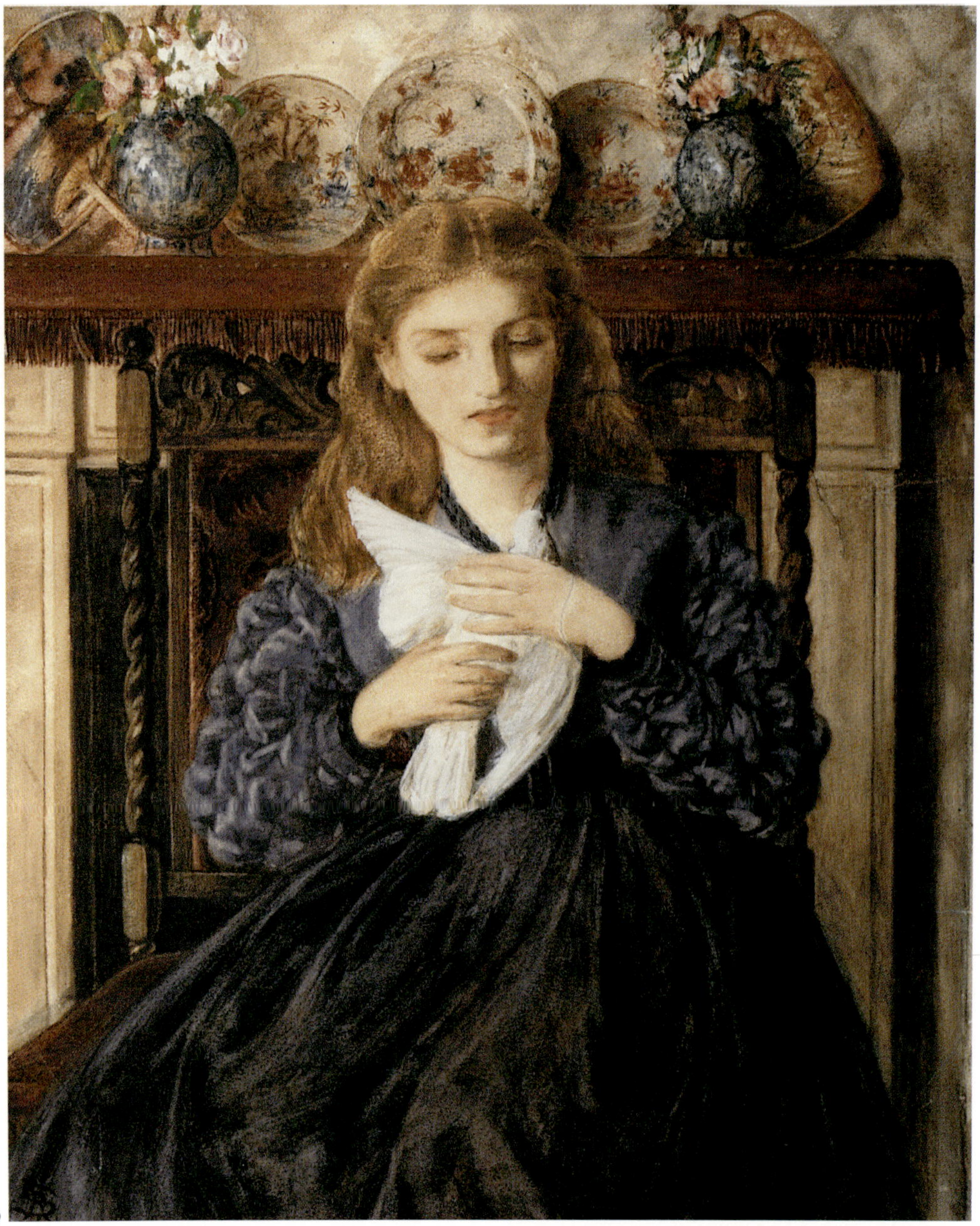

79

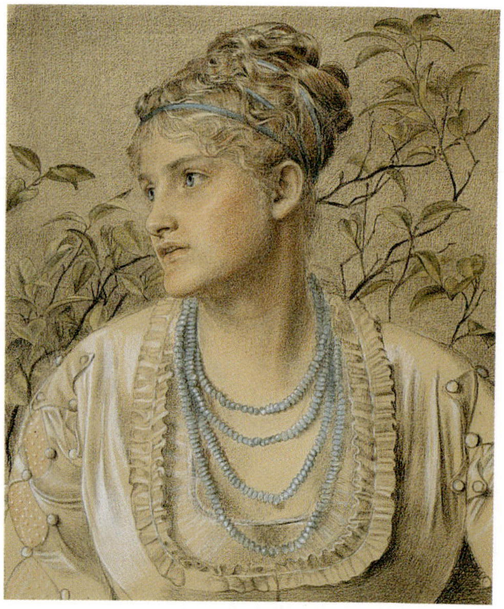

80

80
Frederick Sandys (1829–1904)
Portrait of a Lady (Mary Emma Jones)
c. 1871–73
Coloured chalks on buff paper
48.9 × 39.4 cm (19¼ × 15½ in.)
Birmingham Museums & Art Gallery. Presented by Charles Fairfax Murray, 1904

Although a portrait of Mary Sandys (*née* Jones), this work demonstrates the ambiguity of the model in the later Pre-Raphaelite circle, recognizable yet being used to suggest qualities or ideas rather than a likeness (see Elzea, 2001, p. 249). The emphasis on the details of costume, jewellery and the foliage in the background points to Rossetti's innovations in *Bocca Baciata* (1859, Museum of Fine Arts, Boston); a similar tendency is found in Solomon's pictures of women in the mid-1860s (see cat. 60 and 62).

79
Rebecca Solomon (1832–1886)
The Wounded Dove
1866
Watercolour on thick paper
45.5 × 35.5 cm (17 15/16 × 14 in.)
Signed with monogram
University of Wales, Aberystwyth

Although gaining a reputation with her genre and costume pieces, shown at the British Institution, the Royal Academy and the Dudley Gallery as well as at the annual exhibitions of the Society of Female Artists, Rebecca Solomon sometimes shared 'aesthetic' themes with her younger brother. Cat. 79, which belonged to Simeon Solomon's friend George Powell, demonstrates this occasional closeness in their work. The Chinese plates, fans and fashionable 'advanced' dress are similar to the decorative features in cat. 61, painted the year before.

81
Albert Moore (1841–1893)
Sapphires
1877
Oil on canvas
154.8 × 54.5 cm (61 × 21½ in.)
Signed with anthemion and dated 77 lower left
Birmingham Museums & Art Gallery. Presented by Sir Austen Chamberlain and the Rt Hon. Neville Chamberlain, 1914

One of Moore's "scientifically reasoned chromatic harmonies", as Asleson describes them (Asleson, 2000, p. 140), cat. 81 was shown at the opening exhibition of the Grosvenor Gallery in 1877. For Oscar Wilde, reviewing the exhibition in the Dublin University magazine, Solomon was conspicuous by his absence; Wilde overlooked the fact that his 'fall' some four years earlier meant that he could not have any presence in a respectable exhibition, even at the 'advanced' Grosvenor Gallery. Moore and Solomon converged in various aesthetic experiments and shared models and subjects at the start of their careers.

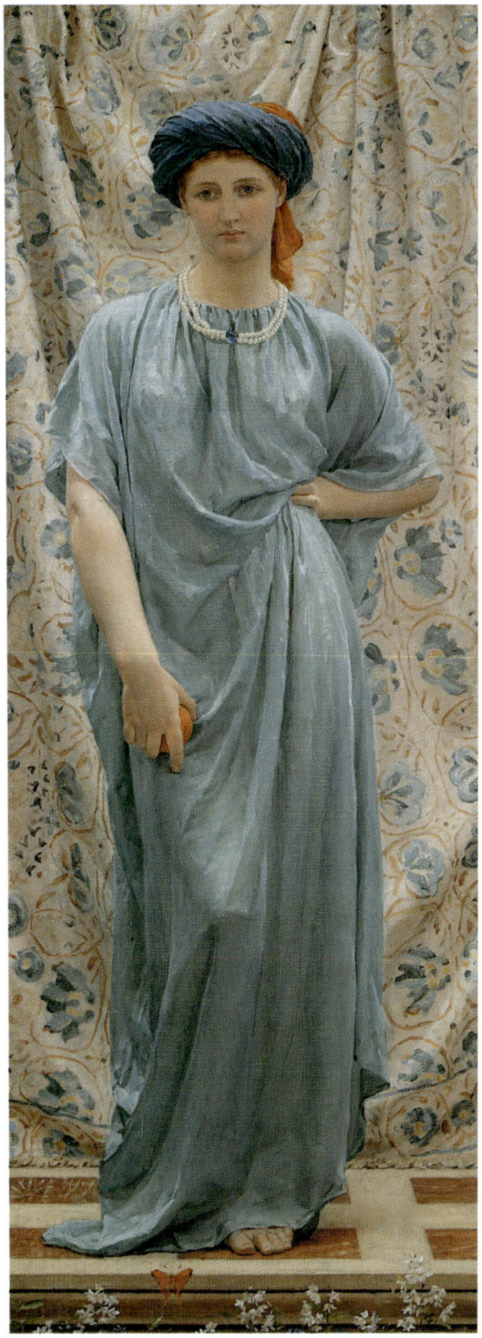

81

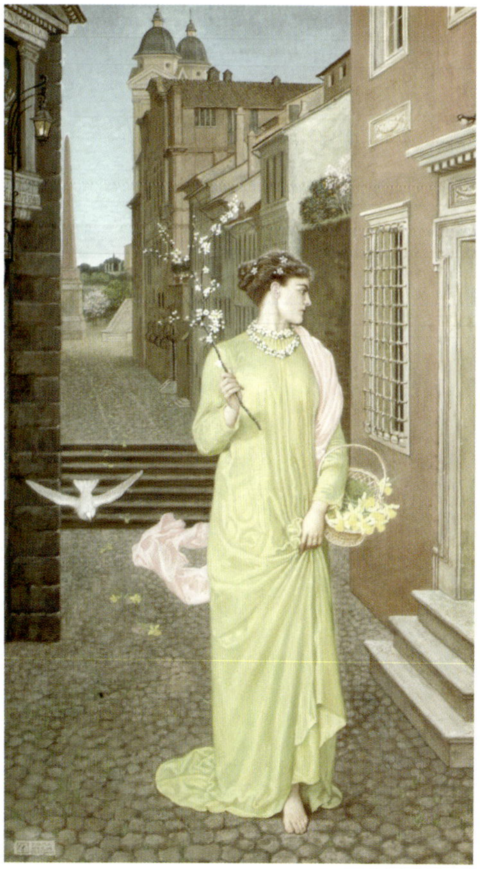

82

82
Walter Crane (1845–1915)
A Herald of Spring
1872
Tempera and bodycolour on paper
59.5 × 32.7 cm (23 7/16 × 12 7/8 in.)
Birmingham Museums & Art Gallery. Purchased (Christina Feeney Bequest Fund) 1929

Crane's technical limitations do not detract from the charm of this allegory, a female figure representing Spring. Cat. 82 has some of the colour harmony ambitions of the work of Moore and Solomon in the previous decade. The wand of blossom held by Spring is reminiscent of Solomon's *A Prelude by Bach* (cat. 69) and other works, and might be evidence of the growing regard for Botticelli, whose *Primavera* is paraphrased in Solomon's painting.

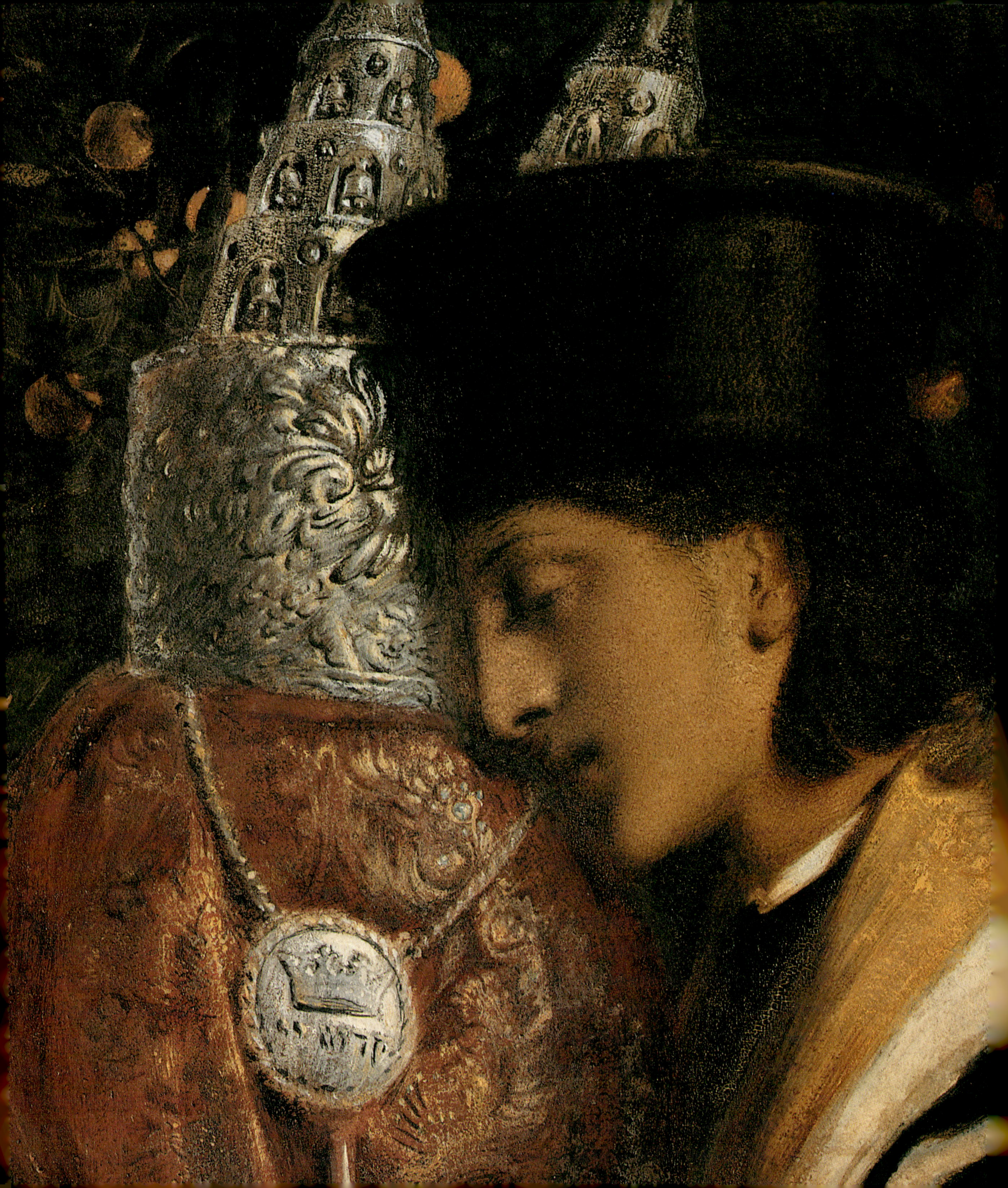

The Dudley and Notoriety

"Unmistakable signs of genius, only run a little mad"

Art Journal, 1868, p. 45

Solomon's paintings had always been greeted with some critical hostility, although that might be accounted for by his identification as a "pre-Raffaelite". These criticisms took issue with 'effeminacy' as well as obscurity of subject-matter. However, this tendency to bad press was intensified as the decade of the 1860s wore on, some critics getting close to libel as they suggested the nature of the artist's temperament and sexuality, some even suggesting madness. The *Illustrated London News* detected "effeminate insanity" in two of the works shown at the Dudley Sixth General Exhibition, which opened in February 1870 (12 February 1870, p. 182).

The Dudley Gallery continued to be the main showcase for Solomon's work; he was briefly a member of the exhibition committee. Solomon became identified as the leader of a new school of figure painting, a kind of Pre-Raphaelitism, but, as the *Times* critic observed,

> a more descriptive title would be 'Archaic', or 'Mediaeval'. It is a school that affects the past in subject, sentiment, and style, down to such minor matters as labelling and framing; its forms are stiff and angular, its colour tending to the funereal or sickly; its ideal of loveliness seems ugliness to the uninitiated, and the last thing it suggests is relish of healthy life, outdoor nature, or cheerful sunlight. It is the outcome in painting of the influences which breed ritualism in worship, what has been called Mort d'Arthurism in poetry, and the worship of Gothic run mad in architecture. ... The minds which continue in it are of the weaklier and more effeminate order.
> (15 February 1869, p. 4)

This section focuses on Solomon's subject paintings featuring male figures, many of them concerning ritual and religion.

94
Carrying the Scrolls of the Law (detail)
1867
Watercolour and bodycolour with varnish on paper
35.5 × 25.4 cm (14 × 10 in.)
Signed and dated *SS Rome 1867*
The Whitworth Art Gallery, University of Manchester

83
Unknown engraver after Simeon Solomon
Two depictions of Jewish ceremonies
1862
Wood engravings
a) **The Marriage Ceremony**
10.4×12.8 cm ($4\frac{1}{8} \times 5$ in.)
b) **Lighting the Lamps, Eve of the Sabbath**
10.2×13 cm ($4 \times 5\frac{1}{8}$ in.)

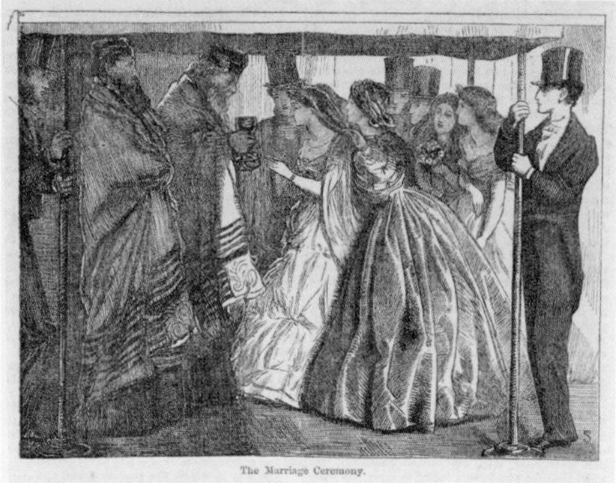

83a

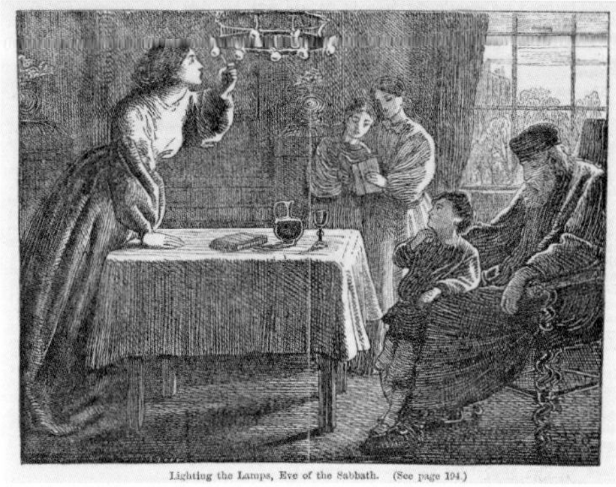

83b

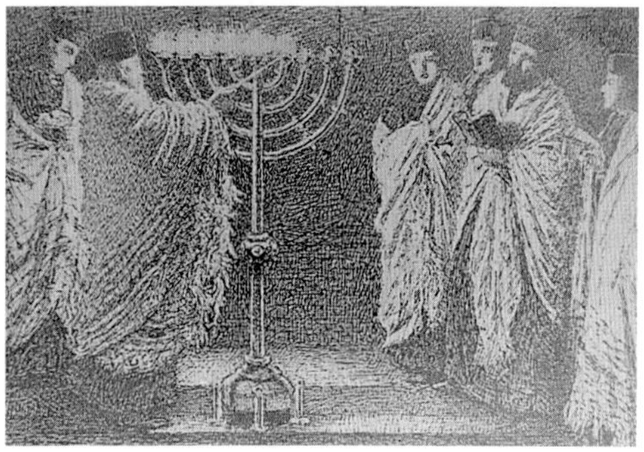

Fig. 37
Coundall, Downes & Co. after Simeon Solomon
The Feast of Dedication (Hanukah)
1862
Photographic print
Courtesy of The Jewish Museum, London

Published in *Once a Week*, VII, 9 August 1862, to illustrate 'Jews in England', pp. 192–93
Birmingham Museums & Art Gallery. Probably bequeathed by J.R. Holliday, 1927

The marriage ceremony takes place beneath a canopy, a *chuppa*, the poles of which are held by male attendants. The *chuppa* symbolizes the groom's home and, on leaving it, the married couple begin their lives anew. In Solomon's illustration much is made of the contrast between the religious garb of the rabbis and the modern, fashionable dress of the bride and her attendants.

The domestic ceremony of the lighting of the lamps defines the aspirations for a peaceful home as well as the continuance of the biblical observance of the Sabbath. The ancient biblical tradition is here acted out in a typical Victorian middle-class setting.

In both illustrations there are observers, a young man in cat. 83a and a child in cat. 83b, a motif introduced early by the artist in descriptions of Jewish ceremonies (see, for example, cat. 8).

In 1862 Coundall, Downes & Co. published ten photographs of Solomon's Jewish subjects (see, for example, fig. 37). Some four years later, Solomon published the images in engraved form in *The Leisure Hour* (XV, 1866, 'Illustrations of Jewish Customs', pp. 73, 168, 217, 329, 377, 476, 540, 604, 653, 823; see fig. 19). These illustrations contain some of Solomon's most intense images of contemporary life. Forrest Reid found them exceptional: "it is a beauty created out of what is not beautiful, which may indeed account partly for its fascination. Its emotion is a kind of nostalgia, a homesickness, a sickness of the soul" (Reid, 1928, p. 104).

84
Dalziel Brothers after Simeon Solomon
Melchizedek Blesses Abram
c. 1863
Wood engraving
17.7×13.5 cm ($6\frac{15}{16} \times 5\frac{5}{16}$ in.)
Signed in the block *SS* (lower left) and *Dalziel* (lower right)
Private collection

Cat. 84 is an engraving made to illustrate the Dalziel Brothers' Bible project. The subject is derived from Genesis 14:17–21.

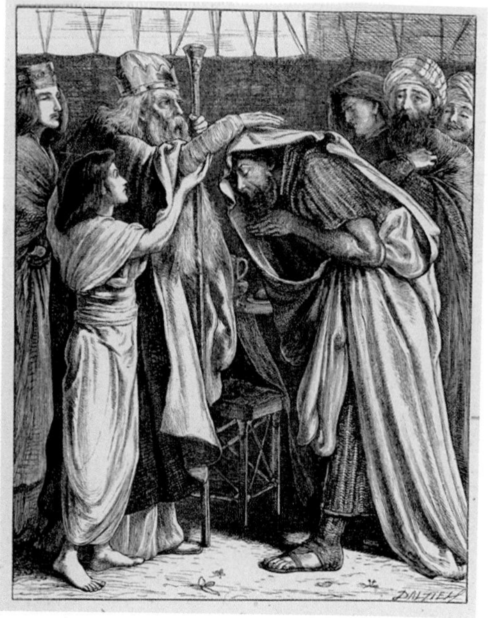

84

The engraving shows the artist's interest in ritual and priesthood, elsewhere depicted in youthful male figures; in this instance, Melchizedek, both king and "priest of God Most High", is distinguished by his age

85
A Deacon
1863
Oil on canvas
35×25.4 cm ($13\frac{3}{4} \times 10$ in.)
Signed with monogram and dated 63 lower right
Birmingham Museums & Art Gallery. Purchased with the aid of a donation in memory of Dr Joseph Li, and supported by the Public Picture Gallery Fund, 2003

Shown at the Royal Academy in 1864 (as no. 273), this painting is one of the artist's first to deal with Catholic or 'High' Anglican religious ritual, although no specific part of the Mass is represented. The emphasis on the dalmatic, the richly embroidered vestment, and on the ritual vessel, probably a pyx or a ciborium, a covered metal vessel containing the reserved eucharistic wafer (the Host), implies that Mass is just about to start and that the Deacon is in the act of placing the Host in the tabernacle on the altar before the priest begins the liturgy. The long, waving hair of the Deacon and his gaunt, ascetic features give him a particularly Pre-Raphaelite appearance, of a kind later to be satirized as typical of the Aesthetic Movement

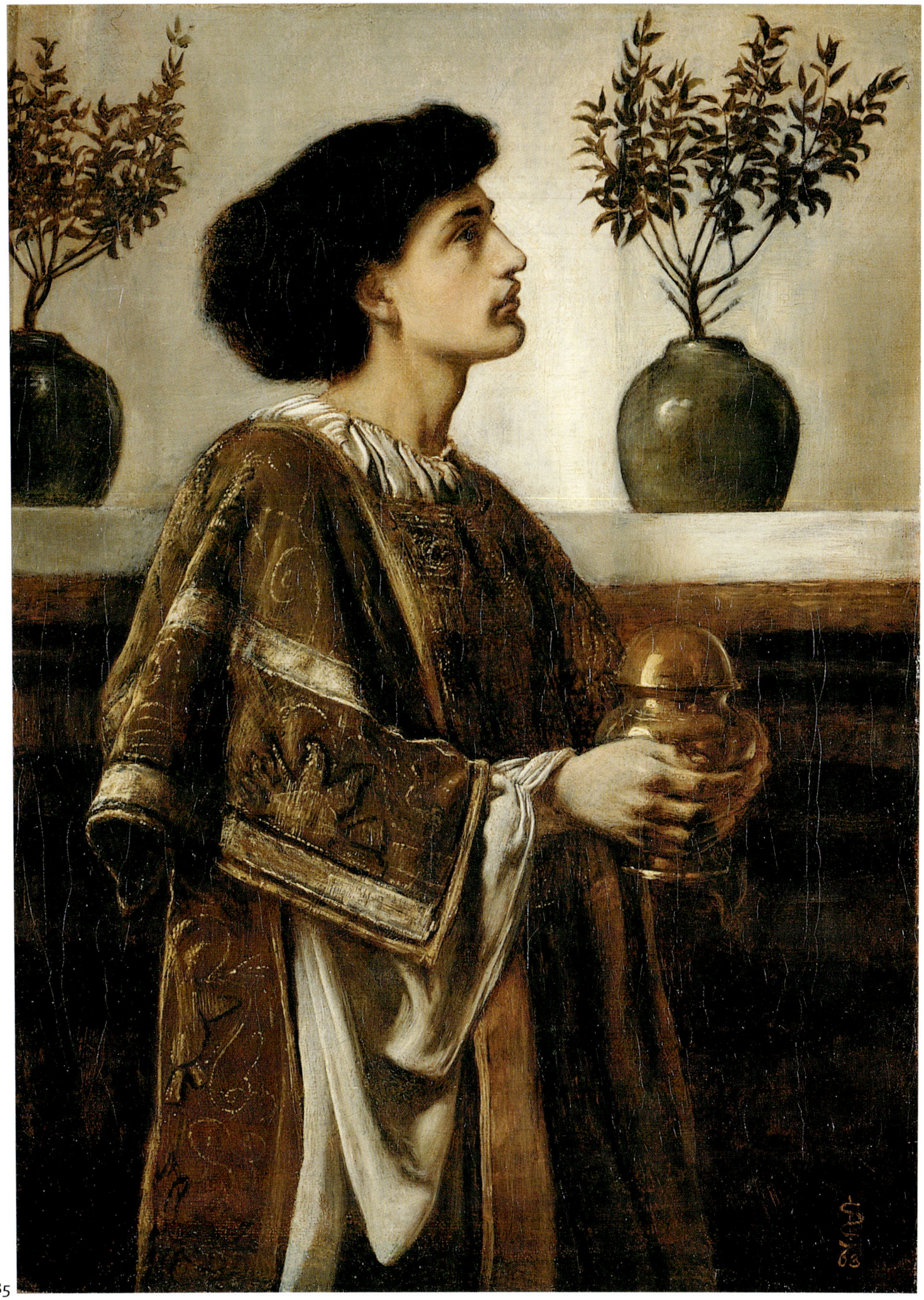

85

male. In this representation Solomon might have been thinking, at least a little, of Father Stanton of St Alban's Church in Holborn, famous for his handsome looks, his austerity and his active role as a leader of the Ritualist movement in the Anglican Church. There might be significance in the choice of green for the vestment, which indicates a particular season in the liturgical calendar, being worn for 'Ordinary Time' after the Epiphany and before Lent or after Pentecost and before the Solemnity of Christ the King. This particular shade of green, a kind of sage, was itself to become one of the Aesthetic Movement's favourites. Some three years after this painting was exhibited *The Times* attacked the Ritualist practices of St Alban's, mentioning the green, gold and yellow vestments, candles and odours as having in them "something almost revolting to an English stomach" (19 October 1866).

Although another painting on religious rituals, Legros's *Ex Voto*, shown at the Royal Academy that same year, was quite extensively reviewed, notices of cat. 85 were sparse. The *Illustrated London News* considered it "originally conceived" (21 May 1864, p. 294), while Francis Turner Palgrave, reviewing the RA for the *Saturday Review*, got the ritual object wrong and clearly thought little of the subject: "Mr Solomon's 'Deacon', a youth holding a censer, is handled with great skill, although with some tendency to blackness in the making out of the forms. We wish that this clever artist would do himself justice by selecting some more important subject" (reprinted in Palgrave, 1866, p. 59). In a letter to her friend Mrs Heimann, Christina Rossetti thought cat. 85 "a fine thing", which, given her own High Church tendencies, might have been expected (Marsh, 1994, p. 208).

86

Two Acolytes, Censing, Pentecost

1863

Watercolour on paper

40.2 × 35 cm (15 13/16 × 13 3/4 in.)

Signed with monogram and dated lower right

The Ashmolean Museum, Oxford

The use of incense, candlesticks and flowers was objected to by a large number of Anglicans between the 1850s and the 1870s. The two acolytes, of contrasting complexions, are treated as portraits, so particular is the treatment of their facial features; one of them has the fashionably long hair of the Pre-Raphaelites, the other, short cropped hair in a style not common at the time. He might be Italian, and the scene might be in a Catholic rather than an Anglican church. The older of the two acolytes is using a thurible full of smoking incense to cense an altar table, a process that takes place after the lighting of the candles (which can be seen in the background). This appears to be a side chapel; the main altar is visible in the background.

The feast of Pentecost celebrates the occasion when the Holy Spirit descended upon the Apostles, following which they dispersed throughout the world to preach the Gospel; its significance here might be that it marked the starting-point or 'birthday' of the Christian Church, hence the solemnity of the young men.

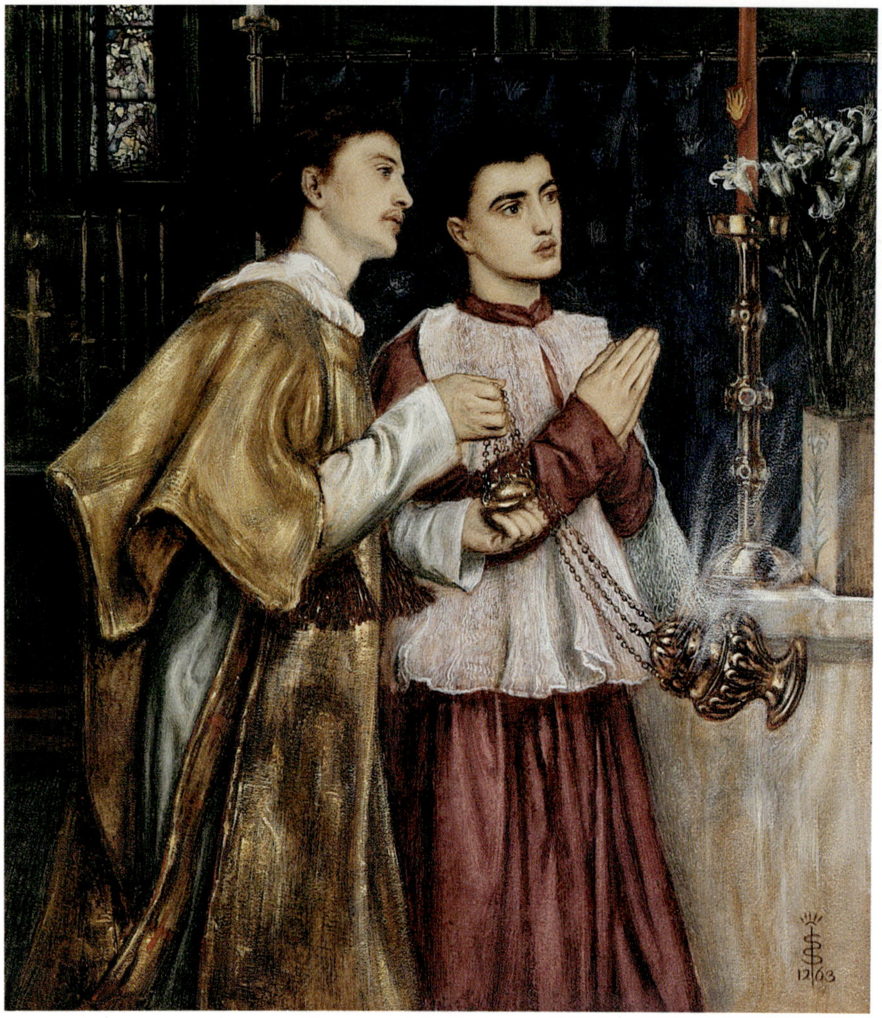

86

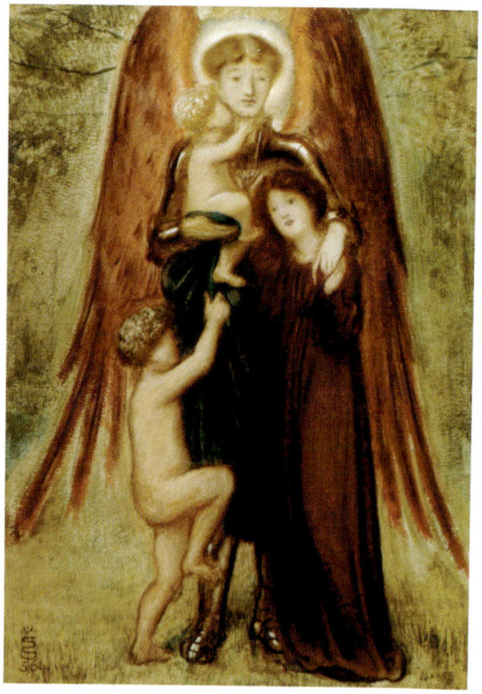

87

87
St Michael of Good Children
1864
Watercolour and gum on paper laid on board
28.8 × 20 cm (11½ × 8 in.)
Signed with monogram and dated *5/64* lower left
Tullie House Museum & Art Gallery

Cat. 87 is a curious work owned by the wealthy industrialist James Leathart, one of the most important patrons of the Pre-Raphaelites. The image of Michael and children might have had special significance for Leathart and might contain a portrait of one of his children. The artist has combined the strong angel image of cat. 40 with the kind of 'gentle' imagery usually associated with Jesus. There are none of the warrior attributes usually associated with Michael the Archangel, the victor over Satan. Michael is, however, venerated by the Jews, so the subject of cat. 87 might have some relevance for the artist himself. Leathart also acquired Ford Madox Brown's *Oure Ladye of Good Children* (1847–61, Tate) at this time and might have sought a companion piece from Solomon.

Cat. 87 is inscribed on the reverse "dedicated to the memory of William Blake". If this is a contemporary inscription, it reminds us that Swinburne was working on his *William Blake: An Essay* at this time, publishing it eventually in 1868 (see also cat. 127), following the participation of both D.G. and W.M. Rossetti in the completion of Gilchrist's *Life of Blake*, published in 1863.

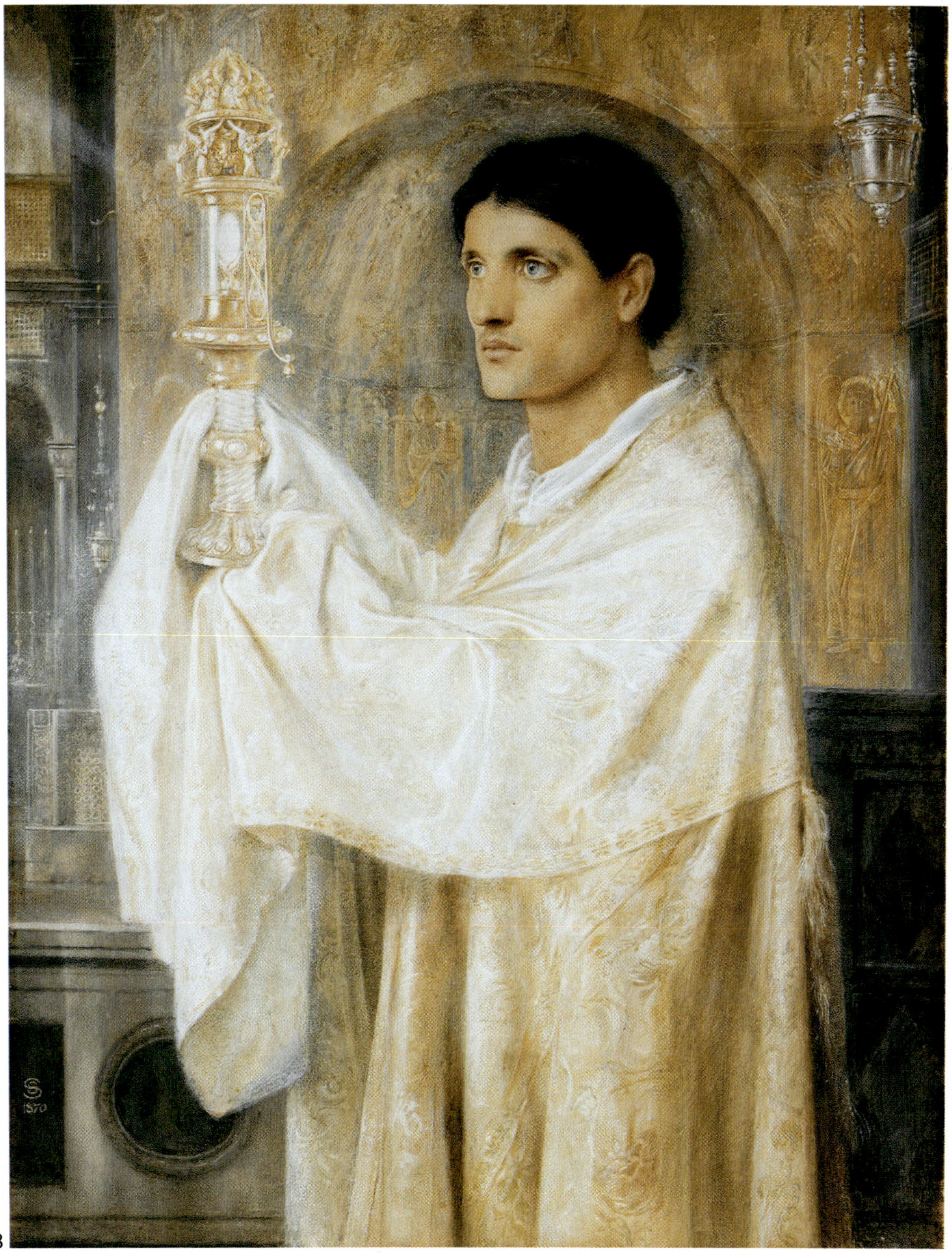
88

88
The Mystery of Faith
1870
Watercolour on paper
50.8 × 38 cm (20 × 14 15/16 in.)
Signed with monogram and dated lower left
National Museums Liverpool, Lady Lever Art Gallery

This most sumptuous of Solomon's paintings is also one of the most subtle, since it is executed almost entirely in white and gold, making it a successor to the 'white experiments' of both Rossetti's *Ecce Ancilla Domini! (The Annunciation)* (1849–50, Tate) and Whistler's *Symphony in White No. 1* (1862, National Gallery of Art, Washington, DC).

Cat. 88 shows a young priest exposing the eucharistic wafer (the 'Host') in a monstrance of curious design, a rock-crystal pillar surmounted by a gold lid in the form of angels with outstretched wings; the occasion would appear to be Benediction (a ceremony of blessing the congregation with the Host) rather than the consecration of the Mass. In both rites, however, the purpose is to convey the central truth that the consecrated Host is the body of Christ in the form of bread. As such it illustrates and reinforces the doctrine of the Real Presence; hence the title of the work. Benediction was a familiar ceremony in the Catholic Church, although it was also practised in All Saints, Margaret Street, as part of a High Anglican ritualistic liturgy.

Shown at the Seventh General Exhibition of Water-Colour Drawings at the Dudley Gallery in 1871 (as no. 89), this work was widely reviewed, most often approvingly. Indeed, its reception marks a high point in Solomon's public career, with reviewers appreciating the deep feeling of the work, the experimental handling of the medium and the colour harmonies.

The *Illustrated London News* said: "It is seldom that so little exception can be taken to a drawing by Mr Solomon as to his 'Mystery of Faith' (89). The mystical tendency of the painter's imagination here finds legitimate expression without resort to symbols of any or no meaning or of objectionable suggestiveness. A priest in the usual golden vestments, and with the usual gleams of light in the background, out of which Mr Solomon always educes artistic harmonies peculiar to himself, stands holding up a monstrance and gazes with speculative eyes at the wafer within. There is very intense and genuine earnestness of expression in the pallid face" (4 February 1871, p. 110).

89
A Coptic Baptismal Procession
1865
Watercolour, bodycolour and gum on paper
26.5 × 42.4 cm (10 7/16 × 16 11/16 in.)
Signed with monogram and dated *65*
Trustees, Cecil Higgins Art Gallery, Bedford

Cat. 89 was shown at the Second General Exhibition of Water-Colour Drawings at the Dudley Gallery in 1866 (as no. 318), with "*vide* Lady Duff Gordon's Letters from Egypt" added to the title. The artist was on the selection committee for this exhibition (but not for the previous or any subsequent exhibition).

The work is unusual in citing a work of travel literature as a source, although the artist might be making the point that such rituals share, to some extent, a common practice throughout the Christian world. The work resembles, too, the design for the *The Rejoicing of the Law* for *The Leisure Hour*, which appeared in the same year (see fig. 38). Cat. 89 was well received by the critics, who noticed it, although it was the exhibition generally, its organization and promise that received most reviewing space.

The *Guardian* critic wrote: "Lady Duff Gordon's Letters from Egypt have suggested to Mr. S. Solomon, in 'A Coptic Baptismal Procession', a subject well suited to his peculiar genius. The priests wear yellow robes and red caps; they carry long tapers, and the light is admitted from above into the corridor along which they are passing" (14 March 1866, p. 289).

The *Art Journal* commented: "The pictures of Mr. Simeon Solomon seldom tread on the confines of the commonplace; ... they generally have about them traits which are decidedly uncommon, and yet perhaps not entirely commendable. 'Medea at Colchis' is certainly strange enough. On the other hand, 'The Coptic Baptismal Procession' has impressive power" (1866, p. 71)

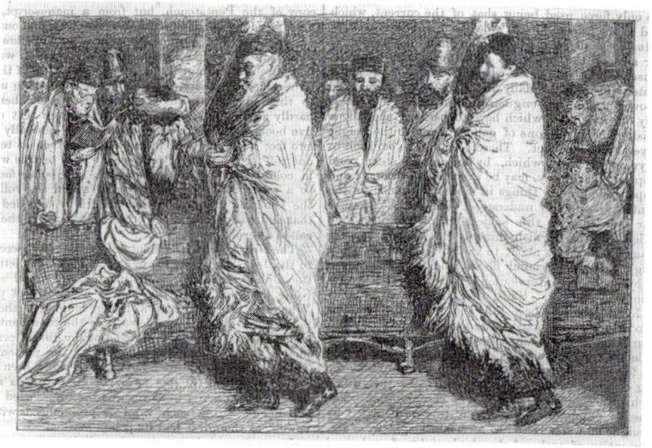

Fig. 38
The Rejoicing of the Law
1866
Wood engraving from a design by Solomon
9.9 × 13.3 cm (3 11/16 × 5 1/4 in.)
Published in *The Leisure Hour*, 1866 (p. 653)
Birmingham Libraries

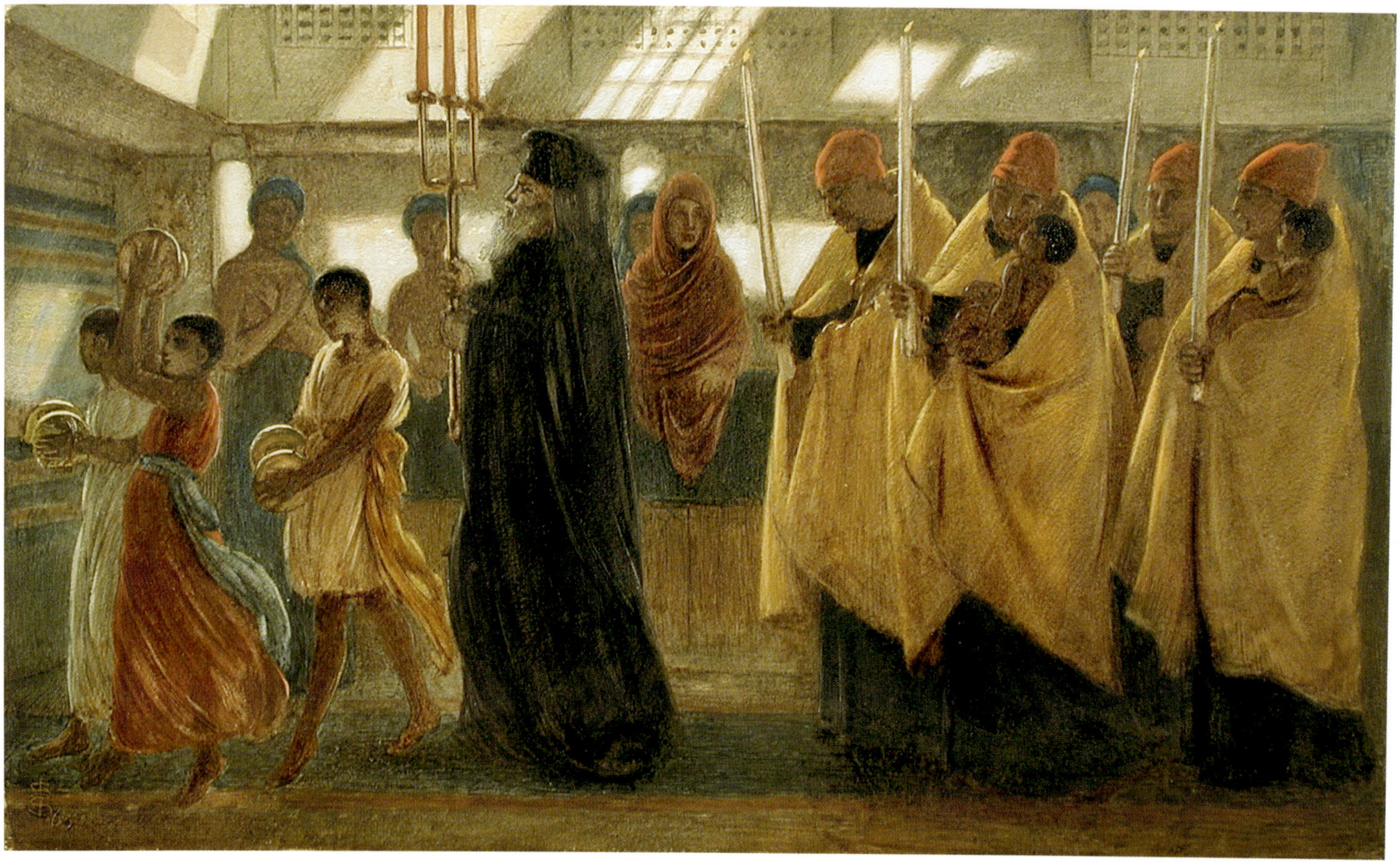

89

90
A Saint of the Eastern Church
1867–68
Watercolour, bodycolour and gum on paper
45.2 × 32.8 cm (17$\frac{3}{16}$ × 12$\frac{15}{16}$ in.)
Signed with monogram and dated *1867–8* lower left
Birmingham Museums & Art Gallery. Presented by the Misses Bunce, 1900

Now known as *A Greek Acolyte*, cat. 90 was first shown at the Fifth General Exhibition of Water-Colour Drawings at the Dudley Gallery in February 1869 (as no. 88), with the title *A Saint of the Eastern Church*. A photograph of the work by Hollyer (example in the Victoria and Albert Museum) bears the title *A Priest of the Orthodox Church*.

The critic of the *Athenaeum* described cat. 90 as "a half-length of a crowned youth holding a flowering branch, and habited in gorgeous Byzantine vestments, and having the long, over-refined face and almond-shaped eyes, to which the artist has often applied his skill. There is a look of luxury about this work which is almost sensual, and is strangely at variance with the assumed monumental character of the ruling idea. If Byzantine art were so voluptuous as this illustration would suggest the face and expression would be apt to the title; as it is, we must accept it, with certain reservations, as a charming study of splendid robes and accessories, with a figure that is almost 'sensational'. It too obviously lacks manliness to satisfy us, even in respect to Art; yet it is very beautiful" (*Athenaeum*, 2154, 6 February 1869, p. 215).

This is one of Solomon's most advanced experiments in colour harmony, confined to brown and black and ochre yet conveying richness and mystery. The iconography is fanciful, with the haloed acolyte, improbably carrying both a thurible and a flowering branch, at once saintly and sensuous. Solomon employs a highly stylized and personal concept of male beauty in which the features combine the stereotypes of Greek Orthodox icons and the emerging classical type of Solomon's imagined ideal.

Cat. 90 was owned by John Thackray Bunce, chairman of the Committee of Birmingham Art Gallery, and given to the gallery by his daughters Kate and Myra. Kate Bunce's best-known work, *Melody* (*c.* 1895, cat. 154), shows a debt to Solomon's painting in its composition and atmosphere of rapt internalization.

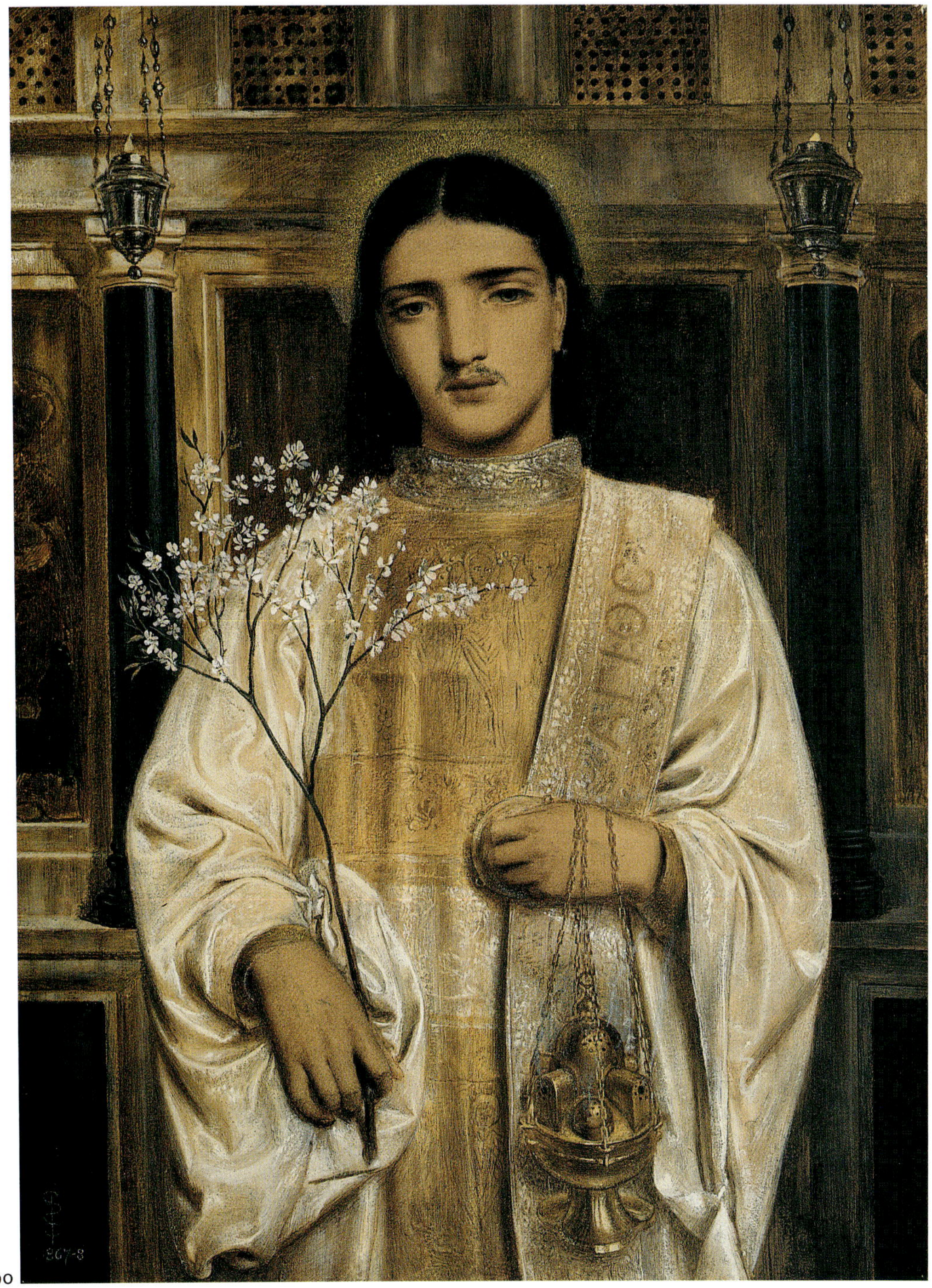

90

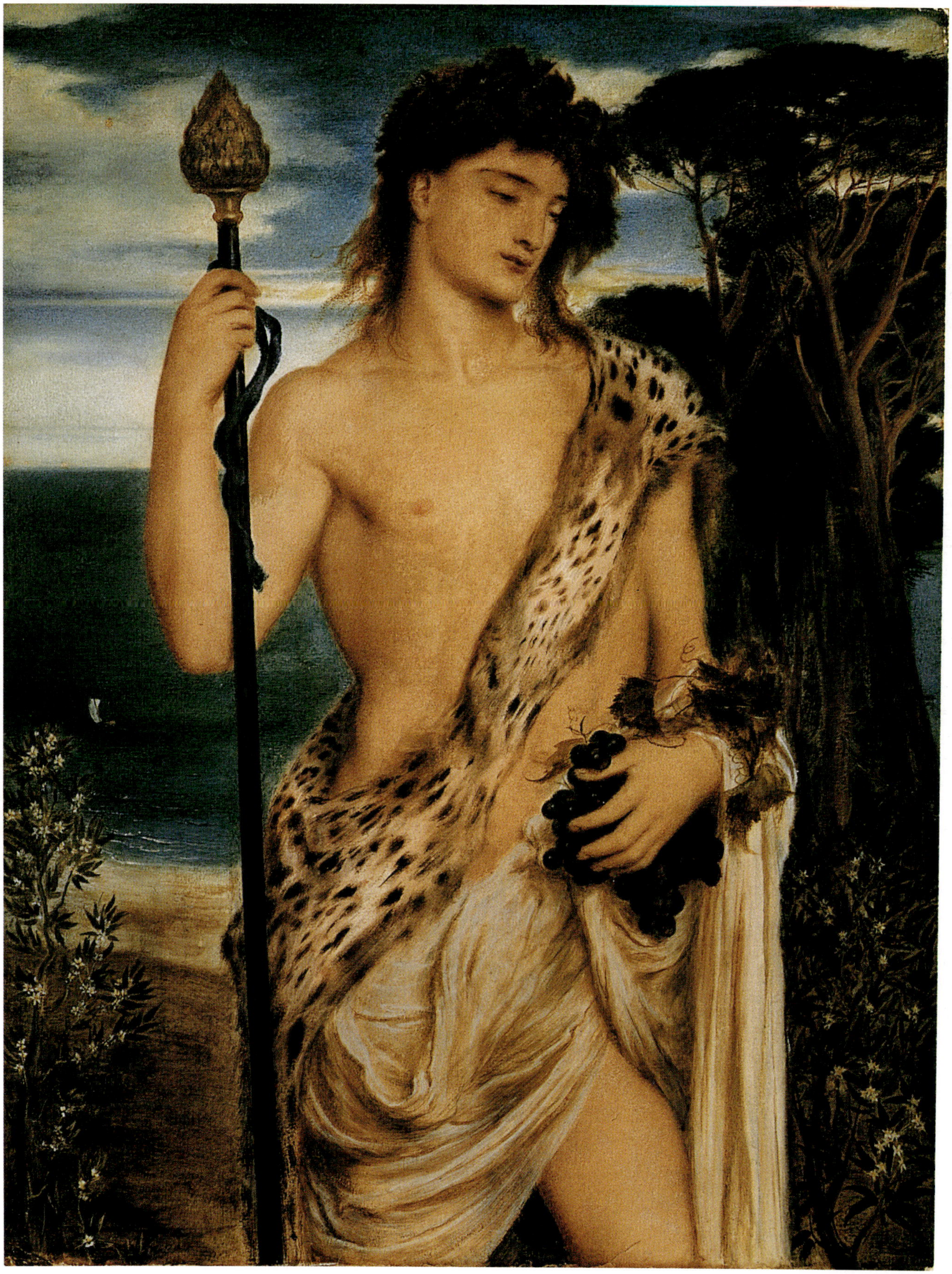

92

91
Bacchus
1867
Oil on wood
50.8 × 37.5 cm (20 × 14¾ in.)
Signed and dated *3/67* lower left
Birmingham Museums & Art Gallery. Bequeathed by Katharine Elizabeth Lewis, 1961

Cat. 91 was first shown at the Royal Academy in the summer of 1867. Although familiar to scholars from Walter Pater's brief but rhapsodic reference in 'A Study of Dionysus', published in *The Fortnightly Review*, xxvi, December 1876, some nine years after its first exhibition (and reprinted in his *Greek Studies* of 1895), cat. 91 was not otherwise reviewed. Pater, who misremembered the year of exhibition, praised Solomon's representation of the god over those of Renaissance painters: "in a 'Bacchus' by a young Hebrew painter, in the exhibition of the Royal Academy of 1868, there was a complete and very fascinating realisation; ... the god of the bitterness of wine, 'of things too sweet'; the sea-water of the Lesbian grape become somewhat brackish in the cup."

The work is oddly compelling, partly because of the ill-matched eyes (a tendency found increasingly in later works by the artist) and the curious shift between naturalism and idealism. The dawn sky might indicate a poetic idea of the coming of Christ, his triumph over paganism and the displacement of Bacchus himself, which would account for the sadness on the face of the young god.

Bacchus is chiefly known as the god of wine, although he originated as a god of fruit trees and fertility, but there were other attributes that might have made him appealing to Solomon and his admirers. While absolutely central to the understanding and worship of nature, Bacchus shares notable characteristics with his other aspect, Dionysus, which would have been known to Solomon's circle. Dionysus was 'effeminate', having been disguised as a girl during a part of his childhood, and bisexual.

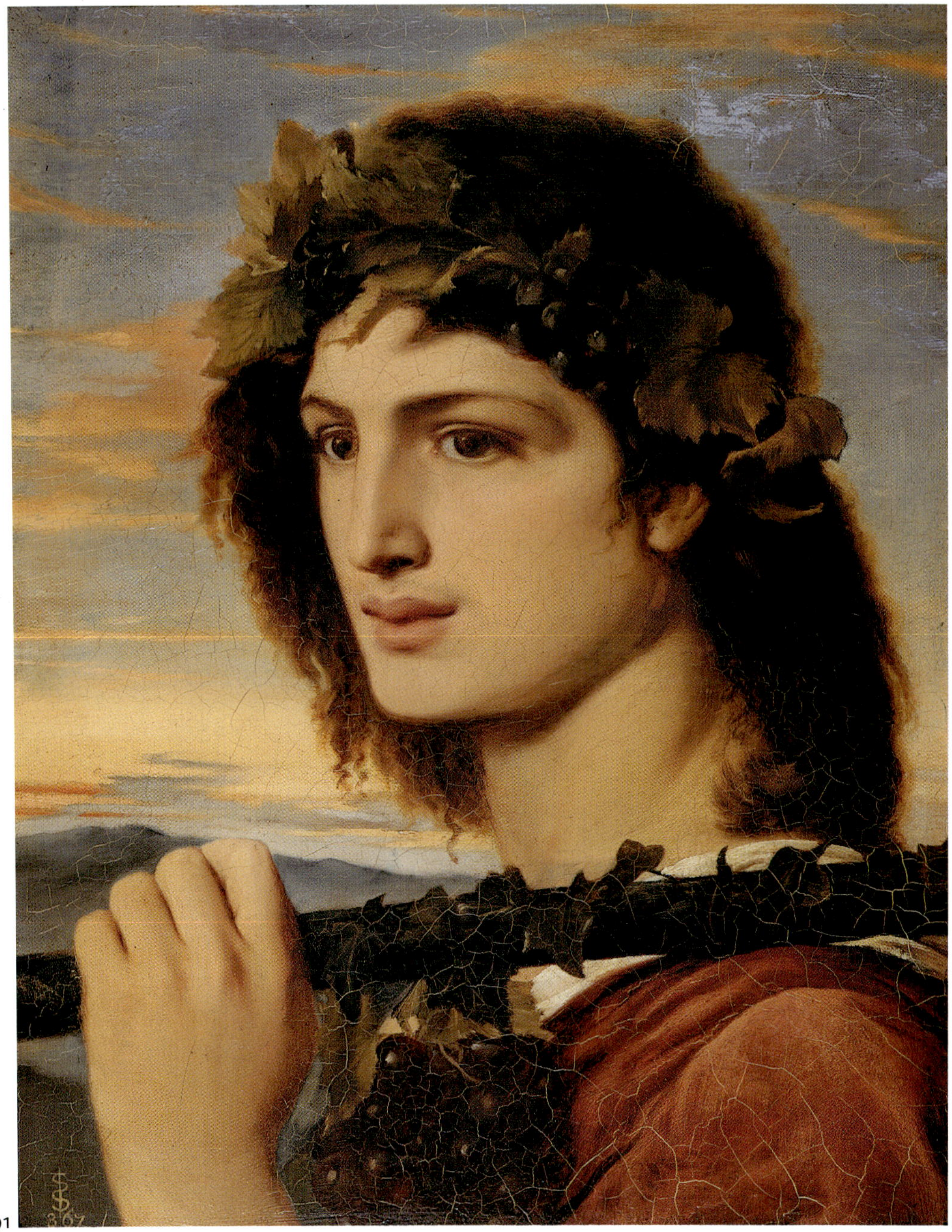

91

92
Bacchus
1867
Watercolour on paper
50.2 × 37.5 cm (19⅜ × 14¾ in.)
Seymour Stein

Cat. 92 was shown at the Fourth General Exhibition of Water-Colour Drawings at the Dudley Gallery in 1868 (as no. 70). The catalogue gives this text from William Morris's *Jason*:

By thee the unnamed smouldering fire
Within our hearts turns to desire,
Sweet, amorous, half-satisfied;
Through thee the doubtful tears untried
Seem fair to us and fortunate,
In spite of death, in spite of Fate.

Solomon recommended Morris's poem to the poet, anthologist and collector Frederick Locker Lampson on his return from Italy in 1867 (undated letter, Beinecke Rare Books Library, Yale University).

The Morris quotation is only tentatively related to the subject of cat. 92, although it might indicate that the picture was intended to represent Antinous, the lover of Emperor Hadrian, dressed as Bacchus. Swinburne noted such a representation: "In the 'Sacrifice of Antinous', he officiates before the god under the divine disguise of Bacchus himself; the curled and ample hair, the pure splendour of faultless cheek and neck, the leopard skin and thyrsus, are all of the god, and godlike; the mournful wonderful lips and eyes are coloured with mortal blood and lighted with human vision. In these pictures some obscure suppressed tragedy of thought and passion and fate seems latent as the vital veins under a clear skin" ('Simeon Solomon: Notes on his "Vision of Love" and Other Studies', *The Dark Blue*, I, July 1871, pp. 573–77).

R. St John Tyrwhitt, writing in *Contemporary Review*, compared Solomon with Leighton: "The same effect [as in Leighton's *Actaea* – a contrast between flesh and sea] is beautifully given in Mr Solomon's Bacchus at the Dudley. We don't know why he is not represented in the Academy, but we think it can hardly be the fault of his picture, if he sent one in" ('Pictures of the Season', *Contemporary Review*, VIII, 1868, p. 340).

93
Heliogabalus, High Priest of the Sun and Emperor of Rome, 118–122 AD
1866
Watercolour on paper
46.4 × 29.2cm (18¼ × 11½ in.)
Signed with monogram and dated *1866* lower right
Private collection

Cat. 93 was shown at the Fourth General Exhibition of Water-Colour Drawings at the Dudley Gallery in 1868 (as no. 252). The title given here appears in the Dudley catalogue.

Cat. 93 shows Elagabalus, who as emperor was known as Aurelius Antoninus, leaning languidly on a plinth; in his left hand he holds an incense-burner, or thurible. His expression, half-closed eyes and secretive smile seem to sum up the Roman Decadence, as does the dark and richly glinting setting of a temple. The subject demonstrates Solomon's interest in religious ritual (see cat. 88 and 90 especially), here given a surprising twist – the ritual of sun-worship. The emperor's cross-dressing and sexual ambiguity are hinted at in the pose and costume.

The artist wrote from Leghorn in Italy to his patron Leyland about the work: "I have at length finished [the] picture of 'Heliogabalus'. I hope to [your] satisfaction. It should have reached you sooner but I have lately been [some]what unsettled in leaving England and coming to Florence where I intend for a time to stay and work" (letter dated September [of probably 1866]; see also Colin Cruise's essay, p. 57).

The Dudley exhibition of that year was generally regarded as challenging. The *Illustrated London News* commented: "A small group of painters we have yet to notice, including Messrs. Solomon, Donaldson, Wooldridge, Bateman, and Stanhope, who adopt a less natural and rational method. For direct, unsophisticated art they seek to substitute a roundabout antiquarianism and those accidents of earlier art so dear to the dilettante charlatan. In a false conception of mediaeval art they retain the Gothic shell and throw away the kernel; servilely imitating the involuntary shortcomings, they ignore the spirit and aims of the primitive painters. The results of this wrong-headed affectation are curiously apparent in the treatment of classical themes" (8 February 1868, p. 134).

The *Art Journal* singled out Solomon in this general tendency in new painting: "Eccentricity has always distinguished the Dudley Gallery. And what can be more singular and abnormal than the productions – clever withal – of Simeon Solomon, Spencer Stanhope, C.P. Slocombe, C. Rossiter, A.B. Donaldson, and H.E. Wooldridge? Solomon is a genius of eccentricity, he can do nothing like other people, and in being exclusively like himself, he becomes unlike to nature. As for choice of subject, most religions of the world have struck by turns the painter's fantastic and splendour-loving fancy. On the present occasion 'Bacchus', 'A Patriarch of the Eastern Church', and 'Heliogabalus, High Priest of the Sun', obtain from the painter about equal favour, whether as to ritual, robes, or anatomies. The latter, however, would not be recognised by the College of Surgeons" (1868, p. 45).

On the other hand, several critics viewed cat. 93 as a picture mostly about colour and experimentation with techniques.

The *Times* critic thought Solomon "an artist of real power, however quaintly and grotesquely employed. He is fond of ringing the changes on special scales or gamuts of colour. Thus, his 'Bacchus', his 'Greek Priest', his 'Heliogabalus', in the glowing robes of a high priest of the Sun, are so many exercises in the key of gold, and very skilfully managed for the most part they are" (4 February 1868, p. 4).

The reviewer of the *Builder* commented: "For manipulative dexterity parts of 'Heliogabalus, High Priest of the Sun and Emperor of Rome 118–22 A.D.' by Simeon Solomon, are a marvel" (8 February 1868, p. 95: 'General Exhibition of Water-colour Drawings').

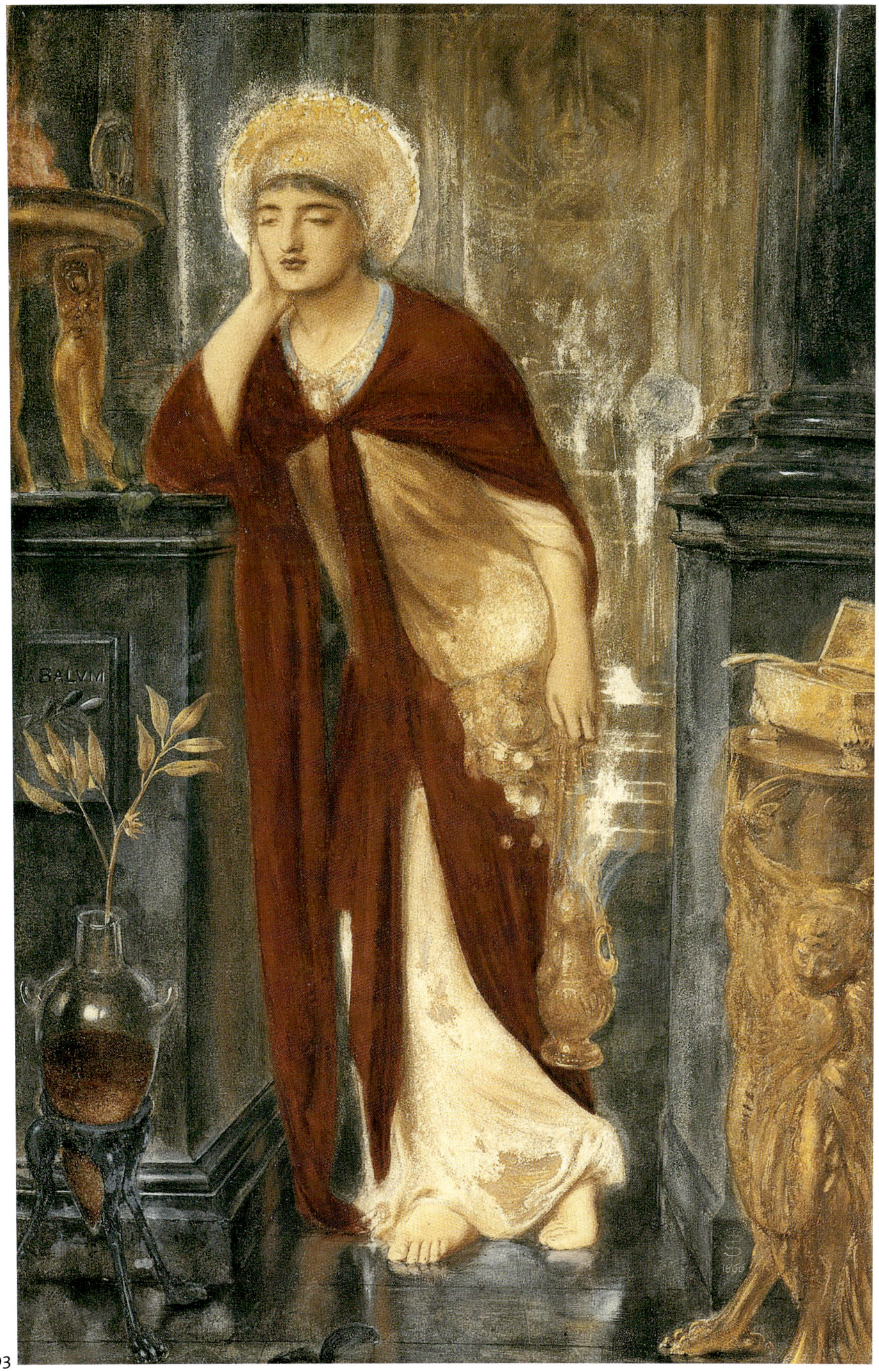

93

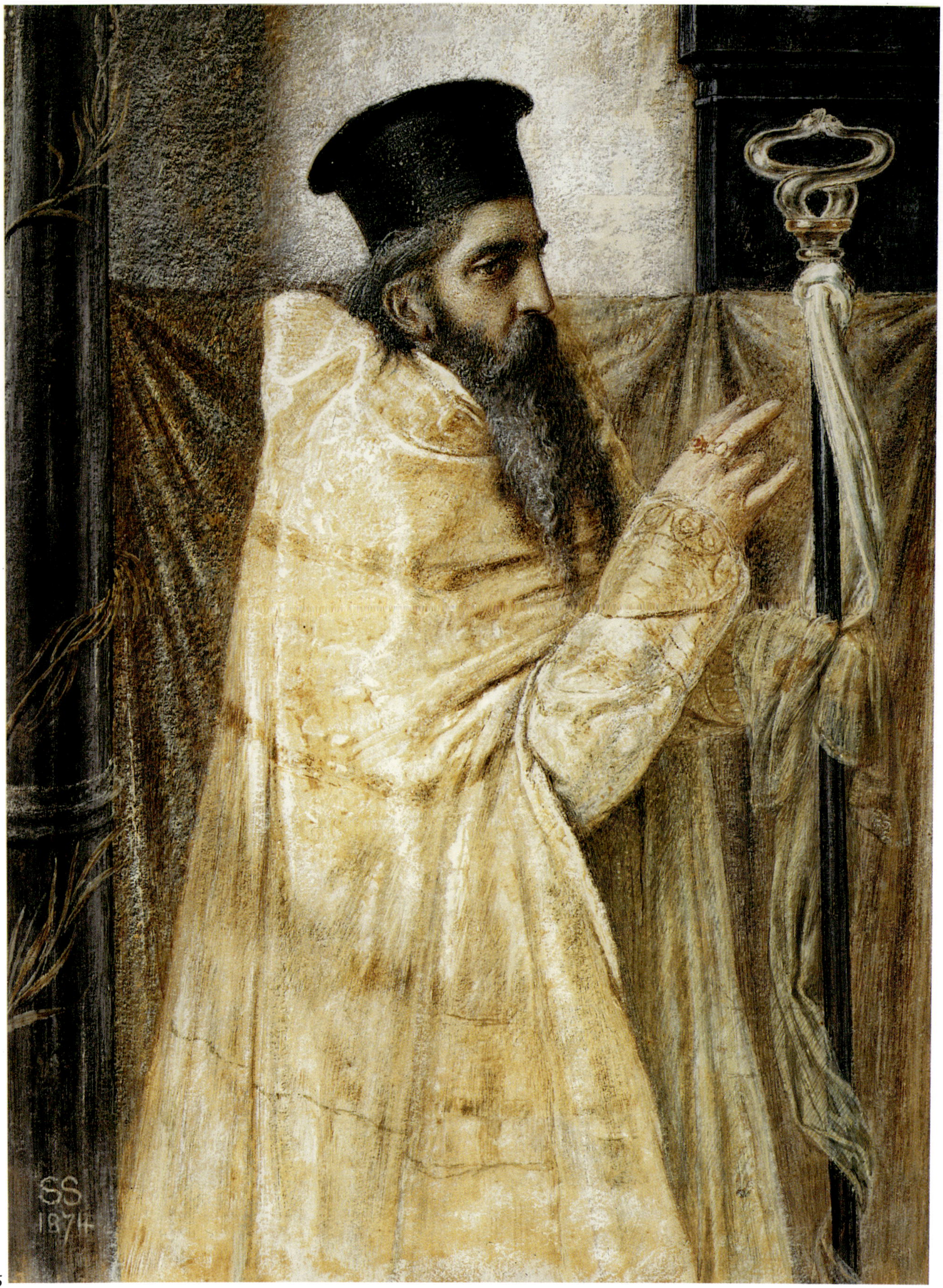

95

reservations about the facial expression of the young rabbi. The *Athenaeum*, for example, observed: "If [the student of technique] looks at *A Young Rabbi carrying the Scroll of the Law* he will enjoy its solidity and courageous dealing with black, and doubt the correctness of the taste which led Mr. Solomon to make the face so sensual, languishing, and sickly. The expression of this head is characteristic of the painter" (2 February 1870, p. 234).

The Spectator was a little more barbed: "The kind of picture which Mr S. Solomon delights to paint is pretty well known. That he is a colorist of remarkable power few will be disposed to deny. His *Young Rabbi carrying the Scrolls of the Law* (51) is a rich assemblage of browns that few could surpass. But the sentiment is remote, not to say hazy, and there is little suggestion of life or reality in the head. Still the picture is free from that repulsive sentiment which too frequently marks Mr. Solomon's compositions" (19 February 1870, p. 237).

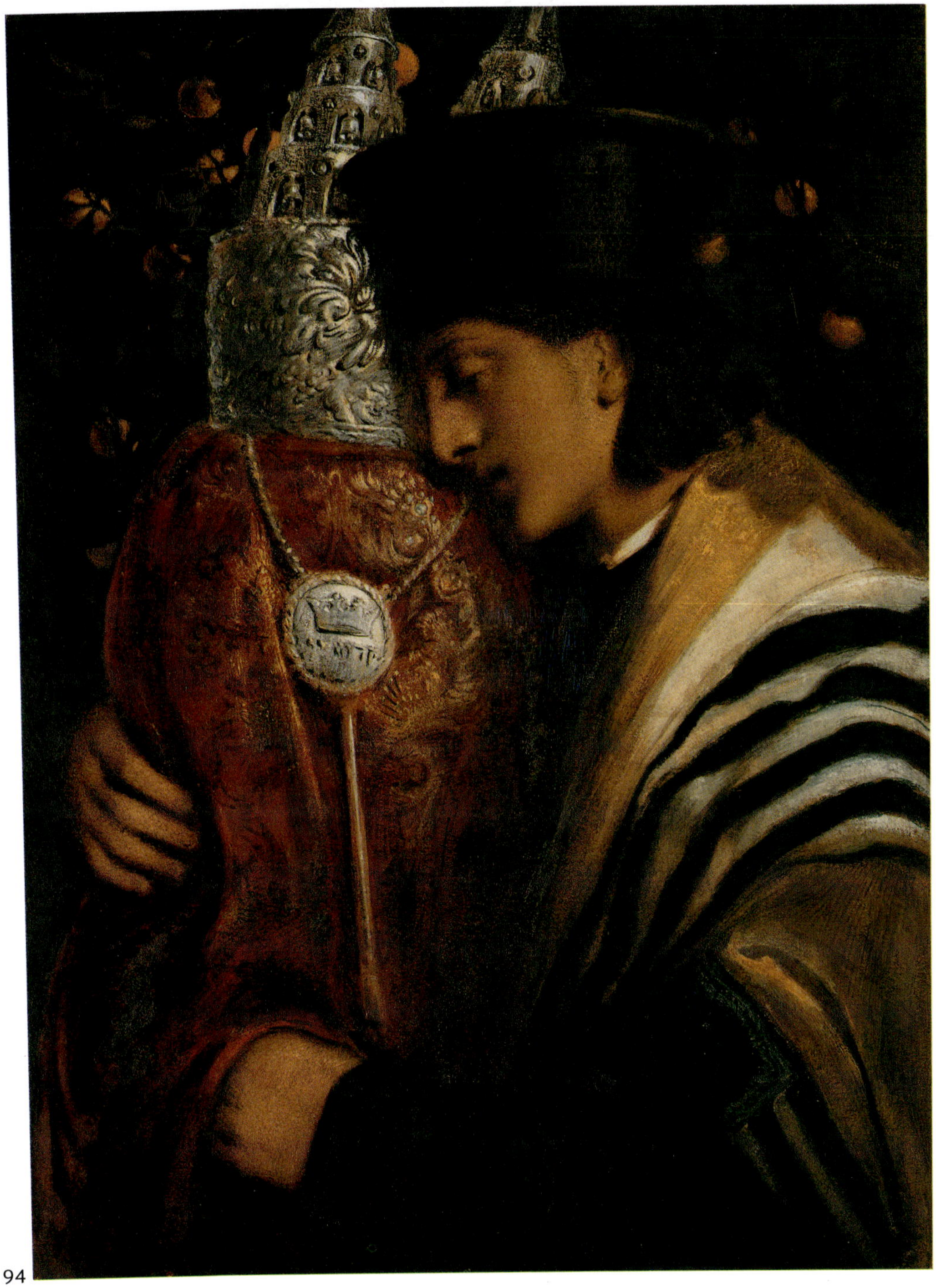

94

94
Carrying the Scrolls of the Law
1867
Watercolour and bodycolour with varnish on paper
35.5 × 25.4 cm (14 × 10 in.)
Signed and dated *SS Rome 1867*
The Whitworth Art Gallery, University of Manchester

Cat. 94 was shown as *A Young Rabbi Carrying the Scrolls of the Law* at the Sixth General Exhibition of Water-Colour Drawings at the Dudley Gallery, 1870 (as no. 51). It is probably Solomon's most succinct version of this subject and one of his most adept and moving works. Its genesis can be seen in his early Jewish ceremony drawings, for example cat. 8.

The painting was well received, although some critics who noted the technical skill had

95
A Bishop of the Eastern Church
1874
Watercolour and bodycolour on paper
30.5 × 22 cm (11¾ × 8½ in.)
Signed with monogram and dated *1874* lower left
Private collection

One of three important watercolours on Greek Orthodoxy (see cat. 90 for an earlier example), this is notable for its colour and handling of the medium; the shimmering effect of light hitting the vestments is achieved by the scumbling of bodycolour over a watercolour base.

Cat. 95 is one of the last of the artist's works to record a Christian ritual in detail; thereafter his works become vaguer, less accurate and more expressive of mysticism. Here the bishop blesses the congregation, an action recorded in *A Greek High Priest* (watercolour, 1868, private collection), which features a similar crozier, the staff denoting the office of bishop, of a design that suggests Solomon's signature of interlocking serpents.

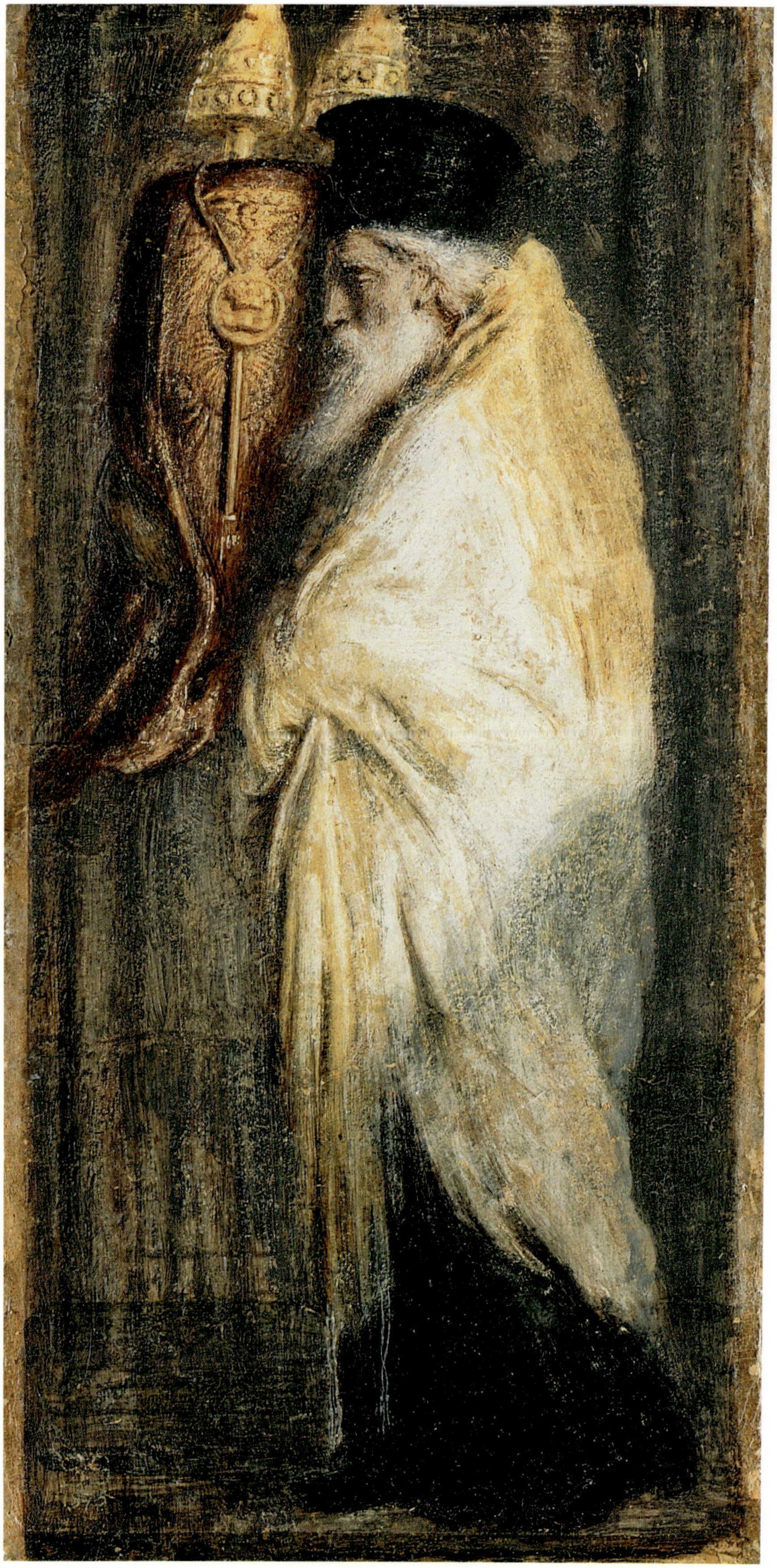

96

96
Aaron with the Scrolls of the Law
1875
Oil on canvas
30.9 × 15.1 cm (12³⁄₁₆ × 5¹⁵⁄₁₆ in.)
Signed and dated *1875*
Southampton City Art Gallery

One of the artist's most atmospheric later oil paintings, cat. 96 shows Aaron in a fanciful depiction anachronistically carrying the Torah in an ornate casing. Aaron was consecrated by Moses as the first High Priest of Judaism (Exod. 29:5–6).

The illustration of Aaron's consecration was undertaken for Dalziels' Bible project by Edward Armitage (1817–1896), although Solomon designed *The First Offering of Aaron* (dated September 1864, cat. 46c) and another Aaronaic subject, *The Burnt Offering*.

97
Frederick Sandys (1829–1904)
Medea
1866–68
Oil on wood
62.2 × 46.3 cm (24½ × 18¼ in.)
Birmingham Museums & Art Gallery. Presented by the Trustees of the Public Picture Gallery Fund, 1925

Begun in 1866 while the artist was staying with Rossetti in Cheyne Walk, cat. 97 would seem to have some of its origins in Solomon's *Habet!* (cat. 75), shown at the Royal Academy the previous year. The two artists shared models, and the swooning woman in *Habet!* has many features in common with Sandys's Medea. Cat. 97 is one of Sandys's greatest works and, as Elzea points out, the last of his major subject paintings (see Elzea, 2001, pp. 184–85). Medea, a sorceress, is seen preparing a poison to kill her rival, Glauké, with whom Jason had fallen in love. The sense of ritual, albeit of magic, is shared with Solomon's religious works of this period.

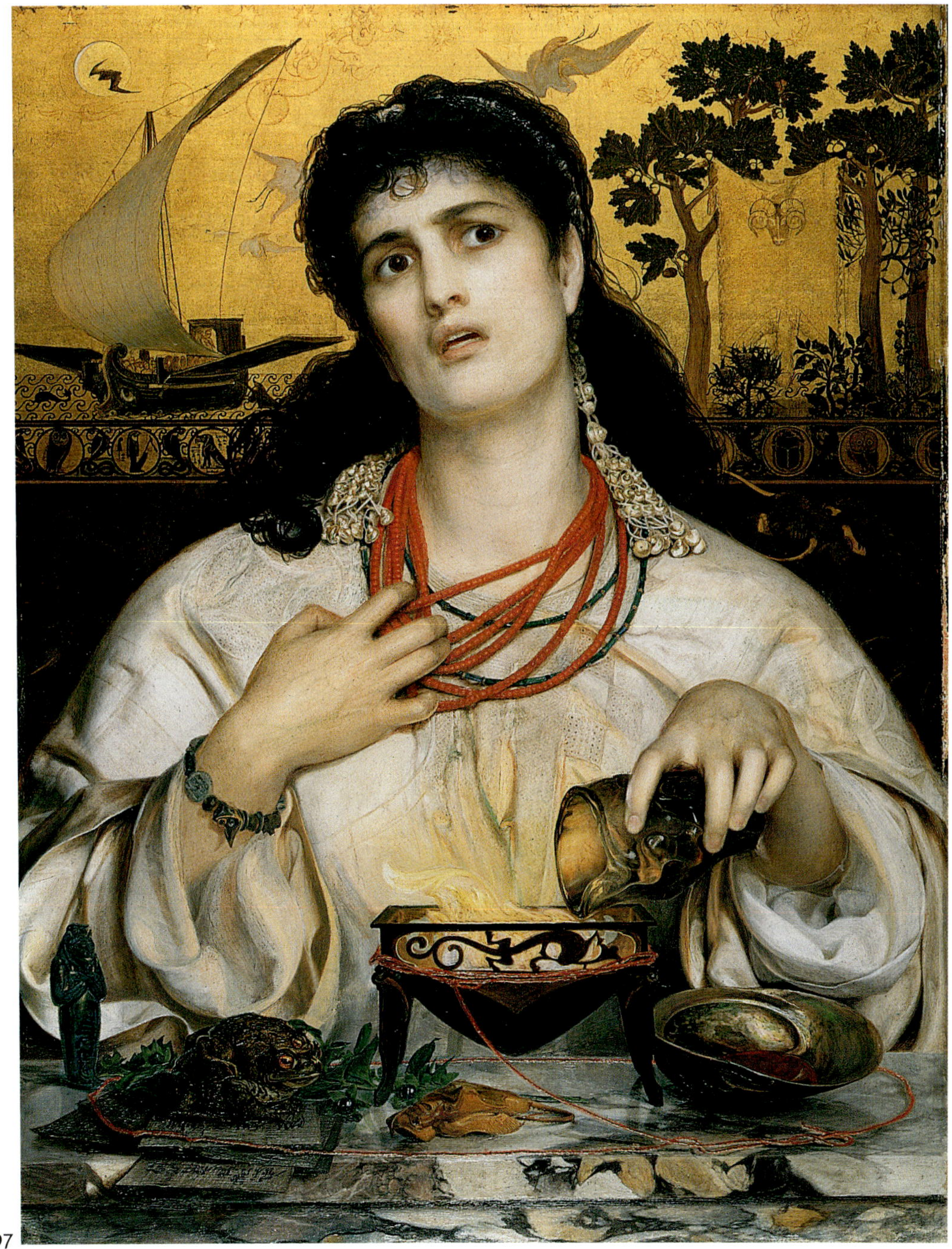

97

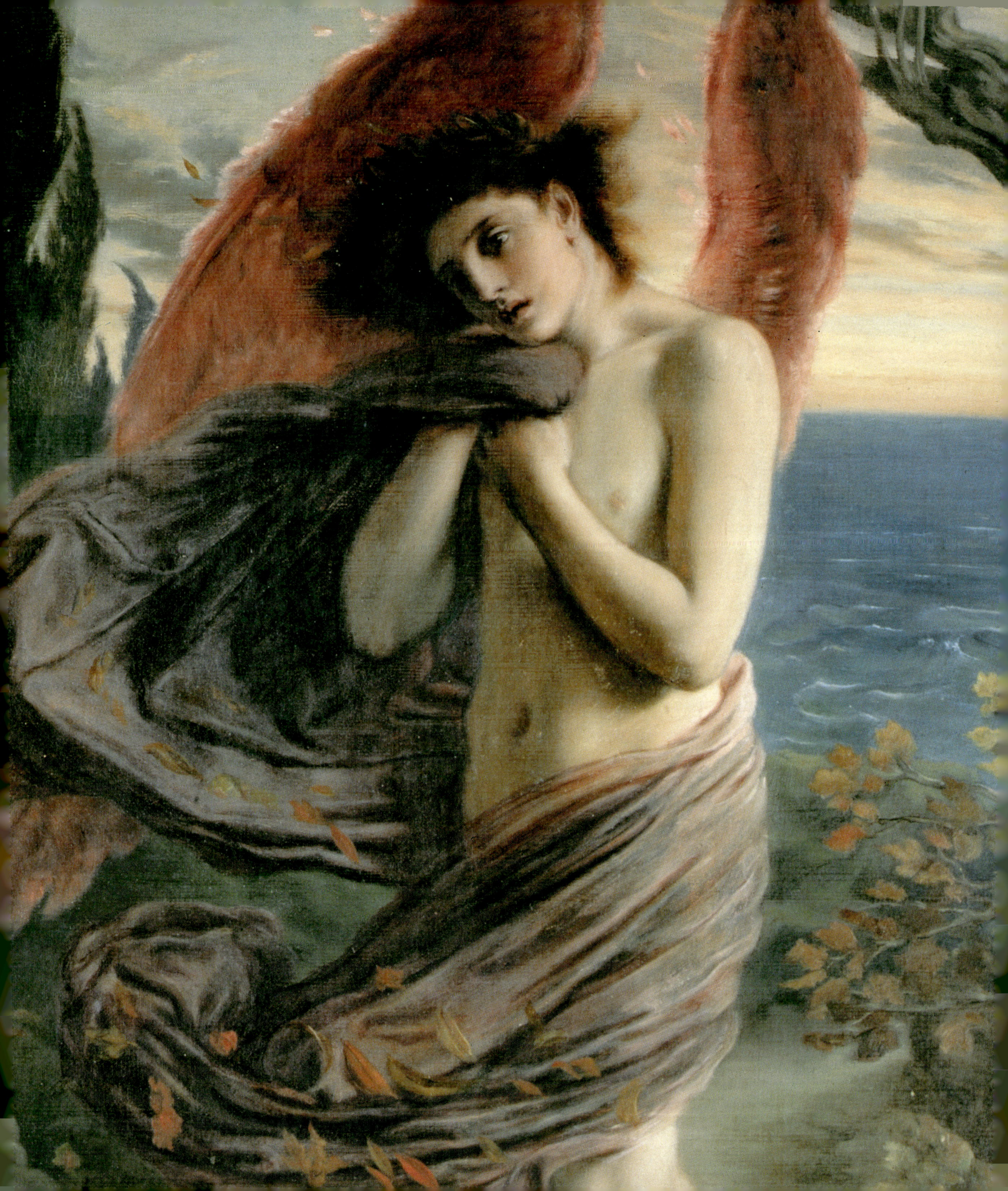

Visions of Love

"Nothing less than genius"

Sidney Colvin, *The Fortnightly Review*, May 1871, p. 675

Although Solomon participated in the new Pre-Raphaelite subject painting of the 1860s with figure compositions showing women in fancy or exotic settings, by far his most original and controversial contribution was in works dealing with the male figure. Part of the new classicism of the period – in many ways inimical to Pre-Raphaelitism – was the reintroduction of the academic nude. This had been particularly contentious in works by Leighton shown at the Royal Academy. Solomon began to formulate a kind of subject painting that combined academic life-drawing practices with symbolism, derived from several sources and given a personal, private and poeticized meaning. The paintings are, in effect, allegories of personal desires, natural phenomena and the human condition. They draw on several sources: biblical and other sacred scriptures, the work of Romantic poets like Shelley and Keats, and Renaissance painters such as Leonardo da Vinci and Botticelli. These allegorical paintings have echoes in the work of Burne-Jones, but Solomon's were both more obscure and more personally revealing; his closeness to Swinburne and to a group of gay patrons, writers and critics such as George Powell and Oscar Browning led him to formulate ever more daring, if somewhat obscure, subjects involving the male nude. These works were received badly, often being objected to on the grounds that they were 'unmanly' or, in some unstated way, immoral.

Adverse criticism culminated in references to Solomon in the infamous critical essay on the poetry of D.G. Rossetti, 'The Fleshly School of Poetry', published anonymously in *Contemporary Review* (and subsequently attributed to the poet Robert Buchanan). Taking Rossetti to task for immorality in his poetry, Buchanan added: "English society of one kind purchases the *Day's Doings*. English society of another kind goes into ecstasy over Mr Solomon's pictures – pretty pictures of morality, such as 'Love dying by the breath of Lust'. There is not much to choose between the two objects of admiration except that painters like Mr Solomon lend actual genius to worthless subjects, and therefore produce veritable monsters – like the lovely devils that danced around Saint Anthony" (p. 340).

Solomon published his own prose work, *A Vision of Love Revealed in Sleep*, in 1871; it bears the imprint of F.S. Ellis, the publisher of Rossetti's *Poems*, although it was privately printed. *A Vision* is short, but it has ambitions to combine both pictorial and literary modes. Swinburne took the opportunity of surveying Solomon's paintings while reviewing his book for *The Dark Blue*. He found the prose unclear and incoherent, but the paintings were highly, even extravagantly praised.

Solomon's career effectively ended in 1873 with his arrest and prosecution (see Gayle M. Seymour, 'The Trial and Its Aftermath', in *Solomon: A Family of Painters*, 1985).

100
Love in Autumn (detail)
1866
Oil on canvas
84 × 66 cm (33 1/16 × 26 in.)
Signed with monogram and dated
1866 Florence
Private collection

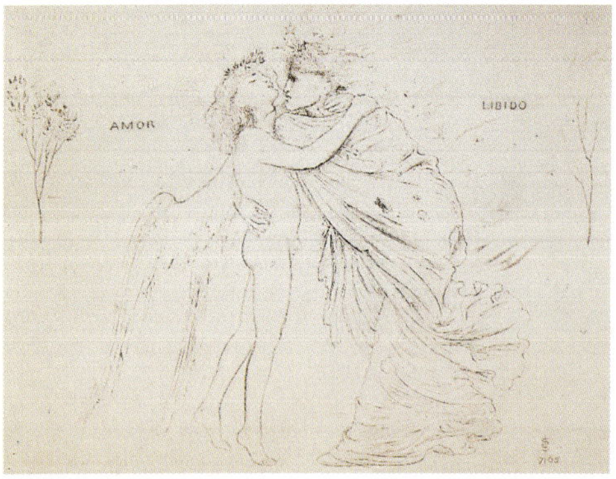

98

98
Frederick Hollyer after Simeon Solomon
Love Dying of the Breath of Lust
Photographic print; original drawing signed with monogram and dated *7 65*
15.7 × 20 cm (6³⁄₁₆ × 7¾ in.)
Private collection

An early drawing of a subject that was to become notorious following Robert Buchanan's attack on Rossetti's poetry in which, in passing, he mentioned Solomon (see the introduction to this section). However, no painted version of the subject appears to have survived, and Buchanan was using journalistic licence when he suggested that it was exhibited at the Dudley Gallery. The original drawing for cat. 98 is untraced.

The title appears in Hollyer's 1906 catalogue (cat. 140), implying that the notoriety did not affect the work's popularity in photographic form.

An enamelled version of the subject exists in a private collection; it is by Ernestine Mills (1871–1959), feminist, craftswoman and editor of *The Life and Letters of Frederic Shields 1833–1911*, London (Longmans, Green) 1912.

99
Frederick Hollyer after Simeon Solomon
The Human Soul
Photographic print; original drawing signed and dated *May 1865*
17.9 × 24.8 cm (7¹⁄₁₆ × 9¾ in.)
Private collection

The title given here is conjectural; the subject does not appear in the 1906 edition of Hollyer's catalogue, and the original drawing is untraced. The subject is a complex allegory of events in the life of the human soul, the 'Anima Humana', depicted as both a male and a female figure. The soul is pursued by Satan and his cohort (the *Sathanaphorae*) as he approaches the Angel of the Lord. Satan carries Innocence on his shoulders, perhaps having stolen it. Sad Love (*Amor Tristis*) accompanies the female figure at the right of the picture. Cat. 99 is inscribed in a scroll: "Invented and drawn by Simeon Solomon for his friend Edward J. Poynter May, 1865". Poynter and Solomon were close friends as students at the RA Schools and shared studio and living accommodation in the 1860s; see cat. 55.

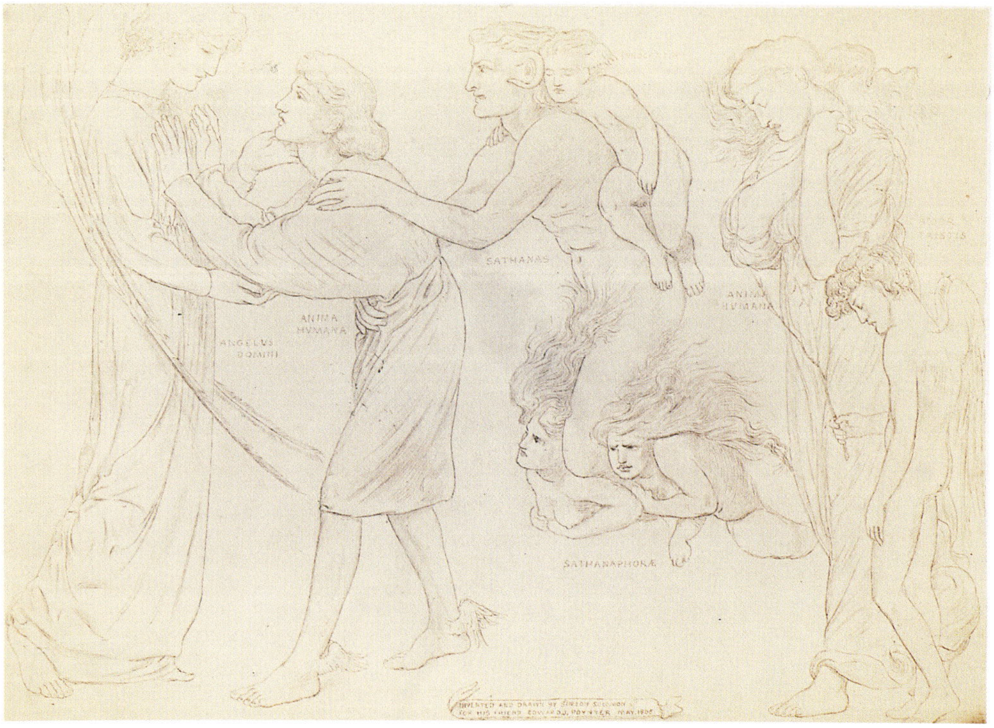

99

100
Love in Autumn
1866
Oil on canvas
84 × 66 cm (33¹⁄₁₆ × 26 in.)
Signed with monogram and dated *1866 Florence* lower left
Private collection

First shown (as no. 96) in the Sixth Winter Exhibition of Cabinet Pictures in Oil, Dudley Gallery, 1872, as *Autumn Love*, cat. 100 was already in the Coltart collection; when sold at the Coltart Sale in 1917 (as Lot no. 87) it was called *Love in Winter* and subtitled in the sale catalogue 'Cupid seeking refuge from the wintry blast'. Solomon wrote to Leyland from Florence, probably in 1866, describing it as showing "Eros being blown by Autumn winds along a place of Cypresses near the Sea" (undated letter, Library of Congress, Washington, DC).

The painting is dated 1866, making one wonder why it took some six years to be exhibited. Perhaps the publication of *A Vision of Love Revealed in Sleep* the year before – in which this subject appears in prose description – prompted the appearance of the work in public exhibition.

The *Art Journal* criticism is typical of the superior tone of most of the reviews: "So entirely now does painting take its themes from domestic sources, that mythology, and even poetry, are but little referred to. There is, however, another mythological conceit, 'Autumn Love', by Simeon Solomon, but so enigmatical as to leave us in doubt as to its reading. The Cupid of the piece is not the chubby child commonly pictured by painters and sung by poets, but a well-grown youth passing through a thicket, subject to the inconveniences of a cold wind which whirls aloft the now sere and yellow leaves. It may, or may not, be the solution of the riddle that love is cold in the autumn of life: under any circumstances the question is scarcely worth propounding as a riddle" (December 1872, p. 309).

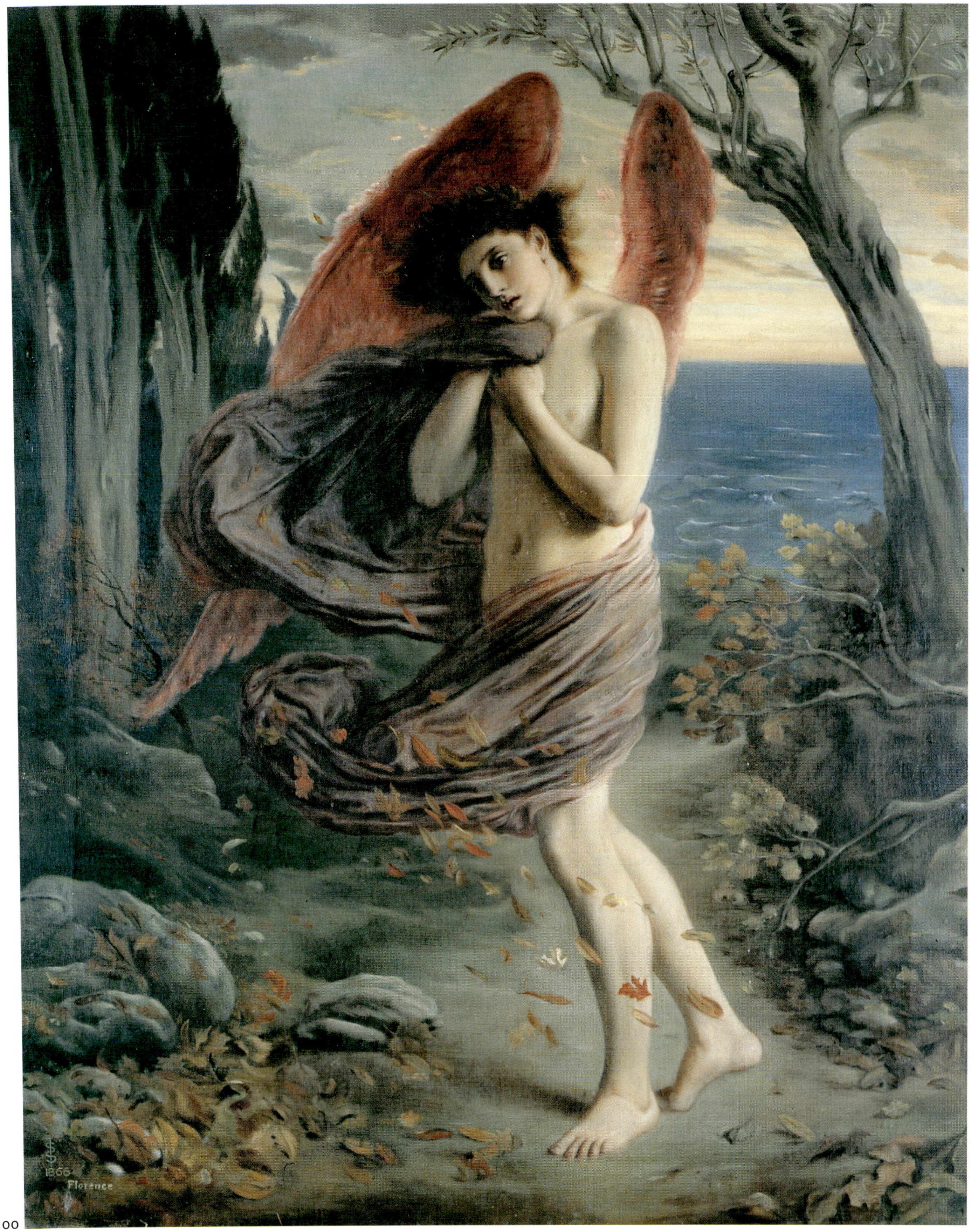

100

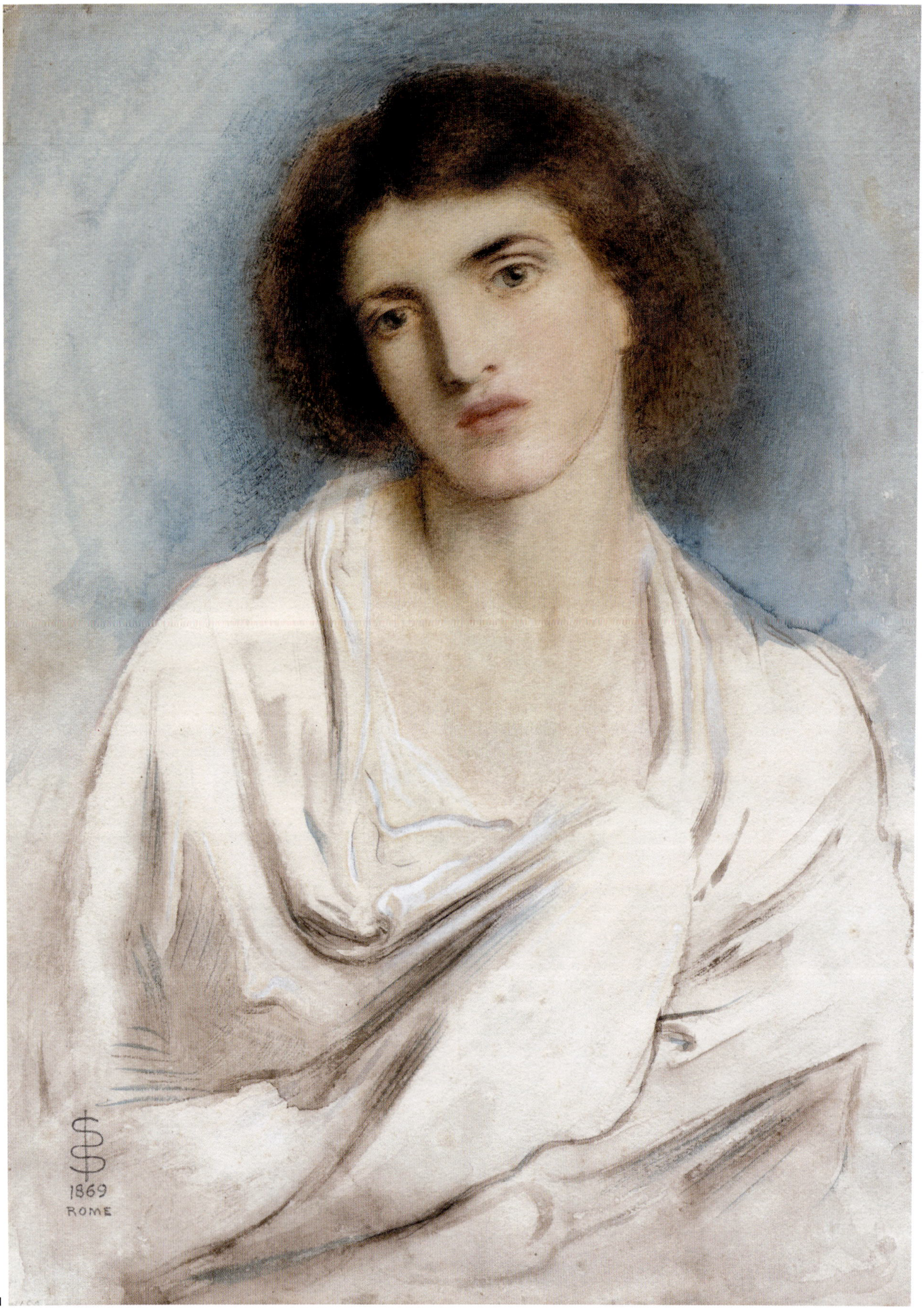

101

Both the *Athenaeum* and *The Times* objected to the work: "A certain 'unmanliness', if we may employ a questionable term, ruins the sentiment of this picture, and the effects to which we have referred are utterly incompatible with exalted fancy, to which nothing is more fatal than badly-drawn legs" (*Athenaeum*, 2 November 1872, p. 569); "Mr. Simeon Solomon's 'Autumn Love' is one of those allegorical designs of his which usually suggest something unwholesome in sentiment, set forth with a finely felt sentiment of colour, but with its forms marred by some more or less palpable failure of proportion. Here the failure is in the lower limbs, which look insufficient to support the figure of the red-mantled, sickly youth, who walks the bleak sea-shore through whistling wind and falling leaves" (*The Times*, 11 November 1872, p. 4).

The mention of the awkwardness of the legs in several reviews may be due to what would appear to be the pictorial origins of the work in Botticelli's *Birth of Venus* (early 1480s, Uffizi, Florence), which Solomon must have seen on his visit to Florence. The figure of Love is a reversed transcription of the figure of a zephyr who floats above Venus and blows her to the shore. There is a striking similarity in the elaborately billowing robes. The zephyr's legs, however, do not bear any weight, and this might have led to the perceived "failure ... in the lower limbs" noted above. Solomon was very early in his appreciation of Botticelli, who was almost completely overlooked in early nineteenth-century surveys of the Renaissance; Solomon was the first artist of the Pre-Raphaelite group to emulate him so openly.

101

Portrait of an Italian Youth

1869

Watercolour on paper

36.4 × 26.3 cm (14⁵⁄₁₆ × 19⅜ in.)

Signed with monogram and dated *1869 Rome* lower left

University of Wales, Aberystwyth

Also known as *An Ideal Head*, cat. 101 is drawn from a model discovered in Italy. The covered hand relates the drawing to both *Until the Day Break and the Shadows Flee Away* (cat. 113) and *The Mystery of Faith* (cat. 88), as well as to other works in which some mystical, sacramental act is to be performed. It suggests that the gesture and facial expression might have been incorporated into one of the 'ritual' works of the 1860s, although the face is more sensual than any of the works in that series.

The model's features had some impact on Solomon, for they appear on two of the male figures in the finished watercolour version of *In the Summer Twilight* (1869, cat. 105) but not in the earlier chalk study (fig. 39).

102

Love amongst the Schoolboys

1865

Pen and ink over pencil on paper

24 × 34 cm (9⁷⁄₁₆ × 13⅜ in.)

Signed with monogram and dated 65 lower right

Private collection

Often believed to have belonged to Oscar Wilde but more probably to Oscar Browning (1837–1923), one of Solomon's closest friends in the 1860s, cat. 102 would appear, because of the quaint outfits, to be set in Browning's school, Eton; Browning had been appointed a master there in 1860.

The winged figure of Love sits on the edge of a table as if interrupting the daily domestic routine of a group of schoolboys who listen with solemn expressions to his message. Some are transformed, like the little boy at the feet of Love, others dreamy, while yet others – like the boy at the extreme right – are more doubtful. The niceties of Love's message are unclear, although from the closeness of the embracing couples it can be presumed to be a more physical version of the Christian instruction to 'love one another'.

The subject-matter of cat. 102 was a matter of some public concern in the 1860s, and Solomon's choice might be seen as both foolhardy and reactionary. The drawing was done at a time of public outrage at the sexual immorality in English public schools and the shift towards morally upright, even priggish, school morals, such as those outlined in Thomas Hughes's *Tom Brown's Schooldays* (1857). In his own way, in cat. 102 Solomon is as sentimental as Hughes. However, it is perhaps an indication of Victorian reform of the public school system that William Cory, the author of *Ionica*, was dismissed from Eton in 1872 and Browning, despite everything a popular master, in 1875; both had developed close friendships with boys.

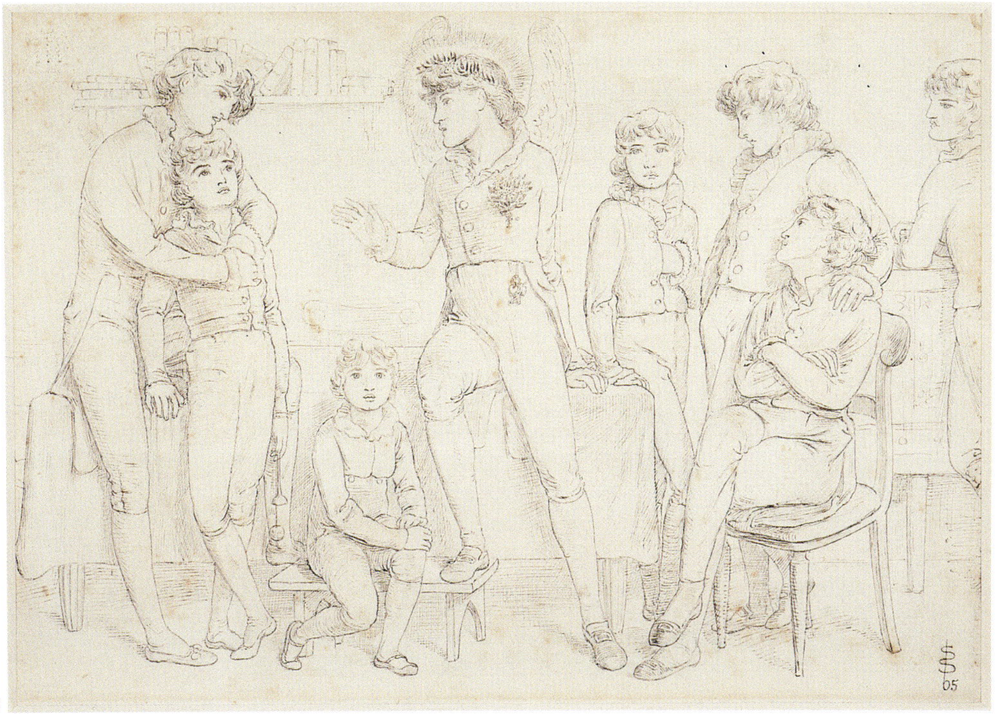

102

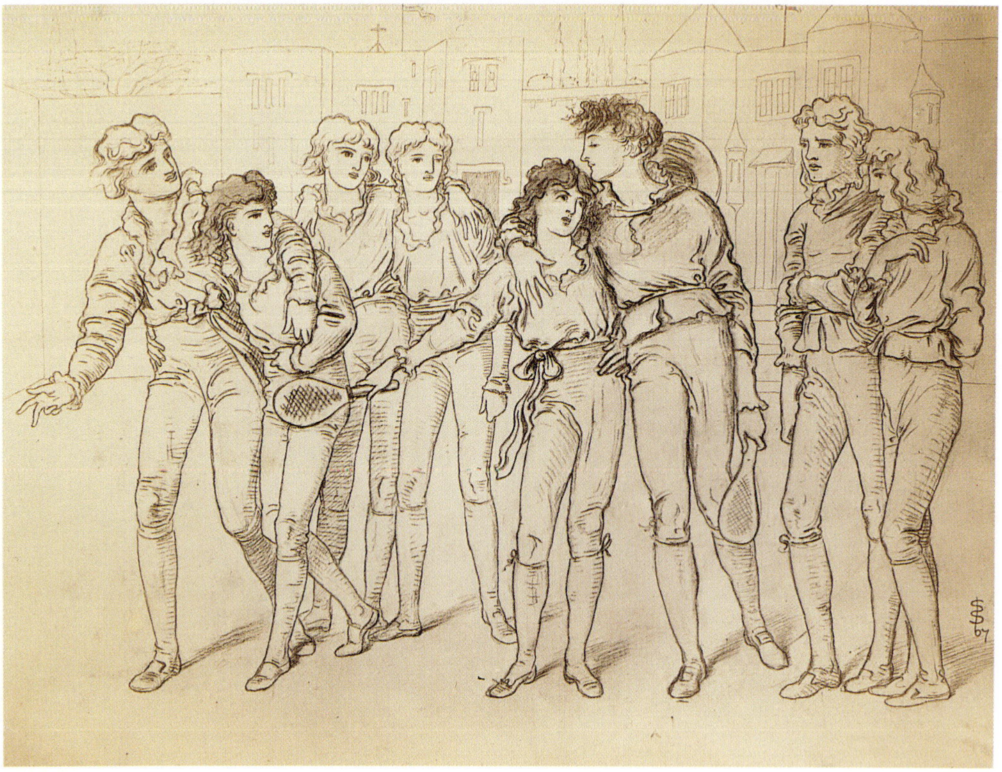

103

104
Socrates and his Agathodaemon
Undated; *c.* 1865
Pen and ink on paper
24.8 × 12.7 cm ($9\frac{3}{4} \times 5$ in.)
Victoria and Albert Museum

The circumstances surrounding the making of this drawing are obscure but the intention seems to be humorous, contrasting the squat plainness of the philosopher with the idealized beauty of his 'better self', a kind of pin-up whose wings add a spiritual, allegorical dimension to the concept. Although the Agathodaemon was a spirit of the crops (a kind of spiritual Bacchus), he was often represented as a snake. Here Solomon uses the Bacchus-like representation of the spirit as a young man, for obvious ends.

103
Frederick Hollyer after Simeon Solomon
Eton Schoolboys
Photographic print; original drawing signed with monogram and dated *67* lower right
18.6 × 24.3 cm ($7\frac{5}{16} \times 9\frac{9}{16}$ in.)
Private collection

This drawing is known only through this, perhaps unique, photographic copy. It depicts some fancifully dressed Eton schoolboys in ruffled shirts, knee-breeches and buckled shoes walking towards the viewer, grouped in embracing couples; two boys hold racquets. Racquets is a traditional game at Eton. In the background is depicted Lupton Tower, one of the school's landmarks. Solomon's interest in the subject developed through his friendship with Oscar Browning.

Cat. 103 possibly predates cat. 105 in its processional, frieze-like composition and in the use of eighteenth-century dress, which also appears in *Love amongst the Schoolboys* (cat. 102).

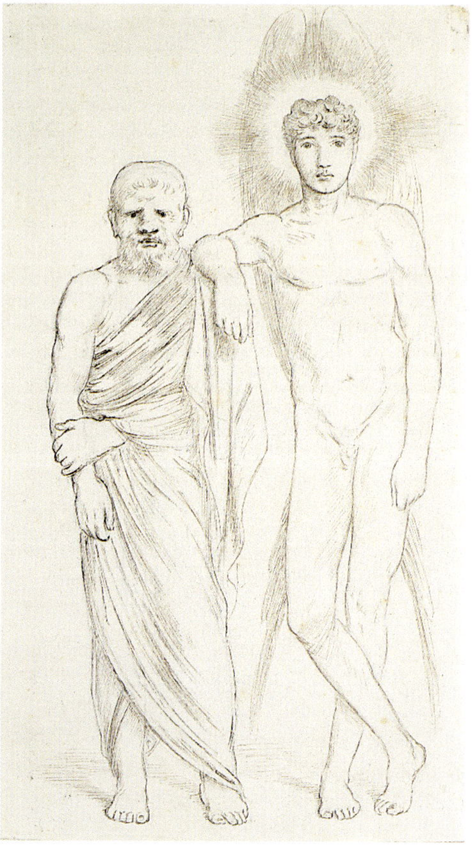

104

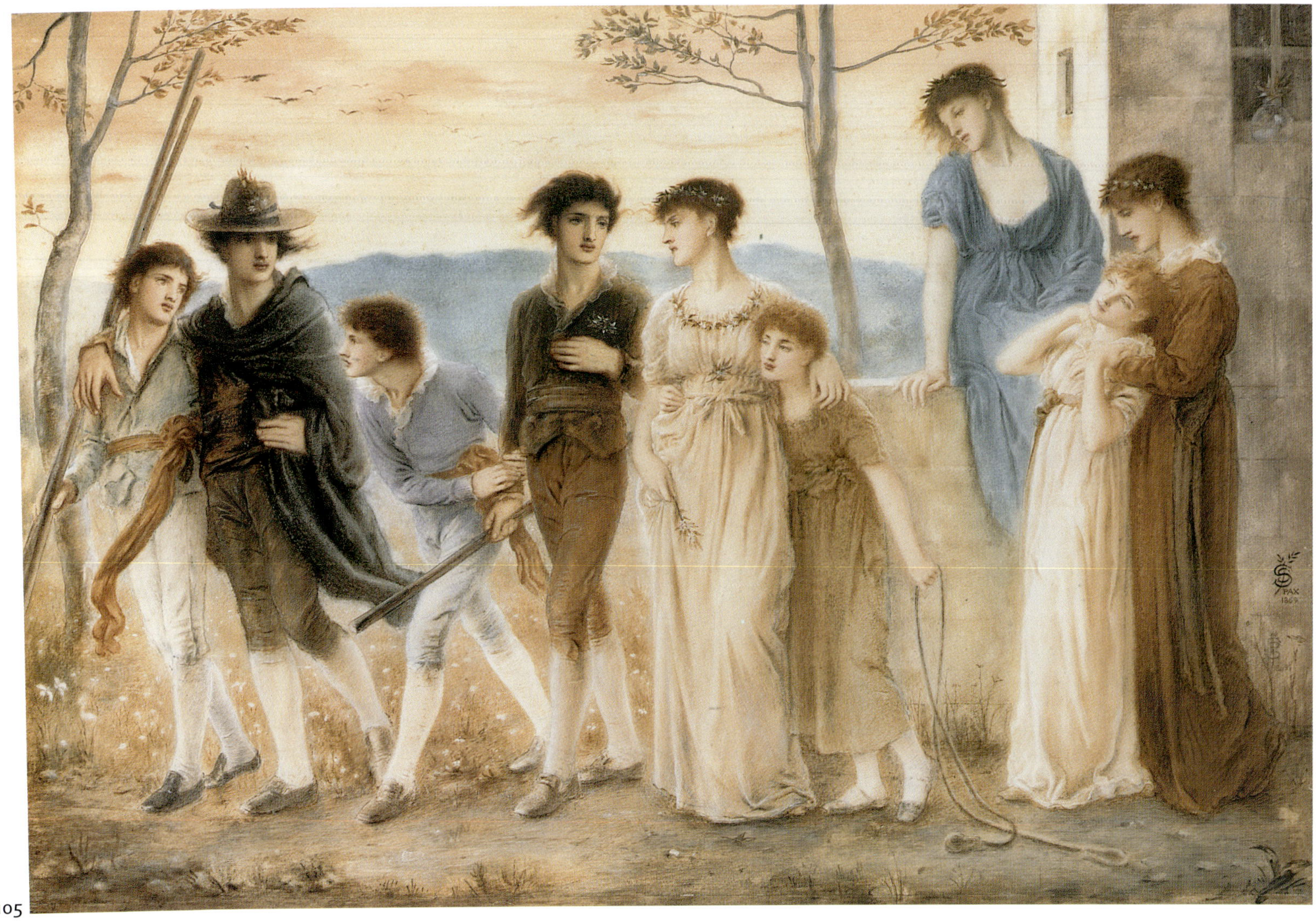

105

105
In the Summer Twilight
1869
Watercolour on paper
50.8 × 69.8 cm (20 × 27½ in.)
Signed with monogram and dated *1869* lower centre right
Seymour Stein

The subject of cat. 105 is obscure, although it is further evidence of the artist's attempt to "paint beautiful things beautifully", in the words of Sidney Colvin, and represents a strain in Pre-Raphaelitism of attempting to paint twilight effects. The odd mixture of clothes suggests a kind of non-specific historical nostalgia that invokes Stothard, Westall and Blake (in his *Songs of Innocence* of 1789), artists from a previous generation who had not yet undergone a fashionable revival. The arrangement of figures, however, suggests an attempt to show the variety of sexual desire taken up more strikingly in other works of this phase, including cat. 69.

Both these aspects were grasped by the critic of the *Builder*: "to what country, to what period, do the youths and maidens belong who are walking in procession, 'In the Summer Twilight'?, whence do they come, and where are they going? In this ... Mr Solomon shows a commingled appreciation of the old master, R. Westall, and the younger originator, – whoever he might have been, – who instituted a peculiar sect of poet-painters! There are instances here, in this gallery, to denote that even a narcoticized dreaminess might be offered as poetry – and the narcotic has been toleration, and even praise sometimes; but it is far easier, always, to emulate the eccentricities of excellence than the excellence itself" (12 February 1870, p. 120).

An earlier study for cat. 105 exists (see fig. 39).

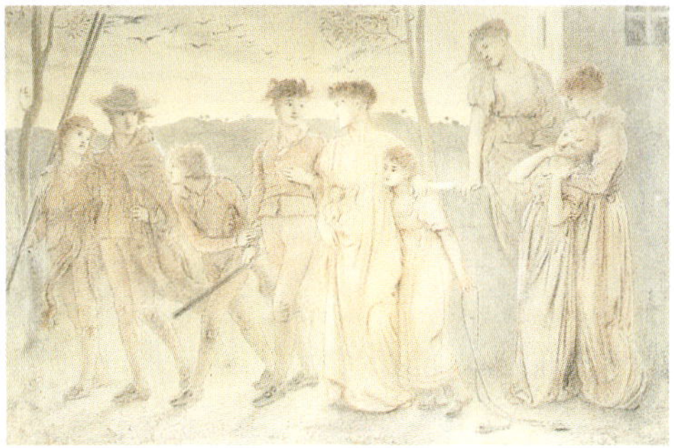

Fig. 39
Study for **In the Summer Twilight**
1866
Coloured chalks and pencil heightened with white on paper
42 × 61.5 cm (16½ × 24¼ in.)
Seymour Stein

106

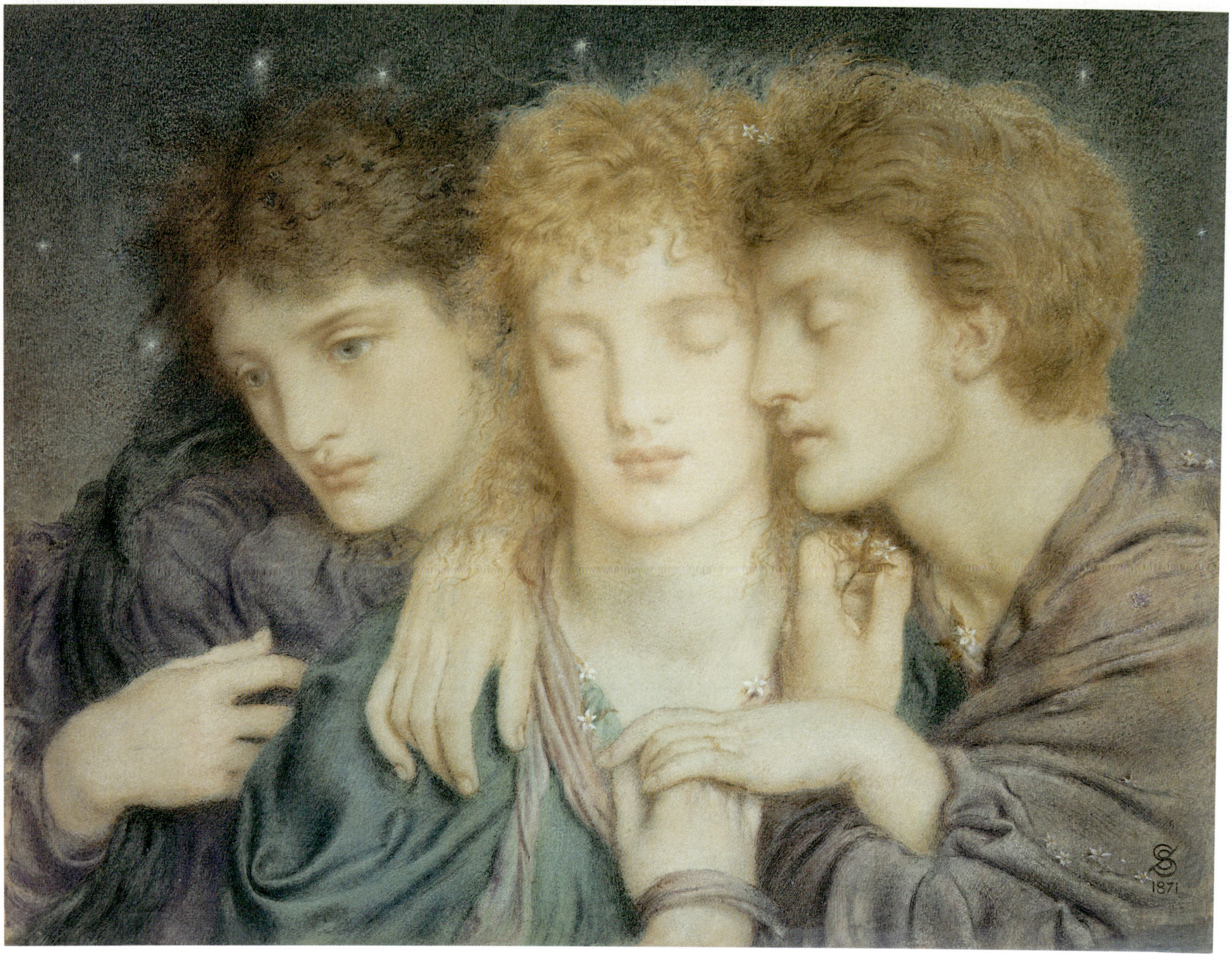

106
The Sleepers and the One who Watcheth
1870
Watercolour on paper
30.7 × 45 cm (12⅙ × 17¹¹⁄₁₆ in.)
Courtesy of the Art Gallery & Museum, The Royal Pump Rooms, Warwick District Council

Shown at the Dudley Gallery's Sixth General Exhibition of Water-Colour Drawings in the winter of 1870 (as no. 625), this impressive watercolour has had a variety of titles; it is one of Solomon's most successful works, satisfyingly combining several motifs and concepts – heads close together, closed eyes, varieties of sexual desire – with colour experimentation. The predomination of blue, grey and green is one of his experiments in producing compositions within a small and closely linked range of colours.

Cat. 106 was not widely noticed in the several reviews that greeted the artist's efforts shown at the Dudley that year: "The artist rises to a higher sphere of thought in 'The Sleepers, and One that keepeth Watch'" (*Art Journal*, 1870, p. 87).

The critic of *The Guardian* saw a connection between this work and *Shadrach, Meshach and Abednego* (see cat. 40) in the same exhibition (9 February 1870, pp. 166–67) and while this is true, there may be some relation between cat. 106 and Courbet's *The Sleepers* (1866, Musée du Petit Palais, Paris), one of the most famous images of same-sex desire in Western art. However, Solomon's title points to some other concerns, more mystical in compass. The term "one who keepeth watch" – the Watcher, represented by the dark, androgynous figure at the left of the composition – is used to describe the race of angels in the Book of Enoch, excluded from the main body of biblical texts in Christian worship since the fourth century; it had provided William Blake with inspiration following its first translation into English in 1821. The only scriptural record of the term is found in Daniel 4:13.

Cat. 106 inspired a sonnet by John Payne, published in his collection of poems *Intaglios* (1871), reprinted in Reynolds, 1985, pp. 99–100.

107
Frederick Hollyer after Simeon Solomon
The Sleepers and the One who Watcheth
Photographic print; original drawing signed with monogram and dated 67 lower right
23 × 35.5 cm (9⅙ × 14 in.)
Birmingham Museums & Art Gallery. Presented by Mrs R.E. Giles, 1931

Cat. 107 is an earlier version of cat. 106 photographed for the artist by Hollyer and included in the portfolio of platinotypes after Solomon designs published in 1869. The original is untraced; it might have been the work shown at the Dudley Gallery in 1872 with the title *Until the Day Break and the Shadows Flee Away*, described by the *Art Journal*: "the text [stands] in the place of a title to a group of three heads, but the relation between the drawing and the text lies in the dim twilight of conjecture. If it point to the consummation of our present disposition, the allusion is not sufficiently perspicuous" (February 1872, p. 75).

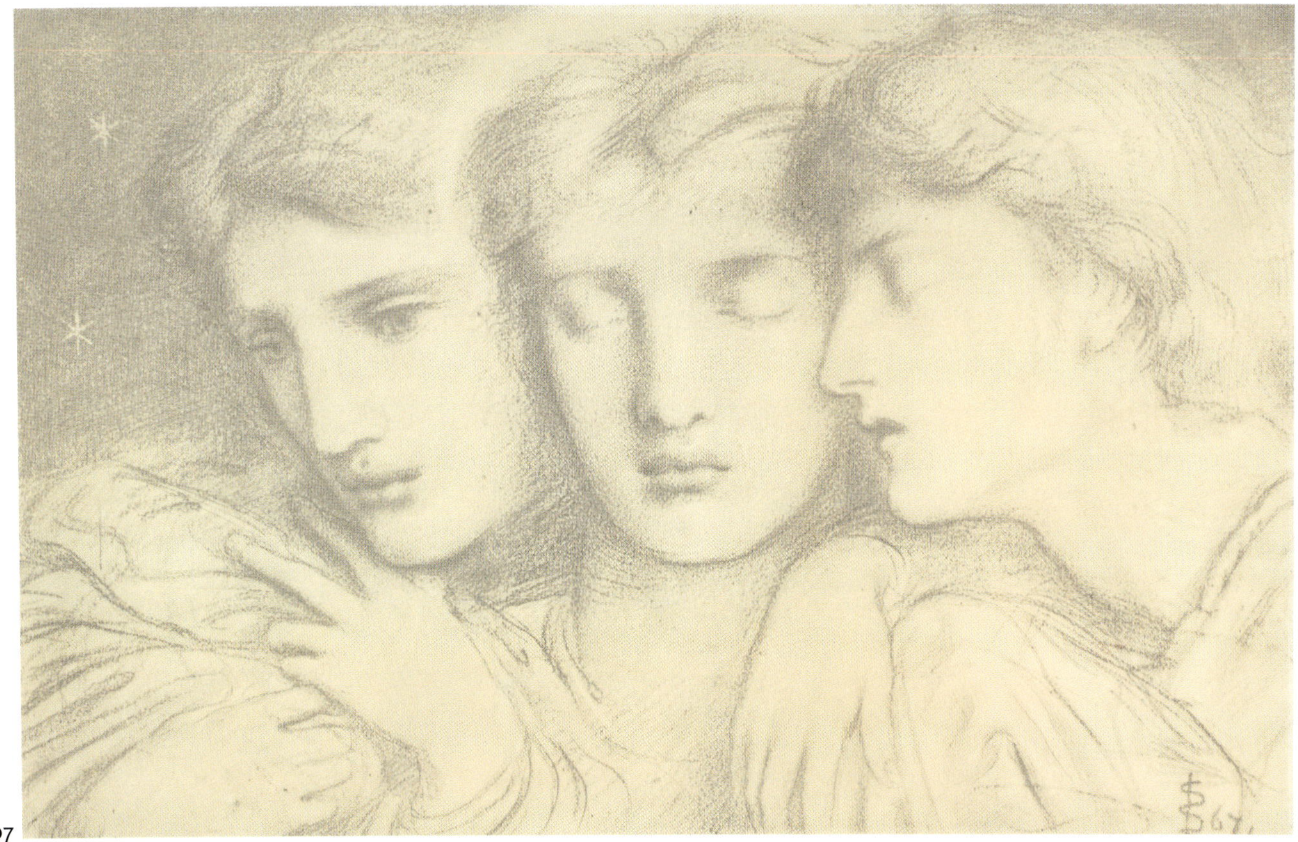

107

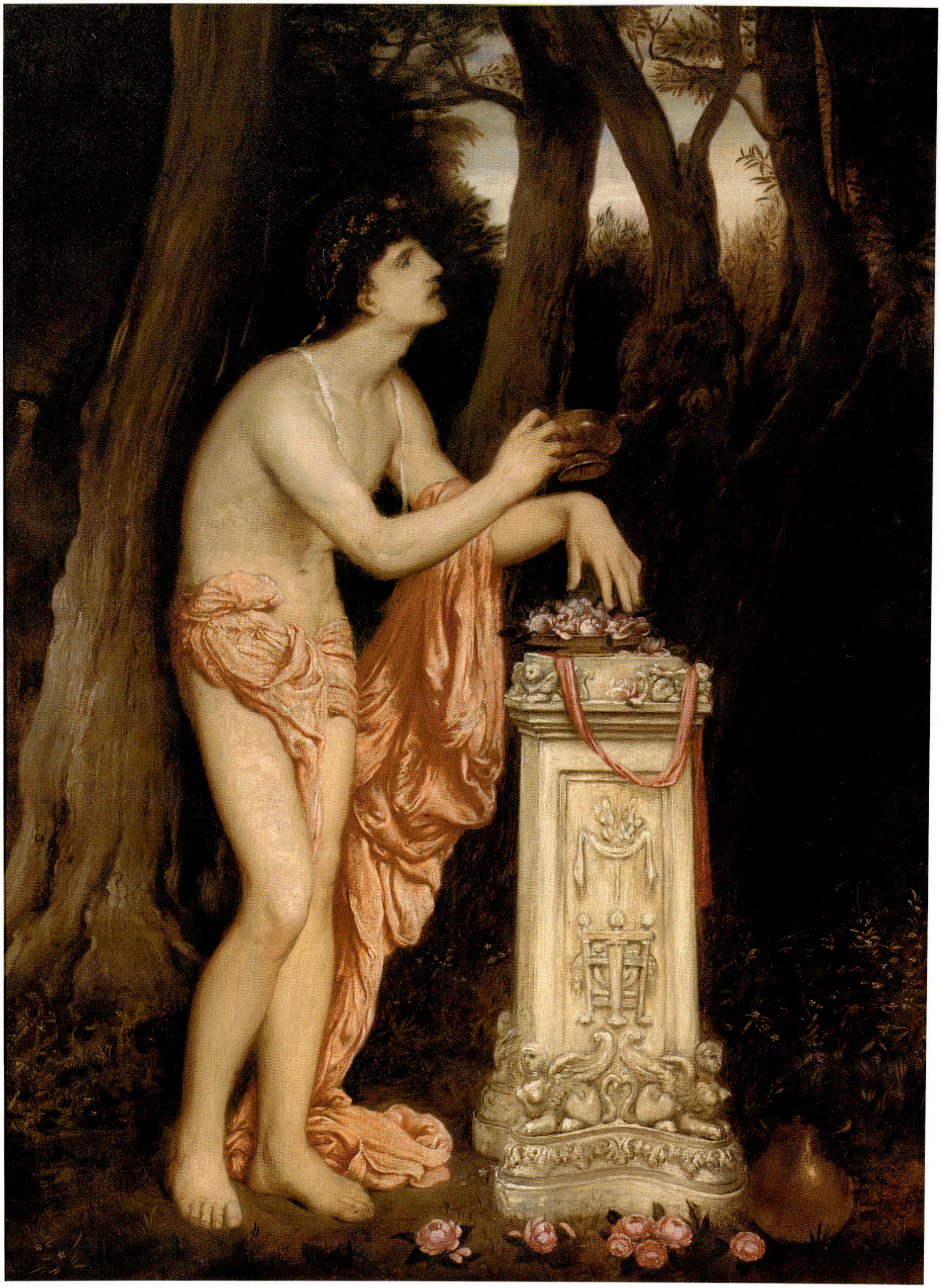

108

108
The Evening Hymn
1870
Oil on canvas
76.2 × 55.9 cm (30 × 22 in.)
Signed and dated lower right
Private collection

One of Solomon's most academic and yet, at the same time, subversive works of this period, cat. 108 was exhibited at the Dudley Gallery's Fourth Winter Exhibition of Cabinet Pictures in Oil (as no. 56) in 1870. It is also known as *An Offering*. Cat. 108 represents a draped youth pouring a libation on a rose-garlanded altar; he raises his head as if in song. It is Solomon's attempt at a full-length male nude, if unorthodox in pose and colour. A contemporary precedent might be found in Leighton's *Daedalus and Icarus*, which had been shown at the Royal Academy in 1869, although there the classical sculptural origins of the proportions of the young man's figure are clear. Solomon's young worshipper seems designed to merge male and female, an experiment fulfilled in *Sacramentum Amoris* (1868, see cat. 114).

Cat. 108 was universally criticized by reviewers, who were quick to point out the effeminacy of the figure, the *Athenaeum* being typical of the general reception: "The art of Mr. S. Solomon does not grow in manliness. 'The Evening Hymn', a youth pouring a libation to Venus on a rose-crowned altar, is neatly but not learnedly, modelled and drawn; accordingly, a powerful sense of grace in the artist's mind being everywhere present, we have ill-drawn, non-natural limbs and trunk, an outrageously long neck, and a face which is antipathetic to all that is masculine" (5 November 1870, p. 599).

The *Illustrated London News* made a connection between the style of the figure and immorality: "we must be permitted to add that, taken in conjunction with the title, 'The Evening Hymn', the conception is worthy of the most corrupt period of the Roman decadence, its covert objectionableness being increased by the rich hues of the flesh and sanguine-hued robe – abstractly artistic in a considerable degree as these are – relieved against the darkling trees" (5 November 1870, pp. 478–79).

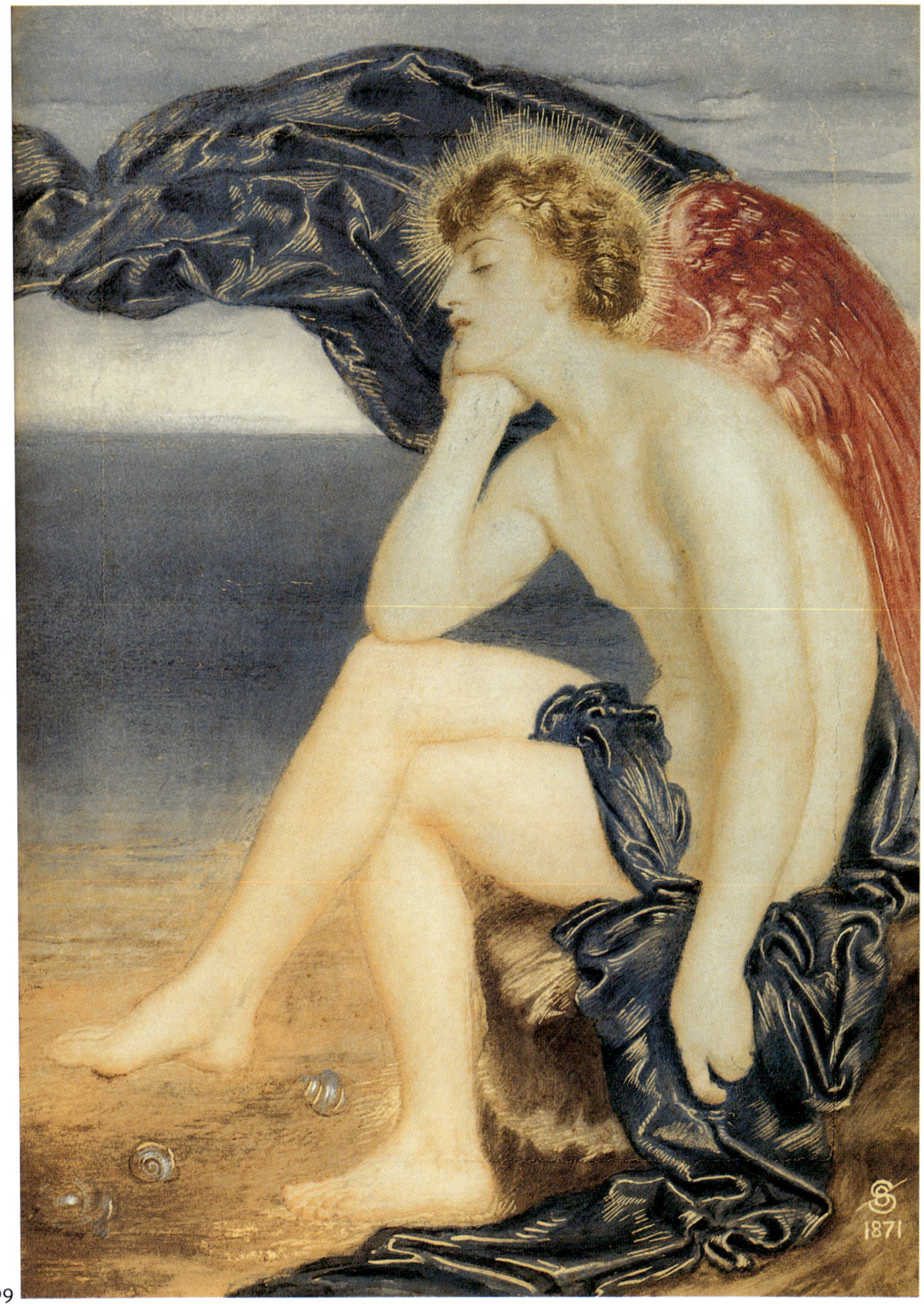

109

109
One Dreaming by the Sea
1871
Watercolour on paper
36 × 26.5 cm ($14\frac{3}{16} \times 10\frac{7}{16}$ in.)
Signed with monogram and dated *1871* lower right
University of Wales, Aberystwyth

Like cat. 77 and 79, cat. 109 belonged to George Powell. Sometimes called *Love Dreaming by the Sea*, the subject of cat. 109 is obscure, although its intention might have been to introduce a 'platonic' element into subject and fancy pictures otherwise dominated by depictions of the female form. Cat. 109 shares with *The Evening Hymn* (cat. 108) a nude male model with an erect nipple displayed and framed by the

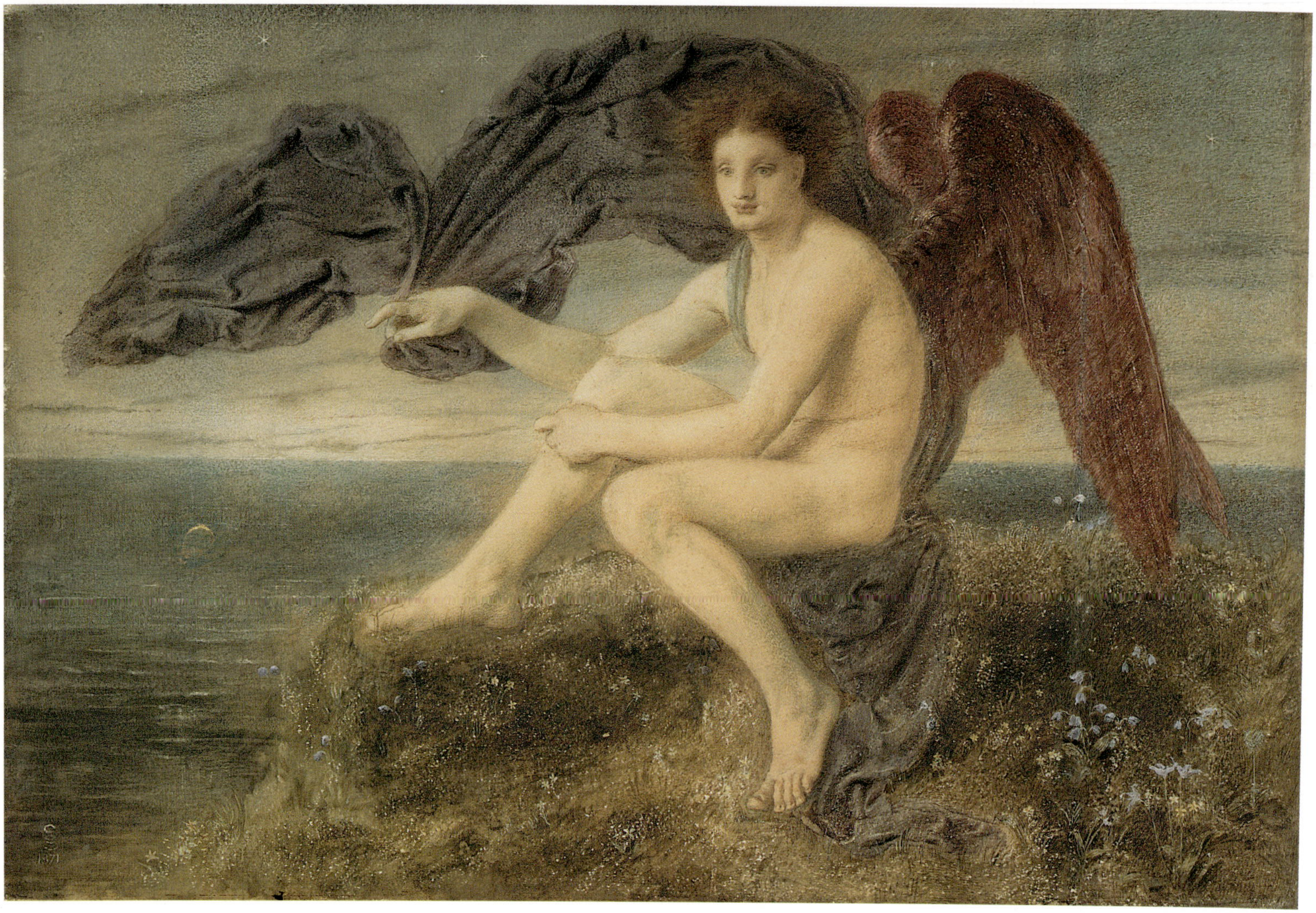

110

crook of the model's arm, a detail that renders the work more personal and erotic than the standard academic life figures of the artist's contemporaries. The work was a commission, and Solomon and his patron corresponded about the details, the painter writing to his patron: "Would you like the ruined temple background to your 'Love' or the sea + sky that we spoke of elsewhere ..." (quoted in Holland, 1997, p. 4).

Cat. 109 was shown at the Dudley Gallery in 1872 (as no. 73) along with several other works with an allegorical tendency. Burne-Jones's *The Triumph of Fortune, Fame, Oblivion, and Love* was shown (as no. 196) at the same exhibition. Together the artists showed a way forward for Pre-Raphaelitism, out of the medievalism of the 1850s and into a classicized subject-matter that was, in part, based on a revival of the nude in painting.

Reviewers were particularly harsh about the new direction in Solomon's work; the *Athenaeum* critic singled out cat. 109 in particular: "Mr. S. Solomon has produced many pictures of a manly and poetical character; but, as these walls show, he is apt to fall into inanities when, we suspect, he thinks himself soaring towards a heaven of fancy, or beguiling us with visions of subtlest imagery. In the category of the latter class of errors, *One Dreaming by the Sea* may be placed. A young person, of uncertain sex, is seated on a stone by a mysterious sea. The figure of such a dreamer, even if seraphic, must be – to satisfy us at least – tolerably well articulated, as surgeons say, and it must be absolutely free from all suspicions of belonging to what have been called 'the Book of Beauty Order of Beings'. Now this emasculated personage is neither articulated nor even moderately well proportioned; notice the poor little feet and the 'dandy's legs'; notice the want of *humanity* in the flesh, and the soulless features" (3 February 1872, p. 150).

110

Dawn

1871

Watercolour and bodycolour on paper

35.3 × 50.7 cm (13⅞ × 19⅞ in.)

Signed with monogram and dated *1871* lower left

Birmingham Museums and Art Gallery. Presented by the Trustees of the Public Picture Gallery Fund, 1909

A watercolour that anticipates the Aesthetic Movement taste for the works of Leonardo da Vinci, cat. 110 contains a reference to his *Virgin of the Rocks* (*c.* 1483, versions in the Louvre, Paris, and the National Gallery, London) in the over-articulated pointing hand. It is evidence of a return to allegory as a painterly concern, one Solomon shared with his friend Edward Burne-Jones.

Cat. 110 was exhibited at the Dudley Gallery in 1872 (as no. 189), together with cat. 109. The critic of *The Guardian* was particularly dismissive of the new direction in the artist's work, observing: "Considering the former contributions of Mr Solomon to the Dudley Gallery, it seems strange to pass by his works without a word of commendation. But he has taken to draw sickly dreams which can give no healthy pleasure, and his imagination feeds on itself instead of gaining tone and strength by vigorous contact with the facts of nature" (3 April 1872, p. 460).

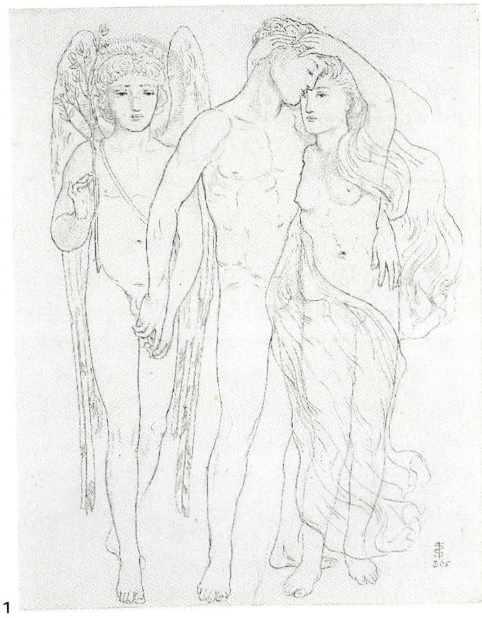

111

111

The Bride, the Bridegroom and Sad Love

1865

Pen and ink on paper

24.8 × 17.1 cm (9¾ × 6¾ in.)

Signed with monogram and dated *3/65* lower right

Victoria and Albert Museum

The subject of cat. 111 is from the Gospel of St John 3:29, although there is an overlay of meaning from the Song of Songs, which had supplied the subject for Rossetti's painting *The Beloved* (1865–66, Tate). The St John text reads: "He who has the bride is the bridegroom. The friend of the bridegroom, who stands and hears him, rejoices greatly at the bridegroom's voice." Solomon's reading is unusual, emphasizing the love, or – more strictly – the sexual desire between two men. As such this is a provocative reading. The 'Sad Love' of the title acts both as an ideal or allegory of rejected love and, because of the positioning of the hands, as the bridegroom's actual deserted sexual partner. The design goes back to Solomon's early sketchbook drawing *The Favourite Apostle* (*c.* 1857, Mishkan Le'Omanut Museum, Ein Harod, Israel). See also cat. 112.

112

Frederick Hollyer after Simeon Solomon

The Bride, the Bridegroom, and the Friend of the Bridegroom

Photographic print; original drawing inscribed with dedication and dated *1868* lower right

23.2 × 17.8 cm (9⅛ × 7 in.)

Birmingham Museums & Art Gallery. Presented by Alan Green, 1981

An alternative version of cat. 111, this is arguably less controversial. The original drawing (1868, Hugh Lane Art Gallery, Dublin), was dedicated to Walter Pater and is inscribed lower right *SS to WP June 1868*. It is often wrongly entitled *The Song of Solomon* (as in Reynolds, 1985, plate 49, and Kolsteren, 1982, fig. 6). The subject is, in fact, derived from the Gospel of St John, the scroll inscription being the Latin version of the verse quoted in cat. 111. There is little sense of rejoicing in the drawing but, instead, a deep sadness.

This photographic copy was owned by the Estonian poet and aesthete Eric, Count Stenbock, who was a friend of the artist and influenced by him (he borrowed Solomon's serpent device for the 'S' of his own surname). Stenbock signed the copy with a dedication, undated: "To Lily, Isabel and Lucy from Stanislaus Eric Stenbock".

A painting of the same subject (untraced) was shown at the Dudley Gallery in the winter of 1869–70 (as no. 19) with the text "And behold, the bush burned with fire, and the bush was not consumed". Several reviews expressed unease with the subject and its treatment: "'The Bride, the Bridegroom, and Friend of the Bridegroom', is a picture of Mr. S. Solomon, and we are grieved to see that a painter, who promised so well, is now exhibiting a work which gives us far more pain than pleasure. The maudlin sentiment, gross affectation, and poverty of form are certainly not cancelled by the beauty of colour or delicacy of tone; whilst the almost blasphemous adaptation of the quotation from Scripture to such a subject as opposed to good taste as it is, is painful to a right-feeling mind" (*Annual Register for 1869*, 1870, 'Art', pp. 359–60).

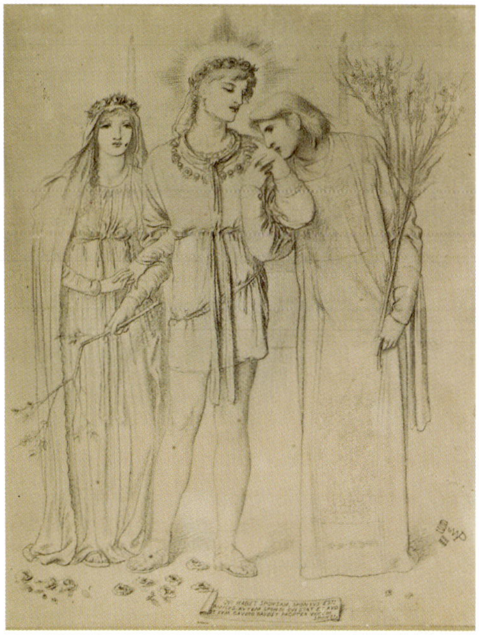

112

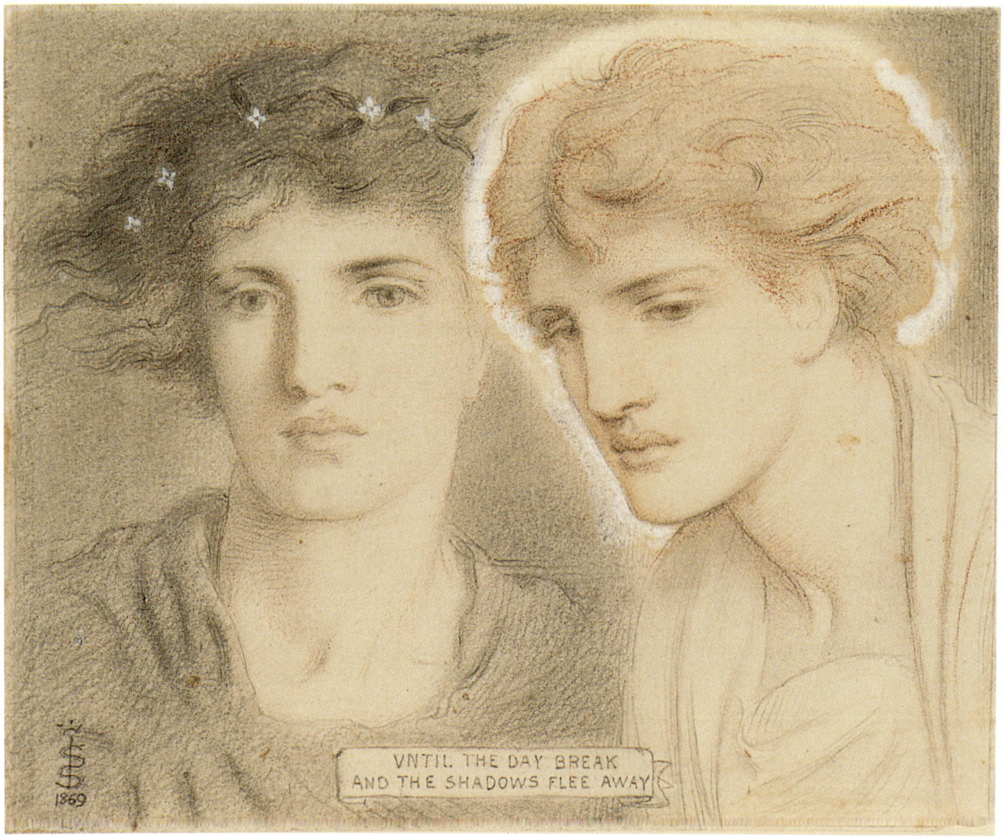

113

113
Until the Day Break and the Shadows Flee Away
1869
Pencil and black chalk with bodycolour and red chalk
12.9 × 15.4 cm (5$\frac{1}{16}$ × 6 in.)
Signed with monogram and dated *1869* lower left
The British Museum, London

Cat. 113 is an early example of what was to become a common compositional device in Solomon's later work (see, for example, cat. 139), the placing of two heads in relation to each other on either side of the picture space. Here the figures make no eye-contact, giving the work a sad, even depressed, atmosphere; the figure on the left stares out of the picture space, beyond the viewer, while that on the right looks downwards and slightly askance. Sidney Trefussis Whiteford suggested that this drawing was "perhaps the most beautiful" of the artist's poetic designs ('A Half-Forgotten Genius' in *The Art Amateur*).

The text is from the Song of Solomon 2:16, although cat. 113 does not illustrate the verse but uses it to suggest an interior state that does not correspond to the ecstatic energy and imagination of the poem. Instead, cat. 113 might be an early pictorialization of the idea central to *A Vision of Love Revealed in Sleep* (1871), in which the same lines are contemplated in the opening paragraph along with two others from "the Wise King" (p. 1). Cat. 113 resembles the drawing reproduced in photographic form as the frontispiece to *A Vision of Love Revealed in Sleep* (see cat. 117).

114
Frederick Hollyer after Simeon Solomon
Sacramentum Amoris
Photographic print; original watercolour dated *1868*
24.8 × 14.8 cm (9$\frac{3}{4}$ × 5$\frac{13}{16}$ in.)
Victoria and Albert Museum

Sacramentum Amoris, arguably Solomon's most controversial work is now lost; cat. 114 is the surviving record of it. The watercolour is well documented in letters to the artist's patron and owner of the work, F.R. Leyland, who objected to the style in which the male figure was painted. Swinburne noted the sexual ambiguity in his survey of the artist's achievements in his review of *A Vision of Love Revealed in Sleep*: "Many of [his figures], as the figure bearing the eucharist of love, have a supersexual beauty, in which the lineaments of woman and of man seem blended as the lines of sky and landscape melt in burning mist of heat and light" (*The Dark Blue*, I, July 1871, p. 574).

The subject appears in the artist's prose poem *A Vision of Love Revealed in Sleep* (see cat. 117) in which Love appears to the wanderer veiled in saffron-coloured cloth and wearing a fawn-skin: "in his hand he carried a staff, which was as the rod of the high priest, for as I looked upon its barrenness burst forth in almond bloom" and his face "glowing with the perfect peace which is shed of Love, for he had borne the Very Love within his hands" (pp. 72–73).

The subject has similarities both to Solomon's ritual works, such as *The Mystery of Faith* (1870, cat. 88), and the 'classical' works like *The Evening Hymn* (cat. 108). The figure bears some resemblance to the monstrance-bearer in Gozzoli's *The Journey of the Magi* (1459–61, Palazzo Medici, Florence), a work that the artist might well have known from his travels in Italy in 1867.

Cat. 114 was the subject of an important exchange of views between the artist and his patron in letters undated but presumably *c.* 1868 to early 1869. For excerpts from this correspondence, see Roberto Ferrari's essay, pp. 47–55. The work, which has subsequently disappeared and might have been destroyed, was luckily photographed on completion by Hollyer and appears here as a platinotype. It was exhibited at the Fifth General Exhibition of Water-Colour Drawings, Dudley Gallery, 1869 (as no. 111); the frame bore the Latin quotation from St John's Gospel that translates as: "The light shineth in the darkness, and the darkness comprehended it not" (1:5). The incomprehension and hostility of critics was striking although not universal. The critic of the *Art Journal*, for example, observed that Solomon "had seldom shown in so great brilliance or – singularity. The artist stands alone although signs appear of a new and rising school in which he might shine as chief. *Sacramentum Amoris* is perhaps the best example of one of the painter's many manners, that of the classic warmed by colour and softened by romance. The drawing and the anatomy are more than usually careful, though the forms still want firmness of articulation, as for example at the knee-joint" (March 1869, p. 81).

The *Illustrated London News* made a moral objection to the work: "To perverted fancy the figure with all its symbols may, of course, be made to yield almost any meaning, but scarcely a wholesome or profitable one" (6 February 1869, p. 135).

115
Study for **Sacramentum Amoris**
1868
Pencil with some watercolour on paper
33.5 × 20.1 cm (13 3/16 × 7 15/16 in.)
The British Museum, London

Cat. 115 is a delicate drawing for the 1868 watercolour (see cat. 114) that emphasizes the dreamy, rapt expression of the monstrance-bearer.

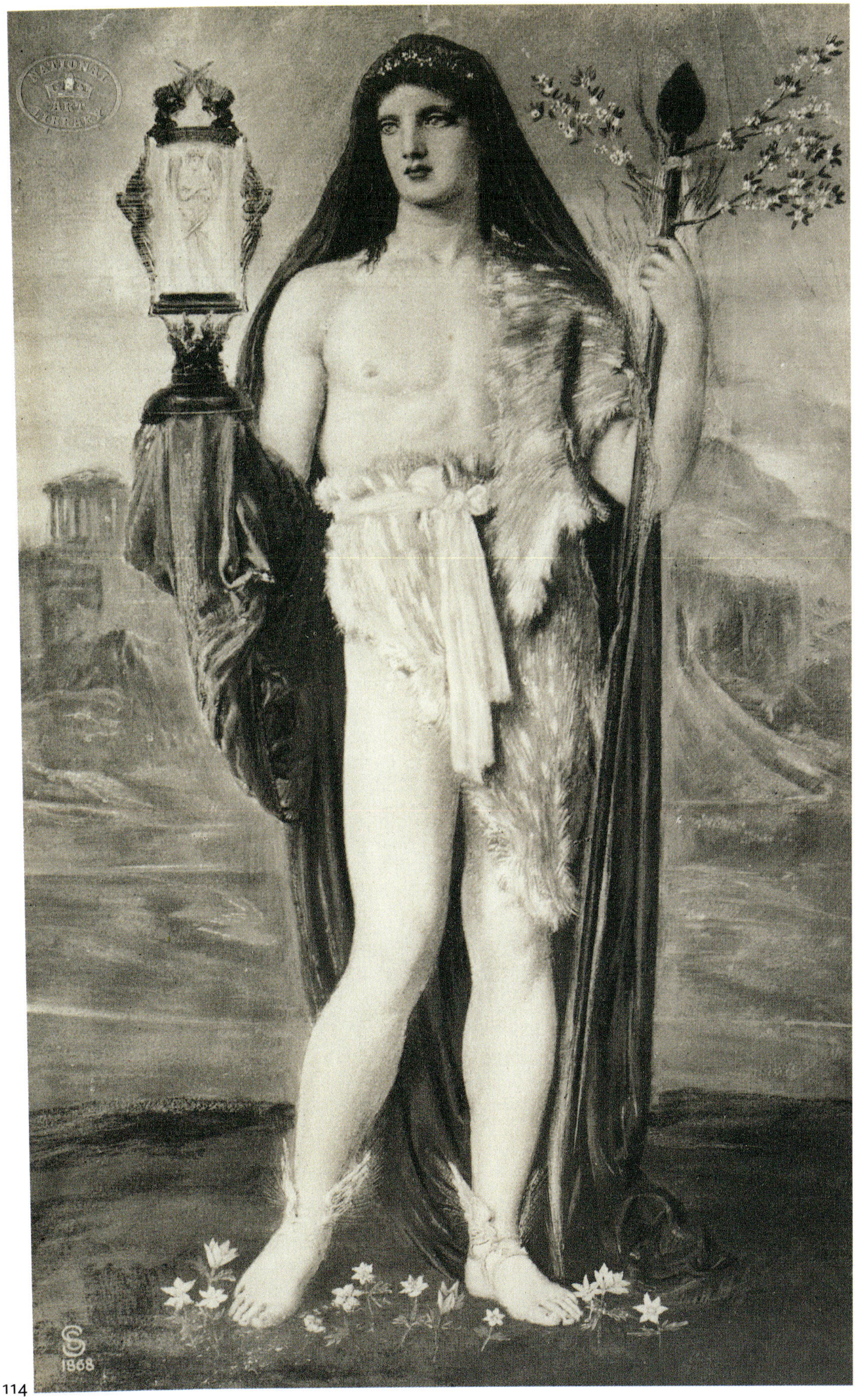

114

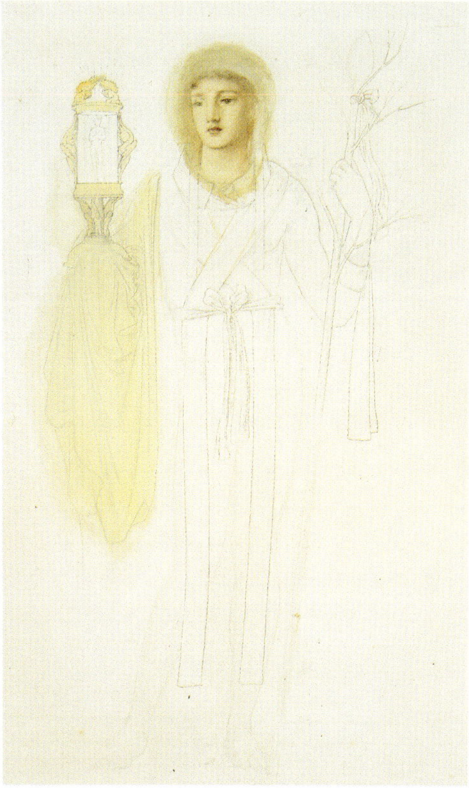

115

116
Frederick Hollyer after Simeon Solomon
Love Bound and Wounded
Photographic print; original drawing signed with monogram and dated *7 1868*
26.2 × 12.3 cm (10⁵⁄₁₆ × 4¹³⁄₁₆ in.)
Private collection

The earliest of several versions of this subject, cat. 116 proves that some of the figures featuring in *A Vision of Love Revealed in Sleep* (see cat. 117) existed in the artist's imagination before the composition of the prose work. Cat. 116, untraced in its original drawn version (probably pen, ink and pencil on paper), exists possibly uniquely in this photographic form by Frederick Hollyer.

The image has at least two functions. One is to provide an allegory of love, marginalized and rejected and, as such, resembling the image of 'Sad Love' that appears in several works of this period (see cat. 111). The other is to depict, in coded form, the sado-masochistic practices of whipping and beating enjoyed by Solomon and Swinburne.

The version shown at the Royal Academy in 1870 (as no. 277) was greeted with some puzzlement, the critic of the *Athenaeum* writing: "*Love Bound and Wounded*, by Mr. S. Solomon, shows a naked young gentleman tied to a tree at his back; it may be said to mean anything, but probably means nothing, so far as the subject or no subject is concerned; technically, it is more valuable, yet the flesh is raw rather than fine in colour, and there is hardly any vitality in the figure" (*Athenaeum*, 2222, 28 May 1870, pp. 713–14).

Gayle Seymour suggests that the figure in the Royal Academy watercolour might be derived from the Praxitelean figure of Eros at the Museo Nazionale, Naples (Seymour, 1986, p. 178), although it relates closely to images of St Sebastian, who was to become something of an icon for early gay art critics and collectors such as André Raffalovich in the 1890s. Solomon might also have been influenced by emblem imagery, such as that found in the engraving *Chastisement of Cupid* attributed to Baccio Baldini (The British Museum, London).

The figure is one of the apparitions of Love in *A Vision*, although the inscription "I saw a wound upon the heart of Love from which flowed blood and roses" does not appear in the published form of the prose poem. Cat. 116 also bears the legend *Vulnerasti Cor Meum* ("Thou hast wounded my heart") on a scroll.

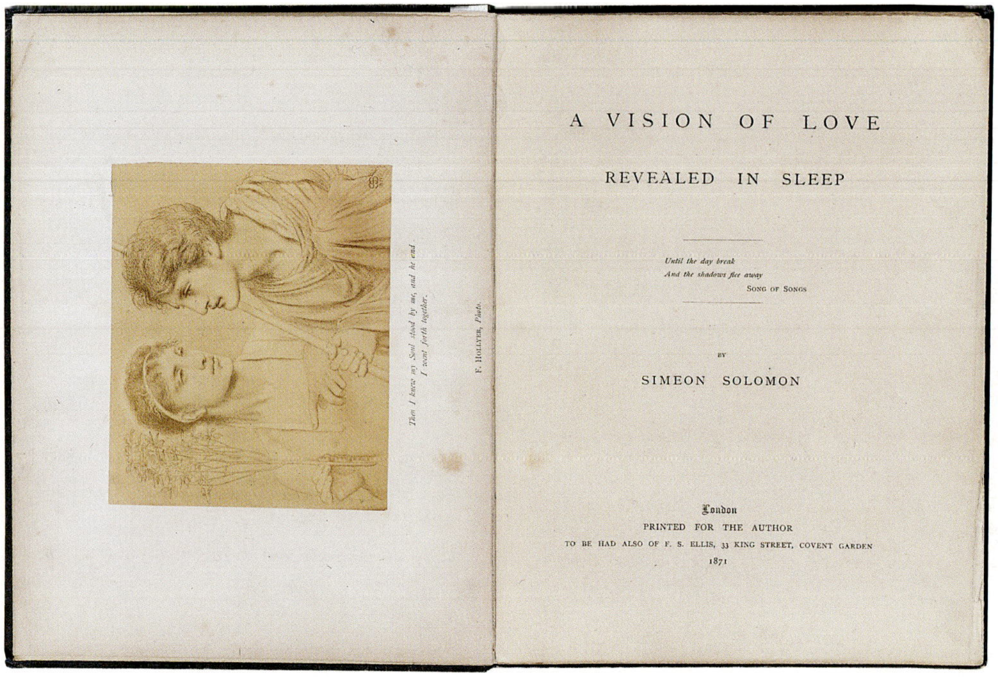

117a

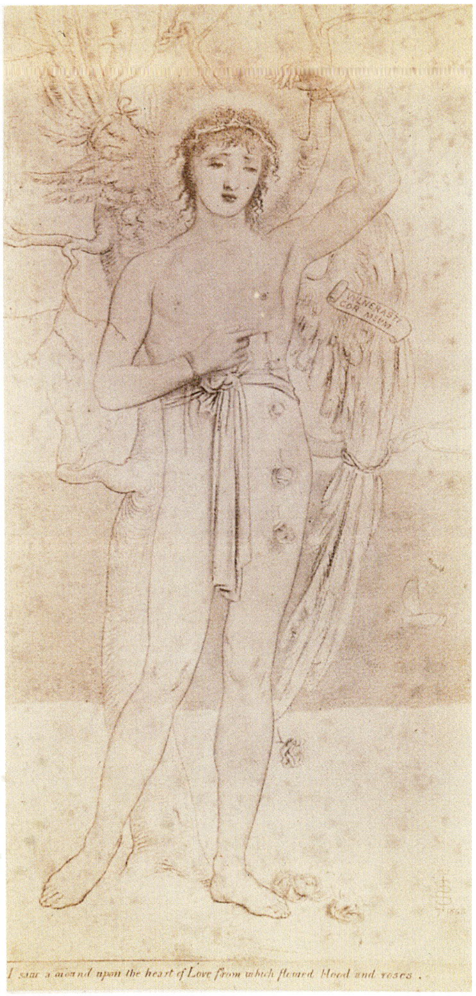

116

117
A Vision of Love Revealed in Sleep
1871
Book
26 × 20 × 0.8 cm (10¼ × 7⅞ × ¼ in.) when closed
a) open at title page; b) closed to show cover
a) Private collection; b) Lionel Lambourne

The genesis of Solomon's short but densely worded allegory is obscure and the sources multiple. Certainly there are direct quotations from the Song of Songs, but other images would suggest sources as diverse as the Old Testament and the *Hypnerotomachia Poliphili* as well as Dante's *Divina Commedia*. The *Roman de la Rose* and other medieval love allegories may also have contributed to the imagery. There is, too, a question of the complex relationship between text and image, exemplified by the existence of images independent of and predating the written text (see, for example, cat. 116).

The book is now regarded as an important early defence of male–male desire, before the popular adoption of terms like 'homosexuality' and its medicalization as a 'condition'. For Solomon it is closer to the type of love defended by Oscar Wilde in his trials in 1895, even if to a hostile and unprepared public. Wilde was to refer

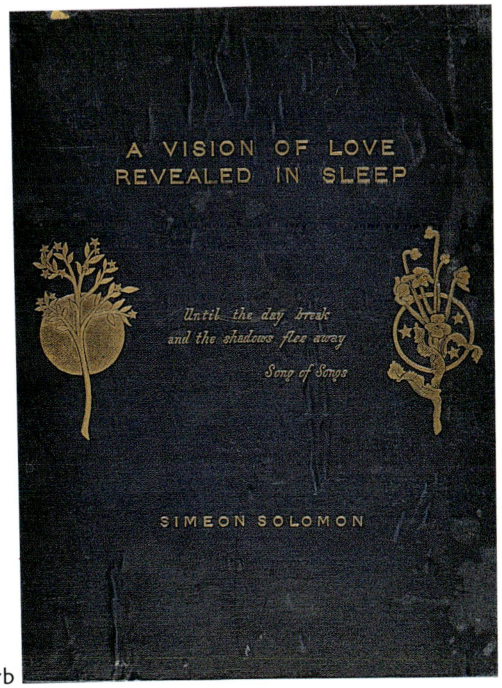

117b

to Solomon in an early essay as "that strange genius who wrote the *Vision of Love Revealed in Sleep*" (*Dublin University Magazine*, July 1877), a daring reference to a disgraced artist. In the 1990s the theatre director Neil Bartlett explored the possibilities of the prose poem as the basis for a series of theatrical performances in an experimental production in London.

There are four recorded reviews of cat. 117. John Addington Symonds, the poet and historian and author of *A Problem in Greek Ethics*, an essay on same-sex desire and its place in modern Western culture, approved of the work, drawing attention to images by the artist that relate to the various scenes described in visionary prose: "In truth, the originality of any poetical or pictorial Mythus, such as is embodied in this vision and in the series of Mr. Solomon's drawings, consists in its creator having viewed an old problem with new eyes, and communicated to the object some of the qualities of his own soul and of the age in which he lives. This, in our opinion, Mr. Solomon has done with eminent and unmistakable distinctness. His Love is not classical, not medieval, not Oriental; but it has a touch of all these qualities – the pure perfection of the classical form, the allegorical mysticism and pensive grace of the middle age, and the indescribable perfume of Orientalism, which, by the way, find a more than usually definite expression in the last scene of this vision" (*The Academy*, 1 April 1871, p. 189). Swinburne, then one of the artist's closest friends, drew attention to a technical flaw in the work in a review that disappointed Solomon: "Dim and vague as the atmosphere of such work should be, this vision would be more significant, and not less suggestive of things hidden in secret places of spiritual reserve, if it had more body of drawing, more shapeliness of thought and fixity of outline" (*The Dark Blue*, I, July 1871, p. 570).

The book's cover was designed by Solomon in a manner developed by Dante Gabriel Rossetti, whose designs influenced the development of book design for the rest of the century. The gold-blocked moon and stars motif echoes Rossetti's stars and comets for William Michael Rossetti's translation of Dante, *The Comedy of Dante Allighieri* [*sic*], London (Macmillan and Co.) 1865.

118
The End of a Month
1871
Wood engraving; original design signed with monogram and dated lower left
Published in *The Dark Blue*, I, 1871, p. 217
10.5 × 15.2 cm (4¼ × 6 in.)
Private collection

Cat. 118 is one of Solomon's most turbulent images of this period, its composition dominated by swirling hair and drapery. It has some of the drama of *Sturm und Drang* illustrations while using much of the 'intensity' of Aesthetic Movement faces – the curled upper lip, the expression of tragic sadness. Two figures, only just identifiable as male and female, stare outwards to their left as if into some bleak future. The tragic atmosphere and sketchy handling prevision Solomon's final manner, adopted in the crayon drawings of the 1880s and maintained until the end of his life.

Cat. 118 illustrates Swinburne's poem 'The End of a Month', which describes the male narrator's feelings at the end of a love affair. (The first stanzas appear opposite the engraving in the open book shown here.) The image, while summing up hectic and conflicting feelings, might illustrate specifically the second stanza: "For the old love's love-sake dead and buried, / One last time, one more and no more, / We watched the waves set in, the serried / Spears of the tide storming the shore."

The letterpress beneath cat. 118 reads "Drawn by S. Salaman".

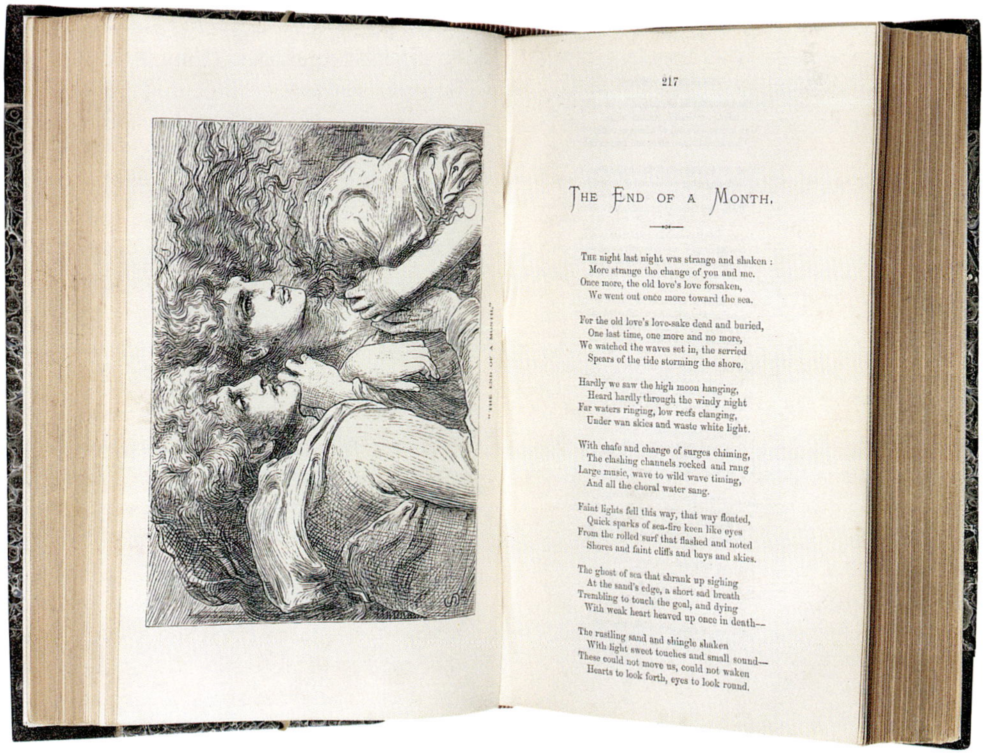
217

THE END OF A MONTH.

THE night last night was strange and shaken :
More strange the change of you and me.
Once more, the old love's love forsaken,
We went out once more toward the sea.

For the old love's love-sake dead and buried,
One last time, one more and no more,
We watched the waves set in, the serried
Spears of the tide storming the shore.

Hardly we saw the high moon hanging,
Heard hardly through the windy night
Far waters ringing, low reefs clanging,
Under wan skies and waste white light.

With chafe and change of surges chiming,
The clashing channels rocked and rang
Large music, wave to wild wave timing,
And all the choral water sang.

Faint lights fell this way, that way floated,
Quick sparks of sea-fire keen like eyes
From the rolled surf that flashed and noted
Shores and faint cliffs and bays and skies.

The ghost of sea that shrank up sighing
At the sand's edge, a short sad breath
Trembling to touch the goal, and dying
With weak heart heaved up once in death—

The rustling sand and shingle shaken
With light sweet touches and small sound—
These could not move us, could not waken
Hearts to look forth, eyes to look round.

118

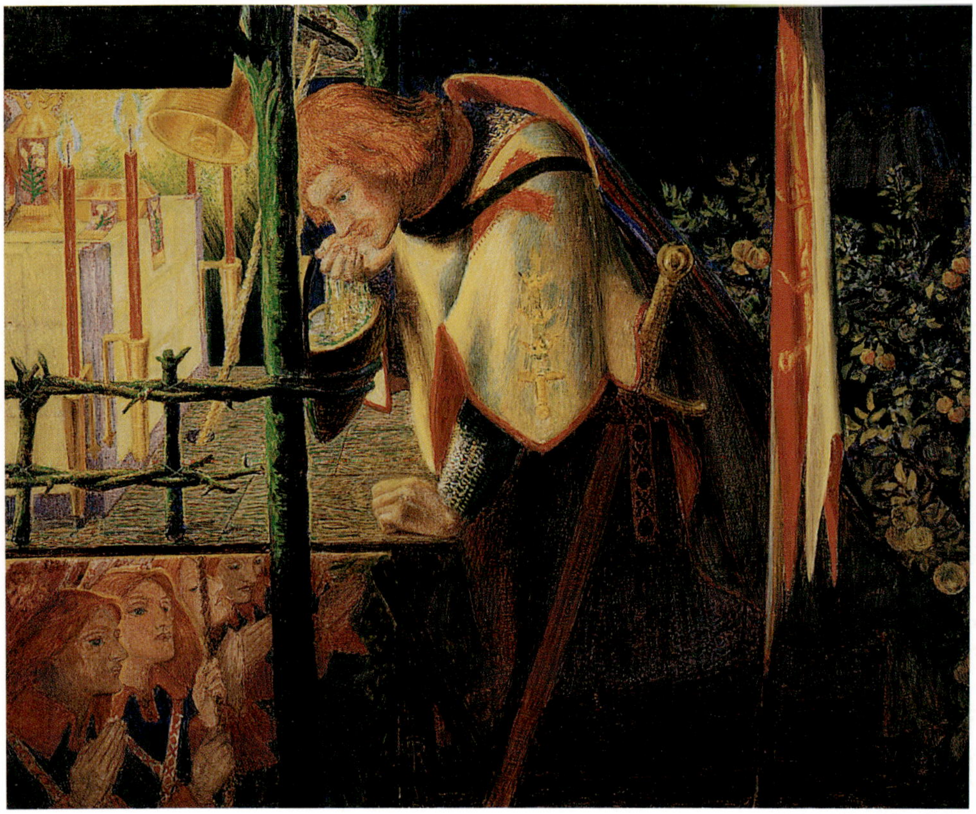

119

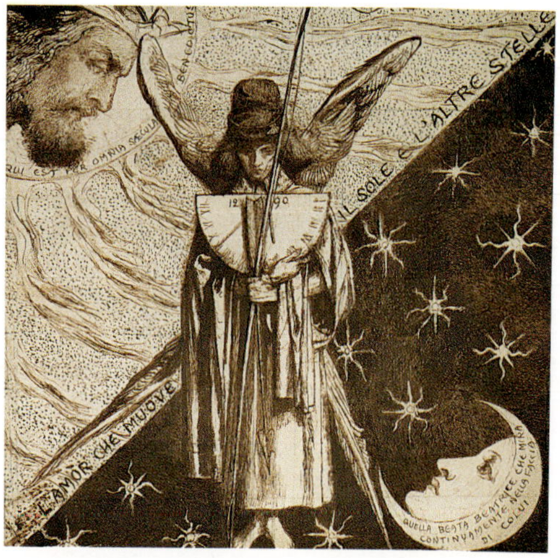

120

119
Dante Gabriel Rossetti (1828–1882)
Sir Galahad at the Ruined Chapel
1859
Watercolour and bodycolour on paper
29.1 × 34.5 cm (11½ × 13½ in.)
Signed with monogram lower centre
Birmingham Museums & Art Gallery.
Purchased 1892

Cat. 119 is based on a design for Rossetti's illustration to Tennyson's 'Sir Galahad' for the Moxon edition (1857). The artist kept many of the features of the original drawing, but the bright light radiating from the altar is given an acidic intensity through the use of watercolour. The details of the altar, the tabernacle and candlesticks, the chalice and ciborium (changed in the illustration from a paten containing bread) with lily-embroidered strips, are elaborations on the description contained in the poem. Here Rossetti prefigures the interest in the altar contained in Solomon's ritual paintings, such as cat. 85 and 86.

The first owner of cat. 119 was James Leathart, the Newcastle-upon-Tyne industrialist, who also commissioned works from Solomon (see cat. 87), probably following Rossetti's advice.

120
Dante Gabriel Rossetti (1828–1882)
Dantis Amor
c. 1860
Pen and brown ink on paper
25.1 × 24.2 cm (9⅞ × 9½ in.)
Birmingham Museums & Art Gallery. Presented by subscribers, 1904

Rossetti made three versions of this subject between 1860 and 1866; this is the most intense. It has strong thematic links with Solomon's *A Vision of Love Revealed in Sleep* (1871) and suggests a precedent for Solomon's *Sacramentum Amoris* (see cat. 114). Although there were no public exhibitions of this design, it was still in Rossetti's possession at the time of his death and would, therefore, have been available for Solomon to study with ease.

The heads of Christ and Beatrice, seen in profile and heavily stylized, face each other with fixed stares as the soul and the traveller do in Solomon's frontispiece to *A Vision of Love Revealed in Sleep* (cat. 117). Rossetti's figure of Love is depicted wearing the cockleshell hat and heavy travelling robe of a pilgrim; he bears a semicircular sundial, a bow and an arrow. The heavily conceptualized figure seems to sink beneath the weight of allegorical accoutrements.

Cat. 120 bears several inscriptions, one of which, *Amor che muove il Sole e L'Altre Stelle*, confirms the absolute power of love. The way 'love' is used pictorially by Rossetti allows for an ambiguous reading: as an emotion and/or as the embodied figure of Love, Amor. It was a quotation that inspired Solomon as well as Burne-Jones, who produced several works bearing Dante's phrase throughout the 1870s.

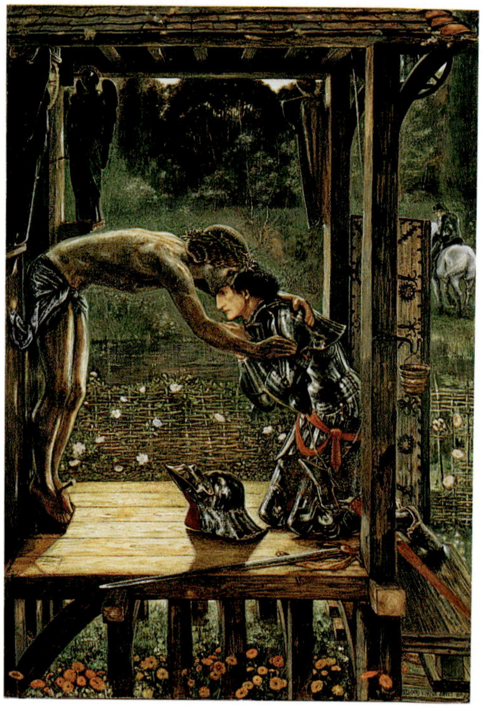

121

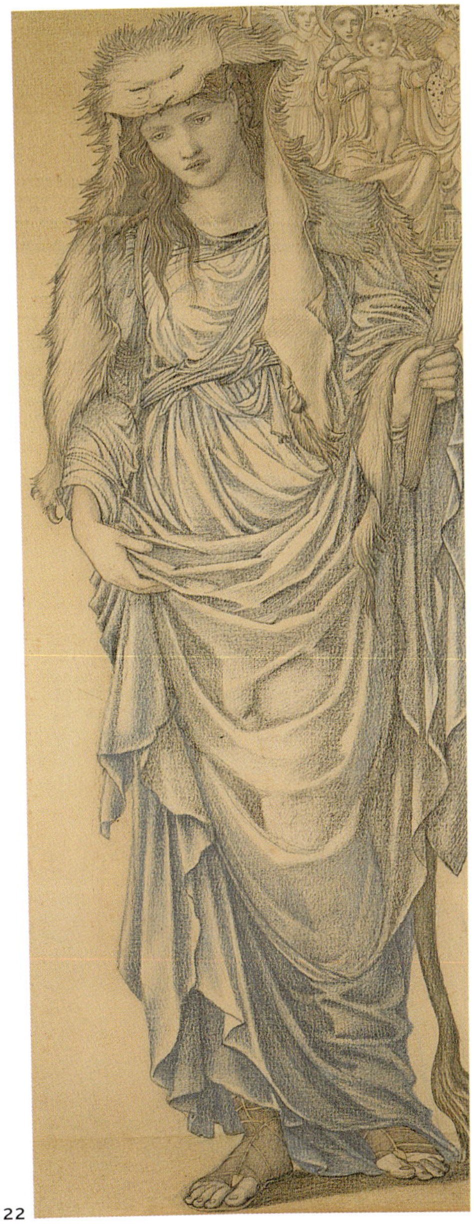

122

121
Edward Burne-Jones (1833–1898)
The Merciful Knight
1863
Watercolour, bodycolour and gum on paper
100.3 × 69.2 cm (39½ × 27¼ in.)
Signed and dated lower right
Birmingham Museums & Art Gallery.
Purchased 1973

With Solomon, Burne-Jones demonstrated the centrality and strength of watercolour for the later Pre-Raphaelite Movement. This work was shown at the Old Watercolour Society in 1864; Burne-Jones was elected an Associate in that year (an accolade sought by Solomon at the same time, although he failed to be elected at this, his only, attempt).

The Merciful Knight, while harking back to the medievalism of the earlier Pre-Raphaelite Brotherhood, suggests a new intensity and mysticism more characteristic of the new Dudley Gallery artists such as Walter Crane and Robert Bateman, as well as Solomon, than those who showed at the Old Watercolour Society. The intensely religious atmosphere of the work depicting the figure of a knight kneeling at a shrine is a further link with Solomon's subjects of the mid-1860s.

122
Edward Burne-Jones (1833–1898)
The Tiburtine Sibyl
1875
Pencil, black chalk, pastel and gold paint on buff paper
111.6 × 45.3 cm (43⅞ × 17 in.)
Birmingham Museums & Art Gallery. Bequeathed by J.R. Holliday, 1927

Cat. 122 is one of two drawings illustrating the mythical Sibyls that became the basis for designs for stained-glass windows. The imposing solemnity of the countenance, the ambiguity of sex and the glowing figures at head height suggest some traces of influence from Solomon's *Sacramentum Amoris* (see cat. 114).

123
Sidney Harold Meteyard (1868–1947)
Hope Comforting Love in Bondage
1901
Oil on canvas
104.2 × 109.2 cm (41 × 43 in.)
Signed and dated bottom right
Birmingham Museums & Art Gallery. Presented by the artist's brother, Mr O.E. Meteyard, 1948

Meteyard was a pupil of, and later taught at, the School of Art at Birmingham. Stephen Wildman points to the "strong Burne-Jonesian influence" both on cat. 123 and a companion piece, *Love in Idleness*, shown in Paris in 1900 (Wildman, 1990, p. 65), but there are striking similarities, too, with the themes that dominated Solomon's work during the late 1860s and for the rest of his career, such as *Love in Autumn* (cat. 100). The colour of cat. 123, with its grape-purple and soft green arrangement, is also reminiscent of Solomon's best paintings, for example *Dawn* (cat. 110).

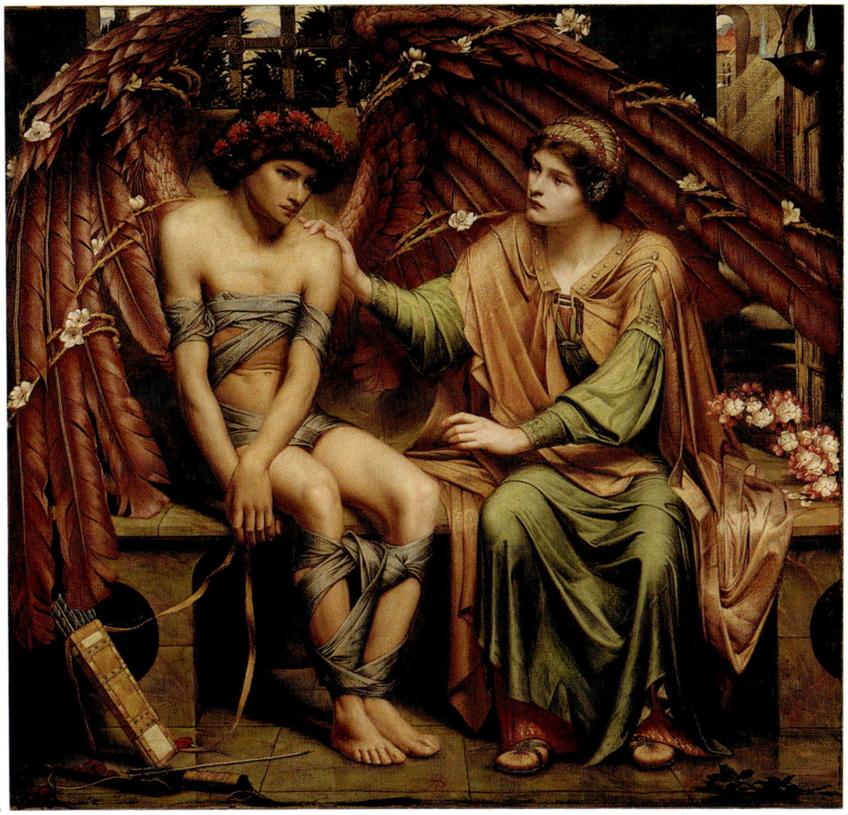

123

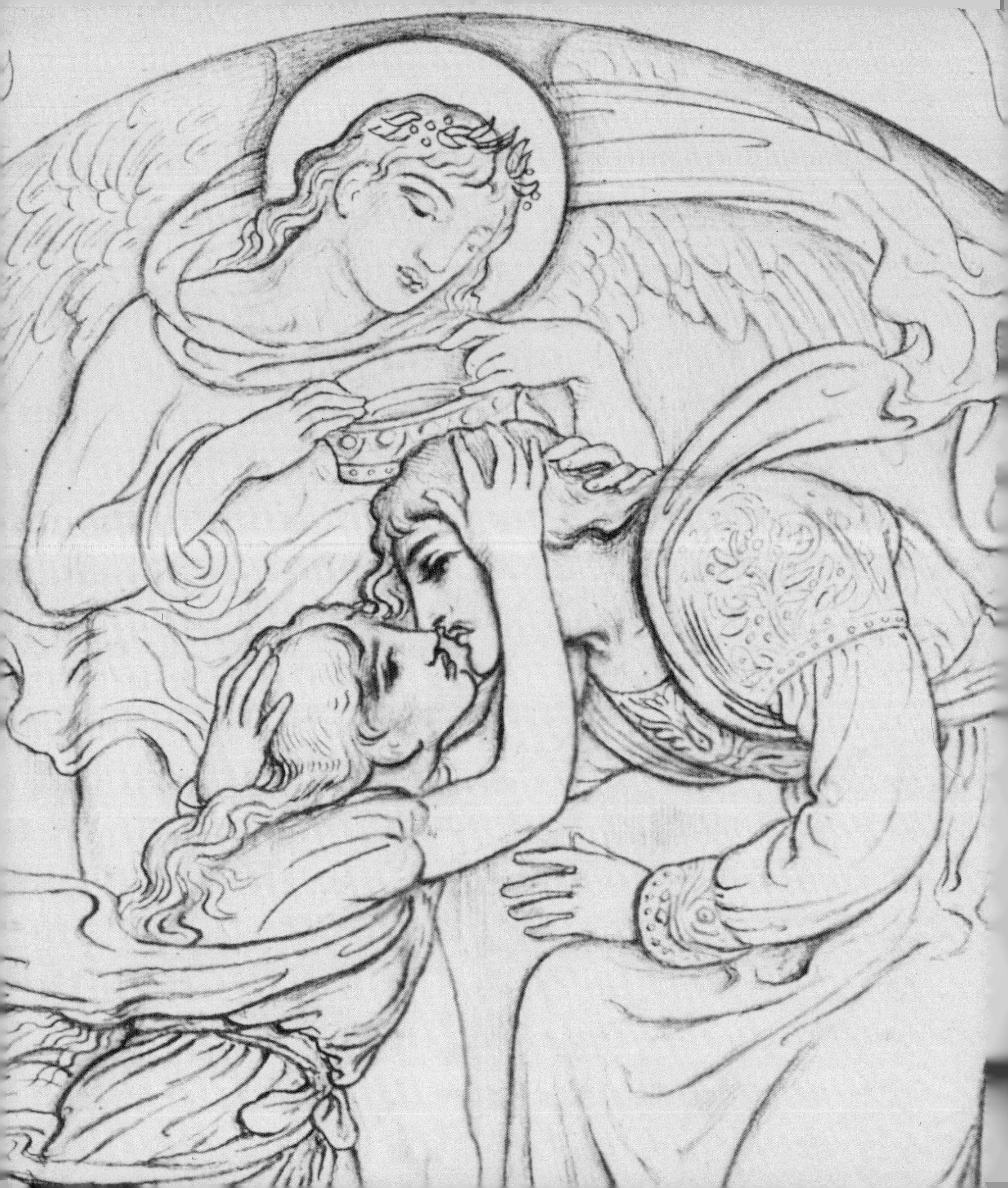

The Late Works

"A shipwreck of a genius"

Arthur Symons writing to Herbert Horne, 19 September 1887

Glimpses of Solomon in the thirty years that followed his downfall are fascinating. Many people thought him dead, but some sought him out partly out of curiosity; others traced him in order to buy drawings from him. Arthur Symons, poet and critic, wrote to Herbert Horne about seeing works on show at the Manchester Exhibition of 1887:

> I was so impressed with their beauty and originality, and a certain morbid grace they have, that I asked one or two people about the man, and finally got the lamentable story from Ellis. One cannot wonder that he has dropped out of sight, and foregone his future; but it is an infinite pity. Do you know him? You say 'he is glad to sell a pencil drawing for a few shillings': what sort of drawings does he do? Is he still capable of fine work? I judge from your remark that he must be almost in destitution: how is that? – would no one patronize or employ him, or has he neglected his art? If you really know much about him you will do me a favour by telling me a thing or two. He *had*, at any rate, a remarkable genius; and there is nothing in this world so pitiful as a shipwreck of a genius.
>
> (Arthur Symons to Herbert Horne, 19 September 1887, quoted in Symons, 1989, p. 30)

Horne himself reintroduced Solomon to an élite group of art enthusiasts by publishing his work in the periodical *The Century Guild Hobby Horse* (see cat. 131).

After some thirty years of living more or less as an outcast, Solomon died suddenly in August 1905, having collapsed in the street in High Holborn earlier in the summer. Following his death Solomon was honoured by two memorial exhibitions, one at the Royal Academy, the other at the recently opened gallery of John Baillie. Shortly afterwards his works were heavily featured at the Whitechapel 'Jewish Art and Antiquities' exhibition. Marion H. Spielmann, writing in the *Jewish World*, thought that "the name of Simeon Solomon will be remembered and honoured as an artist", although he observed that in his later period the artist's "hand and eye had become demoralised" (7 December 1906, p. 626).

Julia Ellsworth Ford claimed that, in 1908, Solomon's fame and popularity were spreading. Perhaps they would have, had it not been for the displacement of Symbolism as a Modernist mode of art practice following the sudden rise of Cubism and Expressionism. Certainly, obituary notices recognized the particular qualities of Solomon's work, his colour sense, the peculiar sadness of the faces and the Symbolist sensibility of his best drawings. He continued to be collected by connoisseurs of Victorian art; Sir Hugh Lane, an important Irish collector, bought several works at auction in the early years of the twentieth century, and surveys of the period included appreciative comments on Solomon's contribution. The reassessment had begun.

145e
Frederick Hollyer after Simeon Solomon
The Desire of the Bride towards the King, and his Glad Response (detail)
1878
Photographic print
20.5 × 16 cm (8 × 6½ in.)
Victoria and Albert Museum

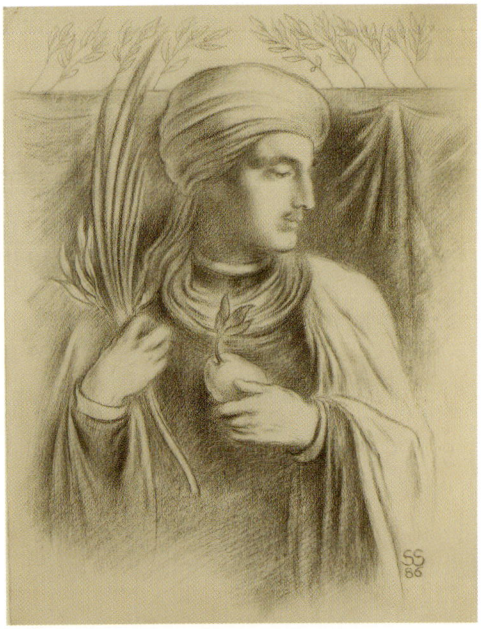

124

124

Man in Turban Holding Lulav and Etrog

1886

Crayon on paper

38.5 × 28 cm (15 × 11 in.)

Signed with monogram and dated *86* lower right

Courtesy of The Jewish Museum, London

The figure holds a *lulav*, a branch of palm, and an *etrog*, a citrus fruit, two of the "four elements" (*arba'ah minim*) central to the Jewish harvest festival, Sukkot (the Feast of Tabernacles). The subject demonstrates the artist's continued reference to Jewish themes at a late stage in his career.

125

David

Undated

Watercolour and bodycolour on paper

27 × 21.6 cm (10⅝ × 8½ in.)

Lent by the Syndics of the Fitzwilliam Museum, Cambridge

This late drawing shows the artist's continued engagement with the history of David, who is here represented as a young turbaned man.

126

The Annunciation

1894

Oil on canvas

37.5 × 62.2 cm (14¾ × 24½ in.)

The Russell-Cotes Art Gallery & Museum, Bournemouth

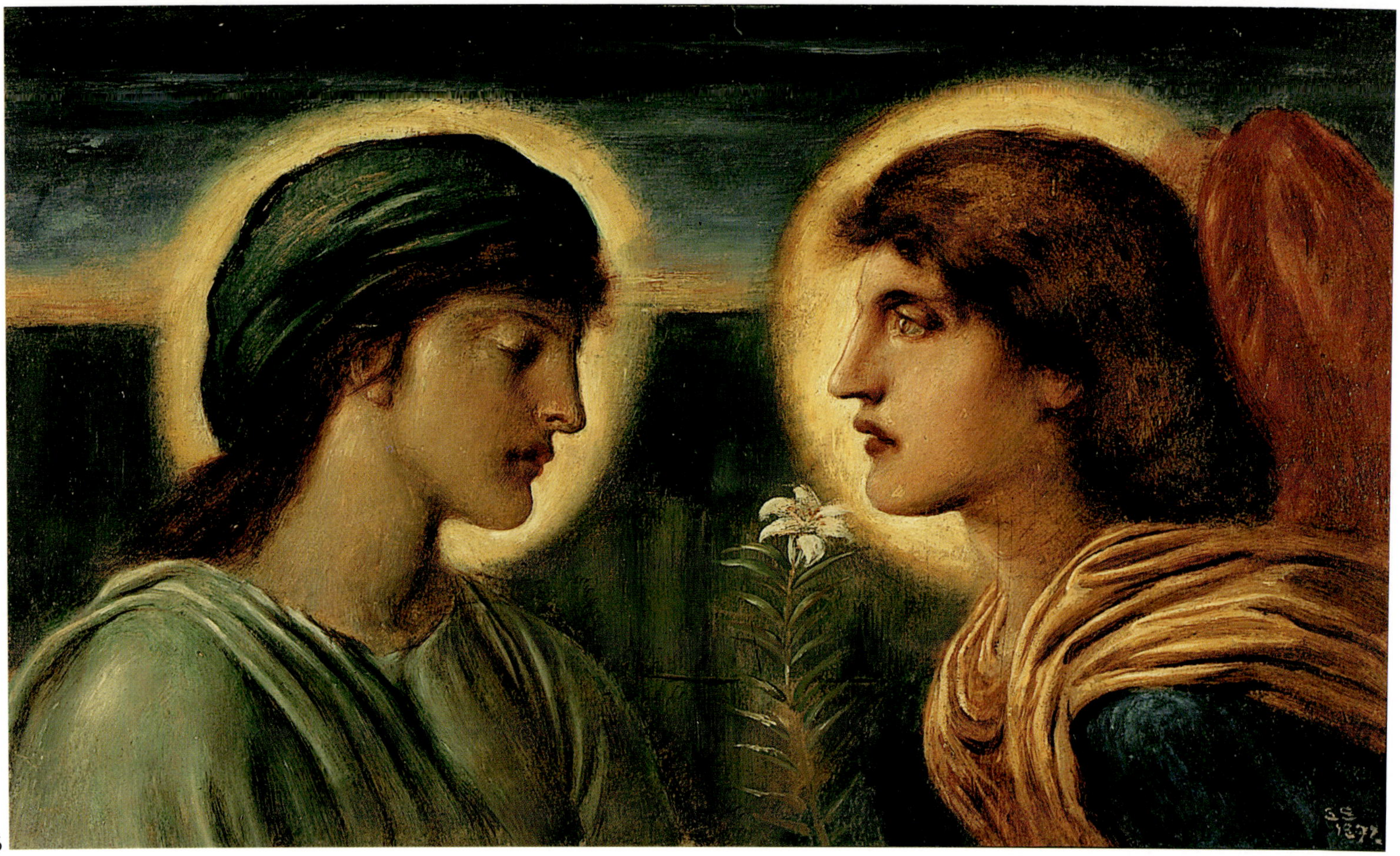

126

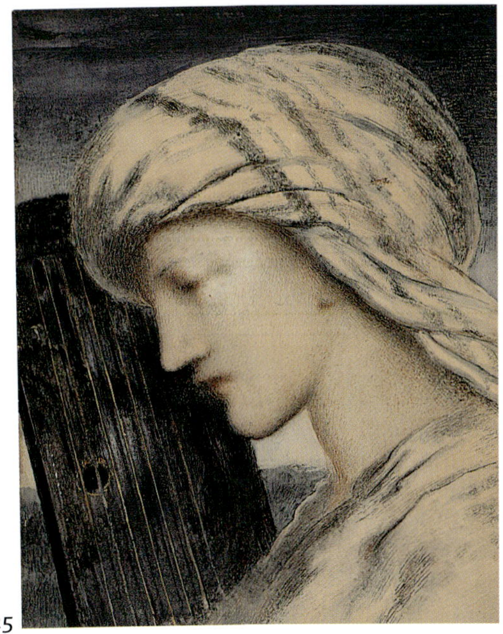

125

This is one of Solomon's several versions of the story of the Annunciation (see, for example, cat. 144), when the Virgin Mary receives from the Archangel Gabriel the news that she will bear the Messiah, Jesus Christ. The subject was a particular favourite of the Pre-Raphaelites, probably because of its importance in Quattrocento 'Christian art'; Rossetti's *Ecce Ancilla Domini! (The Annunciation)* (1849–50, Tate) and Burne-Jones's *The Flower of God* (1862, private collection) are key examples. Solomon did not represent the subject at the time of its greatest vogue among his Pre-Raphaelite contemporaries; his use of the Annunciation at this later stage in his life is evidence of a further exploration of different religious denominations, first undertaken in the 'ritual' works of the 1860s.

It is sometimes assumed in biographical accounts that Solomon converted to Catholicism in the last two decades of his life, although there is no formal record of his having done so. In fact, he was buried as a Jew in the Jewish Cemetery, Willesden, London. He had some connection, possibly as a charitable dependant, to the Carmelite community in Kensington Church Street, whose abbot up to 1870 was Father Hermann, a converted Jew.

127
The Vision of the Doubter
1886
Graphite and coloured pencil on paper
17.2 × 24.2 cm (6¾ × 9½ in.)
Signed with monogram and dated *1886* centre right
Private collection

Cat. 127 is inscribed with the title and "W. Blake's 'Songs of Experience'", although the reference is obscure. The frieze-like procession is derived from Solomon's 'aesthetic' compositions of the 1860s and 70s, for example cat. 63 and 105, and perhaps from Blake's vignettes. Similar compositions can be found in several works of the artist's late career, such as *Good Tidings* (1884; Seymour, 1986, fig. 212) and *The Angel and the Patriarch* (1886, private collection).

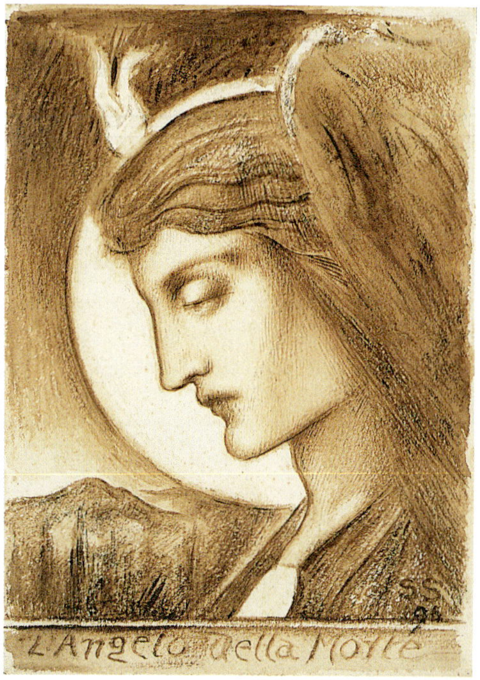

128

128
L'Angelo della Morte (The angel of death)
1896
Watercolour on paper
24.8 × 17.2 cm (9¾ × 6¾ in.)
Signed and dated 96
Dr Dennis T. Lanigan collection, Canada

Cat. 128 shows a calm, severe profile looking downwards sorrowfully, in contemplation, as if towards humanity. It is one of Solomon's most distinctive new themes in his late career, although the subject of death, and its personification as Mors, began to appear in his work in the 1860s (see cat. 68 and 76) and features in *A Vision of Love Revealed in Sleep* (1871, cat. 117).

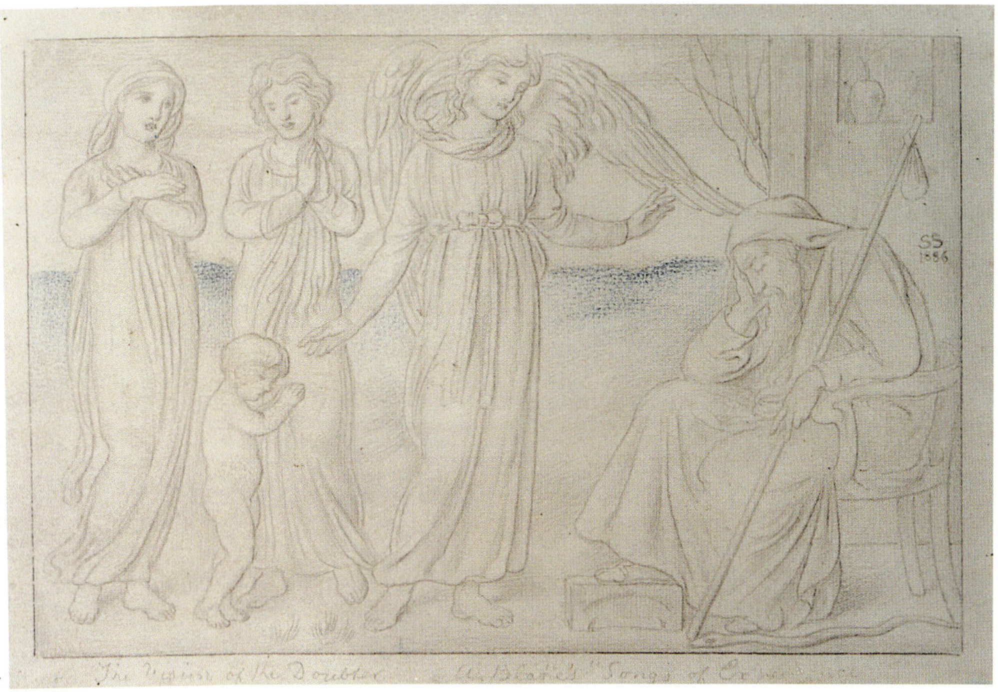

127

129
The Tormented Conscience
1889
Red chalk on paper
40.6 × 30.5 cm (16 × 12 in.)
Inscribed with title in scroll and signed with monogram and dated 89 at lower right
Private collection

Cat. 129 is a version of a recurrent theme in Solomon's later work combining the head of Medusa, the mythical woman whose hair had been replaced by writhing snakes, with an embodied representation of the human conscience that contorts the face and produces tormenting thoughts, forcing the mouth open in pain and disgust. The combination of these motifs is original, although the Medusa theme was one explored by several artists in the latter half of the nineteenth century, particularly in Belgium and France, where Pre-Raphaelitism was an influence on the development of Symbolism. There are strong similarities with one of the most potent Symbolist works, Jean Delville's *Idol of Perversity* (1891, private collection), in which the Medusa suggests a real, yet 'fatal' woman. Here, on the other hand, Solomon's depiction of the Medusa is made more disturbing by the ambiguity of the figure, which is neither male nor female.

Solomon's tendency to combine the Medusa head with other concepts can be seen in his drawing *The Sleep of Remorse* (1886, Harvard University Art Museum, Cambridge MA), which suggests Orpheus, Sleep and the Medusa.

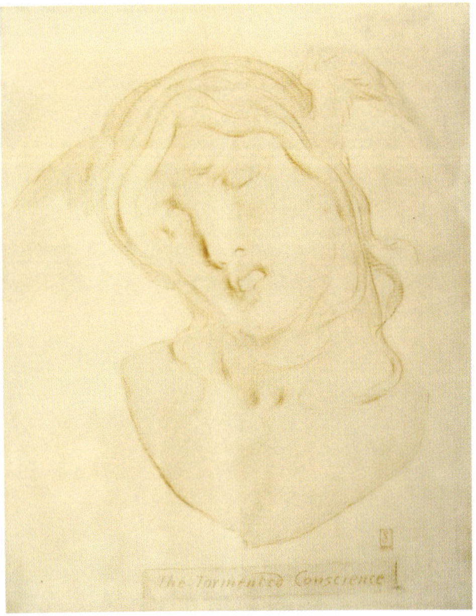

129

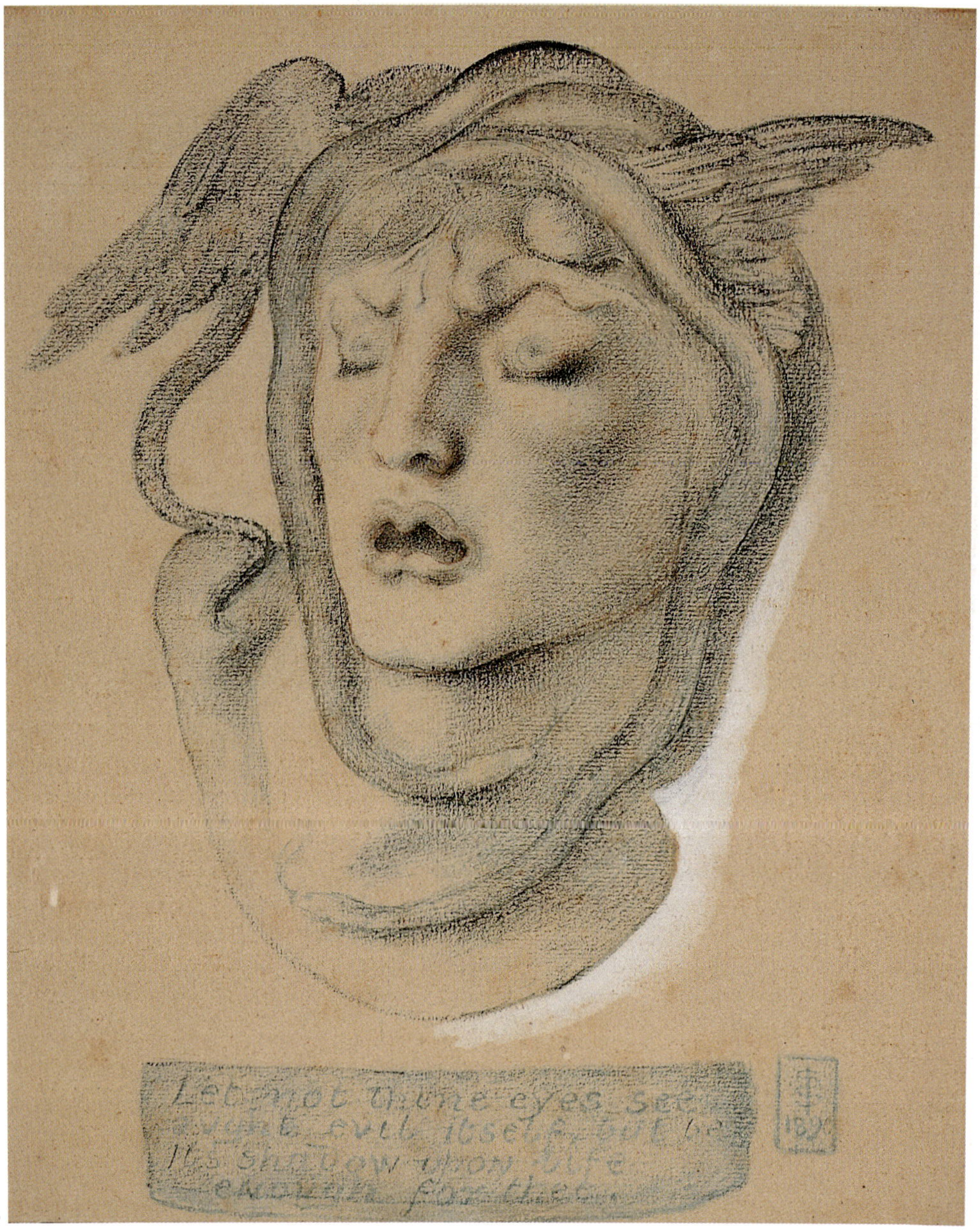

130

130
'Let not thine eyes see aught evil itself, but be its shadow upon life enough for thee'
1890
Coloured chalks on paper
32.5 × 26.3 cm (12 13/16 × 10 3/8 in.)
Private collection

The inscription that gives this work its title is a misquotation (and contraction) of a verse from D.G. Rossetti's poem 'Aspecta Medusa'. Rossetti had begun working on the theme of Medusa in about 1865 but never completed a picture on the subject (although there is a finished study, dated 1868, of Alexa Wilding in the character of the ill-fated heroine of his concept of the story, in the Victoria and Albert Museum). Oddly, Rossetti never satisfactorily realized the depiction of the severed head of the Medusa, the very thing that obsessed Solomon from the 1880s onwards.

While having a clear reference to Classical culture, the Medusa head was used in Jewish communities in Greco-Roman societies (see Goodenough, 1988, pp. 199–200, illustration 40).

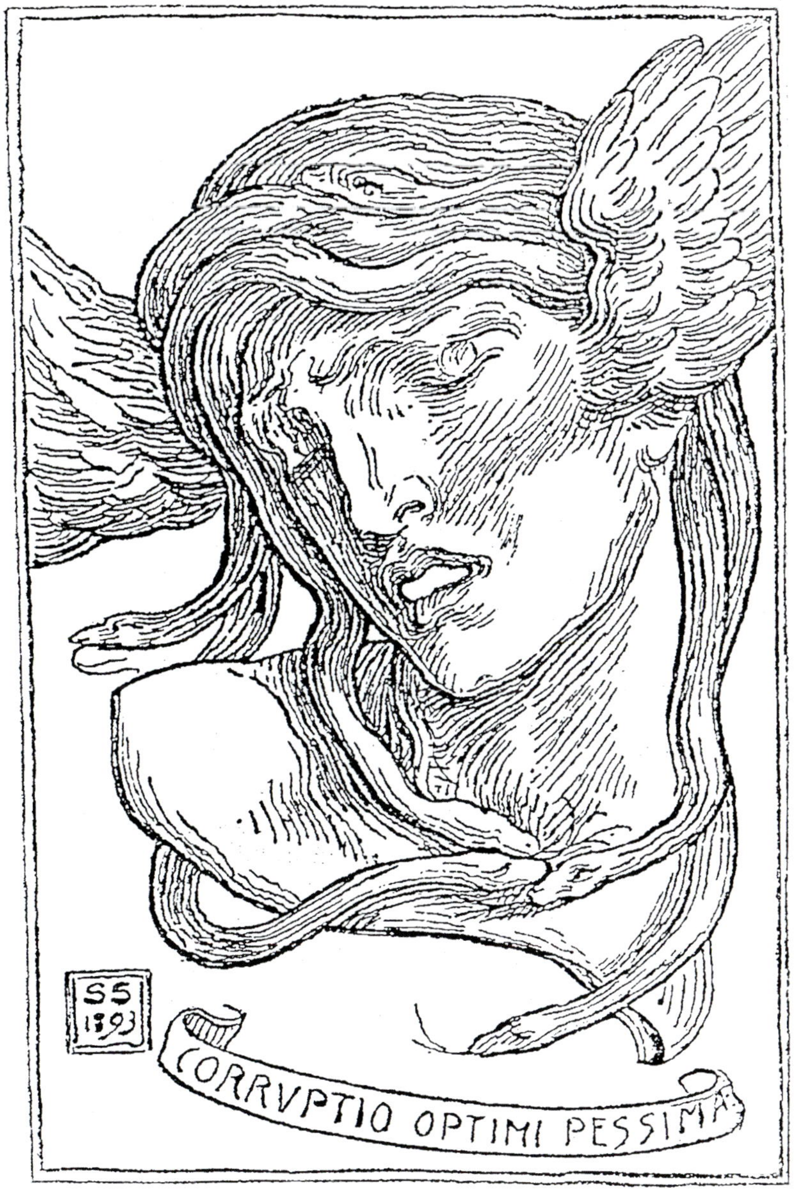

131

132
The Village Wit
1891
Red chalk on paper
35.5 × 24.5 cm (14 × 9½ in.), sight
Signed with monogram and dated *91* lower right and inscribed with title
Private collection

The subject of cat. 132 is obscure and might be a reference to a poem rather than a portrait of an actual person. It is atypical in representing the 'Wit' full face and looking directly out of the picture space. The winsome smile makes the drawing unusual in Solomon's output.

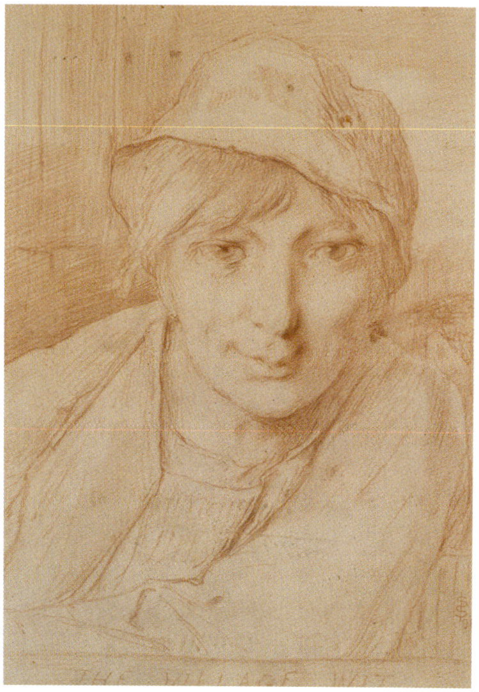

132

131
Corruptio Optimi Pessima
1893
Process reproduction
19.6 × 12.4 cm (7 11/16 × 4 7/8 in.), image
Published in *The Century Guild Hobby Horse*, 1893, following p. 50
Birmingham Libraries

Cat. 131 represents a return to public life after some twenty years. The artist was approached by the designer and author Herbert Horne to contribute to the relaunched Arts and Crafts periodical *The Century Guild Hobby Horse*. This was Solomon's original composition, the other illustration being a photographic reproduction of the painting *Bacchus* (cat. 91) used as the frontispiece to the July 1891 issue.

Solomon's attention to the head is here given a dramatic narrative twist in representing a Medusa-like character with wings and snakes on her head and closed eyelids through which the eyes can still be glimpsed, giving the expression a disturbing stare. Medusa was a recurring motif in Symbolist art throughout Europe at the turn of the nineteenth century, key examples being works by the American painter Elihu Vedder (1836–1923), who knew Solomon in Rome and who exhibited at the Dudley Gallery, and Fernand Khnopff, the Belgian Symbolist (see cat. 155 and 157).

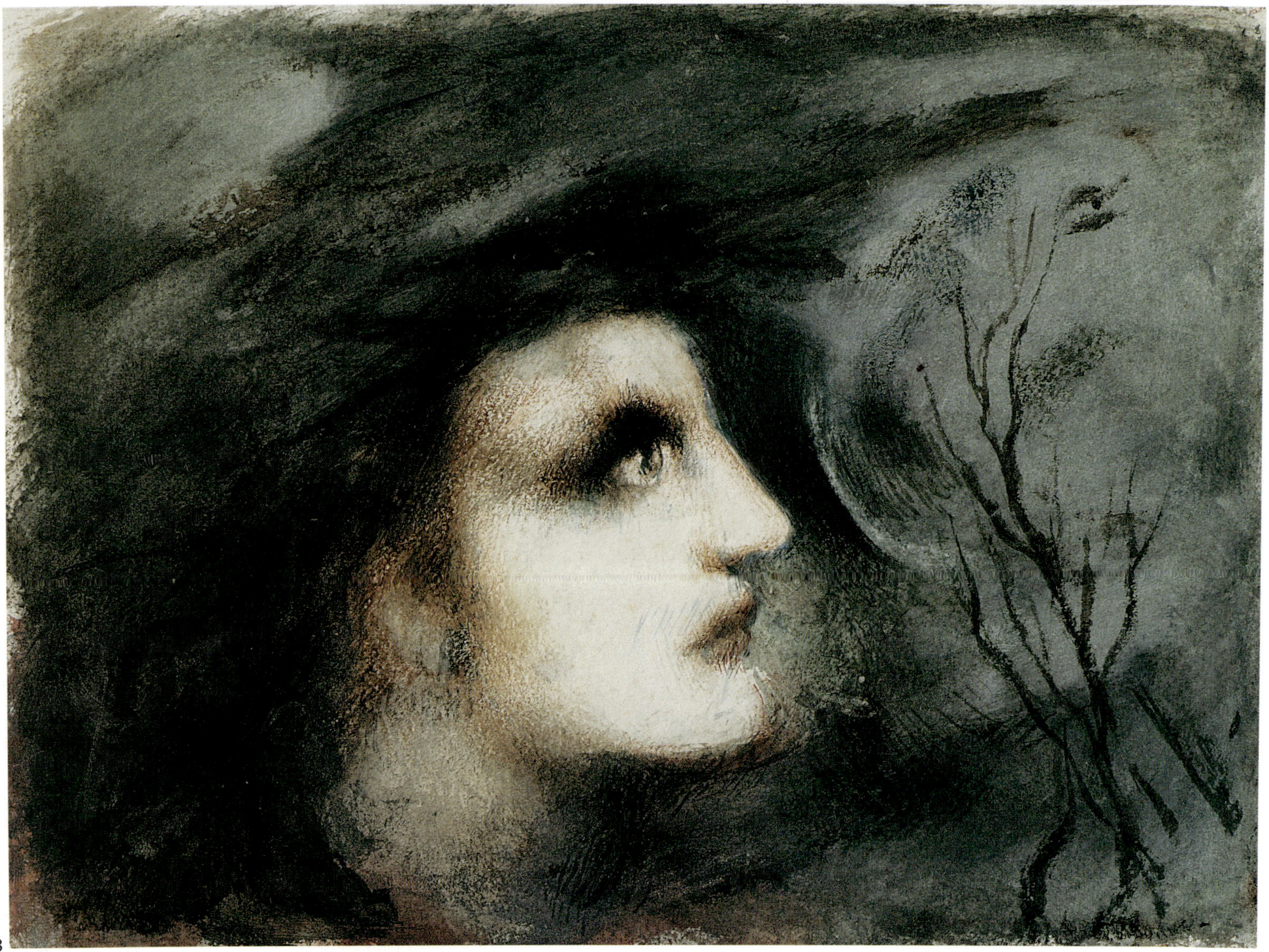

133

133
Creation
Undated, *c.* 1890
Watercolour on paper
22.8 × 27.9 cm (9 × 11 in.)
Victoria and Albert Museum

The title of cat. 133 comes from an inscription on the back in pencil. It is an extraordinarily daring and suggestive work, representing a head in profile staring into a dark, wild space.

134
The Winged and Poppied Sleep
1889
Red chalk on paper
55.3 × 40 cm (21¾ × 15¾ in.)
Signed with monogram and dated *1889* lower right and inscribed with title
Aberdeen Art Gallery & Museums Collections

Cat. 134 bears some resemblance to D.G. Rossetti's famous depiction of his wife, Elizabeth Siddal, as Beatrice in *Beata Beatrix* (1864, several versions, see cat. 149), yet the subject allows Solomon to explore the sparser and more suggestive Symbolist iconography of French and Belgian artists such as Lucien Lévy-Dhurmer (1865–1953), Odilon Redon (1840–1916), whose 'eyes closed' works emphasize internality, Fernand Khnopff (1858–1921) and Jean Delville (1867–1953).

The frame of cat. 134 bears the autograph of Paul Verlaine (1844–1896). Ann Steed suggests that the French poet and the English artist might have met in 1893 (*A Scottish Collection*, 2000, pp. 92–93).

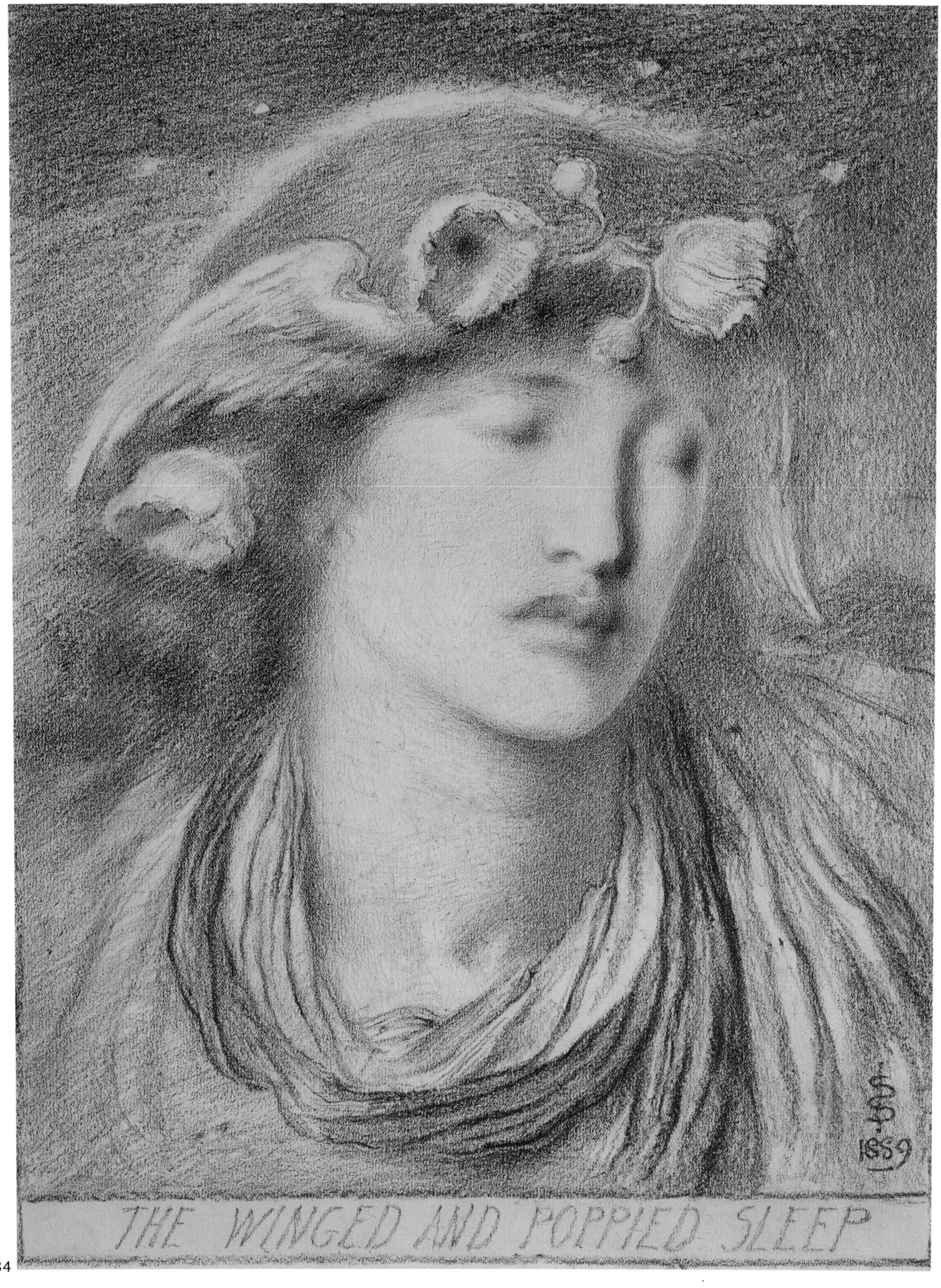

134

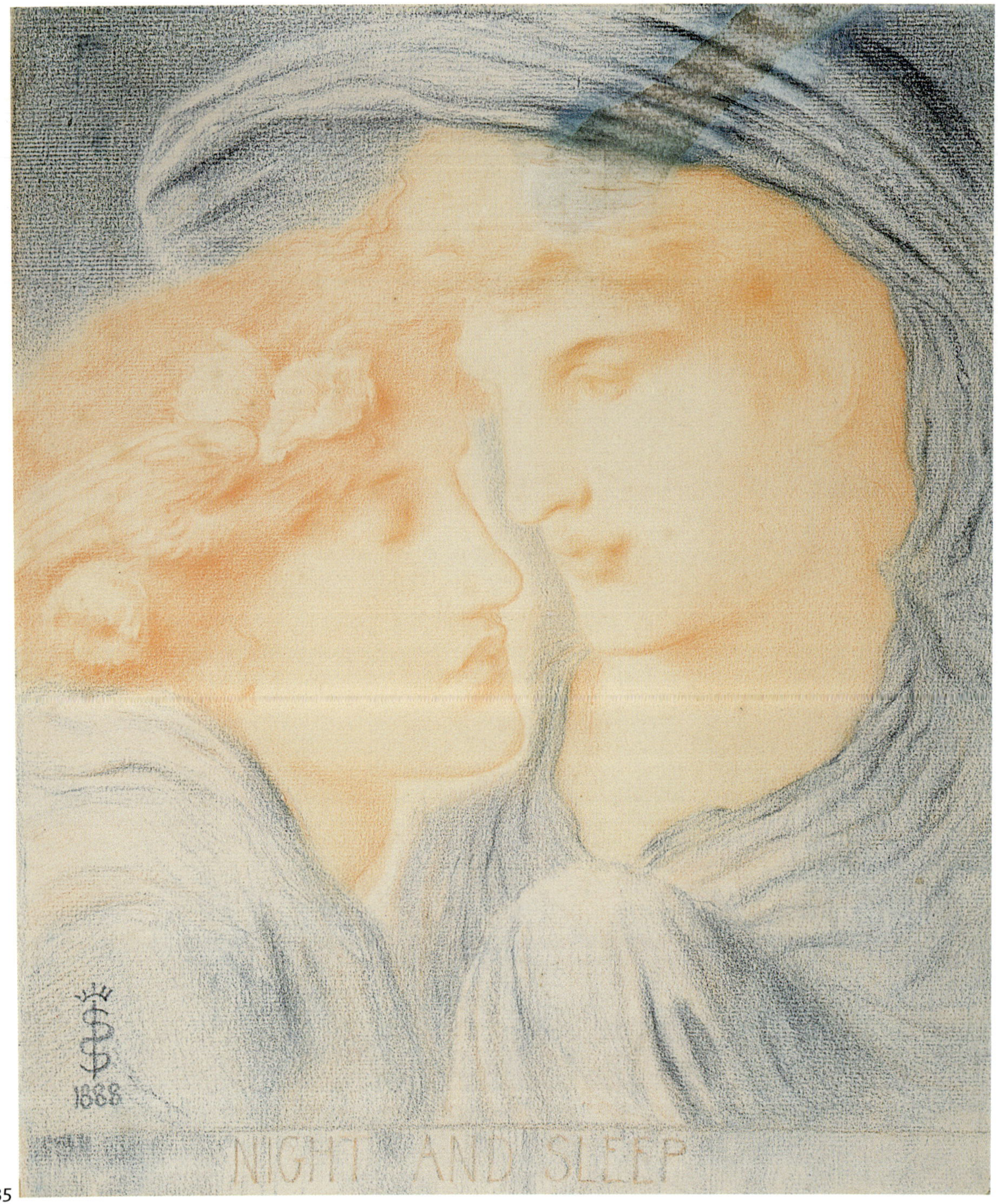

135

135
Night and Sleep
1888
Blue and red crayon on paper
35.7 × 29.5 cm (14 1/16 × 11 5/8 in.)
Signed with monogram and dated *1888* lower left and inscribed with title
Birmingham Museums & Art Gallery. Presented by Cecil F. Crofton, 1908

One of several versions of this subject (see, for example, cat. 141), this drawing exploits the compositional device of heads facing each other in profile that is also used in several works from the 1860s onwards (see, for example, cat. 117a). The concept appears to have been suggested by Shelley, whose *Queen Mab* (1813) opens with the lines: "How wonderful is Death, Death and his brother sleep!"

The poem also suggests the colouration of blue and pink. Shelley was one of Solomon's favourite poets and was still being lauded by him when the artist met Julia Ellsworth Ford on her visit to London in the 1890s.

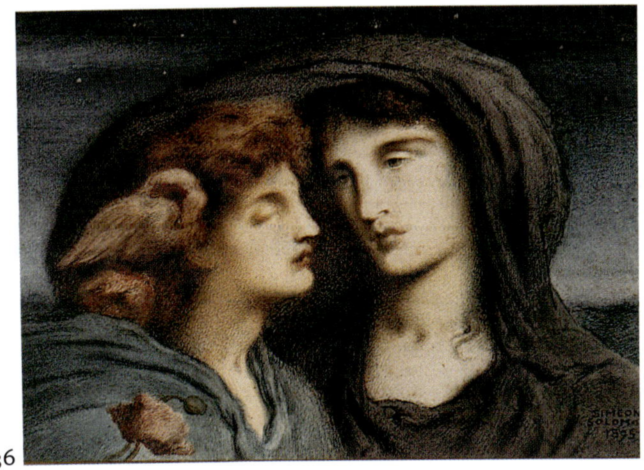

136

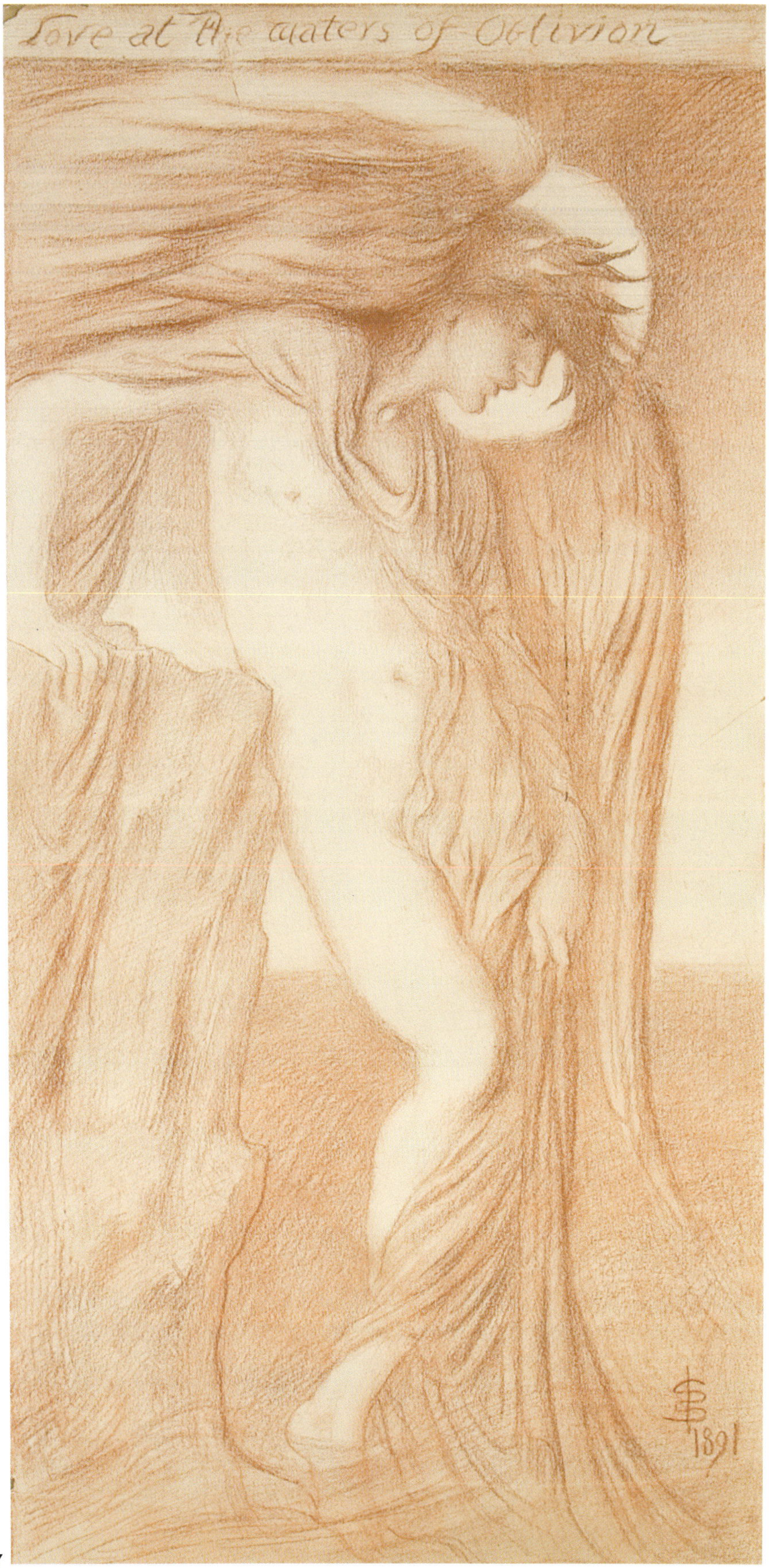

137

136
Night Looking upon Sleep her Beloved Child
1895
Watercolour and charcoal on paper
28.5 × 39 cm (11¼ × 15⅜ in.)
Signed and dated *1895*
Ben Uri Gallery, The London Jewish Museum of Art

Cat. 136 is a later variation on this subject (see cat. 135) and a feminized one, relating this version to Solomon's 'Sapphic' works of the 1860s. The affection of Night for Sleep is palpable. Again the reference seems to be to Shelley, here to stanza IV of 'To Night' (*c.* 1821).

137
Love at the Waters of Oblivion
1891
Red crayon on paper
61 × 30.5 cm (24 × 12 in.)
Signed with monogram and dated *1891* lower right and inscribed with title
The Albert Dawson Collection

Cat. 137 is a subject from *A Vision of Love Revealed in Sleep* but unknown in earlier or alternative versions. This late drawing is stylish and dashing, with linear flourishes reminiscent of Art Nouveau graphics, yet there is a solidity to the figure that indicates a continued interest in Renaissance prototypes, particularly Michelangelo.

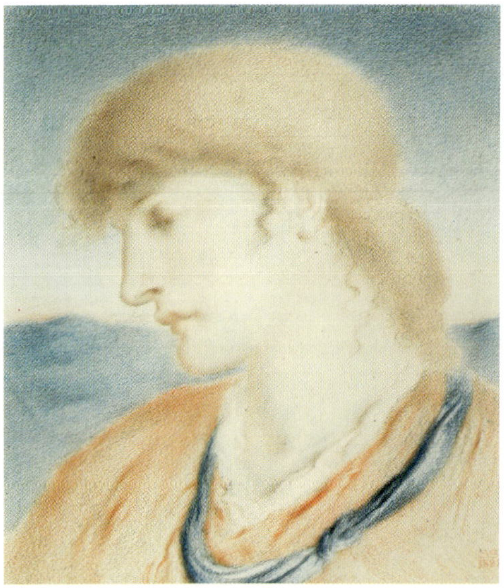

138

138
Head of a Young Man
1888
Blue, red and brown crayon with traces of pencil on paper
29 × 24.5 cm (11⅜ × 9⅝ in.), sight
Signed with monogram and dated *1888* lower right
Birmingham Museums & Art Gallery. Presented by Cecil F. Crofton, 1908

Cat. 138 is one of Solomon's ambiguous heads, the titles of which are vague and interchangeable, but which are often suggestive of deep emotion and interior calm. Several critics pointed out the sexual ambiguity of the sitters: "These faces are without sex: they have brooded among the ghosts of passion till they have become the ghosts of themselves: the energy of virtue or of sex has gone out of them, and they hang in space, dry, rattling, the husks of desire" (Arthur Symons, *From Toulouse-Lautrec to Rodin*, London 1929, p. 156).

The young man in cat. 138 bears some resemblance to representations of St John, the Beloved Disciple.

139
The Moon and Sleep
1894
Oil on canvas
51.5 × 76.3 cm (20¼ × 30 in.)
Signed with monogram and dated *1894* lower right
Tate. Presented by Miss Margery Abrahams in memory of Dr Bertram L. Abrahams and Jane Abrahams, 1973

Cat. 139 is a broadly painted and expressive late oil representing the story of the love of Selene, the goddess of the Moon, for Endymion, allowing the artist a variation on the theme of two heads confronting each other.

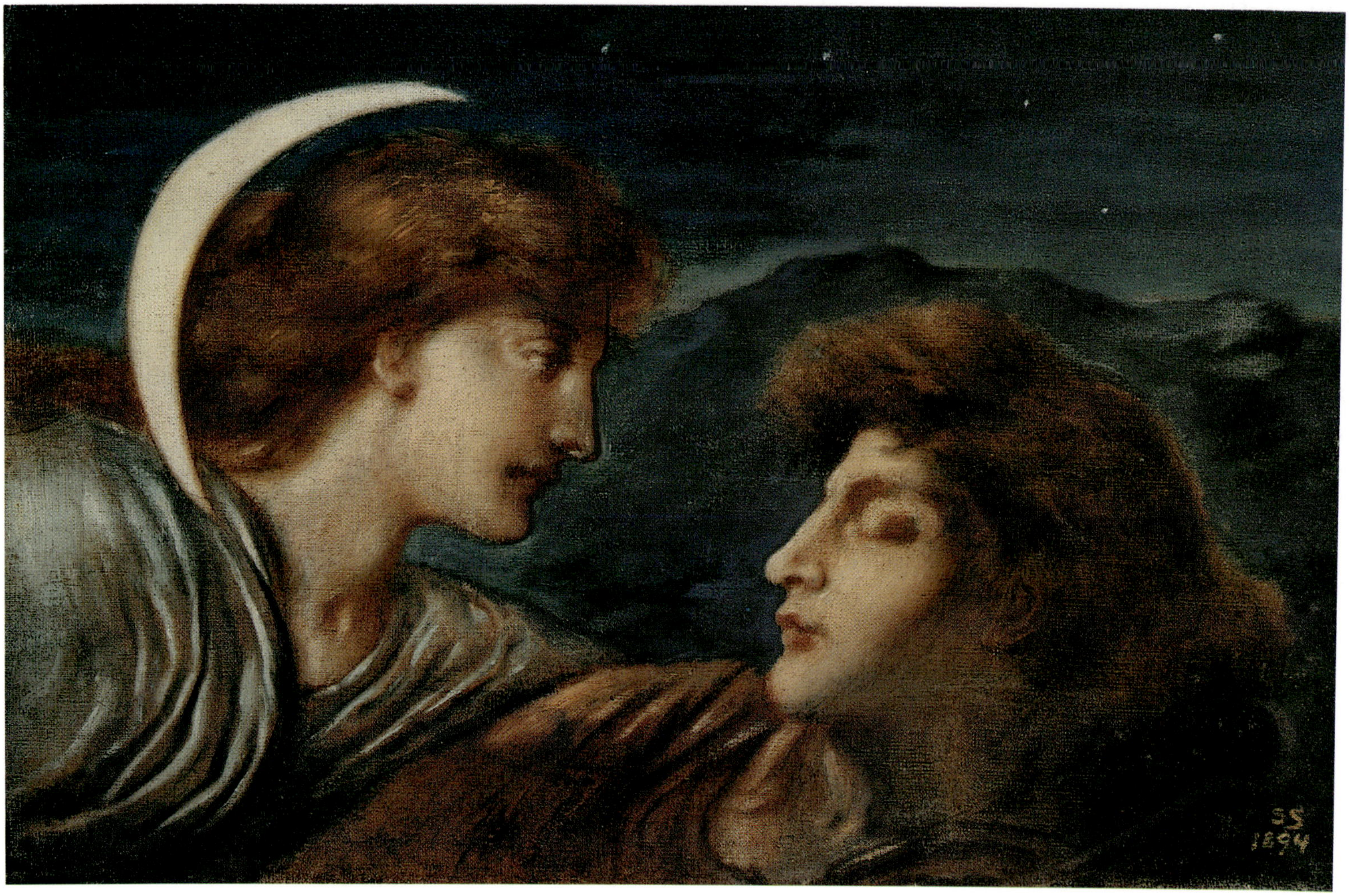

139

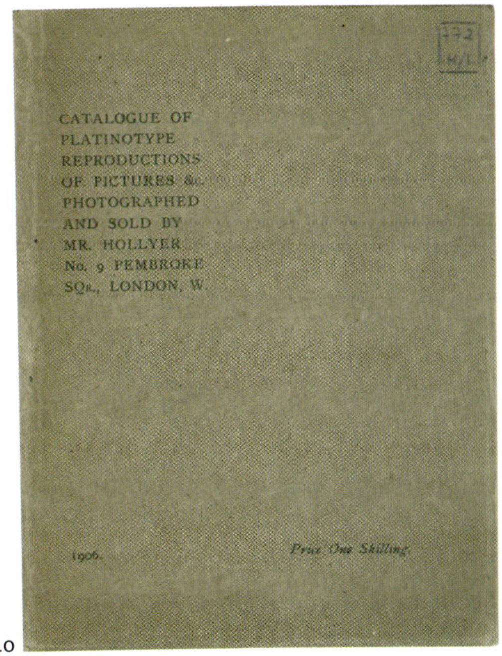

140

140
Catalogue of Platinotype Reproductions of Pictures &c. Photographed and Sold by Mr. Hollyer No. 9 Pembroke Sqr. London, W.
1906
Booklet
19.6 × 14.5 cm (7¾ × 5¾ in.)
Courtesy of the Royal Photographic Society Collection at the National Museum of Photography, Film & Television (by courtesy of the Board of Trustees of the Science Museum)

Solomon was one of the first artists to employ a photographer for the commercial dissemination of his works; his choice of Frederick (sometimes Frederic, as on the illustrated cover to cat. 145) Hollyer (1837–1933) was particularly fortunate. Their first collaboration was made public in 1869 followed by another, "a series of photographs", according to the *Athenaeum* in a scathing review, "by Mr. F. Hollyer, from [Solomon's] sketches and designs". The reviewer commented: "It is a puzzle to us how the author of works such as these can consent to put them before the world in so crude a state. Mr Hollyer's photographs are evidently perfect" (5 February 1870, p. 203). Nevertheless, the artist continued to work with the photographer, who produced the frontispiece to *A Vision of Love Revealed in Sleep* (1871, cat. 117) and was increasingly in demand as a recorder of works of art. On many occasions Hollyer's record of a composition preserves a work now lost or untraced (see, for example, cat. 114).

Hollyer's business grew in the latter half of the century, and his successful studio sold photographic prints of works by Watts, Rossetti, Burne-Jones and other artists, including works of the 'Old Masters', Leonardo, Botticelli and Rembrandt, among others. In the 1870s he perfected the platinotype process that he used for his art reproductions. He became famous, too, as a portraitist and became a member of the exclusive 'Linked Ring' of photographers. In his commercial enterprise he was supported by his son, F.T. Hollyer, who continued the business into the twentieth century.

Although rarely shown in public in its original form after 1873, Solomon's work had considerable commercial value for Hollyer's business. Cat. 140 advertises some 97 different titles of photographic prints for sale as well as, separately, Solomon's pencil portrait of Pater. There is evidence that more than a hundred separate works had been available in previous catalogues, making Solomon's presence conspicuous. (In the same catalogue, for example, Rossetti was represented by 102 items.) Solomon's prints were priced between 7 shillings and 6 pence to one guinea. Four works were reproduced as figures (opposite p. 66), including *Dante's First Meeting with Beatrice* (cat. 16). Robert Ross noted that, at Oxford, "'cultured' undergraduates … would always have a few photographs after Simeon Solomon on their walls – little notes of illicit sentiment to vary the monotony of Burne-Jones and Botticelli". They would be taken down when relatives visited (Ross, 1909, pp. 135–36).

The catalogue entries on Solomon in cat. 140 were preceded by a brief essay by Percy Bate, whose *English Pre-Raphaelite Painters* (1899) had reassessed Solomon in a chapter devoted to "the romantic influence" within the Pre-Raphaelite movement.

For examples of Solomon's work produced after his 'disgrace' in 1873 and photographed, promoted and sold by Hollyer, see cat. 141–46. The photographer's own album of portraits of artists contains two striking images of Solomon (see cat. 148).

141
Frederick Hollyer after Simeon Solomon
Night and Sleep
Photographic print; original drawing signed with monogram and dated *1872* lower left
31.3 × 25.8 cm (12⁵⁄₁₆ × 10⅛ in.)
Birmingham Museums & Art Gallery. Presented by Mrs R.E. Giles, 1931

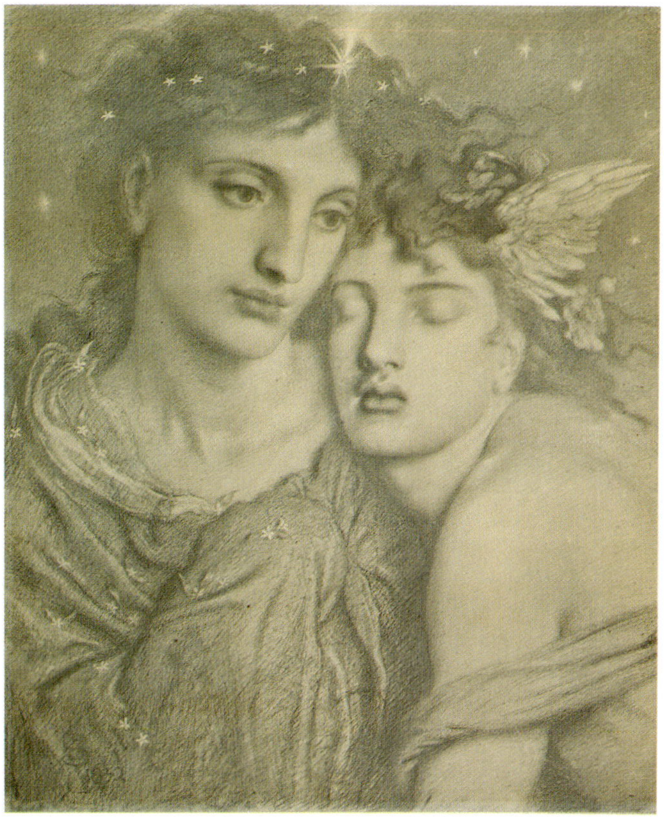

141

142
Frederick Hollyer after Simeon Solomon
Love Confronted by Death
Photographic print; original drawing signed with monogram and dated *1874* upper right
23.2 × 35.7 cm (9⅛ × 14$\frac{1}{16}$ in.)
Birmingham Museums & Art Gallery. Presented by Mrs R.E. Giles, 1931

143
Frederick Hollyer after Simeon Solomon
Somnium
Photographic print; original drawing signed in full and dated *1885*(?) lower right and inscribed with title
33 × 26 cm (13 × 10¼ in.), sight
Collection Dr Michael Richard Barclay

144
Frederick Hollyer after Simeon Solomon
Ave Maria Gratia Plena
Photographic print; original drawing signed with monogram and dated *1888* lower right and inscribed with Latin quotation from the Gospel of St Luke, 1:28
39 × 32 cm (15⅜ × 12⅝ in.), sight
Collection Dr Michael Richard Barclay

The head represents the Angel Gabriel, whose words 'Hail Mary, full of grace', addressed to the Virgin Mary, give the work its title.

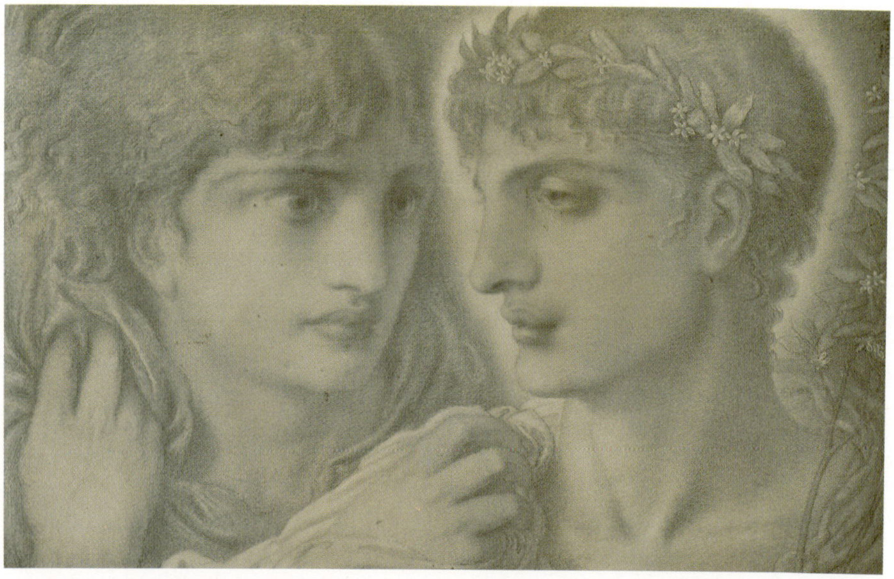
142

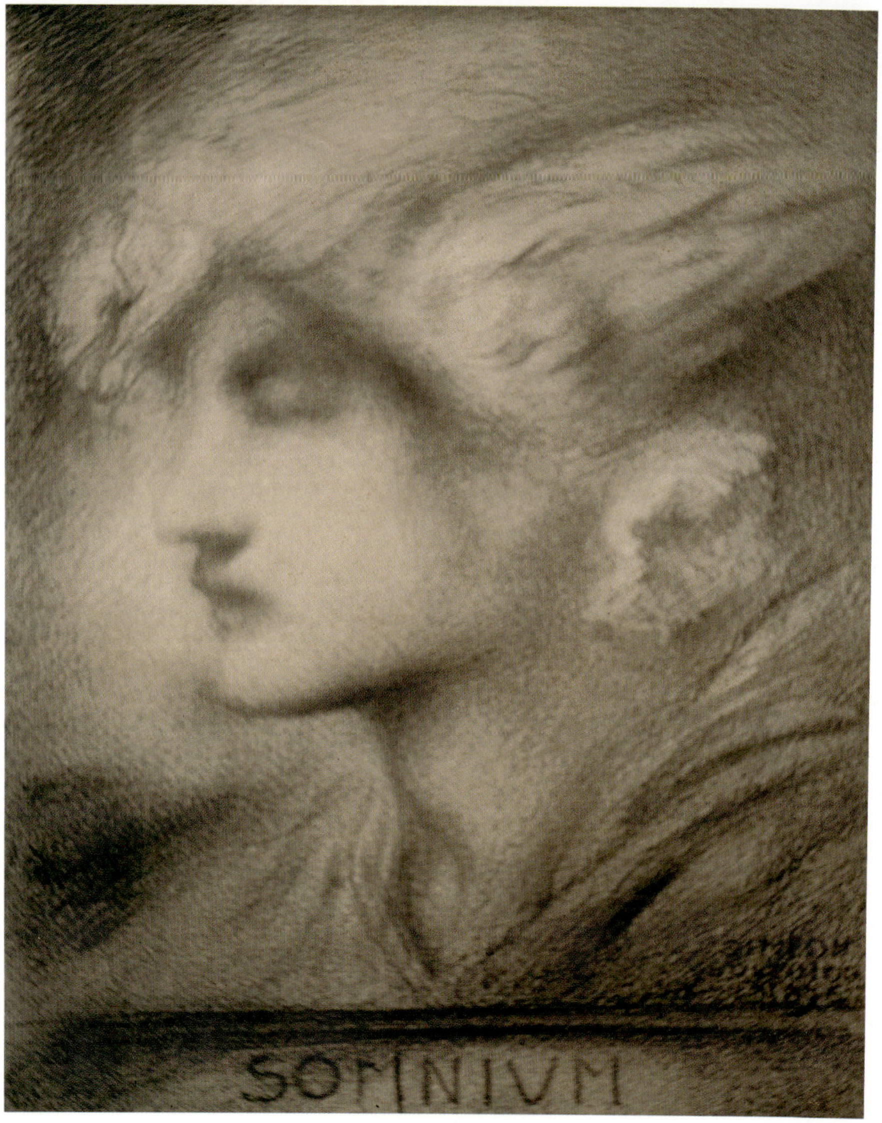

143

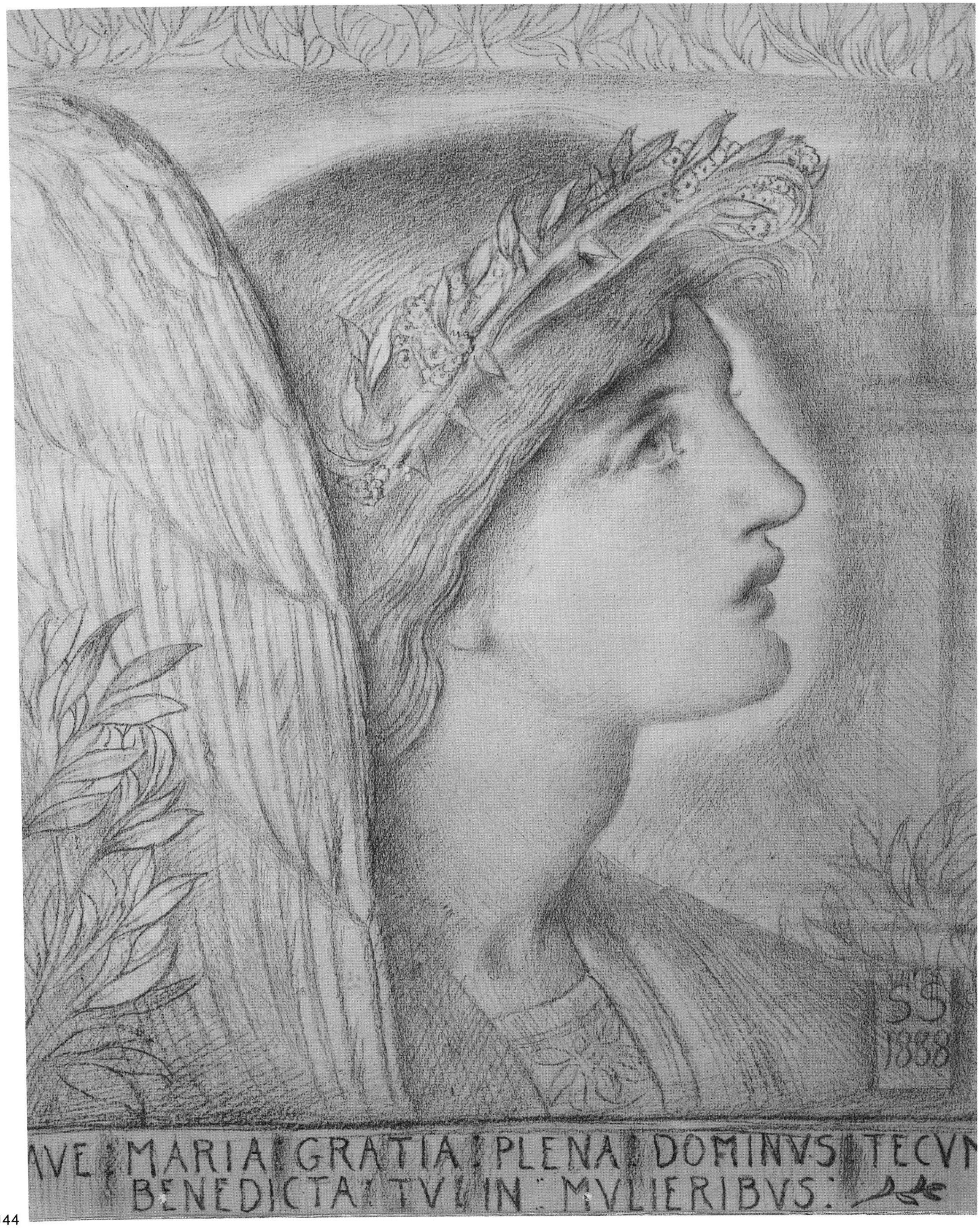
SS
1888
AVE MARIA GRATIA PLENA DOMINVS TECVN
BENEDICTA TV IN MVLIERIBVS

144

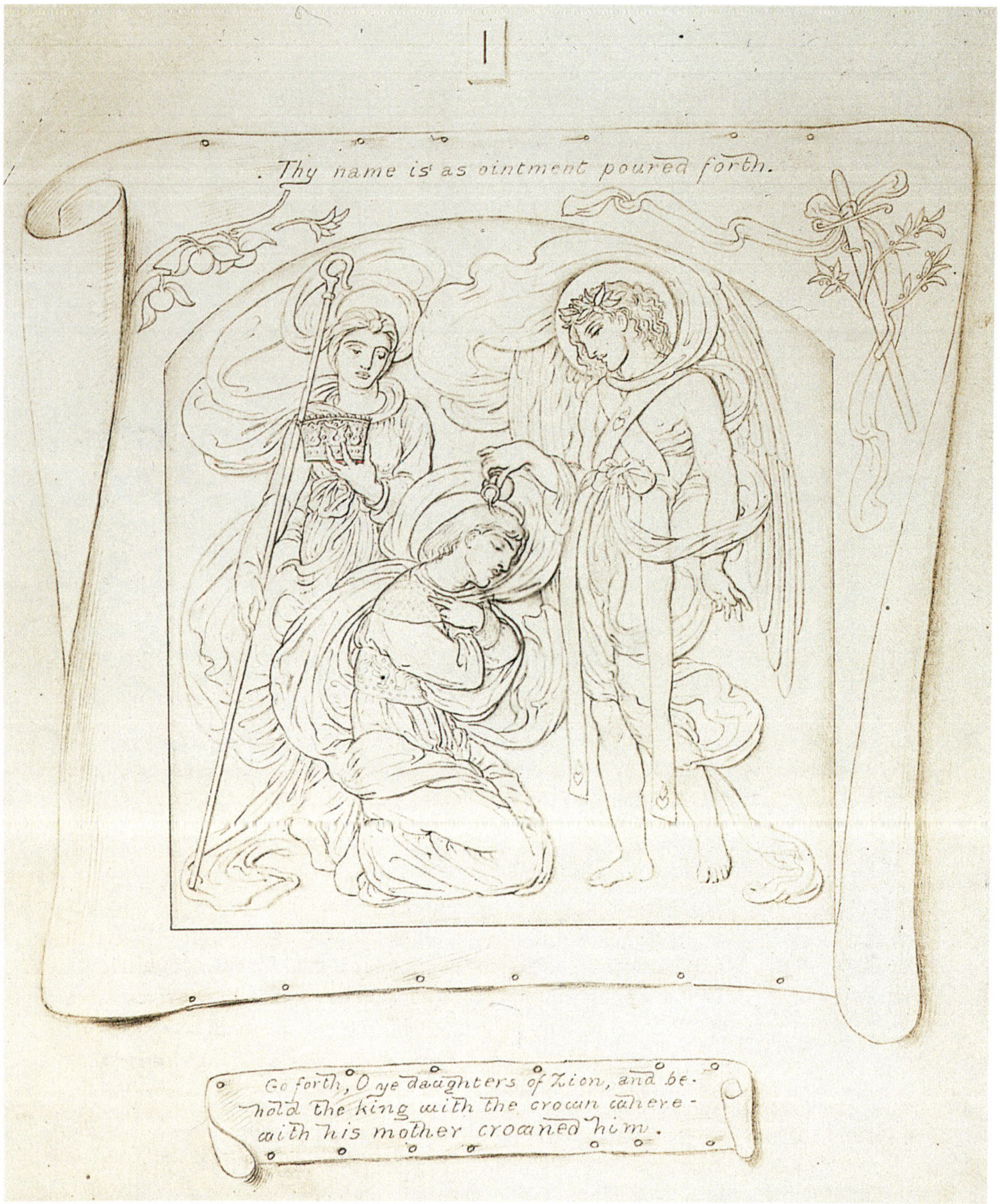

145a

145
Frederick Hollyer after Simeon Solomon
Eight Designs for the Song of Songs
1878
Eight photographic prints with inscriptions, with an illustrated cover and a contents page headed 'Order of Ritual in the Canticles'
Each 20.5 × 16 cm (8 × 6½ in.)
Volume size 36.5 × 28 cm (14½ × 11 in.)
Victoria and Albert Museum

a) **The Consecration and Coronation of the King** ("Thy name is as ointment poured forth")
b) **The Captivity of the Bride and the Arming of the King for her Release** ("A garden enclosed is my sister, my spouse: a spring shut up, a fountain sealed")
c) **The Calling of the Bride** ("I sleep but my heart waketh: it is the voice of my beloved that knocketh, saying, Open to me, my sister, my love, my dove, my undefiled")
d) **The Invitation to the Bride** ("My beloved spake and said unto me, arise my love, my fair one, and come away, for lo, the winter is past")
e) **The Desire of the Bride towards the King, and his Glad Response** ("Thou hast ravished my heart")
f) **The Nuptials of the King and the Bride** ("The day of the gladness of his heart. My beloved is mine and I am his")
g) **The Night of the Nuptials of the King and his Bride** ("His pavilion over me was love")
h) **The Blessing Bestowed upon the King and the Bride** ("My vineyard which is mine is before me")

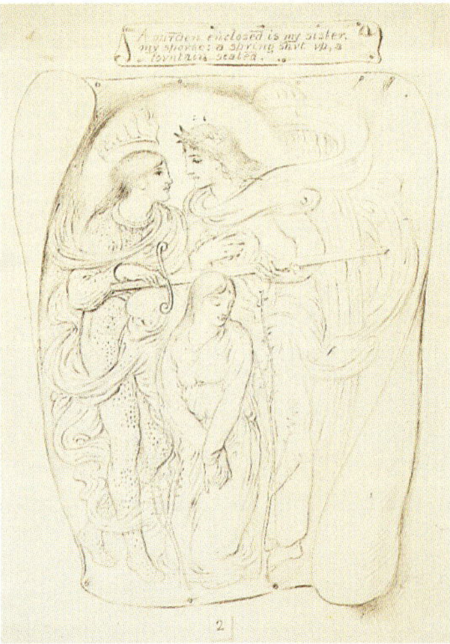

145b

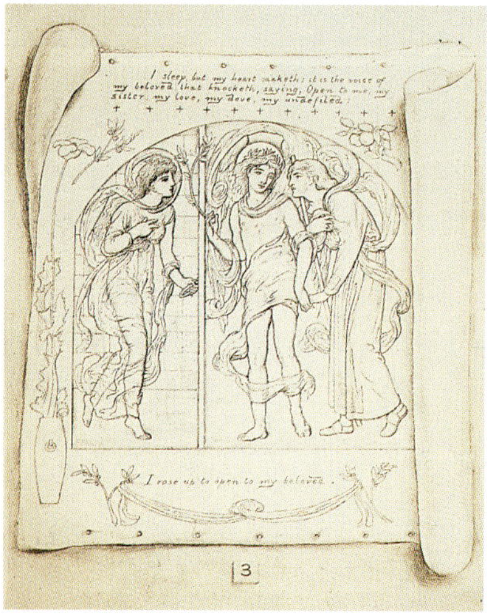

145c

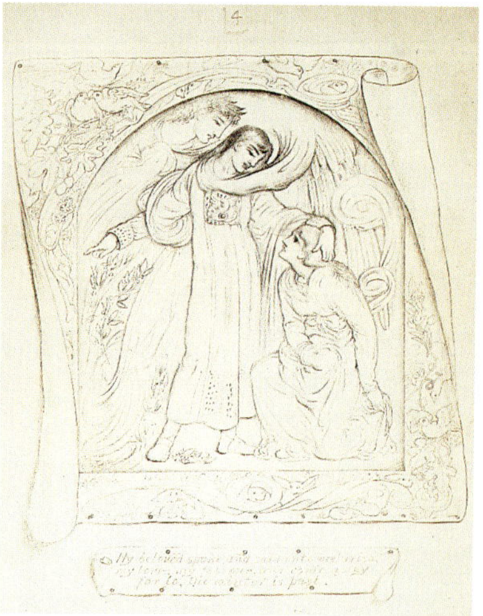

145d

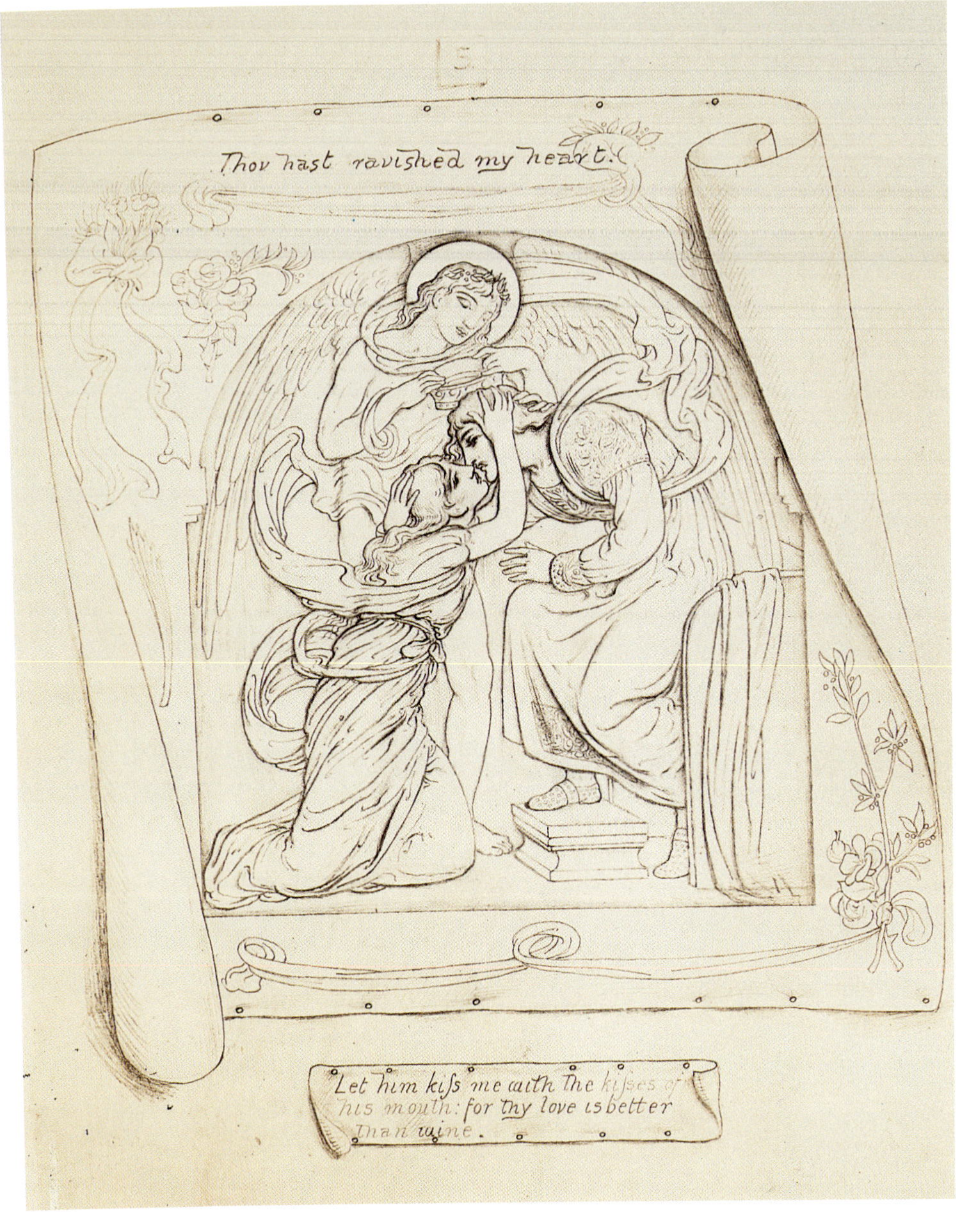

145e

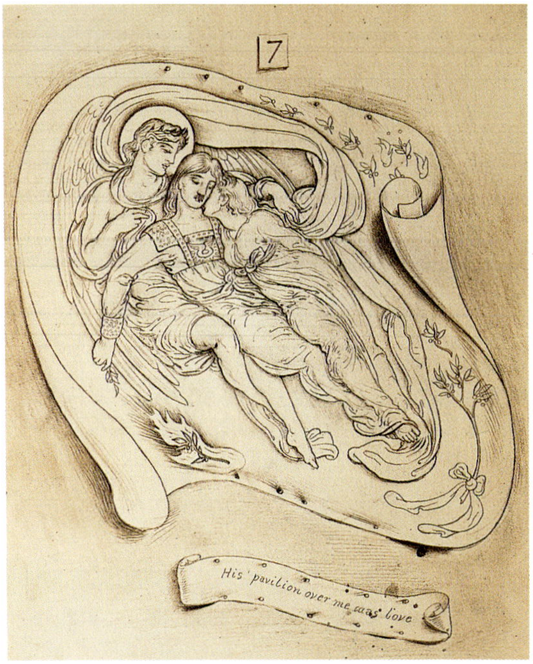

145g

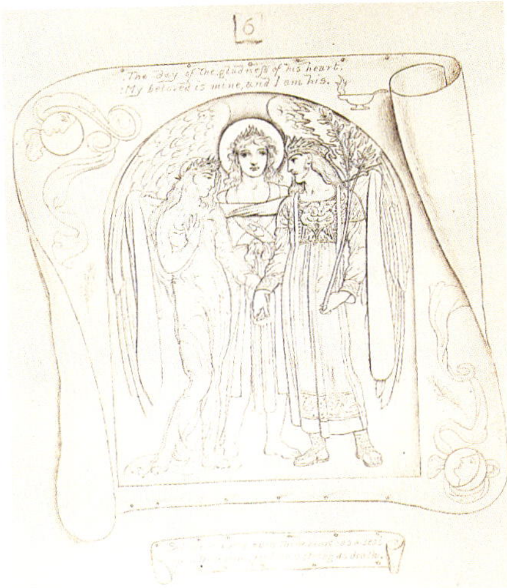

145f

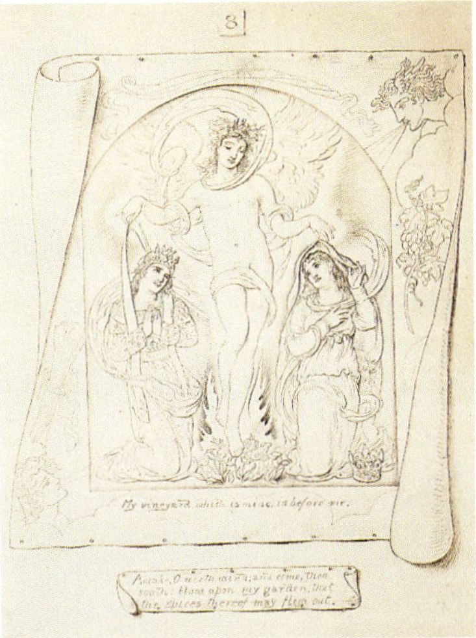

145h

Although dated 1878, these illustrations belong stylistically to an earlier phase of Solomon's career characterized by precise line, complex whole-figure poses and tightly drawn compositions, as, for example, in cat. 99; the facial types and the swirling drapery, however, belong to the later 1870s. The inclusion of the decorative scroll surrounds with their inscriptions and motifs (most often branches, ribbons and bows) is unique in the artist's work. Sidney Trefussis Whiteford observes that these marginal designs "suggest the 'Sibylline Leaves' and the scrolls of mystic import so often spoken of in the Scriptures" ('A Half-Forgotten Genius' in *The Art Amateur*, p. 46).

The subject was taken up several times by Solomon; there are numerous 'bridegroom' subjects (for example, cat. 111 and 112), and a diptych illustrating the scene of the bridegroom knocking on the door and the bride's response, now in the Hugh Lane Gallery, Dublin (unavailable for this exhibition), is dated 1872–73. The plates allow the artist to revisit successful compositions from his previous works; cat. 145a, for example, reworks a composition drawn for the Dalziel Bible project, *Melchizedek Blesses Abram* of *c.* 1863 (cat. 84), while cat. 145g revisits a motif worked out in *The Sleepers and the One who Watcheth* (1867 and 1870, cat. 106 and 107).

Hollyer would appear to have retained the original drawings for this project; works entitled

Eight Designs for the Song of Solomon, owned by him, were shown (as no. 87) at the Baillie Gallery exhibition of the artist's work that opened in December 1905.

Edward Burne-Jones worked on a set of drawings in the 1870s on the same subject (see cat. 151).

146
Frederick Hollyer after Simeon Solomon
The Book of Ruth
1879
Six photographic prints with an illustrated cover
Each 27.8 × 18.4 cm (10$\frac{15}{16}$ × 7 in.)
Volume size 36.5 × 28 cm (14$\frac{3}{8}$ × 11 in.)
Courtesy of The Jewish Museum, London

Cat. 146 is exhibited to show the cover, which represents the biblical heroine Ruth with a sheaf of corn. Solomon's name does not appear on the cover, the project being described as "Illustrated with six designs by SS". The signature on the cover plate is particularly striking, a snake coiled around a tree, set as if in a panel; it is a variation on the snake and staff monogram adopted by Solomon in the previous decade. It anticipates the vogue for including such panels in terracotta in Aesthetic Movement housing schemes.

Evidence of Solomon's continued business partnership with Frederick Hollyer, this portfolio contained six photographs after drawings by Solomon. The subject is an unusual one for the artist at this date in that its central figure is a woman, although, like Esther (see cat. 47), Ruth is emblematic of the Jewish religion and her story of great significance. In histories of the representation of lesbianism her close relationship to Naomi has been seen as an important example of a same-sex union. Their friendship had been recorded by Solomon earlier in his career (see cat. 34).

The plates make use of drapery drawn in a distinctive Baroque style that Solomon employed from the mid-1870s onwards. It is a way of simultaneously articulating the figures and decorating the page.

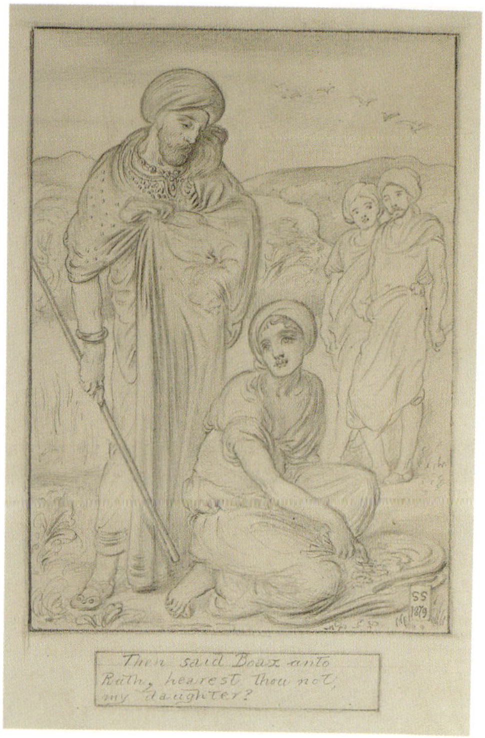

147

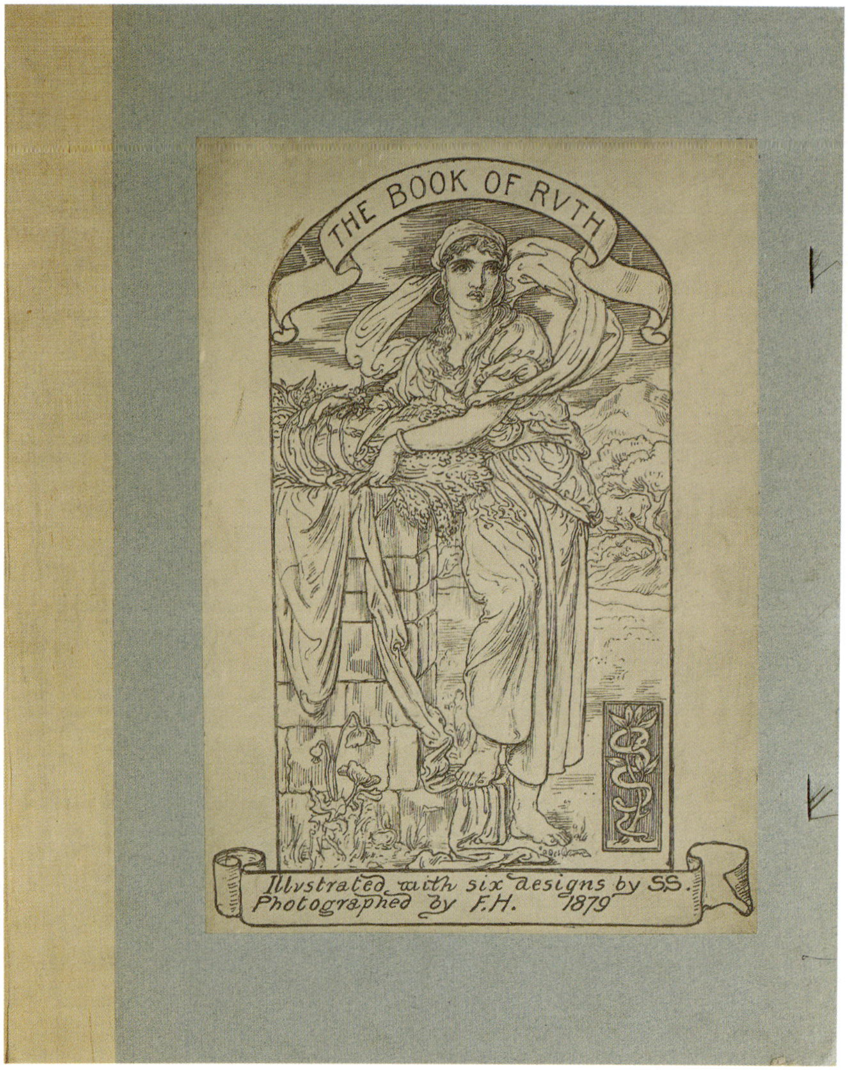

146

147
Ruth and Boaz
1879
24 × 16.5 cm (9¼ × 6½ in.)
Pencil on paper
Signed with monogram and dated *1879* lower right
Courtesy of The Jewish Museum, London

Cat. 147 is the original drawing for the third plate in the portfolio of photographs after drawings by Solomon for *The Book of Ruth*, published in 1879 (see cat. 146). It illustrates the text "Then said Boaz unto Ruth, hearest thou not, my daughter?" (Ruth 2:8), which records the first words said by Boaz to Ruth as she worked in his fields behind the reapers.

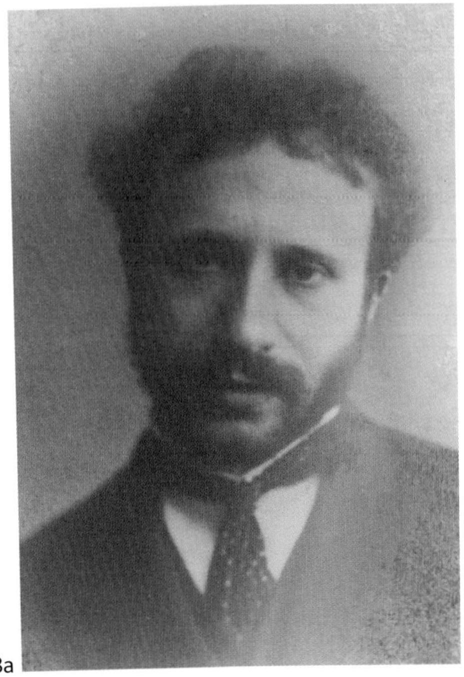

148a

148
Frederick Hollyer (1837–1933)
Two Portraits of Simeon Solomon
c. 1866 and *c.* 1896
Photographic prints mounted in album
a) **Solomon aged 26**
12.7 × 8.8 cm (5 × 3⅝ in.)
b) **Solomon aged 56**
10.8 × 14.2 cm (4¼ × 5⁹⁄₁₆ in.)
Album size 25.3 × 18.5 × 5.8 cm
(9¹⁵⁄₁₆ × 7¼ × 2¼ in.)
Victoria and Albert Museum

These photographic portraits have a particular interest because they are by the photographer who worked closely with Solomon for several decades and who knew him well and collected his works. These factors account for the peculiarly penetrating character studies contained in the portraits; the later of the two, showing him balding and prematurely aged, is a unique record of Solomon's appearance in the last decade of his life. The photographs are pasted into a volume of portraits of artists known to Hollyer, including members of the Pre-Raphaelite circle and the St John's Wood group.

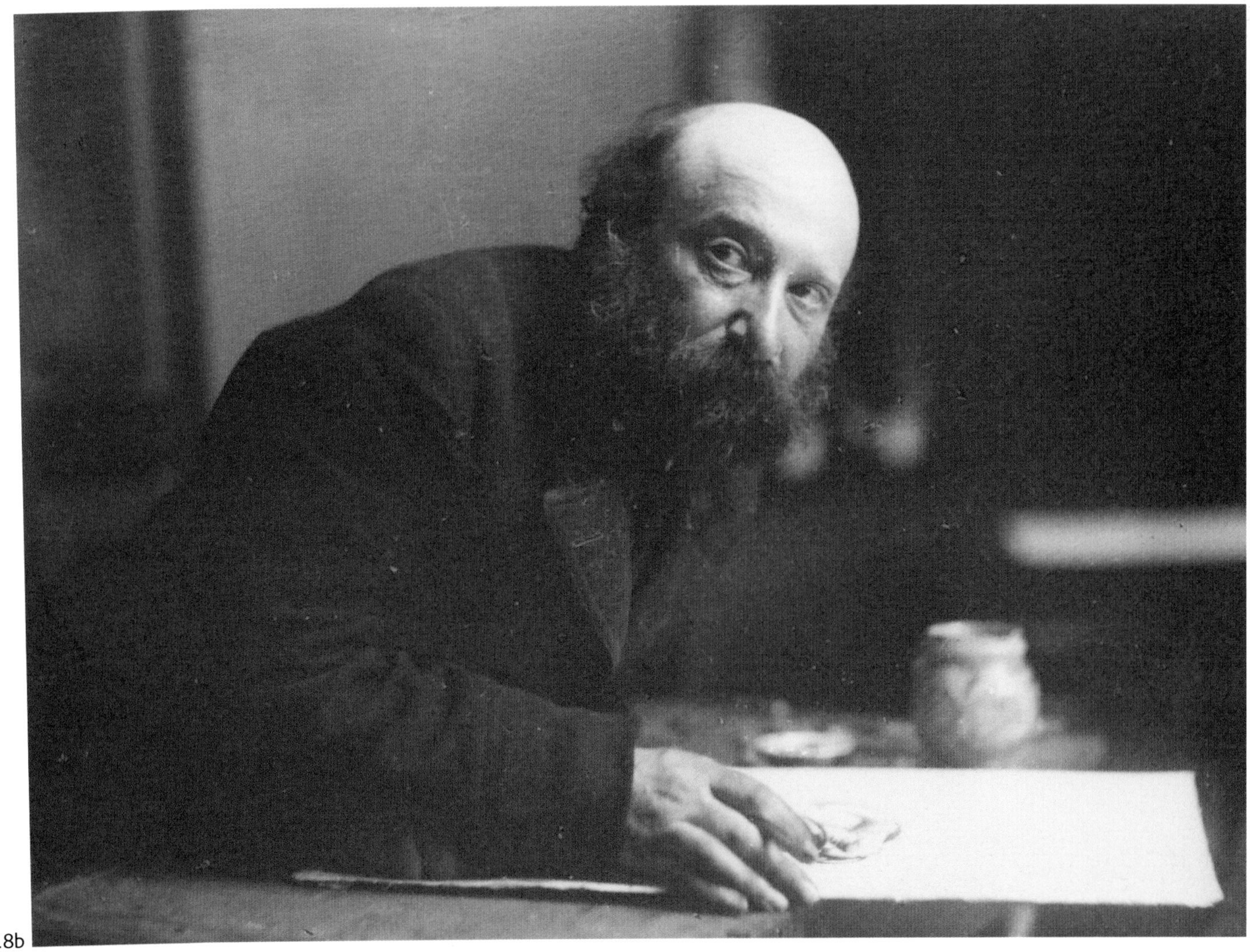

148b

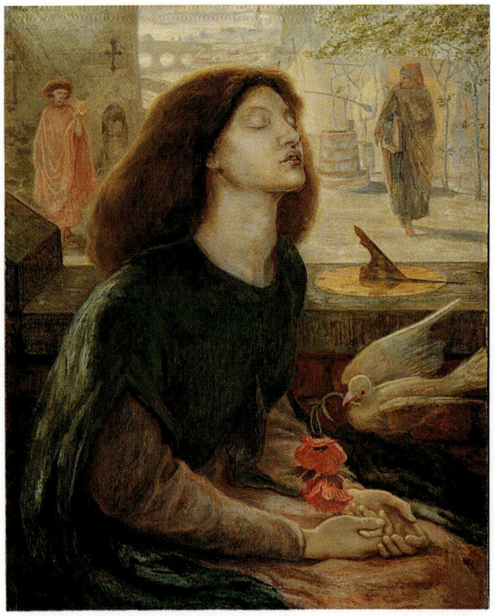

149

149
Dante Gabriel Rossetti (1828–1882)
Beata Beatrix
Begun 1877, left unfinished in 1882
Oil on canvas
86.8 × 68.3 cm (34¹⁄₁₆ × 26¹³⁄₁₆ in.)
Birmingham Museums & Art Gallery.
Purchased 1891

There are four oil versions of this subject, the apparition of Beatrice to her lover Dante on her death. This version was completed by Ford Madox Brown (see Surtees, 1971, 1, p. 96). The composition is one of Rossetti's most potent. Solomon seems to have the work in mind when drawing some of his later mystical works, including *The Winged and Poppied Sleep* (1889, cat. 134).

150
Dante Gabriel Rossetti (1828–1882)
The Question
1875
Pencil on paper
48 × 41.5 cm (18⅞ × 16⅛ in.)
Signed and dated lower right, inscribed with title lower left
Birmingham Museums & Art Gallery. Presented by subscribers, 1904

Rossetti's Oedipus and the Sphinx subject is a complex résumé of various sources, although Solomon's influence has been identified in both the style of the drawing and its content (see *Exposed: The Victorian Nude*, 2001, p. 153). The striking position of the two central figures facing each other finds echoes in Solomon's works illustrating the various tableaux of *A Vision of Love Revealed in Sleep* (cat. 117).

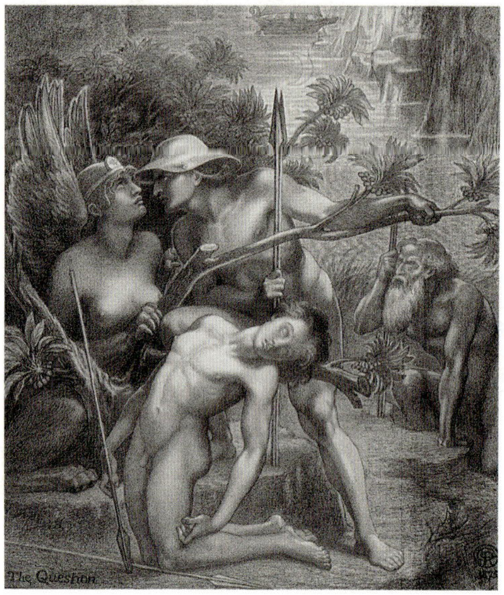

150

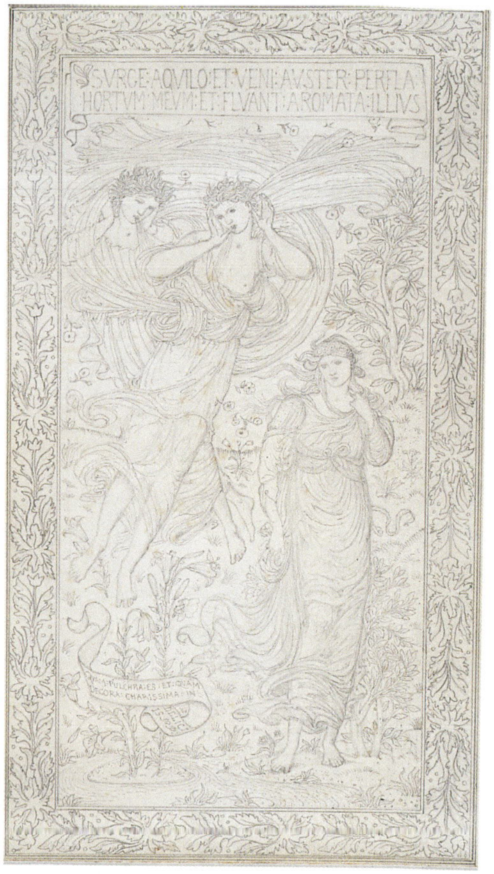

151

151
Edward Burne-Jones (1833–1898)
Awake O North Wind
c. 1875
Pencil on paper
35.5 × 21.2 cm (14 × 8⅜ in.)
Birmingham Museums & Art Gallery. Bequeathed by J.R. Holliday, 1927

Burne-Jones produced five drawings for verses from the Song of Solomon to be translated into embroidery. Cat. 151 illustrates the lines addressed to the North Wind: "Come thou South, blow upon my garden that the spices thereof may flow out", and those that address the beloved: "How fair and pleasant art thou, O Love, for delight".

Cat. 151 is the basis of a large watercolour, *Sponsa de Libano* (1891, Walker Art Gallery, Liverpool).

152
Fred Holland Day (1864–1933)
Hypnos
c. 1896
Photographic print
16.1 × 11.4 cm (6½ × 4½ in.)
Courtesy of the Royal Photographic Society Collection at the National Museum of Photography, Film & Television (by courtesy of the Board of Trustees of the Science Museum)

One of Day's most famous images, an allegorical representation of Sleep, cat. 152 is a study of a young man with a winged headdress; his eyes are closed, and he breathes in the perfume of a poppy. The work has obvious connections with several of Solomon's paintings related to *A Vision of Love Revealed in Sleep* (1871), particularly images of Night and Sleep, such as cat. 135 and 141. Similar influences can be traced in Day's Keatsian subject *Beauty is Truth* (1896).

Day was interested in the avant-garde literary and artistic practices of British Aestheticism, particularly as expressed by Wilde and Beardsley. His experiments with photographic portraiture and nude studies made him a leader in a kind of Symbolism that became known as 'Pictorialism'. His work led him into friendships with the leading American and British photographers of his day, including Gertrude Käsebier and Alfred Stieglitz. He became a member of the Brotherhood of the Linked Ring, whose members included Frederick Hollyer (see Jussim, 1981).

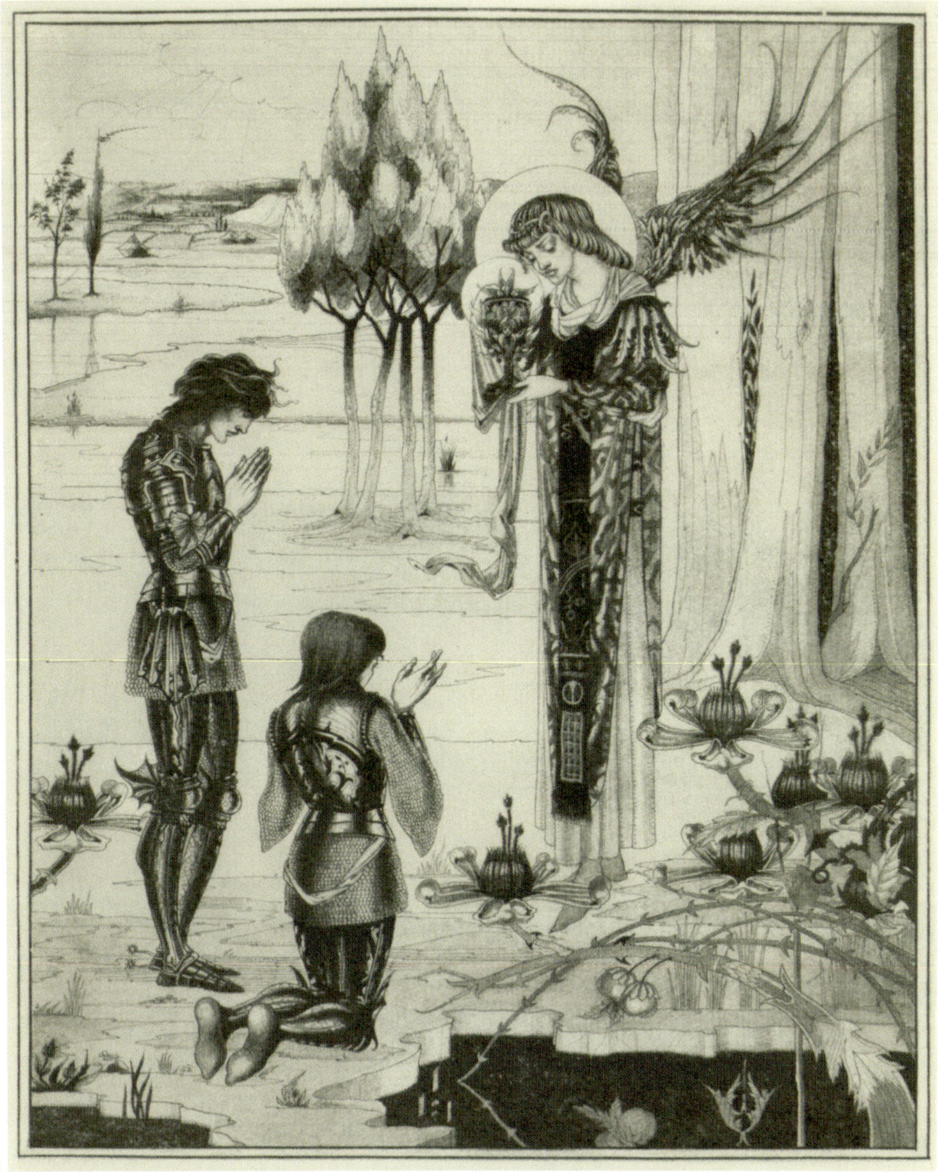

153

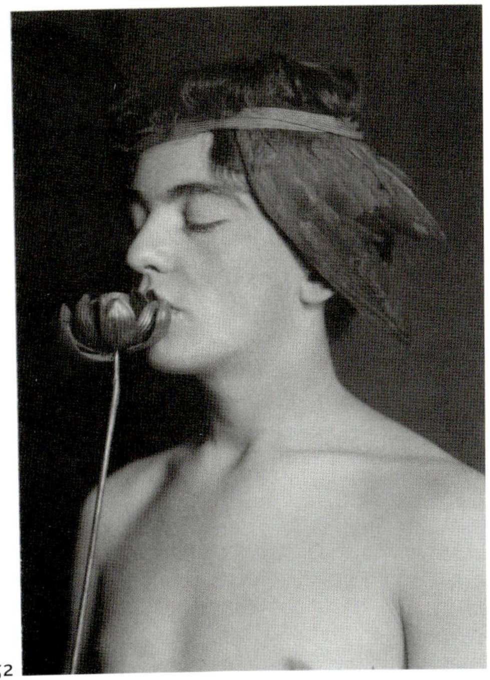

152

153
Aubrey Beardsley (1872–1898)
The Achieving of the Sangreal
Process reproduction
16.7 × 13 cm (6⁹⁄₁₆ × 5⅛ in.), image
Published as frontispiece to volume II of Sir Thomas Malory's *Morte d'Arthur,* London (J.M. Dent & Co.) 1893–94
Birmingham Libraries

Although the debt of Beardsley to Edward Burne-Jones is often recorded, cat. 153, made originally as a sample in 1892 for the publisher J.M. Dent to win the commission for one of the major publishing projects of the 1890s, is closer to Solomon's *Sacramentum Amoris* (see cat. 114) than to Burne-Jones. Stephen Calloway notes Beardsley's interest in Solomon in *Aubrey Beardsley* (1998, p. 38). It is an influence detectable in *Withered Spring* (*c.* 1892, National Gallery of Art, Washington, DC) and other works of Beardsley's early career.

154
Kate Bunce (1856–1927)
Melody
c. 1895
Oil on canvas
76.3 × 51 cm (30$\frac{1}{16}$ × 20$\frac{1}{16}$ in.)
Signed with monogram
Birmingham Museums & Art Gallery. Presented by Sir John Holder, Bart., 1897

Kate Bunce was a leading figure in the Birmingham group of painters at the turn of the century. Her father, John Thackray Bunce, chairman of the Committee of Birmingham Art Gallery, owned Solomon's *A Saint of the Eastern Church* (cat. 90). Cat. 154, also known as *Musica*, has some of the characteristics of Solomon's painting, which would suggest that it might have inspired her, even that it provided her with a compositional template.

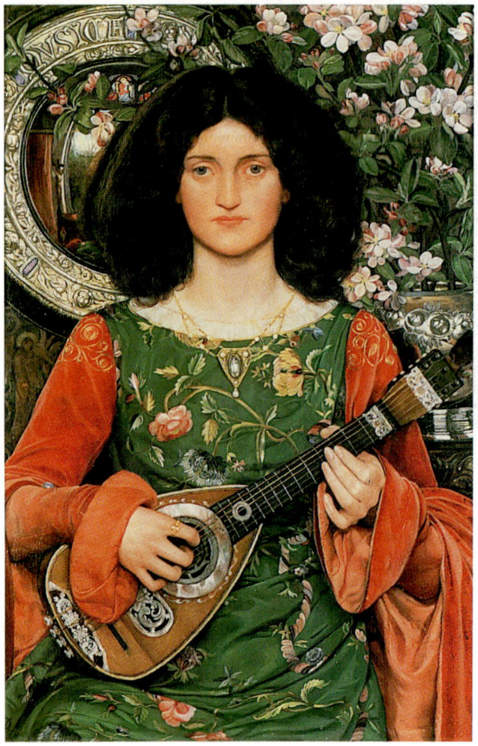
154

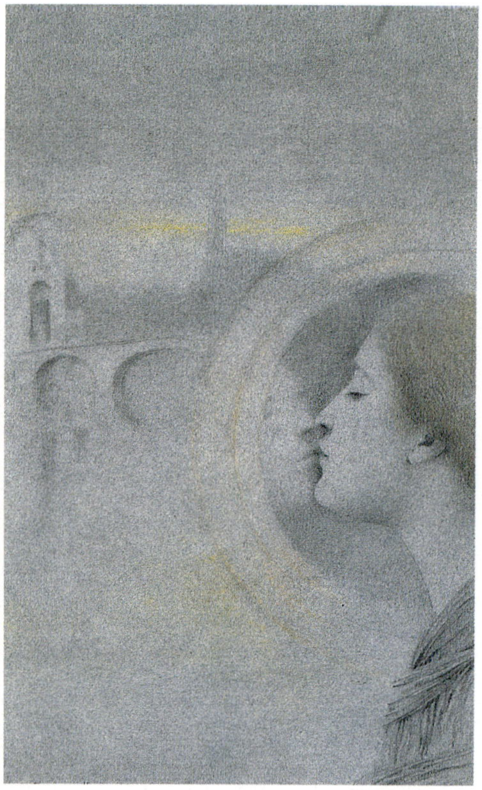
155

155
Fernand Khnopff (1858–1921)
A Grégoire Le Roy: Mon coeur pleure d'autrefois
1889
Pencil, coloured pencil and chalk on paper
23.5 × 14.5 cm (9¼ × 5¾ in.)
The Hearn Family Trust

An image dedicated to the artist's friend Grégoire Le Roy (1862–1941), cat. 155 was designed as the frontispiece to Le Roy's collection of poems of this title ('My heart weeps for days of yore'). The combination of drawing materials, the head seen in profile and the ethereal atmosphere remind us of the impact of English late Pre-Raphaelite art in Belgium, for which Solomon's emphasis on drawing over painting was key.

156
Edward Robert Hughes (1851–1914)
Night with her Train of Stars
1912
Watercolour, bodycolour and gold paint on paper
75.5 × 124.5 cm (29¾ × 49 in.)
Signed bottom left
Birmingham Museums & Art Gallery. Presented in memory of the artist by the E.R. Hughes Memorial Committee, 1915

Cat. 156 is the most famous and popular painting by Hughes, a late example of Symbolist imagery in English art at the start of the twentieth century; it is also a distinguished example of the exhibition watercolour, notable for its scale as well as the handling of the medium – the daring application of bodycolour and gold paint – and the resulting quality of the surface. The imagery relates to Solomon's repeated 'Night and Sleep' images, beginning with *The Sleepers and the One who Watcheth* (cat. 106) and continuing into later chalk drawings such as *The Winged and Poppied Sleep* (cat. 134).

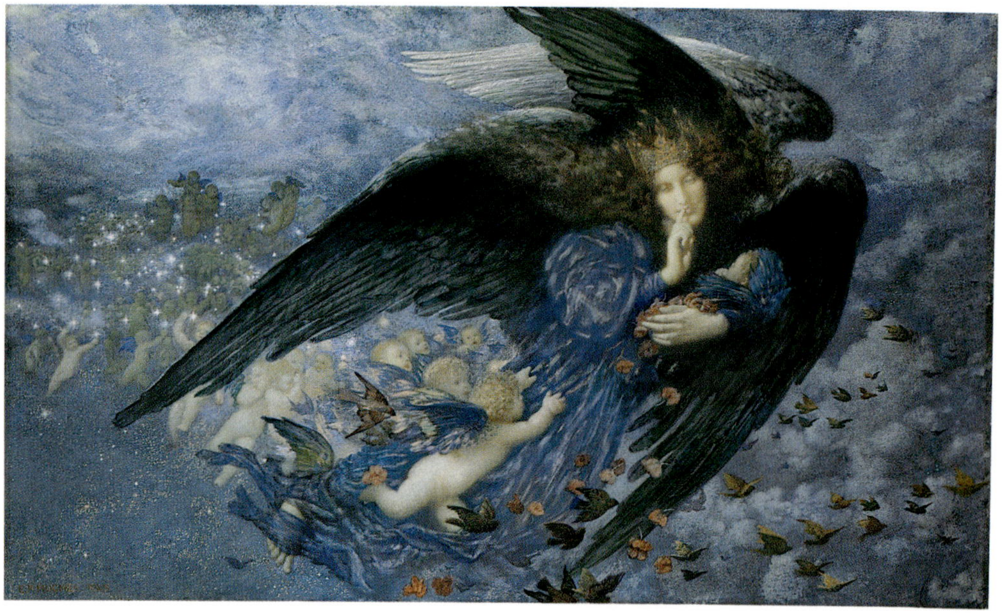
156

157
Fernand Khnopff (1858–1921)
Requiem
1907
Pencil, coloured pencil and black chalk on paper
80.3 × 80.3 cm (31⅝ × 31⅝ in.)
The Hearn Family Trust

One of the most highly finished drawings by Khnopff, cat. 157 covers several themes familiar from Simeon Solomon's work – the androgynous figure, richly robed and holding ritual objects – although a striking feature, not one associated with Solomon, is the complicated perspectival point of view. The date of execution, two years after Solomon's death and one year after the memorial exhibitions of his work in London, might be significant, especially given the title of this work.

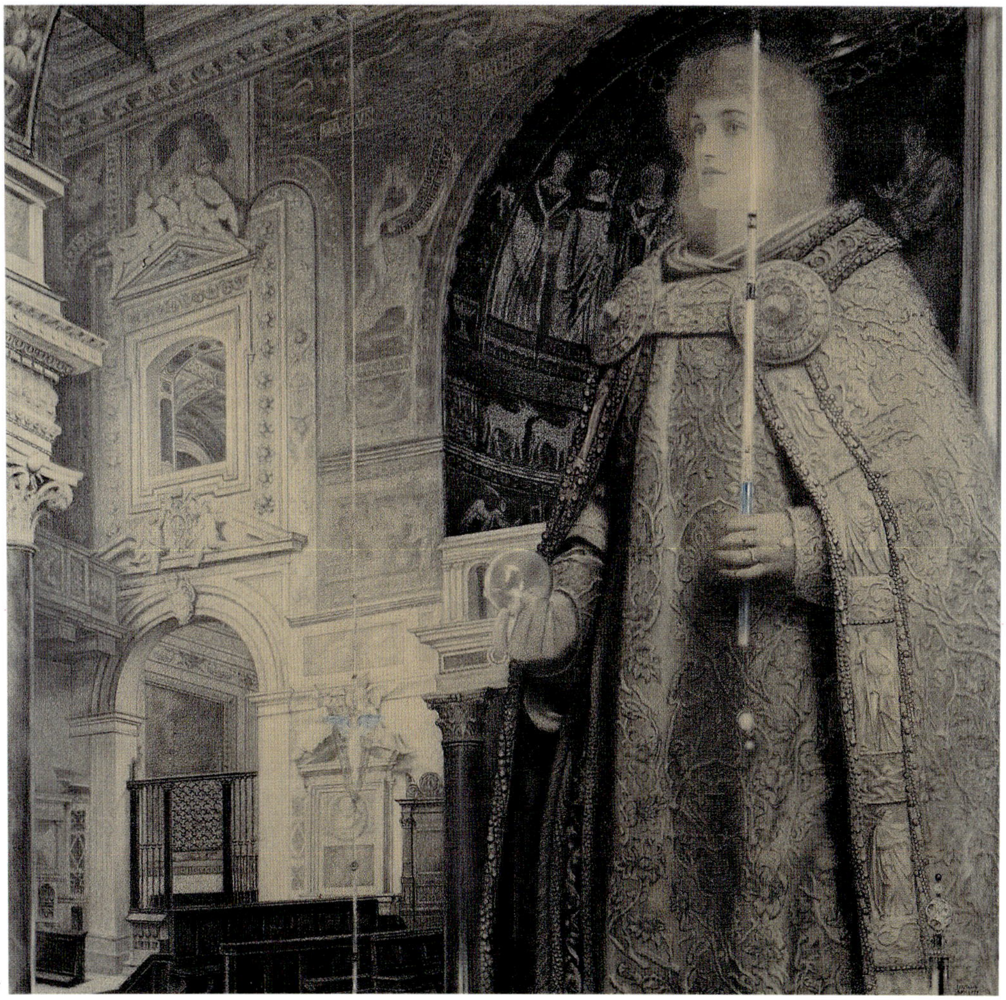
157

Simeon Solomon: A Chronology

1840
9 October: Simeon Solomon is born at 3 Sandys Street, Bishopgate, the last of the eight children of Michael Solomon (born 1779) and his wife, Catherine Levy (died 1886). In the same year, Solomon's father sells the family hat business and establishes a successful factory embossing paper doilies

1841
Abraham Solomon, Solomon's elder brother (born 14 May 1823), exhibits for the first time at the Royal Academy

1852
Solomon studies drawing at F.S. Cary's Academy; he will continue there until he is admitted to the Royal Academy Schools in 1856. His sister, Rebecca (born 26 September 1832), has been attending Spitalfields School of Design. In the same year, she exhibits at the Royal Academy for the first time

1854
5 December: Michael Solomon dies

1856
24 April: Solomon enters the Royal Academy Schools, aged fifteen. That winter, he forms a sketching club with his friends and fellow students Henry Holiday and Marcus Stone; they are later joined by Albert Moore

1857
Having already become friends with George Price Boyce, Solomon meets Dante Gabriel Rossetti late this year or early the following year. Through Rossetti, he later meets Algernon Charles Swinburne and Edward Burne-Jones

1858
Solomon makes his debut at the Royal Academy with his painting *Isaac Offered*. Abraham and Rebecca also both exhibit at the Royal Academy
15 February: Boyce introduces Solomon to William Burges. Solomon will subsequently design panels for Burges's 'Great Bookcase' (1859–62)
Solomon is a member of the Junior Etching Club. He publishes his only known etching, *The Haunted House*, the same year in the club's *Passages from the Poems of Thomas Hood*
November: Solomon exhibits a drawing, *By the Waters of Babylon*, at Gambart's French Gallery's Sixth Annual Winter Exhibition of Cabinet Pictures

1859
By this year, Solomon and others including Burne-Jones, Holiday and Leighton have joined the Artists' Rifle Corps
January: Solomon writes an unpublished, tongue-in-cheek 'PRB Catechism for the Use of Disciples of that School'
November: Solomon exhibits *Dante's First Meeting with Beatrice* at Gambart's

1860
Solomon exhibits *The Mother of Moses* at the Royal Academy
23 June: The picture is praised by Thackeray in the *Illustrated London News*: "A more touching, a more impressive domestic group it would be impossible to imagine"

1861
Solomon exhibits *A Young Musician Employed in the Temple Service During the Feast of Tabernacles* at the Royal Academy

1862
Solomon exhibits *The Child Jeremiah* at the Royal Academy
Coundall, Downes & Co. publishes a set of photographs of Solomon's drawings of Jewish ceremonies
June: Solomon moves to his first studio at 22 Charles Street near Middlesex Hospital. He joins Holiday for a summer holiday in North Wales
August: Two wood-engraved illustrations from designs by Solomon depicting contemporary Jewish life are published in *Once a Week*
19 December: Abraham dies in Biarritz the same day he is elected an Associate of the Royal Academy

1863
Solomon makes his first designs for Morris, Marshall, Faulkner & Co. He exhibits two works, *Juliette* and *The Betrothal of Isaac and Rebekah*, at the Royal Academy
Solomon and Holiday make another trip to Wales, this time joined by William De Morgan, whom Solomon had first met in 1859

1864
February: Solomon fails in an attempt to be elected an Associate of the Old Watercolour Society; Burne-Jones and Boyce succeed
Solomon exhibits *A Deacon* at the Royal Academy
He designs stained glass for windows at All Saints Church, Middleton Cheney, Northamptonshire, for Morris, Marshall, Faulkner & Co. The windows are installed in 1865

1865
The Dudley Gallery opens, allowing Solomon and other artists to exhibit watercolours and works with more liberal subjects
Solomon exhibits *Habet!* at the Royal Academy and illustrates Swinburne's unpublished sadomasochistic novel *Lesbia Brandon*
Frederick Hollyer creates the first set of ten photographs of Solomon's drawings for sale
Solomon discovers the model Gaetano Meo working as a street musician

1866
Solomon exhibits the oil painting *Damon and Aglae* at the Royal Academy
From September this year until August 1867 Solomon travels in Italy, visiting Florence and Rome. Rebecca joins him for part of the trip
Solomon paints *Love in Autumn*, although this will not be publicly exhibited until 1872
The Leisure Hour publishes ten 'Illustrations of Jewish Customs' engraved from designs by Solomon

1867
Solomon exhibits his oil painting *Bacchus* at the Royal Academy
19 April: Holiday joins Solomon in Rome; in May they visit Naples together

1868
Solomon moves into his studio at 12 Fitzroy Street, Fitzroy Square. He is elected a member of the Savile Club
Solomon paints *Sacramentum Amoris* for Frederick Leyland
He exhibits *Heliogabalus, High Priest of the Sun* and *A Patriarch of the Eastern Church* and the watercolour *Bacchus* at the Dudley Gallery

During the course of the year Solomon meets Walter Pater and the Eton master Oscar Browning; both become close friends

1869
Solomon exhibits *The Toilette of a Roman Lady* at the Royal Academy
April: He visits Italy again, with Oscar Browning

1870
March: Sidney Colvin publishes an essay on Solomon in *Portfolio*, the fourth in its series 'English Painters of the Present Day'. The article is published in the *Jewish Chronicle* the same month
Solomon again visits Italy with Oscar Browning. His former friends would later note that he may have been forced to flee for legal reasons, possibly related to his homosexuality. While in Italy, Solomon writes the prose poem that is first published privately as *A Mystery of Love in Sleep: An Allegory*
He exhibits an oil painting, *A Youth Relating Tales to Ladies*, and a watercolour, *Love Bound and Wounded*, at the Royal Academy

1871
March: Solomon's prose poem *A Vision of Love Revealed in Sleep* is published
July: The prose poem is reviewed by Swinburne in *The Dark Blue*. The same issue publishes Swinburne's poem 'The End of a Month', illustrated with a design by Solomon
Solomon exhibits an oil painting of *Carrying the Scrolls of the Law* at the Royal Academy
Solomon is attacked, along with Rossetti and his followers, in Robert Buchanan's essay 'The Fleshly School of Poetry' in *Contemporary Review*

1872
Solomon exhibits *Judith and her Attendant Going to the Assyrian Camp* at the Royal Academy. This is the last time he will exhibit there
He exhibits *Autumn Love* (now known as *Love in Autumn*) at the Dudley Gallery
11 November: *The Times* criticizes *Autumn Love* as "one of those allegorical designs [of Solomon's] which usually suggest something unwholesome in sentiment"

1873
11 February: Solomon is arrested in a public lavatory with another man, George Roberts, and charged with indecent exposure and "attempting to commit sodomy"
12 February: Solomon is remanded in custody
24 February: He appears at Clerkenwell Sessions and is released on bail
24 March: Roberts is sentenced to eighteen months' hard labour. Solomon's sentence of eighteen months of imprisonment with light labour is reduced to a term of police supervision
December: Solomon's former friends hear that he is in Devon giving public readings – apparently of works by Dickens using his own name

1874
3 March: Solomon is arrested in Paris with Henri Lefranc (alias Raphael-Maximilien Dumont) in a public lavatory near the Bourse
18 April: Solomon is sentenced to three months in prison and a fine of 16 francs

1877
Solomon privately publishes a one-act farce entitled *Cleopatra's Needle*

1878
Frederick Hollyer publishes *Eight Designs for the Song of Songs by Simeon Solomon, rendered in Photography by Frederic* [sic] *Hollyer*

1879
Hollyer publishes *The Book of Ruth*, "illustrated with six designs by SS"
October: Swinburne hears that Solomon is selling letters the former had written to him during their friendship

1880
29 February: Rossetti tells Jane Morris in a letter that Solomon has been admitted to hospital "not only ragged but actually without shoes!"

1881
The Dalziel Brothers publish their *Bible Gallery*, which includes six plates designed by Solomon in the 1860s

1885
Solomon is admitted as a 'broken-down artist' to St Giles's Workhouse, Endell Street, where he will live intermittently until his death

1886
20 November: Rebecca Solomon dies after being involved in an accident with a hansom cab in Euston Road
15 December: Kate Levy Solomon dies

1887
Five paintings by Solomon are included in the Royal Jubilee Exhibition of contemporary British painting in Manchester

1892
December: Sidney Trefussis Whiteford publishes the first half of a two-part article on Solomon, 'A Half-Forgotten Genius', in *Art Amateur*. The second part of the article appears the following month

1893
Solomon is approached by the designer and author Herbert Horne to contribute to the relaunched Arts and Crafts periodical *The Century Guild Hobby Horse*; the resulting work is his illustration *Corruptio Optimi Pessima*

1894
The Dalziel Brothers' *Art Pictures from the Old Testament and Our Lord's Parables* is published, including twenty plates designed by Solomon in the 1860s

1895
24 April: Works by Solomon are among the possessions of Oscar Wilde dispersed at his bankruptcy sale in Tite Street, Chelsea. Wilde will later reproach Lord Alfred Douglas with the loss of these works in *De Profundis* (1897)

1897
Two of Solomon's works are included in the London Guildhall exhibition *Victorian Painters* and noted approvingly by the critic of *The Academy*

1905
May: Solomon collapses in the street in High Holborn and is taken back to St Giles's Workhouse, suffering (as the coroner's court was told at the subsequent inquest) "from bronchitis and alcoholism"
14 August: Solomon dies at St Giles's. According to the death certificate, the cause of death is "syncope, sudden heart failure, disease of the aortic valves"
16 August: Solomon is buried in the Jewish Cemetery, Willesden
9 December: One hundred and twenty-two of Solomon's works are exhibited in a retrospective at the Baillie Gallery

1906
Sixteen works by Solomon are included in the thirty-seventh Winter Exhibition of Works of the Old Masters and Deceased Masters of the British School at the Royal Academy. Fifty-three of his works, as well as works by Abraham and Rebecca, are included in an exhibition of paintings by Jewish artists at the Whitechapel Art Gallery

1908
Julia Ellsworth Ford publishes *Simeon Solomon: An Appreciation*, the first monograph dedicated to the artist's work

This chronology has been compiled using information from the following sources:

Cruise, Colin, 'Simeon Solomon (1840–1905), Painter and Draughtsman', entry in *Oxford Dictionary of National Biography*, Oxford (Oxford University Press) 2004
Ferrari, Roberto C., 'Biographical Timeline of Simeon Solomon's Life', *Simeon Solomon Research Archive*. Online. Available http://www.fau.edu/solomon/bio.html (published 20 September 2000; accessed February 2005)
Seymour, Gayle M., 'The Life and Work of Simeon Solomon, 1840–1905', PhD diss., University of California at Santa Barbara, 1986
Solomon: A Family of Painters: Abraham Solomon (1823–1862), Rebecca Solomon (1832–1886), Simeon Solomon (1840–1905), exhib. cat., ed. Jeffery Daniels *et al.*, London, Geffrye Museum (Inner London Education Authority) 1985

Bibliography

Agnew, Geoffrey, *Agnew's 1817–1967*, London (Bradbury Agnew Press) 1967

Alderman, Geoffrey, 'English Jews or Jews of the English Persuasion? Reflections on the Emancipation of Anglo-Jewry', in *Paths of Emancipation: Jews, States, and Citizenship*, ed. Pierre Birnbaum and Ira Katznelson, Princeton NJ (Princeton University Press) 1995, pp. 128–56

Annual Register for 1869, London (Rivingtons) 1870

Arnold, Matthew, *Culture and Anarchy* [1867–68], ed. J. Dover Wilson, Cambridge (Cambridge University Press) 1990

Asleson, Robyn, *Albert Moore*, London (Phaidon) 2000

Barnett, R.D. (ed.), *Catalogue of the Permanent and Loan Collections of the Jewish Museum, London*, London (Harvey Miller) 1974

Bate, Percy, *The English Pre-Raphaelite Painters: Their Associates and Successors*, London (George Bell & Sons) 1899

Bentley, James, *Ritualism and Politics in Victorian Britain: The Attempt to Legislate for Belief*, Oxford (Oxford University Press) 1978

Bland, Kalman P., *The Artless Jew: Medieval and Modern Affirmations and Denials of the Visual Arts*, Princeton NJ (Princeton University Press) 2000

Bohrer, Frederick N., *Orientalism and Visual Culture: Imagining Mesopotamia in Nineteenth-Century Europe*, Cambridge (Cambridge University Press) 2003

Boyce, George Price, *The Diaries of George Price Boyce*, ed. Virginia Surtees, Norwich (Real World) 1980

Brown, Ford Madox, *The Diary of Ford Madox Brown*, ed. Virginia Surtees, New Haven CT and London (Yale University Press) 1981

Buchanan, Robert (writing as 'Thomas Maitland'), 'The Fleshly School of Poetry: Mr. D.G. Rossetti', *Contemporary Review*, XVIII, October 1871, pp. 334–50

Buick, Kirsten P., 'The Ideal Works of Edmonia Lewis: Invoking and Inverting Autobiography', *American Art*, IX, 2, Summer 1995, pp. 5–19

Burne-Jones, Georgiana, *Memorials of Edward Burne-Jones*, 2 vols., London (Macmillan) 1906

Burnham, Patricia M., and Lucretia Hoover Giese (eds.), *Redefining American History Painting*, Cambridge (Cambridge University Press) 1995

Calloway, Stephen, *Aubrey Beardsley*, London (V&A Publications) 1998

Campbell, David A. (trans.), *Greek Lyric*, I, Cambridge MA (Harvard University Press) and London (Heinemann) 1982

Cesarani, David, *The 'Jewish Chronicle' and Anglo-Jewry, 1841–1991*, Cambridge (Cambridge University Press) 1994

Cohen, Richard I., *Jewish Icons: Art and Society in Modern Europe*, Berkeley and Los Angeles (University of California Press) 1998

Colvin, Sidney, 'English Painters of the Present Day: IV. Simeon Solomon', *Portfolio*, I, 3, 1870

Crook, J. Mordaunt, *William Burges and the High Victorian Dream*, London (John Murray) 1981

Cruise, Colin, '"Lovely Devils": Simeon Solomon and Pre-Raphaelite Masculinity', in *Reframing the Pre-Raphaelites: Historical and Theoretical Essays*, ed. Ellen Harding, Aldershot (Scolar Press) 1995

—— 'Reading "Poetry": An Overlooked Painting by Simeon Solomon', *The Review of the Pre-Raphaelite Society*, XI, 1, 2003, pp. 1–13

—— 'Simeon Solomon: A Drama of Desire', *Jewish Quarterly*, Autumn/Winter 1998, pp. 62–67

Davies, Horton, *Worship and Theology in England*, Grand Rapids MI and Cambridge (Eerdmans) 1996

Davis, Whitney, 'The Image in the Middle: John Addington Symonds and Homoerotic Art Criticism', in *After the Pre-Raphaelites: Art and Aestheticism in Victorian England*, ed. Elizabeth Prettejohn, Manchester (Manchester University Press) 1999

DeJean, Joan, *Fictions of Sappho, 1546–1937*, Chicago and London (University of Chicago Press) 1989

Dowling, Linda, *Hellenism and Homosexuality in Victorian Oxford*, Ithaca NY and London (Cornell University Press) 1994

A Dream of the Past: Pre-Raphaelite and Aesthetic Movement Paintings, Watercolours and Drawings from the Lanigan Collection, Toronto (University of Toronto Art Centre) 2000

du Maurier, George, *The Young George du Maurier: A Selection of his Letters, 1860–1867*, ed. Daphne du Maurier, New York (Doubleday & Co.) 1952

Duval, M. Susan, 'F.R. Leyland: A Maecenas from Liverpool', *Apollo*, CXXIV, August 1986, pp. 110–15

Elzea, Betty, *Frederick Sandys (1829–1904): A Catalogue Raisonné*, Woodbridge (Antique Collectors' Club) 2001

Endelman, Todd M., *The Jews of Britain, 1656 to 2000*, Berkeley and Los Angeles (University of California Press) 2002

—— *Radical Assimilation in English Jewish History, 1665–1945*, Bloomington (Indiana University Press) 1990

Exposed: The Victorian Nude, exhib. cat., ed. Alison Smith, London, Tate, 2001

Fairbairn, Patrick, *The Typology of Scripture* [1845–47], Grand Rapids MI (Zondervan) 1967

Falk, Bernard, *Five Years Dead: A Postscript to 'He Laughed in Fleet Street'*, London (Hutchinson) 1937

Feldman, David, *Englishmen and Jews: Social Relations and Political Culture, 1840–1914*, New Haven CT (Yale University Press) 1994

Ferrari, Roberto C., 'To the Rossettis, From the Solomons: Five Unpublished Letters', *Notes and Queries*, LII, 1, March 2005

—— 'The Unknown Correspondence of Simeon Solomon', *The Journal of Pre-Raphaelite Studies*, XII, Spring 2003, pp. 23–34

Finestein, Israel, *Anglo-Jewry in Changing Times: Studies in Diversity, 1840–1914*, London (Valentine Mitchell) 1999

Fone, Byrne R.S. (ed.), *The Columbia Anthology of Gay Literature: Readings from Western Antiquity to the Present Day*, New York (Columbia University Press) 1998

Ford, Julia Ellsworth, *Simeon Solomon: An Appreciation*, New York (Frederic Fairchild Sherman) 1908

Frankel, Jonathan, and Steven J. Zipperstein, *Assimilation and Continuity in Nineteenth-Century Europe*, Cambridge (Cambridge University Press) 1992

Fuller, Jean Overton, *Swinburne: A Biography*, London (Chatto & Windus) 1968; New York (Schocken) 1971

Goldman, Paul, *Victorian Illustration: The Pre-Raphaelites, the Idyllic School and the High Victorians*, Aldershot (Scolar Press) 1996

Goldman, Paul, and Brian Taylor (eds.), *Retrospective Adventures: Forrest Reid, Author and Collector*, Aldershot (Scolar Press) 1998

Goodenough, E.R., *Jewish Symbols in the Graeco-Roman Period*, Princeton NJ (Princeton University Press) 1988

Goodman, Susan Tumarkin (ed.), *The Emergence of Jewish Artists in Nineteenth-Century Europe*, London (Merrell) 2001

Grieve, Alastair, 'The Pre-Raphaelite Brotherhood and the Anglican High Church', *The Burlington Magazine*, XI, May 1969

Hares-Stryker, Carolyn (ed.), *An Anthology of Pre-Raphaelite Writings*, New York (New York University Press) 1997

Held, Julius, 'The Spoken Word in Rembrandt', in *Rembrandt Studies*, Princeton NJ (Princeton University Press) 1991, pp. 164–83

Hertz, J.H. (ed.), *Pentateuch and Haftorahs*, London (Soncino Press) 1981

Hilliard, David, 'UnEnglish and Unmanly: Anglo-Catholicism and Homosexuality', *Victorian Studies*, XXV, 2, 1982, pp. 181–210

Holiday, Henry, 'Memoir of Simeon Solomon' ('Meynell papers'), private collection (unpublished)

—— *Reminiscences of My Life*, London (William Heinemann) 1914

Holland, Neil, 'George Powell of Nanteos', in *To Instruct and Inspire*, Aberystwyth (University of Wales) 1997

Hunt, William Holman, Letter to John Everett Millais, 26 April 1867. University of Manchester, John Rylands Library

—— Letter to Simeon Solomon, n.d. (1860s). London, National Art Library, Victoria and Albert Museum

—— *Pre-Raphaelitism and the Pre-Raphaelite Brotherhood*, 2 vols., London (Macmillan) 1905; 2nd, revised edn, London (Chapman & Hall) 1913

James, William, *Varieties of Religious Experience*, London (Longmans, Green) 1902

Jenkyns, Richard, *The Victorians and Ancient Greece*, Cambridge MA (Harvard University Press) 1981

Jewish Art and Antiquities, exhib. cat., London, Whitechapel Art Gallery, 7 November – 16 December 1906

Jussim, Estelle, *Slave to Beauty: The Eccentric Life and Controversial Career of F. Holland Day, Photographer, Publisher, Aesthete*, Boston (David A. Godine) 1981

Kolsteren, Steven, 'Simeon Solomon and the Song of Songs', *Journal of Jewish Art*, IX, 1982, pp. 47–59

Kushner, Tony (ed.), *The Jewish Heritage in British History: Englishness and Jewishness*, London (Frank Cass) 1992

Lambourne, Lionel, 'Abraham Solomon, Painter of Fashion, and Simeon Solomon, Decadent Artist', *Jewish Historical Society, Transactions*, XXI, 1968, pp. 274–86

—— 'A Simeon Solomon Sketchbook', *Apollo*, LXXXV, January 1967, pp. 59–61

—— 'The Solomon Family', in *Solomon: A Family of Painters: Abraham Solomon (1823–1862), Rebecca Solomon (1832–1886), Simeon Solomon (1840–1905)*, exhib. cat., ed. Jeffery Daniels *et al.*, London, Geffrye Museum (Inner London Education Authority) 1985, pp. 6–8

Lanigan, Dennis, 'The Dudley Gallery: Water Colour Drawings Exhibitions 1865–1882', *The Journal of Pre-Raphaelite Studies*, XII, Spring 2003, pp. 74–96

The Leathart Collection, exhib. cat., Newcastle-upon-Tyne, Laing Art Gallery, 1968

Lee-Wolff, Robert, *Gains and Losses*, New York and London (Garland Publishing) 1977

Lipman, Vivian D., *A History of the Jews in Britain Since 1858*, New York (Holmes & Meier) 1990

McCormack, J.H., *John Gray: Poet, Dandy, and Priest*, Hanover NH (Brandeis University Press) 1991

Macleod, Dianne Sachko, *Art and the Victorian Middle Class: Money and the Making of Cultural Identity*, Cambridge (Cambridge University Press) 1996

Mancoff, Debra N., 'As Others Saw Him: A Self-Portrait by Simeon Solomon', *The Art Institute of Chicago Museum Studies*, XVIII, 2, 1992, pp. 147–55

Marsh, Jan, *Christina Rossetti: A Literary Biography*, London (Jonathan Cape) 1994

—— *Dante Gabriel Rossetti: Painter and Poet*, London (Weidenfield & Nicolson) 1999

Marsh, Jan, and Pamela Gerrish Nunn, *Pre-Raphaelite Women Artists*, London (Thames & Hudson) 1998

Millais, John Guille, *The Life and Letters of Sir John Everett Millais*, 2 vols., London and New York (Methuen) 1899

Ormond, Richard, 'Holman Hunt's Egyptian Chairs', *Apollo*, LXXXII, July 1965, pp. 57–58

Palgrave, Francis Turner, *Essays on Art*, London (Macmillan) 1866

Pater, Walter, 'A Study of Dionysus', *The Fortnightly Review* (new series), XXVI, December 1876, pp. 752–72

A Pre-Raphaelite Collection: D.G. Rossetti, Ford Madox Brown, Holman Hunt, Burne-Jones, Albert Moore, Simeon Solomon, Inchbold, etc. etc., exhib. cat., London, Goupil Gallery, 1896

Prettejohn, Elizabeth, *The Art of the Pre-Raphaelites*, Princeton NJ (Princeton University Press) 2000

—— '"The monstrous diversion of a show of gladiators": Simeon Solomon's *Habet!*', in *Roman Presences: Receptions of Rome in European Culture, 1789–1945*, ed. Catharine Edwards, Cambridge (Cambridge University Press) 1999, pp. 157–72

—— (ed.), *After the Pre-Raphaelites: Art and Aestheticism in Victorian England*, Manchester (Manchester University Press) 1999

Prins, Yopie, *Victorian Sappho*, Princeton NJ (Princeton University Press) 1999

Reid, Forrest, *Illustrators of the Eighteen-Sixties*, London (Faber & Gwyer) 1928

Reynolds, Simon, *The Vision of Simeon Solomon*, Stroud (Catalpa Press) 1985

Ross, Robert, 'Fine Art: Simeon Solomon', *The Academy*, 23 December 1905
—— *Masques and Phases*, London (Arthur L. Humphreys) 1909
Rossetti, Dante Gabriel, *The Correspondence of Dante Gabriel Rossetti*, ed. William Fredeman *et al.*, Cambridge (D.S. Brewer) 2002–
—— *Dante Gabriel Rossetti and Jane Morris: Their Correspondence*, ed. John Bryson, Oxford (Clarendon Press) 1976
—— *The Rossetti–Leyland Letters: The Correspondence of an Artist and his Patron*, ed. Francis L. Fennell, Jr, Athens OH (Ohio University Press) 1978
Rossetti, William Michael, *The Diary of W.M. Rossetti, 1870–1873*, ed. Odette Bornand, Oxford (Clarendon Press) 1977
—— *Selected Letters of William Michael Rossetti*, ed. Roger Peattie, University Park (Pennsylvania State University Press) 1990
Rossetti Angeli, Helen, *Pre-Raphaelite Twilight: The Story of Charles Augustus Howell*, London (Richards Press) 1954
Ruskin, John, *Modern Painters*, 5 vols., Orpington, (George Allen) 1888
Salbstein, M.C.N., *The Emancipation of the Jews in Britain: The Question of the Admission of the Jews to Parliament, 1828–1860*, East Brunswick NJ (Associated University Presses) 1982
Saltzman, Lisa, 'To Figure, or Not to Figure: The Iconoclastic Proscription and Its Theoretical Legacy', in *Jewish Identity in Modern Art History*, ed. Catherine M. Soussloff, Berkeley and Los Angeles (University of California Press) 1999, pp. 67–84
Sarna, Nahum M., *The JPS Torah Commentary: Exodus*, Philadelphia (Jewish Publication Society) 1991
Scott, William Bell, Letter to James Leathart, 11 February 1870. Vancouver, University of British Columbia Library, Rare Books and Special Collections, The James Leathart Collection
A Scottish Collection: Treasures from Aberdeen Art Gallery, exhib. cat., Aberdeen Art Gallery, 2000
Sedgwick, Eve Kosofsky, *Epistemology of the Closet*, Berkeley and Los Angeles (University of California Press) 1990
Sewter, A. Charles, *The Stained Glass of William Morris and his Circle*, New Haven CT and London (Yale University Press) 1975
Seymour, Gayle M., 'The Life and Work of Simeon Solomon, 1840–1905', PhD diss., University of California at Santa Barbara, 1986
—— 'Simeon Solomon and the Biblical Construction of Marginal Identity in Victorian England', co-published simultaneously in *Journal of Homosexuality*, XXXIII, 3/4, 1997, pp. 97–119; and *Reclaiming the Sacred: The Bible in Gay and Lesbian Culture*, ed. Raymond-Jean Frontain, New York (Haworth Press) 1997, pp. 97–119
Silver, Larry, 'Jewish Identity in Art History: Maurycy Gottlieb as Early Jewish Artist', in *Jewish Identity in Modern Art History*, ed. Catherine M. Soussloff, Berkeley and Los Angeles (University of California Press) 1999, pp. 87–113
Solomon: A Family of Painters: Abraham Solomon (1823–1862), Rebecca Solomon (1832–1886), Simeon Solomon (1840–1905), exhib. cat., ed. Jeffery Daniels *et al.*, London, Geffrye Museum (Inner London Education Authority) 1985
Solomon, Rebecca, Letter to Frederick Leyland, 26 October 1866. Library of Congress, Washington, DC, The Pennell Collection
Solomon, Simeon, Letter to Edward Burne-Jones, n.d. (1860s). University of Manchester, John Rylands Library, Fairfax Murray Papers
—— Letter to Henry Holiday, n.d. Collection of Scott Thomas Buckle
—— Letter to Charles Augustus Howell, n.d. Harry Ransom Humanities Research Center at the University of Texas at Austin
—— Letter to Charles Augustus Howell, n.d. University of Manchester, John Rylands Library, Fairfax Murray Papers
—— Letter to William Holman Hunt, n.d. Princeton NJ, Princeton University Library
—— Letters to James Leathart, 1863–*c.* 1868. Vancouver, University of British Columbia Library, Rare Books and Special Collections, The James Leathart Collection
—— Letters to Frederick Leyland, 1866–*c.* 1869. Library of Congress, Washington, DC, The Pennell Collection
—— Letter to D.G. Rossetti, n.d. (1860s). Harry Ransom Humanities Research Center at the University of Texas at Austin
—— *A Vision of Love Revealed in Sleep*, privately printed, London (F.S. Ellis) 1871
Stephens, F.G., 'The Private Collections of England. No. II: Galleries Near Newcastle', *Athenaeum*, 13 September 1871, pp. 342–44
Stirling, A.M.W., *The Richmond Papers*, London (Heinemann) 1926
—— *William De Morgan and his Wife*, London (Thornton Butterworth) 1922
Strazdes, Diana, 'Washington Allston: Great Painting as Mute Poetry', in *Redefining American History Painting*, ed. Patricia M. Burnham and Lucretia Hoover Giese, Cambridge (Cambridge University Press) 1995, pp. 139–57
Suriano, Gregory R., *The Pre-Raphaelite Illustrators*, New Castle DE (Oak Knoll Press) and London (The British Library) 2000
Surtees, Virginia, *The Paintings and Drawings of Dante Gabriel Rossetti (1828–1882): A Catalogue Raisonné*, 2 vols., Oxford (Clarendon Press) 1971
Swinburne, Algernon Charles, 'Simeon Solomon: Notes on his "Vision of Love" and Other Studies', *The Dark Blue*, I, July 1871, pp. 568–77
—— *The Swinburne Letters*, ed. Cecil Y. Lang, 6 vols., New Haven CT (Yale University Press) 1959–62
Symons, Arthur, *Arthur Symons: Selected Letters, 1880–1935*, ed. Karl Beckson and John M. Munro, Iowa City (University of Iowa Press) 1989
—— *Studies on Modern Painters*, New York (William Edwin Rudge) 1925
Visions of Love and Life: Pre-Raphaelite Art from the Birmingham Collection, England, exhib. cat. by Stephen Wildman, Alexandria VA (Art Services International) 1995
Weiner, Julia, '"An artist of strong Jewish feeling": Simeon Solomon's Depictions of Jewish Ceremonies', in *From Prodigy to Outcast: Simeon Solomon – Pre-Raphaelite Artist*, London (Jewish Museum) 2001, pp. 15–22
White, James F., *The Cambridge Movement: The Ecclesiologists and the Gothic Revival* [1962], Cambridge (Cambridge University Press) 1979
Whiteford, Sidney Trefussis, 'A Half-Forgotten Genius', *The Art Amateur*, XXVII, December 1892, pp. 7–9; cont'd XXVIII, January 1893, pp. 46–47
Wildman, Stephen, *The Birmingham School*, Birmingham (Birmingham Museum and Art Gallery) 1990
Williamson, G.C., *Murray Marks and his Friends: A Tribute of Regard*, London (John Lane) 1919
Yates, Nigel, *Anglican Ritualism in Victorian Britain 1830–1910*, Oxford (Oxford University Press) 1999
—— *Buildings, Faith and Worship: The Liturgical Arrangement of Anglican Churches 1600–1900*, Oxford (Oxford University Press) 1991
Zangwill, Israel, *Children of the Ghetto*, Leicester (Leicester University Press) 1977

Index

Page numbers in *italics* refer to illustrations.

Lenders to the Exhibition

Thanks are due to the private owners, named and anonymous, and to the directors and staff of the following museums and galleries for generously lending their works to the exhibition. Works are referred to by their catalogue number.

Aberdeen Art Gallery & Museums Collections 134
Aberystwyth, University of Wales 77, 79, 101, 109
Collection Dr Michael Richard Barclay 143, 144
Bedford, Trustees, Cecil Higgins Art Gallery 89
Birmingham Libraries 131, 153
Birmingham Museums & Art Gallery 15, 17, 18b, 24, 25, 26, 30, 31, 34, 35, 37b, 41, 43, 46, 51, 52, 53, 54, 55, 56, 57, 58, 59, 76, 80, 81, 82, 83, 85, 90, 91, 97, 107, 110, 112, 119, 120, 121, 122, 123, 135, 138, 141, 142, 149, 150, 151, 154, 156
Bournemouth, The Russell-Cotes Art Gallery & Museum 126
Bradford, Royal Photographic Society Collection at the National Museum of Photography, Film & Television 140, 152
Cambridge, The Fitzwilliam Museum 29, 32, 33, 125
Carlisle, Tullie House Museum & Art Gallery 87
Chester City Council, Grosvenor Museum 60, 61
The Albert Dawson Collection 137
Collection Laurin Federlein 37a
The Hearn Family Trust 40, 70, 155, 157
Lionel Lambourne 12, 20, 117b
Dr Dennis T. Lanigan collection, Canada 13, 66, 68, 71, 128
Liverpool, National Museums Liverpool, Lady Lever Art Gallery 74, 88
London, Ben Uri Gallery, The London Jewish Museum of Art 136
London, The British Museum 50, 113, 115
London, The Jewish Museum 1, 2, 3, 4, 5, 6, 7, 8, 9, 124, 146, 147
London, Tate 10, 16, 27, 63, 64, 65, 139
London, Victoria and Albert Museum 21, 44, 73, 104, 111, 114, 133, 145, 148
London, William Morris Gallery 11
Manchester, The Whitworth Art Gallery, University of Manchester 49, 94
Oxford, The Ashmolean Museum 19, 28, 86
Private collection 14, 18a, 22, 23, 36, 38, 39, 42, 45, 47, 48, 62, 67, 69, 72, 78, 84, 93, 95, 98, 99, 100, 102, 103, 108, 116, 117a, 118, 127, 129, 130, 132
Private collection (on loan to Bradford Museums, Galleries & Heritage) 75
Southampton City Art Gallery 96
Seymour Stein 92, 105
Warwick District Council, The Art Gallery & Museum, The Royal Pump Rooms 106

Picture Credits

Aberdeen Art Gallery & Museums Collections 134
Aberystwyth, University of Wales 77, 79, 101, 109
The Ashmolean Museum, University of Oxford 19, 28, 86; figs. 7, 34
Ben Uri Gallery, The London Jewish Museum of Art 136
Birmingham Libraries 131, 153; figs. 19, 38
Birmingham Museums & Art Gallery 15 (also fig. 10), 17 (also p. 64), 18b, 24, 25, 26, 30, 31, 34, 35, 37b, 41, 43, 46, 51, 52, 53, 54, 55, 56, 57, 58, 59, 76, 80, 81, 82, 83, 85, 90, 91, 97, 107, 110, 112, 119, 120, 121, 122, 123, 135, 138, 141, 142, 149, 150, 151, 154, 156; figs. 12, 18, 22, 24, 28, 32, 33, 35
The British Museum, London 50, 113, 115 (also fig. 17); fig. 3
Cecil Higgins Art Gallery, Bedford 89
Christie's Images Ltd 36, 42, 69 (also p. 22), 93 (also p. 38), 100 (also p. 142)
The Albert Dawson Collection/Duncan McNeill Imaging 137
Delaware Art Museum, Wilmington, USA, Bequest of Robert Louis Isaacson;/Bridgeman Art Library figs. 2, 25
Delaware Art Museum, Wilmington, USA, F.V. DuPont Acquisition Fund;/Bridgeman Art Library figs. 13, 36
Collection Laurin Federlein/Birmingham Museums & Art Gallery 37a
The Fitzwilliam Museum, Cambridge 29, 32, 33, 125
Grosvenor Museum, Chester City Council 60, 61
The Hearn Family Trust 40, 70, 155, 157
The Jewish Museum, London 1, 2, 3, 4, 5, 6, 7, 8, 9 (also fig. 20), 124, 146, 147; fig. 37
Dr Dennis T. Lanigan collection, Canada 13, 66, 68, 71, 128
Mishkan Le'Omanut Museum, Ein Harod, Israel figs. 4, 9
National Museums Liverpool, Lady Lever Art Gallery 74, 88 (also p. 56)
Private collection 18a; figs. 6, 8, 11, 21
Private collection/Albert Bowyer 84, 127, 129; figs. 23, 26, 27, 29, 30, 31
Private collection/Bradford Museums, Galleries & Heritage 75 (also p. 106)
Private collection/Rish Durka Photography 12, 20, 22, 23, 39, 48, 67, 72, 78, 98, 99, 103, 116, 117a (also p. 2), 117b, 118, 132, 143, 144
Private collection/Kevin Noble 47 (also p. 82), 102
Private collection/Glen Segal 14, 38 (also fig. 1), 45, 95, 130
The Russell-Cotes Art Gallery & Museum, Bournemouth 126
Science & Society Picture Library 140, 152
Sotheby's Picture Library, London 62, 92 (also fig. 15), 105, 108; fig. 39
Southampton City Art Gallery, Hampshire, UK;/Bridgeman Art Library 96
Tate, London 10 (also fig. 5), 16 (also p. 30), 27 (also back jacket/cover), 63, 64, 65, 139
Tullie House Museum & Art Gallery, Carlisle 87 (also fig. 16)
V&A Images/Victoria and Albert Museum 21 (also p. 12), 44, 73, 104 (also fig. 14), 111, 114 (also p. 46), 133, 145 (also p. 162), 148a (also p. 8), 148b
Warwick District Council, The Art Gallery & Museum, The Royal Pump Rooms 106 (also front jacket/cover)
The Whitworth Art Gallery, University of Manchester 49, 94 (also p. 126)
William Morris Gallery, London 11